Lecture Notes in Artificial Inte

Subseries of Lecture Notes in Computer Science
Edited by J. G. Carbonell and J. Siekmann

Lecture Notes in Computer Science
Edited by G. Goos, J. Hartmanis, and J. van Leeuwen

Springer

Berlin
Heidelberg
New York
Barcelona
Hong Kong
London
Milan
Paris
Singapore
Tokyo

Behnam Azvine   Nader Azarmi
Detlef D. Nauck (Eds.)

Intelligent Systems and Soft Computing

Prospects, Tools and Applications

 Springer

Series Editors

Jaime G. Carbonell, Carnegie Mellon University, Pittsburgh, PA, USA
Jörg Siekmann, University of Saarland, Saarbrücken, Germany

Volume Editors

Behnam Azvine
Nader Azarmi
Detlef Nauck
BT Laboratories
Advanced Communication Engineering
Adastral Park
Martlesham Heath
Ipswich IP5 3RE, UK
E-mail:{ben.azvine/nader.azarmi/detlef.nauck}@bt.com

Cataloging-in-Publication Data applied for

Die Deutsche Bibliothek - CIP-Einheitsaufnahme

Intelligent systems in soft computing : prospects, tools and
applications / Behnam Azvine ... (ed.). - Berlin ; Heidelberg ; New
York ; Barcelona ; Hong Kong ; London ; Milan ; Paris ; Singapore ;
Tokyo : Springer, 2000
   (Lecture notes in computer science ; Vol. 1804 : Lecture notes in
   artificial intelligence)
   ISBN 3-540-67837-9

CR Subject Classification (1998): I.2, D.2, C.2.4, H.5.1, H.3.4, J.1

ISBN 3-540-67837-9 Springer-Verlag Berlin Heidelberg New York

Springer-Verlag Berlin Heidelberg New York
a member of BertelsmannSpringer Science+Business Media GmbH
© Springer-Verlag Berlin Heidelberg 2000
Printed in Germany

Typesetting: Camera-ready by author, data conversion by DA-TeX Gerd Blumenstein
Printed on acid-free paper   SPIN: 10720181   06/3142   5 4 3 2 1 0

Preface

Building intelligent machines has been mankind's dream for decades. There have been many discussions on, and much written about, the impact of machine intelligence on society. Science fiction movies have portrayed both the brighter and the darker aspects of being surrounded on all sides by artificial systems with more intelligence than humans. Building such intelligent machines is, and will remain for the foreseeable future, a dream. The collection of papers that makes up this book, explore the prospects of incorporating intelligent behaviour into software systems. It outlines many promising directions, and describes possible tools and applications for intelligent systems in the near future.

Much effort, time, and money have been spent in the last 50 years in understanding the nature of human intelligence. Why? So that artificial systems can be built that act and work as intelligently as humans. While the realisation of an intelligent machine that is as clever as a human is as yet a technical impossibility, and in some people's view undesirable, we cannot ignore the fact that people nowadays are demanding (intelligent) systems that are useful and can complement their physical or cognitive capabilities. This demand is leading to the creation of a large and lucrative market in intelligent systems, which is naturally spawning the associated information technology industries for building these systems.

The *raison d'être* for this volume is to bring together, within a single publication, a collection of papers describing recent advances in intelligent systems and soft computing, with particular focus on applications. The book is unique in the way it concentrates on building intelligent software systems by combining methods from diverse disciplines, such as fuzzy set theory, neuroscience, agent technology, knowledge discovery, and symbolic artificial intelligence (AI). Traditionally, AI has been trying to solve human-centred problems, such as natural language understanding, speech recognition, and common-sense reasoning. On the other hand, soft computing has been applied successfully in the areas of pattern recognition, function approximation, clustering, and automatic control. The papers in this book explore the possibility and opportunity of bringing these two areas closer together. The first section focuses on future directions and includes contributions from some of the most eminent academics in the fields. The second section aims to provide the reader with an overview of recently developed software tools to aid researchers and practitioners in building flexible intelligent systems. The final section describes a number of developed applications that utilise the theoretical results and software tools described in the first two sections. We hope that the particular combination of the three sections will ensure that the book appeals to a wide audience, ranging from industrial researchers to academic scholars.

February 2000

Behnam Azvine
Nader Azarmi
Detlef Nauck

Acknowledgements

The authors of the papers are the *sine qua non* of the endeavour of creating an edited volume. We are deeply grateful to them and we do apologise if they found us demanding; hopefully it has enhanced the quality of the volume. Our thanks go also to the many reviewers, particularly to David Djian, Kwok Ching Tsui, and Wayne Wobcke. Finally, we wish to acknowledge Graham Davies and David Griffiths of the BT Group Technology Programme for their continuous support of the Soft Computing programme.

Table of Contents

Introduction

In October 1998 we at BT's intelligent systems research group organised a workshop at Adastral Park with the aim of setting up a forum for discussion about new paradigms for building intelligent systems. The feedback from the workshop was extremely encouraging to the extent that we decided to gather together the contributions of the participants. This book is the result of our efforts. Its subject is how to build intelligent systems – systems that can make intelligent decisions in complex situations. The book does not aim to explain what intelligent systems are or should be (as this has been the subject of many recent publications including an edited volume containing a number of contributions from authors represented in this volume entitled Software Agents and Soft Computing [1]), but it tries to offer academics and industrialists a way forward for engineering intelligent systems.

This volume extends and builds upon some of the papers which appeared in BT Technology Journal Vol. 16, No. 3. It is divided into three sections: prospects, tools and applications. The first section includes articles from some of the most prominent academics of our era about future perspectives and new areas of research that will help us in our long search for the nature of intelligence and intelligent systems. The ultimate goal of understanding intelligence is to build artificial systems that behave intelligently and so the second section is devoted to tools that utilise new algorithms and software languages to enable us to build such systems. In the last section a number of papers present recently developed prototypical systems that, by utilising intelligent techniques, will in our view increasingly play a vital role in our lives, fulfilling our information and communication needs in the years to come.

From a technical point of view our aim of compiling this volume has been to build upon the existing work based on well-known symbolic artificial intelligence (AI) by introducing hybrid techniques that borrow from the soft computing paradigm when there is a good reason to do so. Our aim is to demonstrate that such hybrid approaches enable us to provide robust, adaptive and easy-to-interact-with systems that work for, alongside, or on behalf of humans.

1 Motivation

Early attempts at building systems with comparable cognitive capability to the human brain, even in limited domains, have not been as successful as predicted. The problems of knowledge representation, common-sense reasoning, real-time problem solving, vision, speech and language processing have not as yet yielded to classical AI techniques. More research is needed and is being carried out mainly by academia in the areas of pattern recognition, logical representation, search, inference, learning from experience, planning, ontology and epistemology. Despite the difficulties, AI has been successfully applied in areas such as expert systems, classification, planning, scheduling, game playing and robotics.

For the past half century the AI community has aimed to build artefacts that could compete with human level intelligence on various tasks. An alternative view for building intelligent systems is the tool metaphor in which the human is seen as a skilled craft-person with the system trying to provide the tools that fit the capabilities of the user and the task to be performed. In this view, the focus is on systems that can augment the cognitive capabilities of humans, i.e. a human-machine symbiosis or *Human-Centred Intelligent System* (HCIS). HCIS are different in many respects from traditional AI systems in that they do not compete with, or try to match, human level intelligence. Rather, they assist humans in performing cognitive tasks such that the combination of the human and the system has a greater cognitive capacity than each on its own [2].

Looking at the world from a different perspective it can be seen that it is constantly growing in complexity. This complexity manifests itself today, for example, in the form of information overload. In a normal business environment we face an ever growing stream of information from such channels as e-mail, telecommunication devices, Internet-based services, etc. At home with digital, terrestrial and satellite TV we experience a similar situation where we have the choice of hundreds of TV channels. On the one hand, most of this information is useless for us, and on the other hand it becomes more and more difficult to find important information. Intelligent systems can help us cope with this complexity. These are systems that act on our behalf by filtering unnecessary information, dealing with unwanted communication, anticipating and learning our reactions and preferences, actively searching for relevant information for us, scheduling our tasks the way we would, etc.

Symbolic AI techniques mainly do not take uncertainty, imprecision and vagueness into account – even more, they try to avoid them at all cost. This approach consequently leads to systems that require to model all possible states and exceptions resulting in highly complex systems that cannot run in real time on today's computers.

Humans deal with complexity by simplification. Precise representations have a good chance of being wrong or inapplicable most of the time. Furthermore such representations are very brittle and cannot tolerate the small variations or uncertainty that are present in all but a handful of real problems. Simplified rules, and representations that are vague, apply to a whole range of situations, at least to some extent.

Furthermore, precision carries a cost, which is often too prohibitive for real-world problems. By tolerating uncertainty and imprecision we can drastically reduce the complexity of a system. Instead of conceiving rules for every possible precise situation we use vague rules which do not distinguish between similar states.

By building systems that deliberately exploit the tolerance for uncertainty and imprecision in certain situations, we can develop robust intelligent solutions with less cost and effort, two critically important factors in constructing real-world applications.

By assuming the tool-oriented view of HCIS we can concentrate on solving sub-tasks fast and are able to accelerate application development. The main focus in the development of such systems lies on:

- robustness, i.e. applicability under uncertain and vague conditions,
- adaptability, i.e. learning from experience and human intervention,
- autonomy, i.e. acting on behalf of a user without direct intervention, and
- multi-modal interfaces, i.e. making use of human communication channels like vision, speech, and understanding natural language.

In our view soft computing is ideally suited to handle uncertainty, vagueness and learning problems within HCIS.

2 Rationale: Soft Computing

The term *soft computing* was coined by Lotfi A. Zadeh to describe a collection of methodologies that aim to exploit the tolerance for imprecision and uncertainty to achieve tractability, robustness and low solution cost [3, 4]. Zadeh sees fuzzy logic, neural computation and probabilistic reasoning as the main constituents of soft computing, the latter subsuming genetic algorithms, belief networks, chaotic systems and parts of learning theory.

Fuzzy logic is mainly concerned with imprecision, vagueness and approximate reasoning, neural computation with (sub-symbolic) learning and probabilistic reasoning with uncertainty.

According to Bonissone [5] soft computing techniques are drawn together by 'their departure from classical reasoning and modelling approaches that are usually based on Boolean logic, crisp classification and deterministic search.'

Zadeh has selected the term *soft* computing to distinguish the above-mentioned methodologies from traditional *hard* computing which is based on precision, certainty and rigor. Soft computing draws from the idea that precision and certainty carry a cost and that computation, reasoning and decision making should exploit the tolerance for imprecision and uncertainty wherever possible [3].

There are usually trade-offs between precision and robustness and precision and simplicity. If we aim for a very precise system, slight modifications in the input can lead to drastic changes in the system's behaviour. This effect is known as *brittleness* in classical symbolic expert systems. In addition, precision can often only be reached by very complex systems. Complexity, however, can prevent a system from working in real time and a lack of simplicity prevents user-friendliness.

By applying fuzzy systems, for example, a considerable reduction in complexity can be reached. Instead of a large number of individual values, a few fuzzy sets are used to describe a domain. This leads to data compression (granulation), because we refrain from explicitly distinguishing similar values. In addition we can let adjacent fuzzy sets overlap such that slight changes in the input values will not lead to drastically different system outputs.

The performance of soft computing solutions must therefore not only be measured by its precision but also by its simplicity, user-friendliness, robustness, overall cost, etc.

Another important aspect of soft computing is that the mentioned methodologies complement each other. For example, combinations between neural networks and fuzzy systems – so-called neuro-fuzzy systems – are a very well researched area [6, 7]. A neuro-fuzzy system aims at learning a fuzzy system from data, thus combining learning aspects and vagueness handling.

As important as soft computing techniques in the design of HCIS may be, we are convinced that soft computing cannot replace AI. It is important to use both paradigms in building solutions. The Intelligent Assistant that is presented in Section 3 is an example for such a strategy.

3   Outline

The first section of this book contains contributions of well-known researchers from the soft computing community who provide their views of future development in this area.

The second section discusses three well-known tools for soft computing. NEFCLASS-J is an open-source software for learning fuzzy classifiers, FRIL is a commercial system that combines soft computing and AI methodologies and Data Engine™is a commercial data analysis tool with a focus on soft computing techniques.

The third section contains several contributions on the Intelligent Assistant (IA) that was developed within the BT Laboratories at Adastral Park. The IA consists of a suite of integrated assistants that helps the user with communication, information and time management. The assistants use both AI and soft computing techniques to maintain a user model and to learn user preferences.

Section 1 – Prospects

L.A. Zadeh – From Computing with Numbers to Computing with Words – From Manipulation of Measurements to Manipulation of Perceptions – Computing, in its usual sense, is centred on manipulation of numbers and symbols. In contrast, computing with words, or CW for short, is a methodology in which the objects of computation are words and propositions drawn from a natural language, e.g. *small, large, far, heavy, not very likely, the price of gas is low and declining, Berkeley is near San Francisco, CA, it is very unlikely that there will be a significant increase in the price of oil in the near future,* etc. Computing with words (CW) is inspired by the remarkable human capability to perform a wide variety of physical and mental tasks without any measurements and any computations. Familiar examples of such tasks are parking a car, driving in heavy traffic, playing golf, riding a bicycle, understanding speech, and summarizing a story. Underlying this remarkable capability is the brain's crucial ability to manipulate perceptions – perceptions of distance, size, weight, colour, speed, time, direction, force, number, truth, likelihood, and other characteristics of physical and mental objects. Manipulation of perceptions plays a key role in human recognition, decision and execution processes. As a methodology, computing with words provides a foundation for a computational theory of perceptions – a theory which may have an important bearing on how humans make – and machines might make – perception-based rational decisions in an environment of imprecision, uncertainty and partial truth.

J.G. Taylor – Bringing AI and Soft Computing Together – The problem of reconciling what appear as two completely different computing styles, those of AI and of soft computing, is considered in terms of modern brain research. After a brief but general discussion of soft computing relevant to the analysis of the brain, this contribution gives an introduction to neural networks as a modelling framework with which to approach brain processing. The author develops a framework to describe how object perception can arise in the brain and considers how that can help reconcile the two different styles of computing.

J.F. Baldwin – Future Directions for Soft Computing – This paper discusses possible future directions of research for soft computing in the context of artificial intelligence and knowledge engineering. The author uses a voting model semantics to develop ideas for a mass assignment theory which provides means of moving from the case of crisp sets to that of fuzzy sets. The use of fuzzy sets provides better interpolation, greater knowledge compression and less dependence on the effects of noisy data than if only crisp sets are used. The benefits are illustrated in the areas of decision trees, probabilistic fuzzy logic type rules and Bayesian nets.

R. Kruse, C. Borgelt and D. Nauck – Problems and Prospects in Fuzzy Data Analysis – In meeting the challenges that resulted from the explosion of collected, stored, and transferred data, *Knowledge Discovery in Databases,* or *Data Mining,* has emerged as a new research area. However, the approaches studied in this area have mainly been oriented at highly structured and precise data. In addition, the goal to obtain understandable results is often neglected. Therefore the authors suggest concentrating on *Information Mining*, i.e. the analysis of heterogeneous information sources with the prominent aim of producing comprehensible results. Since the aim of fuzzy technology has always been to model linguistic information and to achieve understandable solutions, it is expected to play an important role in information mining.

E.H. Mamdani, A.G. Sichanie and J. Pitt – Soft Agent Computing – Soft agent computing (SAC) draws together the ideas of soft computing with the agent paradigm. This paper considers several issues of fusing these areas from the perspective of agent characteristics and agent architectures. The authors present different abstraction layers of a SAC architecture and describe a practical SAC system based on the beliefs-desires-intention model.

Section 2 – Tools

D. Nauck and R. Kruse – NEFCLASS-J – A Java-based Soft Computing Tool – Neuro-fuzzy classification systems offer a means to obtain fuzzy classification rules by a learning algorithm. It is usually no problem to find a suitable fuzzy classifier by learning from data; however, it can be hard to obtain a classifier that can be interpreted conveniently. There is usually a trade-off between accuracy and readability. NEFCLASS-J is a Java based tool that aims at learning comprehensible fuzzy classifiers. It provides automatic strategies for pruning rules and variables from a trained classifier to enhance its interpretability. NEFCLASS-J is freely available via the Internet at http://www.neuro-fuzzy.de.

T.P. Martin and J.F. Baldwin – Soft Computing for Intelligent Knowledge-based Systems – Knowledge-based systems are founded in the idea that knowledge should be declarative, so that it can be easily read, understood, and altered by a human user as well as by a machine. Logic fulfils these criteria, and logic programming has been widely used for implementing knowledge-based systems. One major shortcoming of logic programming is the lack of a mechanism to deal with the uncertainty inherent in many knowledge-based systems. Soft computing is a key technology for the management of uncertainty. This contribution outlines some of the issues related to the area of soft computing in knowledge-based systems, and suggests some simple problems to test the capabilities of software. FRIL is discussed as an implementation language for knowledge-based systems involving uncertainty, and some of its applications are outlined.

C. Borgelt and H. Timm – Advanced Fuzzy Clustering and Decision Tree Plug-Ins for DataEngine™ – Although a large variety of data analysis tools is available on the market today, none of them is perfect; they all have their strengths and weaknesses. In such a situation it is important that a user can enhance the capabilities of a data analysis tool by his or her own favourite methods in order to compensate shortcomings of the shipped version. However, only few commercial products offer such a possibility. A rare exception is DataEngine™, which is provided with a well-documented interface for user-defined function blocks (plug-ins). In this paper the authors describe three plug-ins they implemented for this well-known tool: an *advanced fuzzy clustering plug-in* that extends the fuzzy c-means algorithm (which is a built-in feature of DataEngine™) by other, more flexible algorithms, a *decision tree classifier plug-in* that overcomes the serious drawback that DataEngine™ lacks a native module for this highly important technique, and finally a *naive Bayes classifier plug-in* that makes available an old and time-tested statistical classification method.

Section 3 – Applications

B. Azvine, D. Djian, K.C. Tsui and W. Wobcke – The Intelligent Assistant: An Overview – The Intelligent Assistant (IA) is an integrated system of intelligent software agents that helps the user with communication, information and time management. The IA includes specialist assistants for e-mail prioritisation and telephone call filtering (communication management), Web search and Yellow Pages lookup (information management), and calendar scheduling (time management). Each such assistant is designed to have a model of the user and a learning module for acquiring user preferences. In addition, the IA includes a toolbar providing a graphical interface to the system, a multi-modal interface for accepting spoken commands and tracking the user's activity, and a coordinator responsible for managing communication from the system to the user and for initiating system activities on the user's behalf. A primary design objective of the IA is that its operation is as transparent as possible, to enable the user to control the system as far as is practicable without incurring a heavy overhead when creating and modifying the system's behaviour. Hence each specialist assistant is designed to represent its user model in a way that is intuitively understandable to non-technical users, and is configured to adaptively modify its user model through time to accommodate the user's changing preferences. However, in contrast to adaptive interface agents built under the behaviour-based paradigm, the assistants in the IA embrace complex AI representations and machine learning techniques to accomplish more sophisticated behaviour.

A. De Roek, U. Kruschwitz, P. Scott, S. Steel, R. Turner and N. Webb – The YPA – An Assistant for Classified Directory Enquiries – The YPA is a directory enquiring system which allows a user to access advertiser information in classified directories. It converts semi-structured data in the Yellow Pages®machine readable classified directories into a set of indices appropriate to the domain and task, and converts natural language queries into filled slot and filler structures appropriate for the queries in the domain. The generation of answers requires a domain independent query construction step, connecting the indices and the slot and fillers. The YPA illustrates an unusual but useful intermediate point between information retrieval and knowledge representation.

K.C. Tsui and B. Azvine – An Intelligent Multi-modal Interface – Research in human/computer interaction has primarily focused on natural language, text, speech and vision in isolation. A number of recent research projects have studied the integration of such modalities. The rationale is that many inherent ambiguities in single modes of communication can be resolved if extra information is available. This contribution discusses issues related to designing and building a multi-modal system. The main characteristics of such a system are that it can process input and output from conventional as well as new channels. Examples of multi-modal systems are the *Smart Work Manager* and the *Intelligent Assistant*. Main components of the two systems described here are the reasoner, the speech system, the non-intrusive neural network based gaze-tracking system, the user presence detector and the integration platforms.

D. Djian – Communication Management – Nowadays, office workers receive an increasing number of communications, mainly through e-mail and telephone. If not handled correctly, these can lead to a communication overload. This paper describes a system which helps a user to manage interruptions from incoming communications. It is based on a generic hierarchical priority model using causal probabilistic networks and taking into account the context of an interruption. The model was implemented in an e-mail and a telephone assistant. These assistants can learn the user's preference in a non-obtrusive manner and we show experimental results of successful adaptation to changing user's needs.

W. Wobcke – Time Management in the Intelligent Assistant – In this contribution, the author discusses in detail issues related to time management in the IA. There are two distinct types of time management relevant to the IA: that concerning the user's management of his or her own time, and that concerning the coordination of actions performed by the various specialist assistants in the system (which affects the overall effectiveness of the system from the user's point of view). To aid the user in managing his or her own time, the IA includes a *Diary Assistant* which acts as a scheduler of tasks with the aim of satisfying the user's combined preferences for start times, durations and deadlines. The Diary Assistant offers ease of use by allowing preferences for a task to be specified using natural language terms such as *morning, afternoon, early morning* and *around 11:00,* which are interpreted by the system using fuzzy functions. To manage the system's time, the IA has a special *Coordinator* for regulating the communication from the system to the user and for planning system tasks. The Coordinator is the only component of the IA capable of scheduling the future actions of the assistants, and incorporates a novel agent architecture based on ideas from reactive scheduling called IRSA (*Intelligent Reactive Scheduling Architecture*). The Coordinator constructs and maintains the system's schedule of tasks using information about the user's schedule obtained from the Diary Assistant.

S. Case, J.F. Baldwin and T.P. Martin – Mood Recognition from Facial Expressions – Facial expressions are an important source of information for human interaction. Therefore, it would be desirable if computers were able to use this information to interact more naturally with the user. However, facial expressions are not always unambiguously interpreted even by competent humans. Consequently, soft computing techniques in which interpretations are given some belief value would seem appropriate. This contribution describes how the mass assignment approach to constructing fuzzy sets from probability distributions has been applied to the low-level classification of pixels into facial feature classes based on their colour.

N.R. Taylor – Modelling Preferred Work Plans – Temporal sequence storage and generation is important during our everyday lives. The sequences of actions that we perform to accomplish tasks are learnt as schemata and are then used in planning solutions. Hence for planning schemata are required to be set up. This contribution describes a system based on a neural network architecture that learns to plan a user's work schedule.

February 2000   Behnam Azvine
BT Laboratories   Nader Azarmi
Adastral Park, Ipswich   Detlef Nauck

References

1. Nwana H. S. and Azarmi N., Eds.: 'Software Agents and Soft Computing'. No. 1198 in Lecture Notes in Computer Science. Berlin, Springer-Verlag (1997).
2. Azvine B. and Wobcke W.: 'Human-centred intelligent systems and soft computing'. BT Technology Journal, Vol. 16(3), pp. 125–133 (1998).
3. Zadeh L. A.: 'Fuzzy logic, neural networks and soft computing'. Comm. ACM, Vol. 37(3), pp. 77–84 (1994).
4. Zadeh L. A.: 'Soft computing and fuzzy logic'. IEEE Software, Vol. 11(6), pp. 48–56 (1994).
5. Bonissone P. P.: 'Soft computing: The convergence of emerging reasoning technologies'. Soft Computing, Vol. 1(1), pp. 6–18 (1997).
6. Jang J.-S., Sun C. and Mizutani E.: 'Neuro Fuzzy and Soft Computing'. Upper Saddle River, NJ, Prentice Hall (1997).
7. Nauck D., Klawonn F. and Kruse R.: 'Foundations of Neuro-Fuzzy Systems'. Chichester, Wiley (1997).

From Computing with Numbers to Computing with Words—From Manipulation of Measurements to Manipulation of Perceptions[1]

Lotfi A. Zadeh

Life Fellow, IEEE

Abstract. Computing, in its usual sense, is centered on manipulation of numbers and symbols. In contrast, computing with words, or CW for short, is a methodology in which the objects of computation are words and propositions drawn from a natural language, e.g. *small, large, far, heavy, not very likely, the price of gas is low and declining, Berkeley is near San Francisco, CA, it is very unlikely that there will be a significant increase in the price of oil in the near future*, etc. Computing with words (CW) is inspired by the remarkable human capability to perform a wide variety of physical and mental tasks without any measurements and any computations. Familiar examples of such tasks are parking a car, driving in heavy traffic, playing golf, riding a bicycle, understanding speech, and summarizing a story. Underlying this remarkable capability is the brain's crucial ability to manipulate perceptions—perceptions of distance, size, weight, color, speed, time, direction, force, number, truth, likelihood, and other characteristics of physical and mental objects. Manipulation of perceptions plays a key role in human recognition, decision and execution processes. As a methodology, computing with words provides a foundation for a computational theory of perceptions— a theory which may have an important bearing on how humans make—and machines might make—perception-based rational decisions in an environment of imprecision, uncertainty and partial truth.

A basic difference between perceptions and measurements is that, in general, measurements are crisp whereas perceptions are fuzzy. One of the fundamental aims of science has been and continues to be that of progressing from perceptions to measurements. Pursuit of this aim has led to brilliant successes. We have sent men to the moon; we can build computers that are capable of performing billions of computations per second; we have constructed telescopes that can explore the far reaches of the universe; and we can date the age of rocks that are millions of years old. But alongside the brilliant successes stand conspicuous underachievements and outright failures. We cannot build robots which can move with the agility of animals or humans; we cannot automate driving in heavy traffic; we cannot translate from one language to another at the level of a human interpreter; we cannot create programs which can summarize nontrivial stories; our ability to model the behavior of economic systems leaves much to be desired; and we cannot build machines that can compete with children in the performance of a wide variety of physical and cognitive tasks.

---

[1] ©1999 IEEE. Reprinted, with permission, from IEEE Transactions on Circuits and Systems-I: Fundamental Theory and Applications, Vol 45, No 1, January 1999.

B. Azvine et al. (Eds.): Intelligent Systems and Soft Computing, LNAI 1804, pp. 3–40, 2000.
© Springer-Verlag Berlin Heidelberg 2000

It may be argued that underlying the underachievements and failures is the un-availability of a methodology for reasoning and computing with perceptions rather than measurements. An outline of such a methodology—referred to as a computational theory of perceptions—is presented in this paper. The computational theory of perceptions, or CTP for short, is based on the methodology of CW. In CTP, words play the role of labels of perceptions and, more generally, perceptions are expressed as propositions in a natural language. CW-based techniques are employed to translate propositions expressed in a natural language into what is called the Generalized Constraint Language (GCL). In this language, the meaning of a proposition is expressed as a generalized constraint, X is R, where X is the constrained variable, R is the constraining relation and isr is a variable copula in which r is a variable whose value defines the way in which R constrains X. Among the basic types of constraints are: possibilistic, veristic, probabilistic, random set, Pawlak set, fuzzy graph and usuality. The wide variety of constraints in GCL makes GCL a much more expressive language than the language of predicate logic.

In CW, the initial and terminal data sets, IDS and TDS, are assumed to consist of propositions expressed in a natural language. These propositions are translated, respectively, into antecedent and consequent constraints. Consequent constraints are derived from antecedent constraints through the use of rules of constraint propagation. The principal constraint propagation rule is the generalized extension principle. The derived constraints are retranslated into a natural language, yielding the terminal data set (TDS). The rules of constraint propagation in CW coincide with the rules of inference in fuzzy logic. A basic problem in CW is that of explicitation of X, R, and r in a generalized constraint, X isr R, which represents the meaning of a proposition, p, in a natural language.

There are two major imperatives for computing with words. First, computing with words is a necessity when the available information is too imprecise to justify the use of numbers; and second, when there is a tolerance for imprecision which can be exploited to achieve tractability, robustness, low solution cost and better rapport with reality. Exploitation of the tolerance for imprecision is an issue of central importance in CW and CTP. At this juncture, the computational theory of perceptions—which is based on CW—is in its initial stages of development. In time, it may come to play an important role in the conception, design and utilization of information/intelligent systems. The role model for CW and CTP is the human mind.

1   Introduction

In the Fifties, and especially late Fifties, circuit theory was at the height of importance and visibility. It played a pivotal role in the conception and design of electronic circuits and was enriched by basic contributions of Darlington, Bode, McMillan, Guillemin, Carlin, Youla, Kuh, Desoer, Sandberg, and other pioneers.

However, what could be discerned at that time was that circuit theory was evolving into a more general theory—system theory—a theory in which the physical identity of the elements of a system is subordinated to a mathematical characterization of their input/output relations. This evolution was a step in the direction of greater generality and, like most generalizations, it was driven by a quest for models which make it possible to reduce the distance between an object that is modeled—the modelizand—and its model in a specified class of systems.

In a paper published in 1961 entitled 'From Circuit Theory to System Theory,' [33] I discussed the evolution of circuit theory into system theory and observed that the high effectiveness of system theory in dealing with mechanistic systems stood in sharp contrast to its low effectiveness in the realm of humanistic systems—systems exemplified by economic systems, biological systems, social systems, political systems and, more generally, man-machine systems of various types. In more specific terms, I wrote:

> There is a fairly wide gap between what might be regarded as 'animate' system theorists and 'inanimate' system theorists at the present time, and it is not at all certain that this gap will be narrowed, much less closed, in the near future. There are some who feel that this gap reflects the fundamental inadequacy of conventional mathematics—the mathematics of precisely-defined points, functions, sets, probability measures, etc—for coping with the analysis of biological systems, and that to deal effectively with such systems, which are generally orders of magnitude more complex than man-made systems, we need a radically different kind of mathematics, the mathematics of fuzzy or cloudy quantities which are not describable in terms of probability distributions. Indeed, the need for such mathematics is becoming increasingly apparent even in the realm of inanimate systems, for in most practical cases the *a priori* data as well as the criteria by which the performance of a man-made system are judged are far from being precisely specified or having accurately-known probability distributions.

It was this observation that motivated my development of the theory of fuzzy sets. starting with the 1965 paper 'Fuzzy Sets' [34], which was published in *Information and Control.* Subsequently, in a paper published in 1973, 'Outline of a New Approach to the Analysis of Complex Systems and Decision Processes,' [37] I introduced the concept of a linguistic variable, that is, a variable whose values are words rather than numbers. The concept of a linguistic variable has played and is continuing to play a pivotal role in the development of fuzzy logic and its applications.

The initial reception of the concept of a linguistic variable was far from positive, largely because my advocacy of the use of words in systems and decision analysis clashed with the deep-seated tradition of respect for numbers and disrespect for words. The essence of this tradition was succinctly stated in 1883 by Lord Kelvin:

> In physical science the first essential step in the direction of learning any subject is to find principles of numerical reckoning and practicable methods for measuring some quality connected with it. I often say that when you can measure what you are speaking about and express it in numbers, you know something about it; but when you cannot measure it, when you cannot express it in numbers, your knowledge is of a meagre and unsatisfactory kind: it may be the beginning of

knowledge but you have scarcely, in your thoughts, advanced to the state of science, whatever the matter may be.

The depth of scientific tradition of respect for numbers and derision for words was reflected in the intensity of hostile reaction to my ideas by some of the prominent members of the scientific elite. In commenting on my first exposition of the concept of a linguistic variable in 1972, Rudolph Kalman had this to say:

I would like to comment briefly on Professor Zadeh's presentation. His proposals could be severely, ferociously, even brutally criticized from a technical point of view. This would be out of place here. But a blunt question remains: Is Professor Zadeh presenting important ideas or is he indulging in wishful thinking? No doubt Professor Zadeh's enthusiasm for fuzziness has been reinforced by the prevailing climate in the U.S.—one of unprecedented permissiveness. 'Fuzzification' is a kind of scientific permissiveness; it tends to result in socially appealing slogans unaccompanied by the discipline of hard scientific work and patient observation.

In a similar vein, my esteemed colleague Professor William Kahan—a man with a brilliant mind—offered this assessment in 1975:

'Fuzzy theory is wrong, wrong, and pernicious.' says William Kahan, a professor of computer sciences and mathematics at Cal whose Evans Hall office is a few doors from Zadeh's. 'I cannot think of any problem that could not be solved better by ordinary logic.' What Zadeh is saying is the same sort of things 'Technology got us into this mess and now it can't get us out.' Well, technology did not get us into this mess. Greed and weakness and ambivalence got us into this mess. What we need is more logical thinking, not less. The danger of fuzzy theory is that it will encourage the sort of imprecise thinking that has brought us so much trouble.'

What Lord Kelvin, Rudolph Kalman, William Kahan, and many other brilliant minds did not appreciate is the fundamental importance of the remarkable human capability to perform a wide variety of physical and mental tasks without any measurements and any computations. Familiar examples of such tasks are parking a car; driving in heavy traffic; playing golf; understanding speech, and summarizing a story.

Underlying this remarkable ability is the brain's crucial ability to manipulate perceptions—perceptions of size, distance, weight, speed, time, direction, smell, color, shape, force, likelihood, truth and intent, among others. A fundamental difference between measurements and perceptions is that, in general, measurements are crisp numbers whereas perceptions are fuzzy numbers or, more generally, fuzzy granules, that is, clumps of objects in which the transition from membership to non-membership is gradual rather than abrupt.

The fuzziness of perceptions reflects finite ability of sensory organs and the brain to resolve detail and store information. A concomitant of fuzziness of perceptions is the preponderant partiality of human concepts in the sense that the validity of most human concepts is a matter of degree. For example, we have partial knowledge, partial understanding, partial certainty, partial belief and accept partial solutions, partial truth and partial causality. Furthermore, most human concepts have a granular structure and are context-dependent.

In essence, a granule is a clump of physical or mental objects (points) drawn together by indistinguishability, similarity, proximity or functionality (Fig. 1). A granule may be crisp or fuzzy, depending on whether its boundaries are or are not sharply defined. For example, age may be granulated crisply into years and granulated fuzzily into fuzzy intervals labeled very young, young, middle-aged, old, and very old (Fig. 2). A partial taxonomy of granulation is shown in Figs. 3(a) and (b).

point of departure: the concept of a granule

informal: a granule is a clump of objects (points) drawn
           together by indistinguishability, similarity,
           proximity or functionality

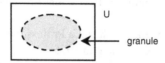

U

granule

formal: a granule is a clump of objects (points) defined
         by a generalized constraint

X isr R

constraining relation

copula

constrained variable

Fig. 1. Informal and formal definitions of a granule.

body	⇒	head + neck + arms + chest + ... + feet
time	⇒	years ⇒ months ⇒ ...
book	⇒	chapters ⇒ sections ⇒ paragraphs ⇒ ...
age	⇒	young + middle-aged + old
size	⇒	small + medium + large
distance	⇒	very near + near + not.near and not.far + far + very far
force	⇒	weak + moderate + strong

Fig. 2. Examples of crisp and fuzzy granulation.

In a very broad sense, granulation involves a partitioning of whole into parts. Modes of information granulation (IG) in which granules are crisp play important roles in a wide variety of methods, approaches and techniques. Among them are: interval analysis, quantization, chunking, rough set theory, diakoptics, divide and conquer, Dempster-Shafer theory, machine learning from examples, qualitative pro-cess theory, decision trees, semantic networks, analog-to-digital conversion, constraint programming, image segmentation, cluster analysis and many others.

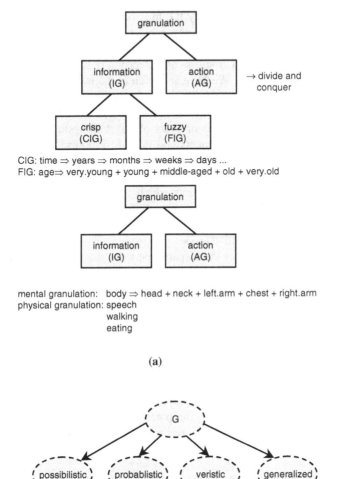

Fig. 3. (a) Partial taxonomy of granulation; (b) principal types of granules.

Important though it is, crisp IG has a major blind spot. More specifically, it fails to reflect the fact that most human perceptions are fuzzy rather than crisp. For example, when we mentally granulate the human body into fuzzy granules labeled head, neck, chest, arms, legs, etc, the length of neck is a fuzzy attribute whose value is a fuzzy number. Fuzziness of granules, their attributes and their values is characteristic of ways in which human concepts are formed, organized and manipulated. In effect, fuzzy information granulation (fuzzy IG) may be viewed as a human way of employing data compression for reasoning and, more particularly, making rational decisions in an environment of imprecision, uncertainty and partial truth.

The tradition of pursuit of crispness and precision in scientific theories can be credited with brilliant successes. We have sent men to the moon; we can build computers that are capable of performing billions of computations per second; we have constructed telescopes that can explore the far reaches of the universe; and we can date the age of rocks that are millions of years old. But alongside the brilliant successes stand conspicuous underachievements and outright failures. We cannot build robots which can move with the agility of animals or humans; we cannot automate driving in heavy traffic; we cannot translate from one language to another at the level of a human interpreter; we cannot create programs which can summarize nontrivial stories; our ability to model the behavior of economic systems leaves much to be desired; and we cannot build machines that can compete with children in the performance of a wide variety of physical and cognitive tasks.

What is the explanation for the disparity between the successes and failures? What can be done to advance the frontiers of science and technology beyond where they are today, especially in the realms of machine intelligence and automation of decision processes? In my view, the failures are conspicuous in those areas in which the objects of manipulation are, in the main, perceptions rather than measurements. Thus, what we need are ways of dealing with perceptions, in addition to the many tools which we have for dealing with measurements. In essence, it is this need that motivated the development of the methodology of computing with words (CW)—a methodology in which words play the role of labels of perceptions.

CW provides a methodology for what may be called a *computational theory of perceptions* (CTP) (Fig. 4). However, the potential impact of the methodology of computing with words is much broader. Basically, there are four principal rationales for the use of CW.

1. *The don't know rationale:* In this case, the values of variables and/or parameters are not known with sufficient precision to justify the use of conventional methods of numerical computing. An example is decision-making with poorly defined probabilities and utilities.
2. *The don't need rationale:* In this case, there is a tolerance for imprecision which can be exploited to achieve tractability, robustness, low solution cost, and better rapport with reality. An example is the problem of parking a car.
3. *The can't solve rationale:* In this case, the problem cannot be solved through the use of numerical computing. An example is the problem of automation of driving in city traffic.
4. *The can't define rationale:* In this case, a concept that we wish to define is too complex to admit of definition in terms of a set of numerical criteria. A case in

point is the concept of causality. Causality is an instance of what may be called an amorphic concept.

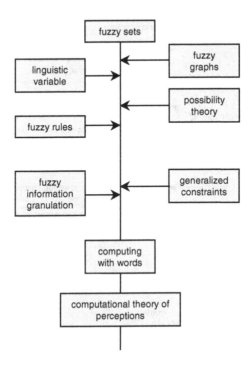

Fig. 4. Conceptual structure of computational theory of perceptions.

The basic idea underlying the relationship between CW and CTP is conceptually simple. More specifically, in CTP perceptions and queries are expressed as propositions in a natural language. Then, the propositions and queries are processed by CW-based methods to yield answers to queries. Simple examples of linguistic characterization of perceptions drawn from everyday experiences are:

Robert is highly intelligent
Carol is very attractive
Hans loves wine
Overeating causes obesity
Most Swedes are tall
Berkeley is more lively than Palo Alto
It is likely to rain tomorrow
It is very unlikely that there will be a significant
     increase in the price of oil in the near future

Examples of correct conclusions drawn from perceptions through the use of CW-based methods are shown in Fig. 5(a). Examples of incorrect conclusions are shown in Fig. 5(b).

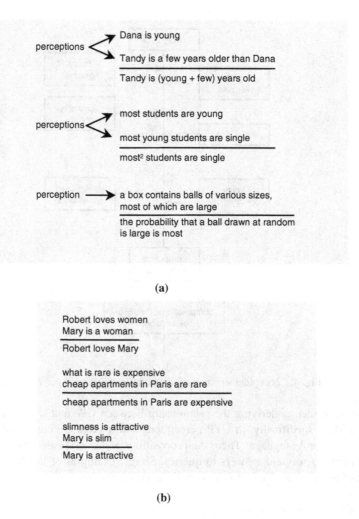

perceptions
Dana is young
Tandy is a few years older than Dana

Tandy is (young + few) years old

perceptions
most students are young
most young students are single

most² students are single

perception → a box contains balls of various sizes, most of which are large

the probability that a ball drawn at random is large is most

(a)

Robert loves women
Mary is a woman

Robert loves Mary

what is rare is expensive
cheap apartments in Paris are rare

cheap apartments in Paris are expensive

slimness is attractive
Mary is slim

Mary is attractive

(b)

Fig. 5. (a) Examples of reasoning with perceptions; (b) examples of incorrect reasoning.

Perceptions have long been an object of study in psychology. However, the idea of linking perceptions to computing with words is in a different spirit. An interesting system-theoretic approach to perceptions is described in a recent work of R. Vallee [31]. A logic of perceptions has been described by H. Rasiowa [26]. These approaches are not related to the approach described in our paper.

An important point that should be noted is that classical logical systems such as propositional logic, predical logic and modal logic, as well as AI-based techniques for natural language processing and knowledge representation, are concerned in a fundamental way with propositions expressed in a natural language. The main difference between such approaches and CW is that the methodology of CW—which is based on fuzzy logic—provides a much more expressive language for knowledge representation and much more versatile machinery for reasoning and computation.

In the final analysis, the role model for computing with words is the human mind and its remarkable ability to manipulate both measurements and perceptions. What should be stressed, however, is that although words are less precise than numbers, the methodology of computing with words rests on a mathematical foundation. An exposition of the basic concepts and techniques of computing with words is presented in the following sections. The linkage of CW and CTP is discussed very briefly because the computational theory of perceptions is still in its early stages of development.

2   What is CW?

In its traditional sense, computing involves for the most part manipulation of numbers and symbols. By contrast, humans employ mostly words in computing and reasoning, arriving at conclusions expressed as words from premises expressed in a natural language or having the form of mental perceptions. As used by humans, words have fuzzy denotations. The same applies to the role played by words in CW.

The concept of CW is rooted in several papers starting with my 1973 paper 'Outline of a New Approach to the Analysis of Complex Systems and Decision Processes,' [37] in which the concepts of a linguistic variable and granulation were introduced. The concepts of a fuzzy constraint and fuzzy constraint propagation were introduced in 'Calculus of Fuzzy Restrictions,' [39], and developed more fully in 'A Theory of Approximate Reasoning,' [45] and 'Outline of a Computational Approach to Meaning and Knowledge Representation Based on a Concept of a Generalized As-signment Statement,' [49]. Application of fuzzy logic to meaning representation and its role in test-score semantics are discussed in 'PRUF—A Meaning Representation Language for Natural Languages,' [43], and 'Test-Score Semantics for Natural Languages and Meaning-Representation via PRUF,' [46]. The close relationship between CW and fuzzy information granulation is discussed in 'Toward a Theory of Fuzzy Information Granulation and its Centrality in Human Reasoning and Fuzzy Logic [53].'

Although the foundations of computing with words were laid some time ago, its evolution into a distinct methodology in its own right reflects many advances in our understanding of fuzzy logic and soft computing—advances which took place within the past few years (see references and related papers). A key aspect of CW is that it involves a fusion of natural languages and computation with fuzzy variables. It is this fusion that is likely to result in an evolution of CW into a basic methodology in its own right, with wide-ranging ramifications and applications.

We begin our exposition of CW with a few definitions. It should be understood that the definitions are dispositional, that is, admit of exceptions. As was stated earlier, a concept which plays a pivotal role in CW is that of a granule. Typically, a granule is a fuzzy set of points drawn together by similarity (Fig. 1). A word may be atomic, as in *young*, or composite, as in *not very young* (Fig. 6). Unless stated to the contrary, a word will be assumed to be composite. The denotation of a word may be a higher order predicate, as in Montague grammar [12, 23].

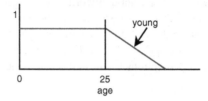

- a word is a label of a fuzzy set

- a string of words is a label of a function of fuzzy sets

    - not very young $\Rightarrow$ (^{2}young)

- a word is a description of a constraint on a variable

    - Mary is young $\Rightarrow$ Age(Mary) is young

Fig. 6. Words as labels of fuzzy sets.

In CW, a granule, g, which is the denotation of a word, w, is viewed as a fuzzy constraint on a variable. A pivotal role in CW is played by fuzzy constraint propagation from premises to conclusions. It should be noted that, as a basic technique, constraint propagation plays important roles in many methodologies, especially in mathematical programming, constraint programming and logic programming (see references and related papers).

As a simple illustration, consider the proposition *Mary is young*, which may be a linguistic characterization of a perception. In this case, *young* is the label of a granule young. (Note that for simplicity the same symbol is used both for a word and its denotation.) The fuzzy set *young* plays the role of a fuzzy constraint on the age of Mary (Fig. 6).

As a further example consider the propositions:

$p_1 = Carol\ lives\ near\ Mary$

and

$p_2 = Mary\ lives\ near\ Pat.$

In this case, the words *lives near* in p_1 and p_2 play the role of fuzzy constraints on the distances between the residences of Carol and Mary, and Mary and Pat, respectively. If the query is: How far is Carol from Pat?, an answer yielded by fuzzy constraint propagation might be expressed as p_3, where:

p_3 = *Carol lives not far from Pat.*

More about fuzzy constraint propagation will be said at a later point.

A basic assumption in CW is that information is conveyed by constraining the values of variables. Furthermore, information is assumed to consist of a collection of propositions expressed in natural or synthetic language. Typically, such propositions play the role of linguistic characterization of perceptions.

A basic generic problem in CW is the following.

We are given a collection of propositions expressed in a natural language which constitute the *initial data set*, or IDS for short.

From the initial data set we wish to infer an answer to a query expressed in a natural language. The answer, also expressed in a natural language, is referred to as the *terminal data set*, or TDS for short. The problem is to derive TDS from IDS (Fig. 7).

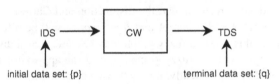

initial data set: {p}   terminal data set: {q}

p, q: propositions expressed in a natural language

{p} = {most students are young, most young students are single}

{q} = {most² students are single}

Fig. 7. Computing with words as a transformation of an initial data set (IDS) into a terminal data set (TDS).

A few problems will serve to illustrate these concepts. At this juncture, the problems will be formulated but not solved.

1) Assume that a function, f, $f: U \rightarrow V$; $X \in U$; $Y \in V$; is described in words by the fuzzy if-then rules:

f: if X is *small* then Y is *small*
    if X is *medium* then Y is *large*
    if X is *large* then Y is *small*.

What this implies is that f is approximated to by a fuzzy graph f^* (Fig. 8), where:

$f^* = small \times small + medium \times large + large \times small$

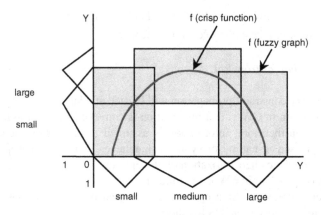

Fig. 8. Fuzzy graph of a function.

In f^*, + and × denote, respectively, the disjunction and Cartesian product. An expression of the form $A \times B$; where A and B are words, will be referred to as a *Cartesian granule*. In this sense, a fuzzy graph may be viewed as a disjunction of Cartesian granules. In essence, a fuzzy graph serves as an approximation to a function or a relation [38, 51]. Equivalently, it may be viewed as a linguistic characterization of a perception of f (Fig. 9).

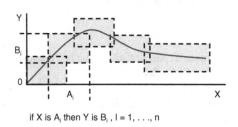

if X is A_i then Y is B_i, $I = 1, \ldots, n$

Fig. 9. A fuzzy graph of a function represented by a rule-set.

In the example under consideration, the IDS consists of the fuzzy rule-set f. The query is: What is the maximum value of f (Fig. 10)? More broadly, the problem is: How can one compute an attribute of a function, f, e.g. its maximum value or its area or its roots, if f is described in words as a collection of fuzzy if-then rules? Determination of the maximum value will be discussed in greater detail at a later point.

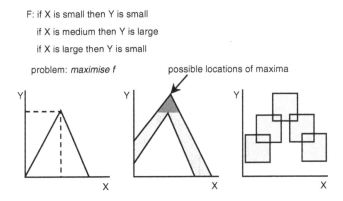

Fig. 10. Fuzzy graph of a function defined by a fuzzy rule-set.

2) A box contains ten balls of various sizes of which several are large and a few are small. What is the probability that a ball drawn at random is neither large nor small? In this case, the IDS is a verbal description of the contents of the box; the TDS is the desired probability.

3) A less simple example of computing with words is the following.

Let X and Y be independent random variables taking values in a finite set $V = \{v_1, ..., v_n\}$ with probabilities $p_1, ..., p_n$ and $p_1, ..., q_n$, respectively. For simplicity of notation, the same symbols will be used to denote X and Y and their generic values, with p and q denoting the probabilities of X and Y, respectively.

Assume that the probability distributions of X and Y are described in words through the fuzzy if-then rules (Fig. 11):

P: if X is *small* then p is *small*
          if X is *medium* then p is *large*
          if X is *large* then p is *small,*

and

Q: if Y is *small* then q is *large*
          if Y is *medium* then q is *small*
          if Y is *large* then q is *large.*

where granules *small, medium* and *large* are values of linguistic variables X and Y in their respective universes of discourse. In the example under consideration, these rule-sets constitute the IDS. Note that *small* in P need not have the same meaning as *small* in Q, and likewise for *medium* and *large*. The query is: How can we describe in words the joint probability distribution of X and Y? This probability distribution is the TDS.

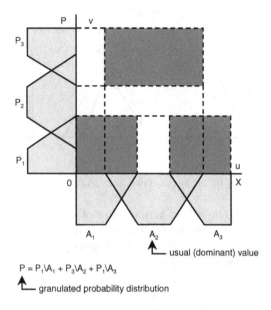

$$P = P_1 \backslash A_1 + P_3 \backslash A_2 + P_1 \backslash A_3$$

— granulated probability distribution

Fig. 11. A fuzzy graph representation of a granulated probability distribution.

For convenience, the probability distributions of X and Y may be represented as fuzzy graphs:

P: *small* × *small* + *medium* ×*large* + *large* × *small*
Q: *small* × *large* + *medium* × *small* + *large* × *large*

with the understanding that the underlying numerical probabilities must add up to unity.

Since X and Y are independent random variables, their joint probability distribution $(P; Q)$ is the product of P and Q: In words, the product may be expressed as [51]:

$(P; Q)$: *small* × *small* × (*small* * *large*)
    + *small* × *medium* × (*small* * *small*)
    + *small* × *large* × (*small* * *large*)
    + ... + *large* × *large* × (*small* * *large*)

where * is the arithmetic product in fuzzy arithmetic [14]. In this example, what we have done, in effect, amounts to a derivation of a linguistic characterization of the joint probability distribution of X and Y starting with linguistic characterizations of the probability distribution of X and the probability distribution of Y.

A few comments are in order. In linguistic characterizations of variables and their dependencies, words serve as values of variables and play the role of fuzzy constraints. In this perspective, the use of words may be viewed as a form of granulation, which in turn may be regarded as a form of fuzzy quantization.

Granulation plays a key role in human cognition. For humans, it serves as a way of achieving data compression. This is one of the pivotal advantages accruing through the use of words in human, machine and man-machine communication.

The point of departure in CW is the premise that the meaning of a proposition, p, in a natural language may be represented as an implicit constraint on an implicit variable. Such a representation is referred to as a *canonical form* of p, denoted as $CF(p)$ (Fig. 12). Thus, a canonical form serves to make explicit the implicit constraint which resides in p. The concept of a canonical form is described in greater detail in the following section.

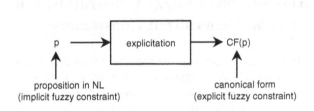

p ——→ explicitation ——→ CF(p)

proposition in NL   canonical form
(implicit fuzzy constraint)   (explicit fuzzy constraint)

Fig. 12. Canonical form of a proposition.

As a first step in the derivation of TDS from IDS, propositions in IDS are translated into their canonical forms, which collectively represent *antecedent* constraints. Through the use of rules for constraint propagation, antecedent constraints are transformed into *consequent* constraints. Finally, consequent constraints are translated into a natural language through the use of *linguistic approximation* [10, 18], yielding the terminal data set TDS. This process is schematized in Fig. 13.

In essence, the rationale for computing with words rests on two major imperatives: 1) computing with words is a necessity when the available information is too imprecise to justify the use of numbers and 2) when there is a tolerance for imprecision which can be exploited to achieve tractability, robustness, low solution cost and better rapport with reality. In computing with words, there are two core issues that arise. First is the issue of representation of fuzzy constraints. More specifically, the question is: How can the fuzzy constraints which are implicit in propositions expressed in a natural language be made explicit. And second is the issue of fuzzy constraint propagation, that is, the question of how can fuzzy constraints in premises, i.e. antecedent constraints, be propagated to conclusions, i.e. consequent constraints. These are the issues which are addressed in the following.

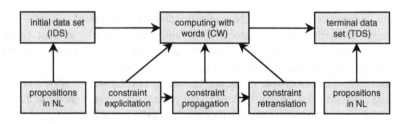

Fig. 13. Conceptual structure of computing with words.

3   Representation of Fuzzy Constraints, Canonical Forms, and Generalized Constraints

Our approach to the representation of fuzzy constraints is based on test-score semantics [46, 47]. In outline, in this semantics, a proposition, p, in a natural language is viewed as a network of fuzzy (elastic) constraints. Upon aggregation, the constraints which are embodied in p result in an overall fuzzy constraint which can be represented as an expression of the form:

$$X \text{ is } R$$

where R is a constraining fuzzy relation and X is the constrained variable. The expression in question is the canonical form of p. Basically, the function of a canonical form is to place in evidence the fuzzy constraint which is implicit in p. This is represented schematically as:

$$P \to X \text{ is } R$$

in which the arrow $\to$ denotes explicitation. The variable X may be vector-valued and/or conditioned.

In this perspective, the meaning of p is defined by two procedures. The first procedure acts on a so-called explanatory database, ED, and returns the constrained variable, X. The second procedure acts on ED and returns the constraining relation, R.

An explanatory database is a collection of relations in terms of which the meaning of p is defined. The relations are empty, that is, they consist of relation names, relations attributes and attribute domains, with no entries in the relations. When there are entries in ED, ED is said to be *instantiated* and is denoted EDI. EDI may be viewed as a description of a possible world in possible world semantics [6], while ED defines a collection of possible worlds, with each possible world in the collection corresponding to a particular instantiation of ED [47].

As a simple illustration, consider the proposition:

$$P = \textit{Mary is not young.}$$

Assume that the explanatory database is chosen to be:

$$ED = POPULATION[Name; Age] + YOUNG[Age; \mu]$$

in which POPULATION is a relation with arguments Name and Age; YOUNG is a relation with arguments Age and μ; and + is the disjunction. In this case, the constrained variable is the age of Mary, which in terms of ED may be expressed as:

$$X = Age(Mary) =_{Age} POPULATION[Name=Mary].$$

This expression specifies the procedure which acts on ED and returns X. More specifically, in this procedure, Name is instantiated to Mary and the resulting relation is projected on Age, yielding the age of Mary.

The constraining relation, R, is given by:

$$R = (^2 YOUNG)'.$$

which implies that the intensifier *very* is interpreted as a squaring operation, and the negation *not* as the operation of complementation [36].

Equivalently, R may be expressed as:

$$R = YOUNG[Age; 1 - \mu^2]$$

As a further example, consider the proposition:

$$p = \textit{Carol lives in a small city near San Francisco}$$

and assume that the explanatory database is:

$$ED = POPULATION[Name; Residence]$$
$$+ SMALL[City; \mu]$$
$$+ NEAR[City1; City2; \mu]$$

In this case:

$$X = Residence(Carol)$$
$$=_{Residence} POPULATION[Name = Carol]$$
and

$$R = SMALL[City\,;\mu]$$
$$\cap_{\text{City1}} NEAR[City2 = \text{San\_Francisco}]$$

In R, the first constituent is the fuzzy set of small cities, the second constituent is the fuzzy set of cities which are near San Francisco, and $\cap$ denotes the intersection of these sets.

So far we have confined our attention to constraints of the form:

$$X \text{ is } R$$

In fact, constraints can have a variety of forms. In particular, a constraint—expressed as a canonical form—may be conditional, that is, of the form:

$$\text{if } X \text{ is } R \text{ then } Y \text{ is } S$$

which may also be written as

$$Y \text{ is } S \text{ if } X \text{ is } R:$$

The constraints in question will be referred to as *basic*.

For purposes of meaning representation, the richness of natural languages necessitates a wide variety of constraints in relation to which the basic constraints form an important though special class. The so-called generalized constraints [49] contain the basic constraints as a special case and are defined as follows. The need for generalized constraints becomes obvious when one attempts to represent the meaning of simple propositions such as:

> Robert loves women
> John is very honest
> checkout time is 11 am
> slimness is attractive

in the language of standard logical systems.

A generalized constraint is represented as:

$$X \text{ isr } R$$

where isr, pronounced "ezar", is a variable copula which defines the way in which R constrains X. More specifically, the role of R in relation to X is defined by the value of the discrete variable r. The values of r and their interpretations are defined below:

e equal (abbreviated to =);
d disjunctive (possibilistic) (abbreviated to blank);
v veristic;

p   probabilistic;
γ   probability value;
u   usuality;
rs   random set;
rfs   random fuzzy set;
fg   fuzzy graph;
ps   rough set;
.   ...

As an illustration, when $r = e$, the constraint is an equality constraint and is abbreviated to = . When r takes the value d, the constraint is *disjunctive* (possibilistic) and isd abbreviated to is, leading to the expression:

$$X \text{ is } R$$

in which R is a fuzzy relation which constrains X by playing the role of the possibility distribution of X. More specifically, if X takes values in a universe of discourse, $U = \{u\}$, then $Poss\{X = u\} = \mu_R(u)$, where μ_R is the membership function of R, and Π_X is the possibility distribution of X, that is, the fuzzy set of its possible values [42]. In schematic form:

$$X \text{ is } R \overset{\rightarrow}{\underset{\hookrightarrow}{}} \begin{array}{l} \Pi_X = R \\ Poss\{X = u\} = \mu_R(u) \end{array}$$

Similarly, when r takes the value v, the constraint is *veristic*. In the case:

$$X \text{ isv } R$$

means that if the grade of membership of u in R is μ, then $X = u$ has truth value μ. For example, a canonical form of the proposition:

$$p = John\ is\ proficient\ in\ English,\ French,\ and\ German$$

may be expressed as:

Proficiency(John)
        isv (1|English + 0.7|French + 0.6|German)

in which 1.0, 0.7, and 0.6 represent, respectively, the truth values of the propositions *John is proficient in English, John is proficient in French and John is proficient in German*. In a similar vein, the veristic constraint:

Ethnicity(John)
        isv (0.5|German + 0.25|French + 0.25|Italian)

represents the meaning of the proposition *John is half German, quarter French and quarter Italian.*

When $r = p$, the constraint is *probabilistic*. In this case,

$$X \text{ isp } R$$

means that R is the probability distribution of X. For example:

$$X \text{ isp } N(m; \sigma^2)$$

means that X is normally distributed with mean m and variance σ^2 : Similarly,

$$X \text{ isp } (0.2\backslash a + 0.5\backslash b + 0.3\backslash c)$$

means that X is a random variable which takes the values a, b, and c with respective probabilities 0.2, 0.5, and 0.3.

The constraint

$$X \text{ isu } R$$

is an abbreviation for:

$$\textit{usually } (X \text{ is } R)$$

which in turn means that:

$$\textit{Prob}\{X \text{ is } R\} \textit{ is usually}$$

In this expression X is R is a fuzzy event and *usually* is its fuzzy probability, that is, the possibility distribution of its crisp probability.

The constraint:

$$X \text{ isrs } P$$

is a random set constraint. This constraint is a combination of probabilistic and possibilistic constraints. More specifically, in a schematic form, it is expressed as:

$$\frac{\begin{array}{c} X \text{ isp } P \\ (X,Y) \text{ is } Q \end{array}}{Y \text{ isrs } R}$$

where Q is a joint possibilitistic constraint on X and Y; and R is a random set. It is of interest to note that the Dempster-Shafer theory of evidence [29] is, in essence, a theory of random set constraints.

In computing with words, the starting point is a collection of propositions which play the role of premises. In many cases, the canonical forms of these propositions are constraints of the basic, possibilistic type. In a more general setting, the constraints are of the generalized type, implying that explicitation of a proposition, p, may be represented as:

$$p \rightarrow X \text{ isr } R$$

where X isr R is the canonical form of p (Fig. 14).

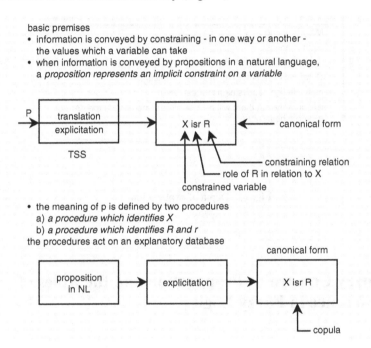

basic premises
- information is conveyed by constraining - in one way or another - the values which a variable can take
- when information is conveyed by propositions in a natural language, a *proposition represents an implicit constraint on a variable*

- the meaning of p is defined by two procedures
  a) *a procedure which identifies X*
  b) *a procedure which identifies R and r*
  the procedures act on an explanatory database

Fig. 14. Representation of meaning in test-score semantics.

As in the case of basic constraints, the canonical form of a proposition may be derived through the use of test-score semantics. In this context, the depth of p is, roughly, a measure of the effort that is needed to explicitate p, that is, to translate p into its canonical form. In this sense, the proposition X isr R is a surface constraint (depth = zero), with the depth of explicitation increasing in the downward direction (Fig. 15). Thus a proposition such as *Mary is young* is shallow, whereas *it is unlikely that there will be a substantial increase in the price of oil in the near future*, is not.

Once the propositions in the initial data set are expressed in their canonical forms, the groundwork is laid for fuzzy constraint propagation. This is a basic part of CW which is discussed in the following section.

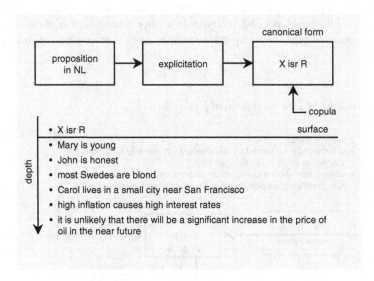

Fig. 15. Depth of explictation.

4.   Fuzzy Constraint Propagation and the Rules of Inference in Fuzzy Logic

The rules governing fuzzy constraint propagation are, in effect, the rules of inference in fuzzy logic. In addition to these rules, it is helpful to have rules governing fuzzy constraint modification, The latter rules will be discussed at a later point in this section.

In a summarized form, the rules governing fuzzy constraint propagation are the following [51]. (A and B are fuzzy relations. Disjunction and conjunction are defined, respectively, as max and min, with the understanding that, more generally, they could be defined via t-norms and s-norms [15, 24]. The antecedent and consequent constraints are separated by a horizontal line.)

Conjunctive Rule 1:

$$X \text{ is } A$$
$$\frac{X \text{ is } B}{X \text{ is } A \cap B}$$

Conjunctive Rule 2: $(X \in U, Y \in B, A \subset U, B \subset V)$

$$X \text{ is } A$$
$$\frac{X \text{ is } B}{(X,Y) \text{ is } A \times B}$$

Disjunctive Rule 1:

$$X \text{ is } A$$
or
$$\frac{X \text{ is } B}{X \text{ is } A \cup B}$$

Disjunctive Rule 1: $(A \subset U, B \subset V)$

$$A \text{ is } A$$
$$\frac{Y \text{ is } B}{(X,Y) \text{ is } A \times V \cup U \times B}$$

where $A \times V$ and $U \times B$ are cylindrical extensions of A and B, respectively.

Conjunctive Rule for isv:

$$X \text{ isv } A$$
$$\frac{X \text{ isv } B}{X \text{ isv } A \cup B}$$

Projective Rule:

$$\frac{(X,Y) \text{ is } A}{Y \text{ is } \text{proj}_V A}$$

where $\text{proj}_V A = \sup_u A$

Subjective Rule:

$$\frac{X \text{ is } A}{(X,Y) \text{ is } A \times V}$$

Derived Rules:

Compositional Rule:

$$X \text{ is } A$$
$$(X, Y) \text{ is } B$$
$$\overline{X \text{ is } A \circ B}$$

where $A \circ B$ denotes the composition of A and B.

Extension Principle (mapping rule) [34, 40]:

$$X \text{ is } A$$
$$\overline{f(X) \text{ is } f(A)}$$

where f, $U \rightarrow V$, and $f(A)$ is defined by:

$$\mu_{f(A)}(v) = \sup_{u|v = f(u)} \mu_A(u)$$

Inverse Mapping Rule:

$$f(X) \text{ is } A$$
$$\overline{X \text{ is } f^{-1}(A)}$$

where $\mu_{f-1(A)}(u) = \mu_A(f(u))$

Generalized modus ponens:

$$X \text{ is } A$$
$$\text{if } X \text{ is } B \text{ then } Y \text{ is } C$$
$$\overline{Y \text{ is } A \circ ((\neg B) \oplus C)}$$

where the bounded sum $\neg B \oplus C$ represents Lukasiewicz's definition of implication.

Generalized Extension Principle:

$$f(X) \text{ is } A$$
$$\overline{q(X) \text{ is } q(f^{-1}(A))}$$

where

$$\mu_q(v) = \sup_{u|v = f(u)} \mu_A(q(u))$$

The generalized extension principle plays a pivotal role in fuzzy constraint propagation. However, what is used most frequently in practical applications of fuzzy logic is the *basic interpolative rule*, which is a special case of the compositional rule of inference applied to a function which is defined by a fuzzy graph [38, 51]. More specifically, if f is defined by a fuzzy rule set:

$$f : if\ X\ is\ A_i\ then\ X\ is\ B_i,\ i = 1,\ ...,\ n$$

or equivalently, by a fuzzy graph:

$$f\ is\ \sum_i A_i \times B_i$$

and its argument, X, is defined by the antecedent constraint:

$$X\ is\ A$$

then the consequent constraint on Y may be expressed as:

$$Y\ is\ \sum_i m_i \wedge B_i$$

where m_i is a matching coefficient,

$$m_i = \sup\ (A_i \cap A)$$

which serves as a measure of the degree to which A matches A_I.

Syllogistic Rule [48]:

$$\frac{\begin{array}{l} Q_1\ A's\ are\ B's \\ Q_2\ (A\ and\ B)'s\ are\ C's \end{array}}{(Q_1 \otimes Q_2)A's\ are\ (B\ and\ C)'s}$$

where Q_1 and Q_2 are fuzzy quantifiers, A, B, and C are fuzzy relations, and $Q_1 \otimes Q_2$ is the product of Q_1 and Q_2 in fuzzy arithmetic.

Constraint Modification Rule [36, 43]:

$$X\ is\ mA \rightarrow X\ is\ f(A)$$

where m is a modifier such as *not, very, more, or less*, and $f(A)$ defines the way in which m modifies A. Specifically,

$$if\ m = not\ then\ f(A) = A'\ (complement)$$
$$if\ m = very\ then\ f(A) = {}^2A\ (left\ square)$$

where $\mu_{2_A}(u) = (\mu_A(u))^2$. This rule is a convention and should not be construed as a realistic approximation to the way in which the modifier *very* functions in a natural language.

Probability Qualification Rule [45]:

$$(X \text{ is } A) \text{ is } \Lambda \rightarrow P \text{ is } \Lambda$$

where X is a random variable taking values in U with probability density $p(u)$, Λ is a linguistic probability expressed in words like *likely, not very likely*, etc, and P is the probability of the fuzzy event X is A, expressed as:

$$P = \int_U \mu_A(u) p(u) du$$

The primary purpose of this summary is to underscore the coincidence of the principal rules governing fuzzy constraint propagation with the principal values of inference in fuzzy logic. Of necessity, the summary is not complete and there are many specialized rules which are not included. Furthermore, most of the rules in the summary apply to constraints which are of the basic, possibilistic type. Further development of the rules governing fuzzy constraint propagation will require an extension of the rules of inference to generalized constraints.

As was alluded to in the summary, the principal rule governing constraint propagation is the generalized extension principle which in a schematic form may be represented as:

$$\frac{f(X_1, \cdots X_n) \text{ is } A}{q(X_1, \cdots X_n) \text{ is } q(f^{-1}(A))}$$

In this expression, $X_1, \ldots, X_n$ are database variables; the term above the line represents the constraint induced by the IDS; and the term below the line is the TDS expressed as a constraint on the query $q(X_1, \ldots, X_n)$: In the latter constraint, $f^{-1}(A)$ denotes the pre-image of the fuzzy relation A under the mapping $f: U \rightarrow V$, where A is a fuzzy subset of V and U is the domain of $f(X_1, \ldots, X_n)$.

Expressed in terms of the membership functions of A and $q(f^{-1}(A))$, the generalized extension principle reduces the derivation of the TDS to the solution of the constrained maximization problem:

$$\mu_{q(X_1, \cdots X_n)}(v) = \sup_{(u_1, \cdots, u_n)} (\mu_A(f(u_1, \ldots, u_n)))$$

in which $u_1, \ldots, u_n$ are constrained by:

$$v = q(u_1, \ldots, u_n).$$

The generalized extension principle is simpler than it appears. An illustration of its use is provided by the following example.

The IDS is:

most Swedes are tall

The query is: *What is the average height of Swedes?*

The explanatory database consists of a population of N Swedes, $Name_1, \ldots, Name_N$. The database variables are $h_1, \ldots, h_N$, where h_i is the height of $Name_i$; and the grade of membership of $Name_i$ in *tall* is $\mu\ tall(h_i)$, $i = 1, \ldots, n$.

The proportion of Swedes who are tall is given by the sigma-count [43]:

$$\sum Count\,(tall \cdot Swedes\ /\ Swedes) = \frac{1}{N} \sum_i \mu_{tall}(h_i)$$

from which it follows that the constraint on the database variables induced by the IDS is:

$$\frac{1}{N} \sum_i \mu_{tall}(h_i) \text{ is } most$$

In terms of the database variables $h_1, \ldots, h_N$, the average height of Swedes is given by:

$$h_{ave} = \frac{1}{N} \sum_i (h_i)$$

Since the IDS is a fuzzy proposition, h_{ave} is a fuzzy set whose determination reduces to the constrained maximization problem:

$$\mu_{h_{ave}}(v) = \sup_{(h_1, \cdots, h_N)} (\mu_{most}(\frac{1}{N} \sum \mu_{tall}(h_i)))$$

subject to the constraint:

$$v = \frac{1}{N} \sum_i h_i$$

It is possible that approximate solutions to problems of this type might be obtainable through the use of neurocomputing or evolutionary-computing-based methods.

As a further example, we will return to a problem stated in an earlier section, namely, maximization of a function, f, which is described in words by its fuzzy graph, f^* (Fig. 10). More specifically, consider the standard problem of maximization of an objective function in decision analysis. Let us assume—as is frequently the case in real-world problems—that the objective function, f, is not well-defined and that what we know about f can be expressed as a fuzzy rule set:

$$f : if \ X \ is \ A_1 \ then \ Y \ is \ B_1$$
$$if \ X \ is \ A_2 \ then \ Y \ is \ B_2$$
$$\cdots\cdots\cdots\cdots\cdots\cdots\cdots$$
$$if \ X \ is \ A_n \ then \ Y \ is \ B_n$$

or, equivalently, as a fuzzy graph:

$$f \ is \sum_i A_i \times B_i$$

The question is: What is the point or, more generally, the maximizing set [54] at which f is maximized, and what is the maximum value of f?

The problem can be solved by employing the technique of α-*cuts* [34, 40]. With reference to Fig. 16, if A_{i_α} and B_{i_α} are α-cuts of A_i and B_i; respectively, then the corresponding α-cut of f^* is given by:

$$f^*_\alpha \ is \sum_i A_{i_\alpha} \times B_{i_\alpha}$$

From this expression, the maximizing fuzzy set, the maximum fuzzy set and maximum value fuzzy set can readily be derived, as shown in Figs. 16 and 17.

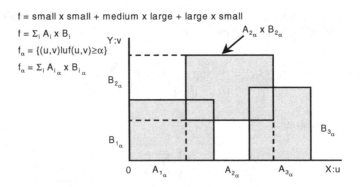

Fig. 16. α-cuts of a function described by a fuzzy graph.

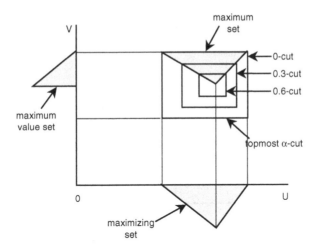

Fig. 17. Computation of maximizing set, maximum set, and maximum value.

A key point which is brought out by these examples and the preceding discussion is that explicitation and constraint propagation play pivotal roles in CW. This role can be concretized by viewing explicitation and constraint propagation as translation of propositions expressed in a natural language into what might be called the *generalized constraint language* (GCL) and applying rules of constraint propagation to expressions in this language—expressions which are typically canonical forms of propositions expressed in a natural language. This process is schematized in Fig. 18.

The conceptual framework of GCL is substantively different from that of conventional logical systems, e.g. predicate logic. But what matters most is that the expressive power of GCL—which is based on fuzzy logic—is much greater than that of standard logical calculi. As an illustration of this point, consider the following problem.

A box contains ten balls of various sizes of which several are large and a few are small. What is the probability that a ball drawn at random is neither large nor small?

To be able to answer this question it is necessary to be able to define the meanings of *large, small, several large balls, few small balls*, and *neither large nor small*. This is a problem in semantics which falls outside probability theory, neurocomputing and other methodologies.

An important application area for computing with words and manipulation of perceptions is decision analysis since in most realistic settings the underlying probabilities and utilities are not known with sufficient precision to justify the use of numerical valuations. There exists an extensive literature on the use of fuzzy probabilities and fuzzy utilities in decision analysis. In what follows, we shall restrict ours to two very simple examples which illustrate the use of perceptions.

Firstly, consider a box which contains black balls and white balls (Fig. 19). If we could count the number of black balls and white balls, the probability of picking a black ball at random would be equal to the proportion, r, of black balls in the box.

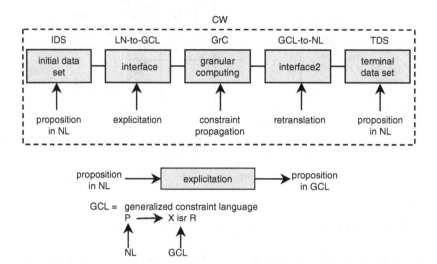

Fig. 18. Conceptual structure of computing with words.

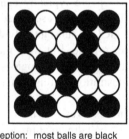

perception: most balls are black

question: what is the probability, P, that a
             ball drawn at random is black?

Fig. 19. A box with black and white balls.

Now suppose that we cannot count the number of black balls in the box but our perception is that most of the balls are black. What, then, is the probability, p, that a ball drawn at random is black?

Assume that *most* is characterized by its possibility distribution (Fig. 20). In this case, p is a fuzzy number whose possibility distribution is *most*, that is:

$$p \text{ is } most$$

Next, assume that there is a reward of a dollars if the ball drawn at random is black and a penalty of b dollars if the ball is white. In this case, if p were known as a number, the expected value of the gain would be:

$$e = ap - b(1-p)$$

Since we know not p but its possibility distribution, the problem is to compute the value of e when p is *most*. For this purpose, we can employ the extension principle [34, 40], which implies that the possibility distribution, E, of e is a fuzzy number which may be expressed as:

$$E = a \, most - b \, (1-most)$$

For simplicity, assume that *most* has a trapezoidal possibility distribution (Fig. 20). In this case, the trapezoidal possibility distribution of E can be computed as shown in Fig. 21.

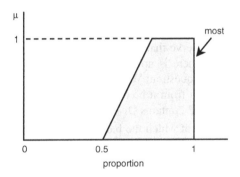

Fig. 20. Membership function of *most*.

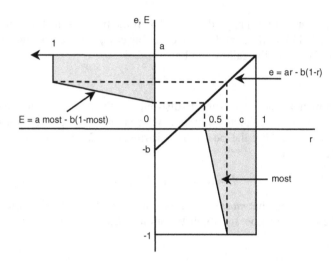

Fig. 21. Computation of expectation through use of the extension principle.

It is of interest to observe that if the support of E is an interval $[\alpha, \beta]$ which straddles O (Fig. 22), then there is no non-controversial decision principle which can be employed to answer the question: Would it be advantageous to play a game in which a ball is picked at random from a box in which most balls are black, and a and b are such that the support of E contains O.

Next, consider a box in which the balls $b_1, \ldots, b_n$ have the same color but vary in size, with b_i, $i = 1, \ldots, n$ having the grade of membership μ_i in the fuzzy set of large balls (Fig. 23). The question is: What is the probability that a ball drawn at random is large, given the perception that most balls are large?

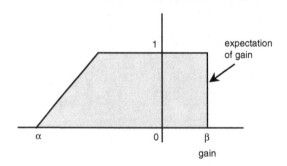

Fig. 22. Expectation of gain.

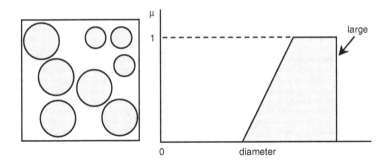

Fig. 23. A box with balls of various sizes and a definition of large ball.

The difference between this example and the preceding one is that the event *the ball drawn at random is large* is a fuzzy event, in contrast to the crisp event *the ball drawn at random is black*.

The probability of drawing b_i is $1/n$. Since the grade of membership of b_i in the fuzzy set of large balls is μ_i, the probability of the fuzzy event *the ball drawn at random is large* is given by [35]:

$$P = \frac{1}{n}\sum \mu_i$$

On the other hand, the proportion of large balls in the box is given by the relative sigma-count [40, 43]:

$$\sum Count\ (large \cdot balls\ /\ balls \cdot in \cdot box) = \frac{1}{n}\sum_i \mu_i$$

Consequently, the canonical form of the perception *most balls are large* may be expressed as:

$$\frac{1}{n}\sum_i \mu_i\ is\ most$$

which leads to the conclusion that:

$$P\ is\ most$$

It is of interest to observe that the possibility distribution of P is the same as in the preceding example.

If the question were: What is the probability that a ball drawn at random is *small*, the answer would be:

$$P \text{ is } \frac{1}{n} \sum v_i$$

where v_i, $i = 1, \ldots, n$, is the grade of membership of b_i, in the fuzzy set of small balls, given that:

$$\frac{1}{n} \sum \mu_i \text{ is } most$$

What is involved in this case is constraint propagation from the antecedent constraint on the μ_i to a consequent constraint on the v_i. This problem reduces to the solution of a nonlinear program.

What this example points to is that in using fuzzy constraint propagation rules, application of the extension principle reduces, in general, to the solution of a nonlinear program.

What we need—and do not have at present—are approximate methods of solving such programs which are capable of exploiting the tolerance for imprecision. Without such methods, the cost of solutions may be excessive in relation to the imprecision which is intrinsic in the use of words. In this connection, an intriguing possibility is to use neurocomputing and evolutionary computing techniques to arrive at approximate solutions to constrained maximization problems. The use of such techniques may provide a closer approximation to the ways in which humans manipulate perceptions.

5.   Concluding Remarks

In our quest for machines which have a high degree of machine intelligence (high MIQ), we are developing a better understanding of the fundamental importance of the remarkable human capacity to perform a wide variety of physical and mental tasks without any measurements and any computations. Underlying this remarkable capability is the brain's crucial ability to manipulate perceptions—perceptions of distance, size, weight, force, color, numbers, likelihood, truth and other characteristics of physical and mental objects. A basic difference between perception and measurements is that, in general, measurements are crisp whereas perceptions are fuzzy. In a fundamental way, this is the reason why to deal with perceptions it is necessary to employ a logical system that is fuzzy rather than crisp.

Humans employ words to describe perceptions. It is this obvious observation that is the point of departure for the theory outlined in the preceding sections.

When perceptions are described in words, manipulation of perceptions is reduced to computing with words (CW). In CW, the objects of computation are words or, more generally, propositions drawn from a natural language. A basic premise in CW is that the meaning of a proposition, p, may be expressed as a generalized constraint in which the constrained variable and the constraining relation are, in general, implicit in p.

In coming years, computing with words and perceptions is likely to emerge as an important direction in science and technology. In a reversal of long-standing attitudes, manipulation of perceptions and words which describe them is destined to gain in respectability. This is certain to happen because it is becoming increasingly clear that in dealing with real-world problems there is much to be gained by exploiting the tolerance for imprecision, uncertainty and partial truth. This is the primary motivation for the methodology of computing with words (CW) and the computational theory of perceptions (CTP) which are outlined in this paper.

Acknowledgement

The author acknowledges Prof. Michio Sugeno, who has contributed so much and in so many ways to the development of fuzzy logic and its applications.

References

1.   Berenji H. R.: 'Fuzzy reinforcement learning and dynamic programming', in 'Fuzzy Logic in Artificial Intelligence', Proc. IJCAI '93 Workshop, ed, Ralescu A. L., Berlin, Germany: Springer-Verlag, pp. 1–9 (1994).
2.   Black M.: 'Reasoning with loose concepts', Dialog 2, pp. 1–12 (1963).
3.   Bosch P.: 'Vagueness, ambiguity and all the rest', in Sprachstruktur, Individuum und Gesselschaft, eds, Van de Velde M. and Vandeweghe W., Tubingen, Germany: Niemeyer (1978).
4.   Bowen J., Lai R., and Bahler D.: 'Fuzzy semantics and fuzzy constraint networks', Proc. 1st IEEE Conf. on Fuzzy Systems, San Francisco, pp. 1009–1016 (1992).
5.   Bowen J., Lai R., and Bahler D.: 'Lexical imprecision in fuzzy constraint networks', Proc. Nat. Conf. on Artificial Intelligence, pp. 616–620 (1992).
6.   Cresswell M. J.: 'Logic and Languages', London, U.K.: Methuen (1973).
7.   Dubois D., Fargier H., and Prade H.: 'Propagation and satisfaction of flexible constraints', in 'Fuzzy Sets, Neural Networks, and Soft Computing', eds, Yager R. R. and Zadeh L. A., New York: Von Nostrand Reinhold, pp. 166–187 (1994).
8.   Dubois D., Fargier H., and Prade H.: 'Possibility theory in constraint satisfaction problems: Handling priority, preference, and uncertainty', J. Appl. Intell., to be published.
9.   Dubois D., Fargier H., and Prade H.: 'The calculus of fuzzy restrictions as a basis for exible constraint satisfaction', Proc. 2nd IEEE Int. Conf. on Fuzzy Systems, San Francisco, CA, pp. 1131–1136 (1993).
10. Freuder E. C., and Snow P.: 'Improved relaxation and search methods for approximate constraint satisfaction with a maximin criterion', Proc. 8th Biennial Conf. of the Canadian Society for Computational Studies of Intelligence, Ont., Canada, pp. 227–230 (1990).
11. Goguen J. A.: 'The logic of inexact concepts', Synthese, Vol. 19, pp. 325–373 (1969).
12. Hobbs J. R. 'Making computational sense of Montague's intentional logic', Artif. Intell., Vol. 9, pp. 287–306 (1978).
13. Katai O, Matsubara S, Masuichi H, Ida M, et al.: 'Synergetic computation for constraint satisfaction problems involving continuous and fuzzy variables by using Occam', in

'Transputer/Occam', Proc. 4th Transputer/Occam Int. Conf., eds, Noguchi S. and Umeo H., Amsterdam, The Netherlands: IOS Press, pp. 146–160 (1992).

14. Kaufmann A and Gupta M M: 'Introduction to Fuzzy Arithmetic: Theory and Applications', New York: Von Nostrand (1985).

15. Klir G and Yuan B: 'Fuzzy Sets and Fuzzy Logic', Englewood Cliffs, NJ: Prentice Hall (1995).

16. Lano K: 'A constraint-based fuzzy inference system', in EPIA 91, 5th Portuguese Conf. on Artificial Intelligence, eds, Barahona P., Pereira L. M. and Porto A., Berlin, Germany: Springer-Verlag, pp. 45–59 (1991).

17. Lodwick W. A: 'Analysis of structure in fuzzy linear programs', Fuzzy Sets and Systems, Vol. 38, No. 1, pp. 15–26 (1990).

18. Mamdani E. H. and Gaines B. R. (eds): 'Fuzzy Reasoning and Its Applications', London, U.K. (1981).

19. Mares M: 'Computation Over Fuzzy Quantities', Boca Raton, FL: CRC (1994).

20. Novak V: 'Fuzzy logic, fuzzy sets, and natural languages', Int. J. Gen. Syst., Vol. 20, No. 1, pp. 83–97 (1991).

21. Novak V, Ramik M, Cerny M, and Nekola J (eds): 'Fuzzy Approach to Reasoning and Decision-Making', Boston, MA: Kluwer (1992).

22. Oshan M. S., Saad O. M. and Hassan A. G.: 'On the solution of fuzzy multiobjective integer linear programming problems with a parametric study', Adv. Modeling Anal, A, Vol. 24, No. 2, pp. 49–64 1995).

23. Partee B.: 'Montague Grammar', New York: Academic (1976).

24. Pedrycz W. and Gomide F: 'Introduction to Fuzzy Sets', Cambridge, MA: MIT Press, (1998).

25. Qi G. and Friedrich G.: 'Extending constraint satisfaction problem solving in structural design', in 'Industrial and Engineering Applications of Artificial Intelligence and Expert Systems', 5th Int. Conf., IEA/AIE-92, eds, Belli F. and Radermacher F. J., Berlin, Germany: Springer-Verlag, pp. 341–350 (1992).

26. Rasiowa H and Marek M: 'On reaching consensus by groups of intelligent agents', in 'Methodologies for Intelligent Systems', ed, Ras Z. W., Amsterdam, The Netherlands: North-Holland, pp. 234–243 (1989).

27. Rosenfeld A, Hummel R. A. and Zucker S.W.: 'Scene labeling by relaxation operations', IEEE Trans. Syst., Man, Cybern., Vol. 6, pp. 420–433 (1976).

28. Sakawa M., Sawada K. and Inuiguchi M.: 'A fuzzy satisficing method for large-scale linear programming problems with block angular structure', European J. Oper. Res., Vol. 81, No. 2, pp. 399–409 (1995).

29. Shafer G.: 'A Mathematical Theory of Evidence', Princeton, NJ: Princeton Univ. Press (1976).

30. Tong S. C.: 'Interval number and fuzzy number linear programming', Adv. in Modeling Anal. A, Vol. 20, No. 2, pp. 51–56 (1994).

31. Vallee R.: 'Cognition et Systeme', Paris: l'Interdisciplinaire Systeme(s) (1995).

32. Yager R. R.: 'Some extensions of constraint propagation of label sets', Int. J. Approximate Reasoning, Vol. 3, pp. 417–435 (1989).

33. Zadeh L. A.: 'From circuit theory to system theory', Proc. IRE, Vol. 50, pp. 856–865 (1961).

34. Zadeh L. A.: 'Fuzzy sets', Inform. Contr., Vol. 8, pp. 338–353 (1965).

35. Zadeh L. A.: 'Probability measures of fuzzy events', J. Math. Anal. Appl., Vol. 23, pp. 421–427 (1968).

36. Zadeh L. A.: 'A fuzzy-set-theoretic interpretation of linguistic hedges', J. Cybern., Vol. 2, pp. 4–34 (1972).

37. Zadeh L. A.: 'Outline of a new approach to the analysis of complex system and decision processes', IEEE Trans. Syst., Man, Cybern., Vol. SMC-3, pp. 28–44 (1973).
38. Zadeh L. A.: 'On the analysis of large scale systems', in 'Systems Approaches and Environment Problems', ed, Gottinger H., Gottingen, Germany: Vandenhoeck and Ruprecht, pp. 23–37 (1974).
39. Zadeh L. A.: 'Calculus of fuzzy restrictions', in 'Fuzzy Sets and Their Applications to Cognitive and Decision Processes', eds, Zadeh L. A., Fu K. S., and Shimura M., New York: Academic, pp. 1–39 (1975).
40. Zadeh L. A.: 'The concept of a linguistic variable and its application to approximate reasoning', Part I: Inf. Sci., Vol. 8, pp. 199–249; Part II: Inf. Sci., Vol. 8, pp. 301–357; Part III: Inform. Sci., Vol. 9, pp. 43–80 (1975).
41. Zadeh L. A.: 'A fuzzy-algorithmic approach to the definition of complex or imprecise concepts', Int. J. Man–Machine Studies, Vol. 8, pp. 249–291 (1976).
42. Zadeh L. A.: 'Fuzzy sets as a basis for a theory of possibility', Fuzzy Sets Syst., Vol. 1, pp. 3–28 (1978).
43. Zadeh L. A.: 'PRUF—A meaning representation language for natural languages', Int. J. Man–Machines Studies, Vol. 10, pp. 395–460 (1978).
44. Zadeh L. A.: 'Fuzzy sets and information granularity', in 'Advances in Fuzzy Set Theory and Applications', eds, Gupta M., Ragade R., and Yager R. R., Amsterdam, The Netherlands: North-Holland, pp. 3–18 (1979).
45. Zadeh L. A.: 'A theory of approximate reasoning', Machine Intelligence, Vol. 9, eds, Hayes J., Michie D., and Mikulich L. I., New York: Halstead, pp. 149–194 (1979).
46. Zadeh L. A.: 'Test-score semantics for natural languages and meaning representation via PRUF', in 'Empirical Semantics', ed, Rieger B., Germany: Brockmeyer, pp. 281–349; also, Tech. Rep. Memo. 246, AI Center, SRI International, Menlo Park, CA (1981).
47. Zadeh L. A.: 'Test-score semantics for natural languages', Proc. Ninth Int. Conf. on Computational Linguistics, Prague, Czech Republic, pp. 425–430 (1982).
48. Zadeh L. A.: 'Syllogistic reasoning in fuzzy logic and its application to reasoning with dispositions', Proc. 1984 Int. Symp. on Multiple-Valued Logic, Winnipeg, Canada, pp. 148–153 (1984).
49. Zadeh L. A.: 'Outline of a computational approach to meaning and knowledge representation based on the concept of a generalized assignment statement', in Proc. Int. Seminar on Artificial Intelligence and Man–Machine Systems, eds, Thoma M. and Wyner A., Heidelberg, Germany: Springer-Verlag, pp. 198–211 (1986).
50. Zadeh L. A.: 'Fuzzy logic, neural networks, and soft computing', Commun. ACM, Vol. 37, No. 3, pp. 77–84 (1994).
51. Zadeh L. A.: 'Fuzzy logic and the calculi of fuzzy rules and fuzzy graphs: A precis', Multiple Valued Logic 1, Gordon and Breach Science, pp. 1–38 (1996).
52. Zadeh L. A.: 'Fuzzy logic = computing with words', IEEE Trans. Fuzzy Syst., Vol. 4, pp. 103–111 (1996).
53. Zadeh L. A.: 'Toward a theory of fuzzy information granulation and its centrality in human reasoning and fuzzy logic', Fuzzy Sets Syst., Vol. 90, pp. 111–127 (1997).
54. Zadeh L. A.: 'Maximizing sets and fuzzy Markoff algorithms', IEEE Trans. Syst., Man, Cybern. C, Vol. 28, pp. 9–15 (1998).

Bringing AI and Soft Computing Together:
A Neurobiological Perspective

John G. Taylor

Department of Mathematics,
King's College, London, WC2R 2LS, UK
john.g.taylor@kcl.ac.uk

Abstract. The problem of reconciling what appear as two completely different computing styles, those of AI and of soft computing, is considered in terms of modern brain research. After a brief but general discussion of soft computing relevant to analyse the brain, an introduction is given to neural networks as a modelling framework with which to approach brain processing. The nature of the two streams of visual processing is then discussed, leading to the problem of how object perception can arise in the brain. A framework is developed to answer that problem, which extends what is termed feature integration theory by introducing the central representation, which includes body information necessary for intention to be achieved. This, along with considerations of brain deficits, leads to a model of the development of an object percept. How this can help reconcile the two different styles of computing is considered in the penultimate section. The paper finishes with a brief summary and conclusions.

1   Introduction

The problem of bringing traditional AI and soft computing together is an important one. On the one hand traditional AI, involved as it is with typically high-level processes in the human brain, is concerned with those aspects of thinking that are correctly ascribed the epithet 'intelligent'. This is especially true of natural language understanding and expert systems. These include particularly the ability to be conscious possessed by the human brain. This is not to say that AI systems are being considered as being aware themselves, but they are mimicking human abilities only in use during consciousness. On the other hand soft computing has developed powerful analytic tools to solve problems involved with levels of processing which can be termed 'pre-intelligent': pattern recognition, prediction, control. Looked at from the point of view of neuroscience, such processes usually take place outside human (or any other) consciousness. These two areas, of soft computing and AI, are therefore apparently very different in level and type or problem being solved.

B. Azvine et al. (Eds.): Intelligent Systems and Soft Computing, LNAI 1804, pp. 41-71, 2000.

Fuzzy logic is often suggested as being a half-way house between AI and the brain; some of the 'fuzzy' assessment rules used in human reasoning can be codified thereby. However, there is no ability yet in a fuzzy system to perform what is more correctly to be regarded as intelligence, defined as the ability to transform meaningful internal representations so as to obtain new ones which satisfy a pre-specified goal. Reasoning systems can be constructed, but all have the problem of giving meaning to the symbols being manipulated; the human (and other higher animal) brain systems are the only ones known to be able to achieve such an ability.

The conclusion from the above arguments on the separation of AI and soft computing are quite incorrect as seen from the neuro-scientific point of view: the two approaches, in the human brain, come seamlessly together, to provide us with the amazingly effective processing powers that have led us to gain enormous understanding of nature and a concomitant ascendency over our less gifted animal colleagues. The intelligent powers we possess at the highest level of awareness, that are being explored by AI, are based on prior processing abilities developed in terms of soft computational abilities which themselves are also of paramount importance. Without effective low-level processing the high-level representations would have no suitably prepared inputs, nor any meaning assigned to them. Thus the question at issue is to attempt to break down that apparent seamless join between AI and soft computing that occurs in our brains. How does soft computing — a pre-intelligent, or sub-symbolic approach — lead to the intelligent, highly symbolic and especially conscious powers of the highest levels of human thought?

The purpose of this paper is to indicate in what way it might be possible to join together these two apparently opposite aspects of brain computing by means of a general framework, one which would allow a glimpse of how these two extremes can be reconciled. The problem being faced here is highly complex, involving as it does several of the most subtle and poorly understood features of brain processing: attention, perspectivalness, intentionality, object coding, and finally consciousness. Especially the latter has very little agreement about its explanation as is evident from the various books now appearing on the subject [1-6]. However, if we try to tackle the problem of consciousness from the viewpoint of the hierarchy of processing in the brain, there must be some sites in the brain more relevant than others for awareness, and these must be tracked down and the value added discerned. Such a search cannot be avoided since without it the divide between the two sides, AI and soft computing, will remain unbridged. AI deals with conscious thought and the relevant processes involved therein. Soft computing as applied to brain processes, on the other hand, is concerned with non-conscious brain states. But how these latter emerge into consciousness, and what that process is in detail, is the point at issue to be solved to bridge the gap between AI and soft computing.

To attempt to solve this very difficult problem it is appropriate to review briefly the two sides of the equation: the processing ongoing at non-conscious and at conscious levels. As noted earlier the former of these involves various still unresolved questions, which, however, are slowly being untangled: object coding, the nature of rewards, the manner in which movements are being made, the nature of skill memory, and how all of these are being learnt in the brain. These are the basis of the soft computing techniques used by the brain, and have led to the development of a number of correspond-ing approaches: reward and Hebbian learning systems, control systems, temporal sequence chunking systems, and also valuable sensor systems using hardware adapta-tions of brain processes. At the same time slower progress is being made on attacking the much harder higher level processes closer to consciousness. Some aspects of this progress will be considered in this paper.

One of the important questions to be answered as part of the analysis of conscious systems is the manner in which consciousness is used to achieve more effective pro-cessing in a system than one in which it is absent. The answer we will try to support here — and one with considerable support in neuroscience — is that consciousness arises from an attentional competition in central cortical regions which are well fed with necessary information for most effective action. In order to be effective there must be suitably high-level coding of inputs, both as to the possible category to which they could belong as well as to the possible actions which can be taken on them. Thus both object models and possible actions on them must be suitably accessible to the competition occurring. At the same time there must be body inputs in order to indicate what is the state of the body at the given time so as to be able to know what are the appropriate actions that can be taken in that state. Similarly there must be access-ible the salience of various competing inputs so as to allow the competition itself to be run most effectively for further survival and goal achievement. Finally there should be available memory of past experiences of the input in order not to make the same mis-take twice. This puts strong criteria on suitable sites in the brain to be possible candi-dates for the emergence of consciousness. We will come shortly to a possible candi-date site and a framework to understand its functionality. This leads us then to con-sider implications for the construction of future computing systems which move to-wards combining soft computing and AI.

The paper begins with a section on soft computing in the brain. It gives a brief dis-cussion of styles of soft computing related to the brain, before turning to a description of neural networks relevant to brain processing. In section 3 is considered early visual processing, and how this is divided into two streams; some of the problems involved in object recognition are then outlined. In section 4 the higher levels of visual pro-cessing are considered, up to the level of object representations. A model of this pro-cessing, that of feature integration [7] is described and a more recent extension of it considered [8] as being able to handle the manner in which active vision occurs across saccades. In section 5 we describe the problem of neglect, where a patient loses awareness of objects on one side of their field of vision. The relevance of this for visual perception is then considered, and a framework for visual awareness developed, based on what is termed the central representation giving a further extension to feature integration theory. This model is used in section 6 to compare the basic processing in a computer to that in the brain, and how the former may be developed so as to provide a class of computers able to implement the overall framework presented here.

2   Soft Computing and the Brain

2.1   General Soft Computing Techniques and the Brain

Presently soft computing denotes a gallimaufry of approaches: genetic algorithms, neural networks of a wide variety of types, Bayesian methods, statistical models, information measure-based approaches, control techniques, together with many more specialised methodologies (Support Vector machines, Gaussian processes, chaos, and so on). Fuzzy logic is also an important component, although its position between AI and soft computing is unclear, as the remarks in the previous section showed; we will not consider it further here due to lack of space. The above soft computing avenues are all being followed up in attacking the problem of the brain, and determining how it computes. It is clearly impossible here to attempt to describe all of these methods, but begin with a brief overview of which of these are expected to be most relevant to help understand the brain, before turning to discuss neural networks in a little more detail.

First on the above list are genetic algorithms. They are of clear importance in our quest: the brain has evolved over geological time. Genetic algorithms are presently being used to help develop hardware versions of intelligent systems, in particular to evolve a neural network which it is hoped will be up to the intelligence of a kitten [9]. This is an ambitious attempt, but meets severe difficulties due to the problem of defining the various environments in which the cost function must be defined in order to achieve its high-level functionality. More low-level attempts to improve present models of various brain processes are presently under consideration. The biggest success for genetic algorithms have undoubtedly arisen from applications to more artificial problems. The use of developmental analysis, attempting to understand how the infant brain develops across various watersheds, has proved more promising for brain science [10]. Part of this has led to a new view of growth spurts as proceeding through low-dimensional chaotic stages before moving into more well-defined dynamical growth (usually of oscillatory form). I will not say more here about the use of genetic algorithms in brain modelling, but note that it is an area to keep under close watch because of its potential importance.

Chaos was mentioned above; it is now more at the centre of the stage in attempting to understand how the brain computes. It has been suggested that the usual dynamics of the brain consists of high-dimensional chaotic motion between incidents of information processing. These occur as the reduction of this chaotic motion to fixed points or oscillatory motions [11, 12]. This vista on the brain in action is highly creative, and has considerable experimental support. In particular, it can explain how the processing can be fast in terms of the motion from the chaotic regime to a fixed point, as compared to processing which only uses fixed points as components of the dynamics. This notion of 'living on the edge of chaos' is one which has attraction, in particular for future processing methods. However, chaos cannot of itself easily give a theory of how the brain functions in a global manner; it is necessary to first specify the underlying dynamics and only then consider the specific chaotic motion which that produces.

There are a variety of information processing methodologies which can be subsumed under the heading of information analysis. This includes the analysis of spike trains to determine their mutual information and the nature of spike codes, of information measures to determine the optimal learning rules to solve given tasks, and numerous statistical approaches to determine significance levels of various hypotheses concerning connectivity in brain activations.

One particular statistical technique becoming of great interest most recently has been that of structural modelling [13]. This is concerned with the analysis of the activities of various modules in the brain measured while subjects are performing a task. The strength of possible connectivities between the various modules is determined by the degree of co-variation in their activities, either across subjects or across time for a given subject. Results from various structural analyses for different tasks are now becoming available and it is increasingly possible to discern the various networks of the brain involved in such tasks and attempt to piece them together [14].

The main technique being used in trying to understand the brain is naturally that of neural networks. This will be described briefly in the next section before we turn to visual processing in the brain.

2.2   The Simplest Artificial Neural Network

An artificial neural network is composed of a set of very simple processing elements. As such, it may be regarded as the most primitive possible parallel computer. Each element is called a neuron; it is often termed an artificial neuron in the literature, but it is useful to drop the epithet 'artificial' both for reasons of space and also because the elements are being modelled in terms of the most essential features of living neurons.

Each of the neurons in a neural network can send a signal, usually normalised to have the value one, to the other neurons in the network of which they are constituents. These signals are sent along connection 'wires' similar to the wires in an electric circuit; in the brain they are called axons. Each neuron then receives the signals from its companions. These signals are rescaled by the so-called 'connection weights', one for each wire coming to a neuron from another one. Thus if the ith neuron receives a signal from the jth, and the connection weight for this wire from neuron j to neuron i has value w_{ij}, then the activity received by the ith neuron will have the amount w_{ij}. The total activity received by the ith neuron, on summing over all of the neurons j from which neuron i receives input, will thus be:

$$A_i = \sum_j w_{ij} u_j$$

where u_j is the output of the jth neuron, being 1 if the jth neuron is active and 0 if it is inactive.

The ith neuron responds with a signal which depends on the value of its activity at that time. This response may be purely a binary decision: give a response (a one) if the activity A_i is positive, otherwise remain silent. The neuron, and its companions, may, on the other hand, respond in a probabilistic manner by giving out a one with the probability $f(A_i)$, where $f(\ )$ is some sigmoidal function of its variable (this is a function which increases monotonically from zero as its variable increases up to some maximum value, when saturation sets in and the neuron then fires at its maximal constant value). The former net is composed of deterministic neurons, the latter of probabilistic ones. Both cases involve passing of zeros or ones only, as occurs for the neurons of the brain, which pass spikes (ones) as brief pulses of electrical activity.

It is also possible to have neurons which pass round real values, and not just zeros or ones; in that case the real-valued output would be:

$$u_i\,(t+1) = f(\,A_i(t)\,) \tag{1}$$

where the activity of the ith neuron at time $(t+1)$ is calculated form the activities $u_j(t)$ at time t, and these quantities are now real valued. The earlier case of a binary output arises from this latter equation by replacing the supposedly sigmoid response function by the sharp step function output (equal to the so-called Heaviside or theta function, which is one if the activation is larger than some threshold value and is zero otherwise). These real-value-passing neurons can be regarded as approximations to the spiking neurons in the brain, where the real value being output by a neuron is the mean firing rate obtained by averaging the number of spikes emitted by a spiking neuron over a suitable length of time; this is an approximation made by many brain modellers to achieve more rapid simulations.

Equation (1), together with its extensions to more complex neurons (involving temporal, geometric, stochastic and nonlinear properties of the intrinsic structure of a neuron), is at the basis of all calculations of ongoing neural network response dynamics in the brain. These neurons have considerably more complex responses than that expressed by equation (1), involving the inherent geometry of the neuron as well as nonlinear response features associated with the signalling between neurons. There are also temporal 'memories' brought about by slow dynamical changes at the synapses where neurons connect with each other. These are thought to have important features for spanning the gaps between the responses to one input and the next. However, modelling such details considerably slows down simulations, so that they are only considered of relevance in modelling relatively small networks in the brain.

The neural net dynamics specified above allows the temporal development of the activities of all of the neurons of a given net to be calculated in terms of their initial activities (at time 0, say) and the values of the connection weights. These activities may be used for various processing tasks which are achieved by means of various specialised types of connectivity or network architecture, either for artificial tasks or to model different parts of the brain. External inputs also have to be included, but these have been excluded for simplicity in equation (1); their inclusion is achieved by adding them directly to the activities $A_i(t)$ in the function on the right hand side of (1).

2.3   Neural Network Architectures

There are two extreme architectures for neural networks.

- Feedforward nets are those where the neurons are laid out in successive layers, 1, 2, 3, etc, and activity feeds through from the input at layer 1 to layer 2, then to layer 3, and so on — such a feedforward net can set up transforms of one pattern (entered on the input) into another as output:

$$x \rightarrow y \tag{2}$$

  where x is the input pattern and y the output (not necessarily of the same dimension). The layers which do not feed to the output directly are termed 'hidden', since their outputs are not observed directly by an outsider. Such a transformation as (2) can be used in classification (when y may be a binary vector serving as a classifier) or to achieve more generally an associative memory (where a given input x_i leads to its associated output y_i).

  This feedforward style of processing is clearly observable in the brain, and for many years it was thought that such a processing style was prevalent. More recently interest has turned to the manner in which feedback lines, observable neuroanatomically by various techniques, are involved in the processing. We therefore turn to consider feedback or recurrent networks.

- Recurrent nets are those where the output of any layer may be fed back to itself and to earlier (or later) layers. The activity of such a net then 'settles' or 'relaxes' to a stable or fixed point, sometimes called an attractor. The most well-known of such recurrent nets is the single layer Hopfield net, with all-to-all connectivity, with a symmetric connection matrix, $w_{ij} = w_{ji}$, with $w_{ii} = 0$. In this case it is possible to obtain a lot of information about the activity of the net, and even to specify how the connection matrix must be chosen in order to obtain a given set of attractors of the net. The net then acts as a 'content addressable memory', so as to complete or fill in noisy or degraded versions of patterns. This is achieved by starting the network off in states of the neurons corresponding to a noisy version of the input pattern and waiting till the net settles down into a persistent state; the connections can be chosen so that this final activity is a cleaned up version of the input pattern, and equals the desired output pattern.

  There are numerous feedback lines in the brain, and, in general, many modules, both at sub-cortical and cortical level, feed to a given area or module. However, recent brain imaging shows that the networks involved in high-level processing are well defined, and not all of the brain 'lights up' when perceptual or cognitive processing is occurring. This selectivity arises since the different modules have been selected by reason of their suitably high connection strengths to others in the relevant network. We therefore turn to consider how network connection strengths can be modified so as to solve certain tasks.

2.4   Neural Network Training

The question that must now be answered about a neural net is how the connection matrix is chosen to be effective in the solution of a given task; choices have been mentioned above but there is an important criterion to be imposed on them; they are to be obtained by training the net, and not by using 'hard-wiring'. This is particularly important in order to enable the network to be developed to be effective on tasks for which the hard-wired solution is unknown. Such learning is crucial, for this reason, in the present neuro-biological context, although some hard-wiring (corresponding to genetic coding) may occur. It is also possible to apply genetic training algorithms to neural networks, although that approach will not be considered here.

The most popular net, the feedforward one, has been used to attempt to solve the following problem.

Choose the best set of connection weights so that the network approximates most effectively (say in the mean square sense) the mapping of some given data set:

$$x_i \rightarrow y_i \tag{3}$$

for a given training set of pairs $\{x_i, y_i\}$, for $1 \le i \le N$, for some N.

That such a choice is possible, for a suitably large net composed of nodes, emitting and receiving real values, is the result of the important Universal Approximation Theorem, which states that a single hidden layer net, with a suitably large number of hidden nodes, can approximate any suitably smooth function:

$$y = F(x) \tag{4}$$

Such results lead to confidence that a neural net can always be found to get a good approximation to any function (4).

The most basic technique is that of back-error propagation, which is a so-called gradient descent technique on the mean square error function (which assesses how different the actual output $F(x_i)$ of the network on a given input value is from the desired one y_i):

$$E = \sum_i [y_i - F(x_i)]^2 \tag{5}$$

In gradient descent each weight is reduced by a small amount proportional to the gradient of E with respect to the weight of interest; this enables the error (5) gradually to be reduced by 'descending' the surface given by (5) as a function of the weights along the steepest path in weight space. This training method allows for the error caused by an incorrect choice of connection weights to be reduced gradually so as to ultimately bring it below any criterial value.

Another alternative training method, which is known to be an approximation of gradient descent, is called reinforcement learning, in which a reinforcement signal is given to change the weights if the output of the net is a good approximation to the desired output, while the weights are penalised by moving them away from their present values if the output is not close to the desired value.

All of these methods assume that a given set of input-output pairs for the network, as given by (3), is known so that the error function (5) can be constructed.

Such an approach, in which a given training set (3) is assumed available, is called a supervised training paradigm. Outputs are expected to be specified for a given set of inputs. More biologically realistic is the alternate unsupervised paradigm in which there is no specification of the input-output responses of the net; it must attempt to extract, by its learning, suitable features of its inputs so as to be able to respond effectively and solve whatever tasks it has been set (such as extract features from the input, or survive). In particular, it has to be able to create a suitable internal representation of its environment so as to help other modules (if they exist) to take suitable actions.

One specification of how to achieve such internalisation of the environment for a neural net has been hinted above for the Hopfield net. This uses a version of what is termed Hebbian learning, after the Canadian psychologist Donald Hebb who introduced it, as roughly: "A synapse is changed by an amount determined by the afferent input and the actual output of the cell." This learning law involves no external supervisor to indicate any conditions on the output of the cell in order that the synaptic weight be in fact updated; it is thereby completely unsupervised, in distinction to the more popular but artificial supervised learning law described above.

The Hebbian learning law is moreover local in character, depending only on the activities relevant to the synapse in question and not on those of neurons in remote parts of the net or in other modules. As such the Hebbian learning paradigm is extremely attractive as a possible form of biological learning law. There is also a considerable literature on experimental support for such a law being used in living neurons.

When applied in its simplest form to the neuron of Fig. 2 the learning law for w_{ij} becomes:

$$\Delta w_{ij} = \varepsilon u_i\, u_j - \mu\, u_i \tag{6}$$

where the first term is that of Hebbian learning and the last is a decay term to avoid increasingly large weights as learning proceeds. This training algorithm leads, in the Hopfield net, to the weight matrix being a sum of the previously experienced patterns and the response to a new pattern determined by the closeness of this pattern to each of the stored ones. Thus the pattern space is divided up into segments, called basins of attraction, according to the various stored patterns.

A new input imposed initially on the states of a recurrent net trained in this manner will modify its activation pattern over the neurons of the network as time passes until the state of activity will end up as one of the attractors on which the net was trained.

2.5   Biological Realism for Neural Network Learning Laws

Numerous variants of the learning law (6) have been proposed so as to make the network able to extract various features of its inputs. Thus inserting a factor equal to the square of the output of the neuron i in the decay term of the right hand side of equation (6) allows the neuron to extract the most important information-theoretic aspect of its environment, termed the principle components. Modifying the learning so it takes place after a competition between neurons, being won by the most active, and then only allowing learning for a neighbourhood of the winner, leads to topographic maps of the input space on an ordered array of the neurons; this is termed the self-organising feature map (SOFM) [15].

These approaches have been used to develop nets which have a similarity to networks in the visual and somato-sensory cortex in terms of their topographically ordered response patterns.

On the other hand reinforcement learning has proved more popular and appropriate for modelling of frontal lobe motor and working memory systems, with considerable understanding being built up in terms of coupled modules and their learning. This has been particularly associated with the use of dopamine, which has particular medical import in its progressive loss in Parkinson's disease. Learning laws incorporating some features of dopamine effects have been developed in association with what is called remporal difference learning [16]. It is to be noted also that supervised learning approaches have been used in modelling frontal systems so as to determine neural architectures (with suitable recurrence) which would solve frontal tasks such as delayed response or the Wisconsin Card Sorting Test, but these have now been superseded by the more biologically realistic architectures and learning laws noted above [17, 18].

2.6   Summary

In conclusion, a neural network is a system of input-output nodes whose strengths of connections between each other are able to be trained so that the network produces an effective response to a set of inputs. Simple models of neural networks are being increasingly used to understand the brain. As part of this program, more global tasks, such as a rise in visual processing, are being tackled by neural network modelling. We turn to describe the nature of visual processing and a general framework for visual perception, before moving on to consider what insights it can provide for bridging the gap between soft computing and AI.

3   Visual Processing

3.1   Introduction

The development of a machine vision system as powerful as that possessed by humans has not yet been possible. We can effortlessly recognise complex objects in our visual field and perform manipulations on them, the like of which no machine is anywhere near being able to be created to achieve. Therefore human visual processing has been much studied over the years to attempt to understand how we achieve such decidedly difficult tasks.

The results indicate that our visual powers arise by both breaking down the retinal image into component parts and recombination of those parts to activate previously stored templates ('binding') so as to allow identification of objects and make appropriate action responses. Such processing has been found to have been achieved by splitting the visual input into a number of streams so as apparently to make the task simpler; how exactly that simplification is achieved is still unclear, but progress is being made in unravelling it.

In the following, two visual streams will be considered, starting with their identification at the sub-cortical level, since that is the most primitive and therefore is in some sense the bedrock of the total system. Cortical processing can be regarded in some sense as the 'icing on the cake'. We will then turn to the two main cortical streams, the 'what' for object processing and the 'where' for spatial and motion analysis. The manner in which these might be combined will then be described briefly; the story here is decidedly poorly understood yet, but important progress is being made.

Retinal output is itself composed of two streams, termed P and M. The P stream is more sensitive to slow movement of objects and has finer spatial sensitivity than the M stream. This division of visual output from the retina into P and M streams is now accepted as leading to an important separation of the further cortical visual processing into two streams, termed the dorsal (or M) stream and the ventral (or P) stream, fed from the corresponding streams from the retina just mentioned. These two streams are not completely separate in cortex but have interchanges between each other, but in general seem to process separate aspects of the visual input in quite different ways. There is now understanding of this difference between the two streams from neuro-anatomical connections, from deficits in humans and primates, from single cell recordings and most recently by non-invasive techniques.

The differences between the two streams is shown in terms of the hierarchically arranged cortical areas through which they pass (see Mishkin et al [19], and DeYoe and Van Essen [20]). The first of these references argues for such a separation from the deficits produced in monkeys in object discrimination (on removal of the temporal lobe) and in landmark discimination (on bilateral removal of posterior parietal cortex). The second [20] then argues that object processing and recognition involves much interaction between these two pathways at several stages in the processing hierarchy. Let us consider each of the pathways in turn and then consider them more globally.

3.2   The Ventral 'What' Stream

The P stream, the so-called ventral stream (since it goes down ventrally in the brain to the inferotemporal lobe and the limbic system including hippocampus) travels to the so-called 'blobs' and the 'inter-blobs' in V1, as seen from their characteristic staining patterns observed when cytochrome oxidase has been applied to the cortex. The blobs contain cells mainly sensitive to colour, possessing wavelength sensitivity in the form of R-G or B-Y opponency (excitation to red shone centrally versus inhibition below the spontaneous level to green shone in the surround, for example). This strand sends outputs directly to the thin stripes (as determined by cytochrome oxidase staining) in the next area V2 and then on to the further inferotemporal area V4. This strand outputs through the upper layers 2/3 in V1 (as is common in cortical processing from one area to the next one up in the processing hierarchy) of the six-layered cortex (see Figs. 1 and 2).

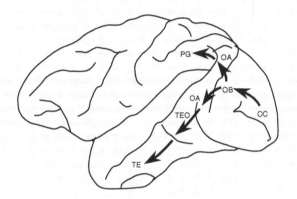

Fig. 1. Lateral view of the left hemisphere of the rhesus monkey. Arrows schematise two cortical visual pathways, each beginning in primary cortex (areas OA and OB) and then coursing either ventrally into the inferior temporal cortex (areas TEO and TE) or dorsally into the inferior parietal cortex (area PG). Both cortical visual pathways are crucial for higher visual function, the ventral pathway for object vision and the dorsal and ventral streams (involving the M and P streams also discussed in the text) being clearly delineated. The details of the selective functionality of the two streams are shown more fully in Fig. 2.

The P stream also sends input to orientation-sensitive cells in V1 (in the interblob areas in V1), some of which also have binocular response properties. These send their output to the interstripe areas (as observed by cytochrome oxidase staining) in V2 which preserve the properties of the V1 cell, at the same time giving more complex responses in some cases, such as through the 'end-stopped' cells, which are sensitive to the ends of lines and are thought to be involved in the construction of analysis of illusory conjunctions [21]. These cells also send their output mainly to the cells in V4 to combine with those of the blob/thin stripe cells of the colour-sensitive strand.

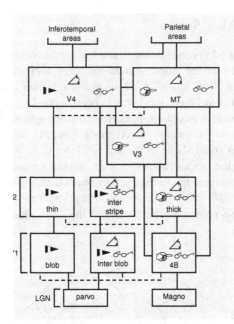

Fig. 2. Schematic diagram of anatomical connections and neuronal selectivities of early visual areas in the macaque monkey. LGN = lateral geniculate nucleus (in the thalamus). Divisions of V1 and V2: blob = regions which produce blobs when stained under cytochrome exidase; 4B = layer 4B; thin = thin (narrow) cytochrome oxidase strips; intersripe = cytochrome oxidase-poor regions between the thick and thin strips; thick = thick (wide) cytochrome oxidase strips; V3 = visual area V3; V4 = visual area(s) V4; MT = middle temporal area. Areas V2, V3, V4 and MT have connections to other areas not explicitly represented here. Heavy lines indicate robust primary connections. Dotted lines represent observed connections that require additional verification. Icons: rainbow = tuned and/or opponent wavelength selectivity; angle symbol = orientation selectivity; spectacles = binocular disparity selectivity and/or strong binocular interactions; pointing hand = direction of motion selectivity.

The assignation of V4 as 'the' colour area in the brain by Zeki [22] has been somewhat controversial but is now to some extent accepted (although it is very debatable that colour awareness actually arises from activity in V4). However, the importance of V4 to colour vision is now well established both through deficits and non-invasive analysis. The story of the painter who had a very difficult time coming to grips with his loss of colour experience after suffering a head injury in a car crash is well known [23], and just an extreme example indicating the importance of that region in colour sensitivity of cortex.

The end point of the ventral stream is thus posited as V4. This has cells which are variously colour sensitive, orientation sensitive and have binocular disparity selectivity or strong binocular interactions. In the process of input being transformed from one area to the next there is an increase of the size of receptive fields of the relevant cells from about 1 degree in V1 to 2-4 degrees in V2 to about 8 degrees in V4. This increase is thought to arise from simple serial fan-in as one proceeds up the processing hierarchy.

The ventral stream arises from the foveal component of the retinal input (the inner 3-4 degrees of the visual field) with greatest acuity for analysis of the input. This is to be compared with the M stream which contains more peripheral input analysed with far less precision [24]. Let us turn to that now.

3.3   The Dorsal 'Where' Stream

The motion-sensitive cells of the cortex start in layer 4B of the striate area V1, being fed by the retinal motion M stream from the retina, and thence through the thalamus. This input is fed out directly from that same layer 4B in V1 (and is not processed in the higher layers 2/3 as the P stream input is) to the thick stripes in V2 and then on to the area MT or directly to that area without interruption. Area MT is well known now to be crucial for the response to motion in various forms. Thus non-invasive experiments have shown very clearly the extreme form of sensitivity of the area to moving stimuli as compared to the earlier area V1 [25]. There is even a 60% response of MT cells to moving stimuli which only have a 1.5% contrast against background as compared to a few percent response of V1 cells to the same input.

The area MT is thought to be of importance in helping explain the response of patients with loss of V1, or parts of it, to moving images — the phenomenon of 'blindsight' [26]. In this phenomenon the subject, in spite of being blind, in the sense of having no awareness of a moving spot in his/her blind field of view, will be able to indicate above chance level in which direction the spot has been moving. This may require some encouragement, since the patient is embarrassed to 'guess' when they have no direct 'experience' on which to base their response. It is thought that there is direct input to MT which has been spared in whatever injury caused their loss of cortex, so that this region can allow knowledge to be obtained on which the 'guess' can be based. However, there are some subjects who have direct awareness of the moving spot, in spite of that experience not allowing them to say what the spot looked like. Thus MT is an important area in the processing hierarchy towards motion awareness.

Numerous relatively succesful neural models of V1 and MT have now been constructed. Those for V1 mainly concentrate on explaining the origin of the orientation sensitivity of the majority of cells in V1, especially by training synapses for inputs to the cortical sheet by Hebbian learning, with particular use of lateral connections so as to enable the learnt synapses responsive to different inputs to be regularly spaced out across the cortex in V1. Careful simulations have allowed considerable understanding to be obtained of the mechanisms of orientation sensitivity [27, 28]. Models for MT have been constructed to explain the directional and velocity sensitivity of the cells there [29], although these have all used orientation sensitivity inserted by hand. In any case there are important features of the responses of some MT cells to the motion of the global field of view which indicate that such cells may be involved in scene segmentation for differently moving objects, and these have yet to be modelled. There are also models of further areas, like MST, which is sensitive to the heading direction of the subject, and is thought to be extracting signals on self-motion. As with the MT cells the models are still too simple to account for all of the important features of cells in these areas.

One especially important problem is that of the function of feedback from higher to lower areas; thus there is extensive feedback from MT to V1, yet its function is unknown [30]. It has been conjectured that such feedback may be important in constructing the response patterns of MT cells to the global flow pattern to which they are being exposed, although there may also be extensive lateral connectivity which can also help provide explain this complex response [31].

As indicated above, the further areas beyond V1 in the dorsal stream help solve a number of tasks:

- further analyse the moving input to achieve segregation into figure and ground (which in general will have different movement characteristics);
- analyse the shapes of the various parts of the input;
- analyse the positions of the parts of the input;
- transform the retinal co-ordinates into body-centred ones for actions to be made;
- give information to the frontal eye-fields (especially area 8) in order to direct eye movements to a new position in the visual field;
- direct attention to any new and salient input which has recently entered the peripheral visual field;
- co-ordinate or update visual input with actions about to be or in the process of being made.

These (and others not mentioned) form an important set of tasks that need to be performed in order for actions based on the needs of the person and of their visual input to be made. That explains why there are numerous areas in the dorsal stream in the extra-striate visual and parietal cortex. These are only now being explored fully; some of the latest results are contained in Thier and Karnath [32].

3.4   The Stable Object Representation

The manner in which objects are coded by the action of the two visual streams described above is still unclear. Given the problems already described above concerning the early visual areas, it would seem premature to attempt to move on to this problem. Yet some understanding of processing in the higher level areas may help clarify what occurs at lower levels, especially with respect to the function of the feedback lines. Such higher level processing also has considerable interest in its own right. Let us then move on to discuss how object representations may arise.

The main set of object representations are supposedly stored in later processing stages in the inferotemporal lobe, as determined by the loss suffered by patients with deficits in those areas. On the other hand loss of the dorsal stream will give rise to processing deficits involving action and motion [33], but not object recognition; loss of temporal lobe will cause recognition deficits that tend to be severe, even though motion and action deficits may be low.

The work of Tanaka and colleagues [34] has been important in elucidating the nature of some aspects of object representations. He has shown that in the monkey dorsal processing stream:

$$V1 \rightarrow V2 \rightarrow V4 \rightarrow TEO \rightarrow TE \qquad (7)$$

there is a build up of 'elaborate' cells, which respond to comparatively complex stimuli, composed of circles with strips emanating from them or other non-trivial stimulus shapes. Moreover it ensues that there is roughly a hyper-column of cells, vertical to the cortical surface and with a diameter of about 400-600 microns, which codes for very similar 'elaborate' inputs. This is very reminiscent of the coding for orientation in V1, for which there are similar hypercolumns encoding orientation sensitivity to oriented bars of steadily changing orientation (but the same position in space) as one moves across the hypercolumn. This similarity in coding is to be expected, although the manner in which object representations are then constructed is not clear.

What is needed in this construction is:

- segmentation of the object of interest from others in the input so that it can be processed at a higher level;
- binding of the activities in the various codes (colour, motion, shape, texture, binocular disparity) in order to build a unified object percept;
- activation of stored templates to compare with the just-constructed percept;
- transfer of the resulting identified concept to frontal lobes so as to allow for suitable actions to be taken relevant to the goals of the subject.

The first problem is the famous 'binding' problem, for which numerous solutions have been suggested. Thus the use of coupled oscillatory neuronal activities (suggested as being at about 40 Hz) has been favoured for a time. This has now been reduced to the use of synchronous activations of the different codes for a given object stimulus. Another alternative is to use motion as a basic segregator, since as mentioned earlier there are cells in MT which are sensitive to background motion relative to that of the local motion coded for by the cell, and other cells there sensitive to total motion of the whole field. This would lead to relative inputs across these cells which would allow for very fast figure-ground segregation. Since there are good connections between the relevant dorsal and ventral pathways [35], then such information is very likely easily available to the ventral object stream, leading to activation of commonly moving parts of the visual field being sent from the dorsal to the ventral areas. These latter must then be trained (or genetically wired) so as to be sensitive to the correct set of common strong inputs; such a possibility is not difficult on use of Hebbian learning.

Moreover, it is noted in Baizer et al [36] that "...both parietal and inferotemporal cortices receive common inputs from extensive regions in the anterior STS which may play a role in linking the processing occurring in these two cortical subdivisions of the visual system." Such linking may allow common activations to achieve binding in a manner dependent on both the P and M stream common activations.

A final approach to the binding problem, with some overlap with the other techniques, is that of Triesman's 'Feature Integration Theory' [7]. In this, attention applied to a 'master map' of locations is used to bind together different activations on the feature map spaces, such as the colour and orientation maps, so that they are encoded in a temporary object representation file. This is then compared to a stored description of objects, held in permanent memory (in a task such as visual search for a given stimulus). Thus here binding is achieved by attention in an inexplicable manner; this leaves the final solution to the binding problem still open. However, the notion of 'temporary object files' is very close to the associated one of a buffer store, supposedly occurring in posterior cortex as part of the working memory system [37].

This still leaves open the sites of such object files, both for the buffer and for the permanent storage modules. The former has now been observed by non-invasive techniques in specialised posterior cortical sites, and the latter are thought to be placed in mesial temporal lobe systems, such as suggested in Triesman [7]. However, it is emphasised there that such coding is not local and may more likely involve representations which involve relationships with other objects rather than single object representations.

4   A Framework for Visual Perception

There are various questions raised in the previous section to which we will try to give a preliminary answer here. We will do that by using knowledge about the effects of various brain lesions on the experience of a subject. This will guide us both to where in the brain might be the site most crucial for visual perception and then to use that to relate back to the feature integration theory [7] described above. This will lead us to a general framework for perception and consciousness, and so enable us to glimpse a style of computation bringing soft computing and AI together.

4.1   Neglect

After a stroke that destroys the right dorsal portion of the brain, especially in the parietal lobe, a patient will lose awareness of various forms of sensation [38-40]. Neglect is not simple to describe precisely, and can easily be confused with extinction, in which a patient is unable to report a stimulus on their right hand side if two stimuli, one to the right and one to the left sides of the subject are presented; the patient can, however, report one stimulus presented on its own. Neglect can, for example, be detected by the inability of a patient to cancel all of the items in a visual array, say of letters or of symbols. Failure to notice items on the left indicates hemi-spatial neglect.

It has been shown experimentally that extinction can arise from loss of the superior parietal lobe. The parietal lobe is shown in Fig. 3, and its superior part contains regions devoted to eye movement control and grasping and reaching and planning.

Neglect is now being considered as arising from damage more precisely to the inferior parietal lobe [38].

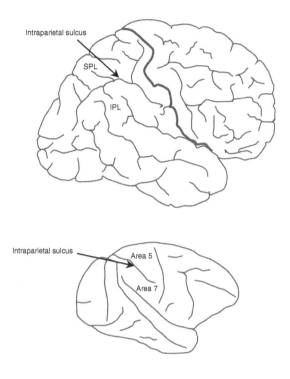

Fig. 3. Diagrammatic views of the lateral surface of the human and macaque cerebral hemispheres, showing the location of the intraparietal sulcus in each case (SPL, superior parietal lobule; IPL, inferior parietal lobule).

Neglect is known to arise from processing involved with information from the body. Thus when a patient has their ear stimulated by ice cold water they lose their neglect for a period. A similar amelioration occurs when the neck of the patient is vibrated, or they twist in their chair so that neck muscle activity impinges on the relevant degraded parietal area. These results are of great importance in understanding the manner in which the body enters perception. It is clear that in the parietal lobe there are important signals received from the body so as to allow rapid planning of actions to be taken, using the most appropriate co-ordinates already modified for bodily configuration.

Several neural models have been constructed of this phenomenon (see Pouget and Sejnowski [39] and references therein). They both use nonlinear modifications of visual inputs as determined by body inputs, and can be shown to be effective in explaining the manner in which the various extra body inputs noted above can help reduce the neglect experienced by a patient.

4.2   An Extended Feature Integration Theory

The question of the persistence of the visual scene through saccades is one which has produced important extensions of the understanding of visual processing. We will consider here such an extension before developing it further to adumbrate a framework from which to approach the problem of joining together soft computing and AI; we turn to this in the following section.

The original model of feature integration [7], described earlier, assumed that an input was initially encoded on a set of feature maps (for separate colour, texture, motion, etc) and its spatial position on a master 'spatial' map. An 'object file', acting as a temporary object representation, was also set up by the input on a separate module. This object file used spatio-temporal coding as well as other attributes (such as the name) of an object to give it identity. Attention drawn to a particular position on the master spatial map caused correlated activations at the same positions on the feature maps and integrated them together to bind with the activation in the object file.

We extend the above model in terms of a modified version of the feature integration theory presented in Henderson [8], which includes the manner in which information about objects is stored across saccades; it reduces the object files solely to having space-time co-ordinates. Further information on semantic categories and object models are in quite separate modules in the ventral pathway. This modification is based on numerous psychophysical experiments to assess the level of storage of visual inputs both across saccades and across short delays. The experiments that supported the extension of the feature integration theory used pairs of objects (letters, together with shape distractors) which were either shown at a central visual position within a single eye fixation, viewed across a saccade movement, or viewed at different retinal and spatial locations over time. Information about the objects was observed in subjects to be maintained over time both by episodic object representations (the 'object files') and by long-term memory representations (the 'object models'). Neither of these were found to code specifically for sensory information, and as Henderson wrote: "Object files can be thought of as episodic object tokens that are individuated by spatio-temporal co-ordinates." Thus the master map of space and the object files are equated in Henderson's version of feature integration theory [8].

The use we make here of this model is as follows. Firstly the spatial nature of the object files labels supports their being placed in the inferior parietal lobe (IPL); involvement of parietal lobe in the process of feature integration had already been suggested in Triesman et al [41]. Neglect is a loss of awareness and happens, as noted above, precisely in those patients with inferior parietal lobe damage. Secondly, and more importantly, the placement of the spatial object files in the the inferior parietal lobe leads to the proposal that visual awareness arises in the object files map itself. This is through a competition taking place there [42]. Thirdly the sensory components of the object files encoded in earlier visual processing stages are made accessible to awareness, we propose, through feedback coupling to the inferior parietal lobes.

An extension of Henderson [8] is now appropriate in terms of the identification of the object files module, containing essential information from the body to give 'perspectivalness'. This we do by means of what we call the 'central representation'. This we now develop.

4.3   The Central Representation

Evidence from neglect studies and brain imaging on healthy subjects has been presented above to implicate the inferior parietal lobe (IPL) as playing an important role in controlling attention and awareness. Both of these attributes can occur in a range of possible frames of reference: neglect can be observed tied to an object, or to a trunk-centred frame of reference or a variety of other reference frames, as noted earlier [38]. This implies that the IPL is very likely composed of a set of modules, each carrying information from the environment as well as modulation by possible body input. Thus the IPL is eminently suited to carry what is termed the 'Central Represen-tation.' This is defined as follows:

> "The central representation is the combined set of multimodal activations involved in fusing sensory activity, body positions, salience and intention-ality for future planning; it involves a competitive process between the various modules it contains to single one out to enter consciousness and be used for report to other working memory sites for further planning or ac-tion."

There are several important features of the central representation (CR) defined above that need discussion.

1) The CR must have access to sensory input, such as in vision, coded at a high level. Thus it must have good access to temporal lobe representations, so as to use the categorisation built there to guide action.

2) It also must have access to the bodily input needed to guide actions in terms of the intentionality coded in the superior parietal lobe. It was noted already that such intentionality is coded for various sorts of actions: of the limbs, eyes, head or fingers. This intentionality must be furnished with the parameters of the objects on which the actions must be taken; thus cerebellar and vestibular input, with important information on the state of the body, is also needed to be accessible to the central representation, as it is indeed uniquely in the parietal lobes.

3) Salience of the inputs in the sensory field is an important attribute for the guidance of actions; that arises from limbic input already activated to provide saliencies of inputs from the orbitofrontal cortex by way of the cingulate. This is compounded by activations in the retrosplenial gyrus, encoded as parts of episodic memory [43, 44]. Such connections have been especially emphasised by Mesulam, who wrote, in discussing the important limbic connections to the parietal lobe involved in neglect: "However, the cingulate and retrosplenial projections are much more selective and may be related to more complex and learned aspects of motivation." Both this and the aspects noted under points 1) and 2) above sup-

port the inferior parietal lobe as the site for the CR, since the IPL has good connections to the temporal lobe as well as to body inputs.

4) There are several modules involved in the CR in the IPL; the total activity must undergo an overall competition, possibly aided by thalamo-nucleus reticularis thalami processing (where the nucleus reticularis thalami is a thin sheet of inhibitory neurons wrapped around the thalamus and acting as a set of 'gatelets' to cortical throughput). A simulation of such a model has been given earlier [45, 46]. The existence of such competition is supported by attentional deficits observed in subjects with pulvinar lesions.

5) Siting the emergence of awareness in the IPL, as the product of the competition ongoing there, is supported by a simulation of the data of Libet and colleagues [46]. This involved the creation of sensory experience (that of a gentle touch on the back of the patient's hand) by direct stimulation of cortex in patients being operated on for dyskinesia and related movement problems. The simulation [48] used a simplified model of the cortico-thalamo-nucleus reticularis circuit, and led to the observed dependence of the delay of awareness on the strength of the threshold current for experiencing the touch on the back of the patient's hand.

6) Such a competition has also been suggested [49] as occurring to explain experimental results of subliminal effects on lexical decision response times obtained by Marcel [50]. The experiment involved measurement of the reaction times of subjects to deciding if a letter string was a word or not. Prior subliminal exposure to priming words occurred, with the presentation of polysemous words such as 'palm', on which the lexical decision had to be made. The prior exposure caused the decision to be speeded up or delayed in characteristic ways according to the semantic relation of the prior word to the later one; the simulation was able to explain these results by means of a competition assumed to occur on the phonological store (known to be in the IPL), aided and abetted by activations from a prior semantic memory store.

In conclusion, we site the CR in the IPL as the confluence of information on salience, episodic memory, high-level coding of inputs and information on body state; the update of Henderson's model [8] is given in Fig. 4.

We add that the further prefrontal and sensory area contributions to the model of Fig. 4, beyond the feature integration theory [7, 8] incorporate aspects from the early and late processing (in sensory and prefrontal cortical areas). The various additional modules in Fig. 4, beyond the central one of the CR, give the extra contents of consciousness. Thus the process of the development of awareness of an object according to the above model occurs through the following stages.

1) Early visual coding leads to activations of feature representations in V4, MT and similar early visual areas in both the ventral (temporal lobe) and dorsal (posterior parietal lobe) streams.

2) A set of possible intentions for motor actions on the objects of the visual scene is set up in the superior parietal lobe.

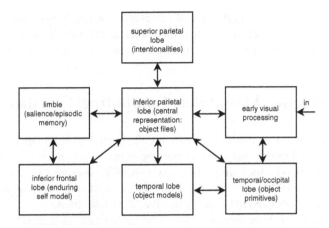

Fig. 4. The updated version of the feature integration theory, including the central representation and other supporting modules.

3) Emotional salience and earlier relevant episodic memories associated with the inputs are activated in the limbic system, especially the cingulate and retrosplenial gyrus, by inputs being fed subcortically to the amygdala and hippocampus and so activating the limbic system preconsciously.

4) Object models are also activated at a preconscious level in the temporal lobe on the basis of previously encoded categories.

5) Attentional focus and awareness of the object at the centre of the fovea arises by the process of winning the competition between various activations (object files) still present on IPL in the central representation, and those just created by new visual inputs which have just arrived there. These activities consist of representations which are encoded in a spatial form, as is basic to the feature integration theory [7, 8].

We conclude that the central representation is spatial, but previously mentioned evidence indicates that it is not retinotopic. The various component modules of the central representation are thus expected to have a spatial encoding of sensory inputs, modulated by body inputs in the manner discussed earlier. There is thus a set of spatial maps in the central representation for various sensory inputs. Consciousness of inputs arises through activations in the central representation, with suitable recurrent connections to the sensory areas providing sensory detail for reports missing from the central representation.

We underline the crucial feature of the central representation in comparison to the feature integration theories [7, 8]: the object file module has been fused with both the master map of spatial locations and the attentional module. Awareness of an input arises by the representation on the object file winning a competition there. This leads in general to identification of initial awareness of an input with its 'token', as a specific object, not its 'type' or category. The identification of the type of an input will be expected to take longer, since there has to be conjoint activation of the object model module in conjunction with the central representation, and then resulting activation of the relevant working memory, such as the phonological store for verbal report. Similar object-specific coupling to the sensory feature maps must also be enhanced.

5   Bringing AI and Soft Computing Together

How can the new framework incorporating the central representation and attentional control be developed to help narrow the gap between AI and soft computing? AI is here considered to be the computational system which uses directed attention throughout, while soft computing allows the detailed content of consciousness and attention to be prepared and sculpted to be most effective for task solution.

There are many discussions on how to bridge the gap between soft computing and AI, sometimes called the complete reduction problem [51]. The basic problem is that of giving meaning in the external world to the symbols being manipulated by AI systems. This has been attempted by using forms of neural or other systems and their styles of learning which are remote from the brain. From the general viewpoint of the whole range of tools of soft computing there is not much concern with attempting to use brain-style processing, especially at a global level, to build a bridge from symbols down to the sub-symbolic level. We have here a different slant on the problem of bridging the gap: the brain allows us a glimpse of at least one feasible solution. How can we move across this division from what we have considered so far?

There are various levels of difficulty at which solutions to this task can be developed. At one level is considered insertion of the central representation architecture of Fig. 4 into a standard stored program computer system. Various ways of achieving this will be discussed shortly. At the next higher level is the development of a hybrid system fusing the soft computing paradigm for attentional control described in the previous section with the higher level AI systems also mentioned earlier. At the most ambitious level is the attempt to 'go it alone' with the attentional system, by additional action-based systems, developed still using soft computing. We consider each of these in turn over the next three subsections.

5.1   Standard Computer Enhancement

The model presented in the previous section involved numerous modules computing by unsupervised soft techniques. These led to a set of feature modules activated in parallel for a given segregated input, with an additional module for representations of categorisations of that input, termed object models. There is also a module for analysis of the global input, in terms of the set of possible actions that could be made on the inputs. Finally there is the overarching attentional module, which runs a competition between its inputs, these being smoothed spatial representations of the global input. Such an attentional system was suggested as valid for vision and touch inputs, and can be applied to sound inputs by tonotopic coding of input sound traces.

To relate to a standard computer architecture, and in particular to assess how that could be extended by some of the features we have uncovered as part of the attentional system, we make a correspondence between the two systems by the relations:

Central Representation (attentional module) ↔ Control Processing Unit in the
    Central Processing Unit

Feature maps ↔ Software preprocessing filters

Object models ↔ ROM memory

Intentional maps ↔ Arithmetic logic unit

Working memories for Report ↔ Output devices

Buffer working memories ↔ Cache memories

Although the overall relationship is suggestive, especially for the global control modules, it is imperfect in the manner in which information is stored and passed around. For a neural network this is achieved by storage in attractor networks; information is not handed on in its original attractor form from one module to other modules where it is needed. In a neural network there are transformations at each stage of the processing, such as in the case of the manner of fusion of bodily and visual inputs in the parietal lobe described earlier. Such transformations of input are far from the identity map. For a standard computer architecture the information is directly passed unchanged from external memory into the CPU registers, being preserved in exact detail in the process. It is in the CPU that data is modified by the ALU. This difference is important, but could be dealt with by allowing transformation of data, using well-defined rules, to occur in a standard computer even when the data is being transferred.

Independently of that extension, in order to put the above analogy to work, the present points of weakness of the standard computer architecture need to be assessed. To explore this, let us consider working memory and its analogue of cache memory. From the present understanding of human working memory [37], cache memory systems could be extended and be developed as specialised memories for particular input domains. However, the 90-95% hit ratio of cache memories reported in modern computer systems indicates little need for such an update [52, 53]. This would be changed if specialised data domains were introduced, involving also specialised software preprocessing system for each data input domain; such changes could benefit from the use of the earlier analogy.

Another important area is that of long-term memory, one under intense investigation in neuroscience. But the present situation here for computer systems is similar to that described earlier for cache memory: improvements of long-term memory structures appear unnecessary, since paging allows arbitrary extension of memory at little additional cost (given the cheapness of RAM memory). However, the Principle of Locality is known to lead to the grouping of pages [52]; the understanding being gained of long-term memory in the brain is expected to be of importance in improving the way paging can be used optimally.

One area of present problems in using standard computer architecture is parallel computing: job partitioning is proving of great difficulty. Modern software is not yet able to handle tasks involving very large problems, such as a rise in fluid dynamics or geophysics; it is sometimes more effective to handcraft solutions to specific tasks in these and similar domains. The task of job partitioning is similar to that faced by a human in a complex environment. That is solved by filtering achieved by attention. This process is based on the competition being run on the central representation module. Development of a similar module in a parallel computer would achieve considerable improvement in solutions to the job partitioning task. Suitable information would need to be sent to the competitive module so as to achieve optimal ordering of jobs. A solution would be a software program designed to store the relevant information on salience of jobs (which itself would require a separate subprogram) and to run the competition between the jobs, indexed by their saliences.

It is clear that in all of these possible developments the symbol grounding problem has not been considered directly, if at all. We turn to the approach trying to ground existent symbols in a sub-symbolic framework based on soft computing.

5.2   Hybridisation

At the next level of difficulty, then, we meet the problem of fusing together the presently successful soft computing techniques with those of AI. We encounter again the gap between the two: soft computing is sub-conceptual, AI is conceptual. A considerable amount of work has now been done on developing soft computing versions of expert systems [54-57]. However, there are still problems in the development of systems able to create databases containing knowledge which is used by humans in communication but which is difficult to codify in logical (or even fuzzy) terms. Such a problem, for example, is that of building an expert system able to recognise and make decisions about the emotionality of faces and their associated speech [58].

Consider a sequence of facial expressions on a person's face as observed by a colleague as they converse. The speaker is providing to their conversant considerable information about their own emotional state during the exchange: their feeling of pleasure or displeasure in recounting some story, their similar response to further questions about the story and possible anger or dismay if being told they were not believed or were strongly disagreed with. The emotional responses are fleeting, especially being specified by the movements of facial muscles indicating certain emotions. But there is in addition the more general undertow of the emotional state the person is in at the outset of the encounter — be it positive or negative. It is only possible to detect the particular signs of emotions by use of specialised feature detectors.

At the same time the nature of emotion is not well defined. To be able to construct an expert system of a hybrid form to be able to make deductions about the emotional state of someone from their facial expressions (and speech structure), not only must the relevant feature detectors be used on the visual (and auditory) inputs but there must also be a transform from the subsymbolic distributed representations of outputs from the set of feature detectors (which may be upwards of 50 or so) to a set of symbols needed to describe the emotional state of the speaker. But there is no easy classification of a suitable set of emotional states. Instead it may be better to proceed by constructing a set of viewer/listener responses classifying the emotional content of the communications from their colleague in terms of what the viewer perceives as various energy/activity/directionality (or other) components that the speaker is trying to signal to their companion. Thus the symbolic coding of the output of the feature detectors is in terms of the probabilities of certain key signals. These are then to be used to make certain deductions concerning the viewer/speaker by existing probabilistic techniques.

This is an example of an attempt to relate more closely together human processing and the nature of information being signalled between humans so as to enable better human/computer interaction to be achieved. However, in so proceeding, we are forgetting the task from which we started: to develop a link between soft computing and AI from neuroscience by means of symbol grounding through the central representation. The approaches described above in this sub-section are not intelligent (in a grounded manner) in the sense defined earlier: the ability to transform representations to others in a goal-directed manner, that we hope to achieve by the deployment of the central representation, possessing as it does both attention and intentionality.

The neuro-scientific model — based on the central representation developed by soft computing styles of processing in the brain — is not yet up to the job set it, since it has very little intellectual power, even if it has arguably better attentional ones. In order to be able to relate to the problems routinely being considered by AI, such as language translation and rule deduction by expert systems, some form of thinking must be introduced into the neural system. That takes us to the highest level, in problem difficulty, of all. We turn to that finally.

5.3   Towards Thinking by Soft Computation

To develop any semblance of thought in soft computers, we have to move on from the basic architecture of the central representation outlined earlier and in Fig. 4 towards that able to handle sequential processing with stored internal representations. This is because thinking involves the use of working memory [37], including systems able to make transformations on internally held activations over periods of seconds. That is the executive component of working memory. We must therefore consider internally directed actions on internally held representations. This is a task solved by the working memory systems in our frontal lobes, so it is natural to look at the architecture and processing styles used there to achieve its effectiveness in thought processes.

Neural models of frontal lobe sequence processing have been developed by us elsewhere [17, 18], on the basis of a cartoon of the frontal lobes termed the ACTION network. This is considered in more detail by Neill Taylor in his paper later in this volume, to which the reader is referred for further details. The basic idea is to use recurrent loops to preserve activity for as long as needed. This persisting activity can be used, when it has attained a certain threshold level or after a GO signal, to activate a further temporally persisting neural activity, this new one turning off the previous one. In this manner a temporal sequence can be played out in the output nodes; learning the sequence can be achieved by use of reward learning, mentioned earlier.

The ACTION network is a simple model of frontally sited working memory. However, it must be coupled to posterior brain sites so as to be sculpted by the earlier representations there so as to be able to communicate with them. This is not to say that the frontal systems are able to accept posterior data automatically; the frontal ACTION-type system has to be trained by soft computing techniques to allow proper interaction between the ACTION net and the posterior sites coding for object recognition and preparation for action on objects.

We place an ACTION network in interaction with the attentional control system of the previous section. In so doing we are assuming the following processes can occur:

1) intentionalities of actions can be used to transform representations in the frontal ACTION network;

2) control of attention by the central representation can be extended to be effective over activations in the ACTION net;

3) connection of the salience net to the ACTION net is achievable to give support to ACTION network activity;

4) encoding of object-like representations in the ACTION network, so as to be able to have temporally extended activations of them (through continued activation from the ACTION net to the object model module).

The addition of the ACTION net is made in order to allow the total system, including the attentional control system, to achieve the overall functionality possessed by a thinking brain, one able to make transformations on its internal representations in order to achieve specific goals. That, I claim, is the most basic feature, apart from attentional control of selection and coherence of distributed attributes of inputs, which distinguishes AI systems from those based only on soft computing. To attain this ambitious end, it is necessary to consider each of the above numbered processes and how they might be implemented.

Firstly, in order to be able to use intentionalities of actions to transform ACTION network representations, these latter must be encoded in a similar manner to those in the object model module. Actions to be taken on the objects that the system can recognise have been assumed to have been learnt as part of the overall training of the attentional control system (the central representation). Similar training is assumed to be possible to extend these intentionalities to act frontally.

Secondly, it is also required that the competition on the attentional net can be extended to take account of input from the frontal system. This could be hard wired, although fine-tuning by Hebbian learning would be necessary to make this be able to account for the details of representations constructed on the ACTION network.

Thirdly, the salience net is needed to extend its influence over the ACTION network, especially since this is to be used as a relatively free-standing system able to perform at the 'centre of attention', so capturing the competition being run on the central representation (by means of suitable ACTION net connectivities).

Finally, the object models must be able to be accessed by the ACTION net (but not duplicated there) so that these object models can be used, when suitably activated, to provide constraints on the activity dynamics on the ACTION net.

This processing has been developed along solely soft computing lines, neglecting all of the advances made by AI and also not considering the earlier attempt to map traditional computers to the attentional system of section 5.1 and of hybridisation in section 5.2. This does not mean these two approaches are unimportant. The second could be used to implement, at least at a preliminary stage, high-level processing structures beyond the abilities of the combined attentional system and ACTION network. In addition it is very important to attain an effective mapping from the attentional/ACTION net system on to a traditional computer to be able to implement the computing style of the brain more effectively than on specialised computer systems. Thus the possibilities mentioned in section 5.1 would enable more effective brain-style computing on enhanced standard computers.

6   Conclusions

This is a very brief description of an ambitious plan of new styles of computers, based loosely on understanding being obtained from the brain. Their constructions involve solving some very hard problems, including that of constructing suitably computationally efficient detailed implementations of the architecture of Fig. 4 (architectures for the ACTION net are described in Neill Taylor's paper later in this volume). Let me summarise why such systems are relevant to consider, given all of the difficulties inherent in their construction — in particular why it is not too soon to attempt such ambitious undertakings.

To begin with, the architecture being considered is based on certain tried and tested neural architectures. The ACTION net is effective for temporal sequence learning and generation. Sequences of increasing length can be learnt by a chunking methodology which has some relation to brain maturation. Then parts of the posterior modules are able to be simulated: the attentional net (as a winner take all, especially using a continuum-style of neural network, being found increasingly effective as a simulation style for control and vision problems modelling parts of the brain). Thirdly, the salience map, as represented by the amygdala in the brain, is known to have a crucial function in giving affective value to inputs, and is importantly related to learning processes in cortex of the resulting valuation [59]. Neural models of the amygdala are now becoming increasingly detailed, but are already at a level of being able to simulate various of the effects observed [59]. Fourthly, the earlier visual processing modules are also being modelled increasingly effectively, as mentioned earlier. There are also models of intentionality [60] and of long-term memory involvement.

All of the relevant modules have one or several existent neural models. The time is becoming ripe for an attempt to combine these models to produce a neural system able to begin to bridge the gap between AI and soft computing. At this point it would seem that the system under consideration completely replaces AI, since it is only based on neural networks with suitable training. No AI high-level systems are involved. That indeed seems to be correct, but the crucial step being attempted here has been to bridge the gap at a conceptual level, which has been achieved by attempting to answer the question: can a neural system be constructed so as to be able to think? In developing our answer, we have followed a trail through the development of object percepts so as to be able to construct a system that can attend to, and think about, such objects. In order to do so it has to build suitably powerful object representations and associated attentional systems to determine when to allow relevant access to them. It can then be regarded as a putative but low-level expert system, able to argue about and solve problems in a particular domain. Further training and development then moves it into the domain of AI systems. The organisation of hybrid systems is then possible, since the attentional/ACTION net system has already crossed over towards the AI side of the divide, and can access reasoning systems using words or other symbols used sequentially. In fact the system under consideration is a solution to the problem of grounding the symbols in an AI expert system. As such, then, it would accomplish exactly the purpose set up initially: to bridge AI and soft computing.

The answer we arrive at, then, is in terms of a trainable attentional/ACTION net system to begin to learn the symbol grounding of the AI system and to improve certain aspects of standard computers. Much will have to be done to put such systems in operation.

References

1. Block N., Flanagan O. and Guzeldere G.: 'The nature of Consciousness', Cambridge MA: MIT Press (1997).
2. Chalmers D.: 'The Hard Problem of Consciousness', Cambridge: Cambridge University Press (1998).
3. Penrose O.: 'The Emperor's New Mind', Oxford: Oxford University Press (1989).
4. Dennett D.: 'Consciousness Explained', Cambridge: Cambridge University Press (1991).
5. Crick F.H.C.: 'The Astonishing Hypothesis', London: Simon & Schuster (1994).
6. Damasio A.: 'Descartes Error', New York: Basic Books (1994).
7. Triesman A.: 'Features and objects: The fourteenth Bartlett Memorial Lecture', Quart. Journal of Experimental Psychology, Vol. 40A, pp. 201-237 (1998).
8. Henderson J.M.: 'Two Representational Systems in Dynamic Visual Identification', Journal of Experimental Psychology: General, Vol. 20, pp. 410-426 (1994).
9. de Garis A.: 'Private communication' (1998).
10. Johnson M. H.: 'Cortical Maturation and the Development of Visual Attention in Early Infancy', Ch 10, in 'Brain Development and Cognition', ed., Johnson M. H., pp. 167-194, Oxford: Blackwell (1993).
11. Freeman W.A.: 'Mass Action in the Nervous System', New York: Academic Press (1975).
12. Whittle P.: 'Neural Networks and Chaotic Carriers', London: Wiley (1998).
13. McIntosh A. R. and Gonzalez-Lima F.: 'Neural network interactions related to auditory learning analysed with structural equation modeling', Human Brain Mapping, Vol. 2, pp. 23-44 (1994)
14. Mesulam M.: 'From sensation to cognition', Brain, Vol. 12, pp. 1013-1052 (1998).
15. Kohonen T.: 'Associative Memories', Berlin: Springer (1996).
16. Schultz W.: 'Reward Responses of Dopamine Neurons: A Biological Reinforcement Signal', Proc ICANN '97, eds., Gerstner W., Germond A., Hasler M. and Nicoud J-D., pp. 1-12, Berlin: Springer (1997).

17. Taylor N. and Taylor J.G.: 'Experimenting with Models of the Frontal Lobes', pp. 92-101 in 'Connectionist Models in Cognitive Neuroscience', eds., Heinke D., Humphreys G. W. and Olson A., London: Springer (1998).

18. Monchi O. and Taylor J.G.: 'A hard-wired model of coupled frontal working memories for various tasks', Information Sciences, Vol. 113, pp. 231-243 (1998).

19. Mishkin M., Ungerleider L.G. and Macko K.A.: 'Object vision and spatial vision: Two cortical pathways', Trends in Neuroscience, Vol. 6, pp. 414-417 (1983).

20. DeYoe E. and Van Essen D.C.: 'Concurrent processing streams in monkey visual cortex', Trends in Neuroscience, Vol. 11, pp. 219-226 (1988).

21. Peterhans E., von der Heydt R. and Baumgartner G.: 'Neuronal responses to illusory contours stimuli reveal stages of visual cortical processing', in 'Visual Neuroscience', eds., Pettigrew J. D., Sanderson K. J. and Levick W. R., pp 343-351, Cambridge: Cambridge University Press (1986).

22. Zeki S.: 'The representation of colours in the cerebral cortex', Nature, Vol. 284, pp. 412-418 (1980).

23. Sachs O.: 'The Man Who Mistook his Wife for a Hat', (1995).

24. Wandell B.A.: 'Foundations of Vision', Sunderland, MA: Sinauer Associates (1995).

25. Tootell R. B. H. et al: 'Functional Analysis of Human MT and Related Visual Cortical Areas Using Magnetic Resonance Imaging', Journal of Neuroscience, Vol. 15, pp. 3215-3230 (1995).

26. Weiskrantz L.: 'Blindsight', Oxford: Oxford university Press (1986).

27. Somers D.C., Nelson S.B. and Sur M.: 'An Emergent Model of Orientation Selectivity in Cat Visual Cortical Simple Cells', Journal of Neuroscience, Vol. 15, pp. 5448-5465 (1995).

28. Ben-Yishai R., Lev B-O and Sompolinsky H.: 'Theory of orientation tuning in visual cortex', Proceedings of National Academy of Science, Vol. 92, pp. 3844-3848 (1995).

29. Nowlan S.J. and Sejnowski T.: 'A Selection Model for Motion Processing in Area MT of Primates', Journal of Neursocience, Vol. 15, pp. 1195-1214 (1995).

30. Salin P. A. and Bullier J.: 'Corticocortical Connections in the Visual System: Structure and Function', Physiological Review, Vol. 75, pp. 107-154 (1995).

31. Tootell R. J. B. et al: 'Organization of Intrinsic Connections in Owl Mokey Area MT', Cerebral Cortex, Vol. 7, pp. 386-393 (1997).

32. Thier P. and Karnath H.O. (eds.): 'Parietal Lobe Contributions to Orientation in 3D Space', Berlin: Springer (1997).

33. Milner A. and Goodale M.: 'The Visual Brain in Action', Oxford: University Press (1995).

34. Tanaka K.: 'Inferotemporal Cortex and Object Vision', Annual Reviews of Neuroscience, Vol. 19, pp. 109-139 (1996).

35. Morell A. and Bullier J.: 'Anatomical segregation of two cortical visual pathways in the macaque monkey', Visual Neuroscience, Vol. 4, pp. 555-578 (1990).

36. Baizer J. S. Ungerleider L. G. and Desimone R.: 'Organization of Visual Inputs to the Inferior Temporal Posterior Parietal Cortex in Macaques', Journal of Neuroscience, Vol. 11, pp. 168-190 (1991).

37. Baddeley A.: 'Working Memory', Oxford: Oxford University Press (1986).

38. Milner A. D.: 'Neglect, extinction and the cortical streams of visual processing', in 'Parietal Lobe Contributions to Orientation in 3D Space', eds., Thier P. and Karnath H.O., pp. 3-22, Berlin: Springer (1997).

39. Bisiach E: 'The spatial features of unilateral neglect', in 'Parietal Lobe Contributions to Orientation in 3D Space', eds., Thier P. and Karnath H-O., pp. 465-496, Berlin: Springer (1997).

40. Karnath H.O.: 'Neural encoding of space in egocentric coordinates? Evidence of and limits of a hypothesis derived from patients with parietal lesions and neglect', in 'Parietal Lobe Contributions to Orientation in 3D Space', eds., Thier P. and Karnath H-O., pp. 497-520, Berlin: Springer (1997).

41. Triesman A., Cavanagh P., Fischer B., Ranachandran V. S., and von der Heydt R.: 'Form Perception and Attention: Striate Cortex and Beyond', Ch 11, in 'Visual Perception: The Neurophysiological Foundations', pp. 273-316, San Diego: Academic Press (1990).

42. Taylor J. G.: 'The Race for Consciousness', Cambridge, MA: MIT Press (1999).

43. Mesulam M.: 'Attention, Confusional States and Neglect', Ch 3, in 'Principles of Neuro-biology', ed., Mesulam M., pp. 125-168, Philadelphia: FA Davis Co (1985).

44. Stein J.: 'The representation of egocentric space in the posterior parietal lobe', Behav, Brain Sci., Vol. 15, pp. 691-700 (1992).

45. Taylor J. G. and Alavi F.: 'A global competitive network for attention', Neural Network World, Vol. 5, pp. 477-502 (1993).

46. Taylor J. G. and Alavi F.: 'A global competitive neural network', Biol. Cybernetics, Vol. 72, pp. 233-248 (1995).

47. Libet B. et al: 'Production of threshold levels of conscious sensation by electrical stimulation of human somatosensory cortex', J of Neurophsyiology, Vol. 27, pp. 546-578 (1964).

48. Taylor J. G.: 'A competition for consciousness?', Neurocomputing, Vol. 11, pp. 271-296 (1996).

49. Taylor J. G.: 'Breakthrough to awareness: a preliminary neural network model of conscious and unconscious perception in word processing', Biol Cybernetics, Vol. 25, pp. 59-72 (1996).

50. Marcel A. J.: 'Conscious and preconscious recognition on polysemous words: locating the selective effects of prior verbal contexts', in 'Attention and Performance VIII', ed., Nickerson R.S., Hillsdale NJ: Lawrence Erlbaum (1980).

51. Haugeland J: 'The nature of plausibility of cognitivism', Behaviour and Brain Science, Vol. 2, pp. 215-260 (1978).

52. Wilkinson B.: 'Computer architecture', London: Prentice-Hall (1996).

53. Gorse D.: 'Lecture Notes on Computer Architectures (B10)', Department of Computer Science, University College London, unpublished, (1999).

54. Gallant S.: 'Neural Network Learning', Cambridge, MA: MIT Press (1993).

55. Gallant S.: 'Connectionist Expert Systems', Communications of the ACM, Vol. 31, No. 2, (1998).

56. Omlin C.W. and Giles C.L.: 'Extraction of Rules from Discrete-time Recurrent Neural Networks', Neural Networks, Vol. 9, pp. 41-52 (1996).

57. Alexandre F. (ed): 'Connectionist-Symbolic Processing: From Unified to Hybrid Approaches', Hillsdale, NJ: Lawrence Erlbaum (1997).

58. Kollias S., Gielen S., Apolloni B., Cowie R. and Taylor J. G.: 'Principled Hybrid Systems: Theory and Applications', (PHYSTA) EC Project ERB 4061 PL 97-0238 (1997).

59. LeDoux J.: 'The Emotional Brain', London: Weidenfeld & Nicholson (1998).

60. Fagg A. H. and Arbib M. A.: 'Modeling parietal-premotor interactions in primate control of grasping', Neural Networks, Vol. 11, pp. 1277-1304 (1998).

Future Directions for Soft Computing

Jim F. Baldwin

Advanced Computer Research Centre and
Engineering Mathematics Department
University of Bristol, Bristol BS8 1TR, UK
`jim.baldwin@bristol.ac.uk`

Abstract. In this paper we discuss possible future directions of research for soft computing in the context of artificial intelligence and knowledge engineering. Fundamental issues are presented with basic ideas emphasised rather than detailed accounts of algorithms and procedures.

The use of fuzzy sets to machine learning, computer intelligence and creativity are discussed in relation to the central problems of creating knowledge from data, pattern recognition, making summaries, user modelling for computer/ human interfaces, co-operative learning, fuzzy inheritance for associative reasoning.

A voting model semantics for fuzzy sets is used to develop ideas for a mass assignment theory which provides the means of moving from the case of crisp sets to that of fuzzy sets. The use of fuzzy sets in this way will provide better interpolation, greater knowledge compression, and less dependence on the effects of noisy data than if only crisp sets were used. We will see how easy and useful it is to use successful inference methods such as decision trees, probabilistic fuzzy logic type rules, Bayesian nets with attributes taking fuzzy values rather than crisp values.

The mass assignment theory provides a unified approach to handling both probabilistic uncertainty and fuzzy vagueness.

1   Introduction

As a society we collect so much data but do so little effectively with it. Supermarkets collect data concerning customer transactions, report distribution difficulties, and provide financial accounts. Hospitals carry out tests and hold patient records. Data is provided in engineering projects to provide models for analysis and design. Financial institutions provide records of potential customers, collect statistics of existing customer performances. Traffic behaviour, market surveys, product performance are recorded to improve management and performance decisions. Data is cleaned and processed, studied and moved from place to place, visualised and communicated, stored in data banks. We collect with enthusiasm hoping that the data will provide us with the answers we require. Data mining is a new subject area with journals, conferences, and books describing case studies and recalling methods of analysing and visu-

B. Azvine et al. (Eds.): Intelligent Systems and Soft Computing, LNAI 1804, pp. 72-94, 2000.

alising data. Methods are available for answering questions of a single source of data by forming rules to predict the answers, generalising from those cases in the database. Neural net methods, Bayesian nets and decision trees are some of the more sophisticated approaches to provide these generalisations. So often background knowledge is ignored, applications are rather simple and constrained, and the methods are not robust for noisy data and for data in which attributes are continuous variables. We can answer simple queries about one attribute when given values of some or all the others in the database. We can find simple patterns in the data. The tuples in the database are used as learning examples and how good the predictions and classifications are depend on how representative this data is of the situation in hand.

Ideally we would wish to throw the data away and replace it with a summary in the form of knowledge sentences which fully represented all the relevant knowledge contained in the data. This summary would form part of a larger knowledge base made up of similar summaries from other database sources. We could then converse with the knowledge base in the same way as we might wish to talk to a human expert. The knowledge base could be used to provide deductive inferences, probabilistic inferences, analogical inferences, associative and inheritance inferences. We are far from this ideal but we need to move towards it.

The central question for this paper is to ask how can soft computing help and is it really necessary. I will ask the more specific question. How can fuzzy sets be of help in our pursuit for creating knowledge summaries from databases? This avoids the difficulty of deciphering what we actually mean by soft computing.

The world is not fuzzy in any way. We can look out and see the precision of a leaf on a tree, the curvatures of the road, the shading of a car, the detail of a person's face, the clouds in the sky. But this precision which we can see with our eyes if we want is often unwanted detail when it comes to labelling and categorising and classifying and clustering the real world into groups which we can label. We give labels to such objects as people, clouds, cars, fields, good paintings, happy faces, etc, because we wish to talk about these objects in terms of their common properties within their group. It is a necessary part of our understanding of the world to label and give names to these labels and use them in natural language.

A crisp set is a set of elements which satisfy all our criteria for belonging to the set. An even set of dice values is {2, 4, 6} because the numbers 2, 4, and 6 are all even and are dice values. A fuzzy set is a set of values with memberships in the range [0, 1] where the membership value is in some sense a measure of how well the element satisfies what we mean by small dice value. A fuzzy set of small dice values might be {1 / 1, 2 / 0.8, 3 / 0.3} where 2, for example has membership of 0.8 in the fuzzy set 'small' associated with dice values. We will later discuss the semantics of this fuzzy set in more detail.

In moving from crisp to fuzzy sets we need only introduce the membership function as having possible values in the range [0, 1] instead of in the set {0, 1} as for the crisp case. Most people would accept this change. The controversy of fuzzy sets has little to do with this definition. People might ask how can we choose the actual membership values and this is a sensible question which somehow we must answer. The controversy of fuzzy set theory lies with the calculus used for such operations as intersection, union, etc, But there is really a more fundamental question which is asked before worrying about the calculus. Is it really necessary to complicate our modelling world by introducing fuzzy sets in addition to existing crisp sets? We will now discuss this important question.

Every one will accept that humans use fuzzy concepts. In fact, almost all our concepts are fuzzy. This contrasts with the mathematical world which uses precisely defined concepts. Why do we use fuzzy concepts, concepts that we cannot define exactly. We have no definition for tall and yet we use the term and find it easy to apply. When is an object a bush rather than a tree? These questions have been asked many times and over several years. Do we really need to discuss them now? We do need to discuss them to answer why we require fuzzy sets for the purpose of converting large data sets into knowledge bases. We must look more closely at the semantics of a fuzzy set, study in more detail how we should modify those methods which use only crisp sets to accommodate fuzzy sets and indicate the real gain in using these more complicated ideas. No one would wish to complicate for the sake of it. There has to be a good reason for introducing fuzzy concepts.

Fig. 1 could be the membership function for tall.

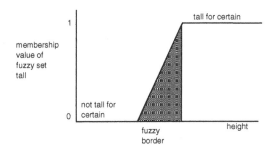

Fig. 1. Possible membership function for 'tall'.

This concept of a fuzzy set intuitively appeals and the basic concept of fuzzy borders makes good sense. We need to understand more fully why and how this fuzzy region is important and should not be ignored.

Fuzzy labels occur so very often in the vocabulary of the natural language we use. We have a subjective judgement of the degree to which a particular label is appropriate. Fuzziness arises because of human labelling and subjective judgement. It is not present in the raw real world before labels are given.

We will try to answer why we need fuzzy sets before discussing their semantics and what calculus we should use. This will provide motivation for studying them in more detail. Most instrument measurements provide us with exact numbers — these numbers may be approximate and would be better interpreted as a mean of some probability distribution. Attributes of databases mostly have exact values in their tuples. There may be missing information and sometimes only a range of possible values given.

Sometimes the value may be described by a probability distribution. Only very infrequently would an attribute be given a fuzzy value. Why should we therefore bother with fuzzy sets?

Consider an attribute, which can take a continuum of values in some range. We would expect every object or data tuple which had attributes with similar values to be similar in respect to classification and predictions for any unknown attribute. We would like to group values of an attribute together and give them a label to distinguish this group from others. We could use precise groupings, intervals defining possible ranges of values. We could then group tuples together which had the attribute values in the same intervals. Tuples whose values belong to the same intervals would then be indistinguishable. If a certain classification were associated with one, we would also associate it with the others. Similarly we would provide the same prediction for all. A tuple would belong to a cell in a multidimensional space. All tuples with the attribute values lying in the same intervals would belong to the same cell. A classification or prediction would be given to each cell. No account can now be given to the fact that one tuple may lie on the edge of one cell and near other cells. You would expect tuples near the edge of the cell to be a little similar to those belonging to neighbouring cells. If we took this into account it would be equivalent to some form of multidimensional interpolation. This would obviously provide greater accuracy for prediction. In more complicated situations we would not have a definite classification associated with each cell but a probability distribution over the set of possible classifications. In this case the multidimensional interpolation would change the probability distributions of tuples belonging to the same cell by taking into account the distributions of the neighbouring cells. We see, therefore, that the multidimensional interpolation provides better accuracy for both prediction and classification.

The formation of cells and the grouping of tuples with the multidimensional form of interpolation provide a natural method of generalisation. We have classification and prediction for any point in a given cell even though the database only provides a selection of points in the cells.

How can we obtain the multidimensional interpolation easily and naturally? If we use fuzzy sets as defining our intervals rather than crisp ranges then we will have the required variation across the intervals by means of the membership function of the fuzzy set. Points in the centre of the interval will be given high membership and those at the edges low membership with intermediate values in between. Thus instead of dividing up a line into crisp intervals we can define the intervals using such fuzzy sets as **small**, **medium** and **large**. This will provide us with the required variation and interpolation effect. We will discuss exactly how in a later section.

This use of fuzzy sets is not restricted to attributes with continuous variables. The same arguments apply to the case where we have a discrete set of possible values for an attribute. For example we can replace the dice values {1, 2, 3, 4, 5, 6} with the groupings {**small**, **medium**, **large**} where **small**, **medium** and **large** are fuzzy sets defined in the space of dice values.

The fuzzy sets we will label as words. We can still use the methods we might use with crisply defined groupings with these fuzzy groupings. How we do this, and what modifications we have to make so that we can deal with fuzzy labels we will discuss in a later section. For now it is enough to say that this can easily be done.

The effect of using multidimensional interpolation not only increases the accuracy but will allow us to use fewer rules if we are using rules as our form of knowledge representation, smaller decision trees if this is the form of knowledge representation, or more simple graphs if we use causal nets. The use of fuzzy sets to provide groupings for our data thus gives better accuracy, greater data compression and natural generalisation. This is our motivation for using fuzzy sets. The additional complication introduced by using fuzzy sets rather than crisp intervals pays off because of the greater accuracy and compression.

What we do later is consistent with probability theory — no conflict should exist for probability theorists. The labels on the groupings are words represented with fuzzy sets. A modified counting procedure will be established and used to compute probability distributions over the set of classifications. Prediction problems will be treated as classification problems in which each class is given a fuzzy set label. We will derive a probability distribution over these fuzzy classes and use this distribution with the mass assignment interpretation of fuzzy sets to derive a point value for the prediction. Thus prediction is fuzzy classification plus defuzzification.

We will discuss ID3 type approaches using attributes with fuzzy groupings for constructing decision trees. Bayesian Nets with variables taking word values defined by fuzzy sets and neural nets with inputs depending on fuzzy word groupings will also be discussed. The approach to be discussed is also relevant to inductive logic programming methods with probabilistic conditioned rules in which predicate variables can be instantiated to fuzzy sets. The approach has been used successfully with ID3 type methods and applied to many application areas and test examples. These will be discussed briefly later.

We will also discuss other extensions such as prototype modelling using knowledge structures which can be used to make inferences where only some of the prototypes are applicable and where only a partial match with several prototypes can be made. Answers from each prototype will be obtained and these must be fused together to obtain the final solution.

The fusion problem is most important and has been discussed for several years. The following is an example of a fusion problem. We see colours in a three dimensional colour space. If we damage one of the dimensions, we effectively project on to one of the three two-dimensional spaces. There are three types of colour blindness corresponding to each of these two-dimensional projections. Imagine we have three such colour blind persons viewing a colour scheme. Each provides a colour description from their two-dimensional point of view. Can we construct a correct three-dimensional view point from these descriptions?

This problem arises often in data mining because we have too many attributes, too many variables, and too many dimensions to cope with. We can project on to lower dimensional spaces and do our classification with respect to each of these smaller dimensional points of view. We must then fuse the answers together to obtain the solution for the full dimensional space. The fusion can take various forms from simple conjunctive fusion, a weighted average sort of fusion, to the more complex case in which no simple formula-based fusion can be assumed and we have to learn the rules of fusion for the case in hand from examples.

Maybe the most important problem we have is how to select the most appropriate attributes. The primary attributes of the database may not be the most appropriate and combinations of these primary attributes would form a better discrimination. The combination can be algebraic, relational and combinations of these. How can we select these more appropriate attributes? We will suggest genetic programming where trees representing language constructs depicting relational and algebraic combinations are formed to satisfy some fitness measure. The choice of this fitness measure is most important. We cannot use the success of a construct on a test set because this would be computationally too severe. We need some form of discrimination measure that would indicate possible success. The mass assignment theory will supply such a measure.

We have indicated in this introduction that fuzzy sets can be used effectively to provide considerable enhancement to those methods that are already used but with crisp groupings. New approaches will also be suggested. Because we are using fuzzy groupings it is important that necessary modifications to existing methods should be simple extensions. Changing from crisp to fuzzy intervals or groupings should not require radical rethinking or radically different methods. Methods we use with the fuzzy groupings will always have their counterpart with crisp groupings. All we wish for in using fuzzy groupings is that we obtain better accuracy and greater compression.

2   Voting Model Semantics

This is essential to the arguments we put forward in this paper and to the methods we discuss. We give only a brief account of the least prejudiced distribution since this is essential to the whole of the discussion.

Consider a fair dice and let us introduce the words **small**, **medium**, **large** in the context of the set of values which the dice can show, namely $\{1, 2, 3, 4, 5, 6\}$. These words are fuzzy because not everyone will agree with the same subset of the value domain as satisfying a given word when asked to accept or reject each value. If they did we could write down precise definitions of **small**, **medium** and **large** in this context. If we are to use words like these in our computer linguistic statements then we must provide them with semantics appropriate for humans to be able to interpret them properly.

Suppose we have a representative set of people who are asked to accept or reject the value x as satisfying the word **small**. Of course, the person can have a partial acceptance but we are forcing the person to make a binary decision. A person is not allowed to abstain and if he/she has accepted already y as small then he/she must also accept x as small if x < y. Suppose everyone accepts 1 as **small**, 80% accept 2 as **small** and 20% accept 3 as **small**. We will then define the fuzzy set **small** as:

small = 1 / 1 + 2 / 0.8 + 3 / 0.2

where the membership value for a given element is the proportion of people who accept this element as satisfying the fuzzy set. A person can accept the same element as belonging to any number of fuzzy sets. We might also get the fuzzy sets:

medium = 2 / 0.2 + 3 / 1 + 4 / 1 + 5 / 0.2
large = 4 / 0.2 + 5 / 0.8 + 6 / 1

using a similar voting procedure for accepting a score as satisfying **medium** and **large** respectively.

We call this the voting model semantics for a fuzzy set. The assumption that a voter who accepts a given value will also accept other values having a greater membership value in the fuzzy set is called the 'constant threshold constraint'.

We do not record the exact voting pattern for each person for the different values. If we are given the proportions for each element in the fuzzy set **medium**, for example, the voting pattern, with the constant threshold constraint, will look like:

1	2	3	4	5	6	7	8	9	10	persons
3	3	3	3	3	3	3	3	3	3	
4	4	4	4	4	4	4	4	4	4	
2	2									
5	5									

The 5s must have the same voters as the 2s since a voter who accepted 2 must also accept 5 since the membership of 5 is less or equal to the membership of 2.

Suppose you are told that the dice score is **medium**. What probability distribution would you accept for the dice score? Does this question make sense. Consider that you are told that the dice score is even and you are asked for a probability distribution. You would conclude that the dice value could only be 2, 4 or 6. Further, you would assume these to be equally likely in the absence of further information and conclude:

$$Pr(2) = Pr(4) = Pr(6) = 1/3.$$

If you do not wish to make the equally likely assumption then you could only say that the dice value was in the set $\{2, 4, 6\}$. This is equivalent to a distribution over the power set of the dice values. The power set S of S is the set of all subsets of S including the null set $\emptyset$. In this case the distribution is:

$$\{2, 4, 6\} : 1$$

This corresponds to a family of distributions over S which is defined by:

$$1 : 0, 2 : Pr(2), 3 : 0, 4 : \{r(4), 5 : 0, 6 : Pr(6)$$
where $Pr(2) + Pr(4) + Pr(6) = 1$

A probability distribution over S corresponds to a family of distributions over S.

The only difference between this and the fuzzy case above is that we are told the dice value is a crisp set, even, rather than the fuzzy set. So the question makes sense and we must find a way to modify what we can do with crisp sets to the case of fuzzy sets.

We can think of one of the persons from the representative set being chosen at random and we will know that the score is one of the values accepted by that person as being **medium**. Thus if we choose person 1 it would be a value from $\{2, 3, 4, 5\}$ while if we choose person 10 it would be a value from $\{3, 4\}$. Without further assumptions we cannot give a distribution over the set of dice values but we can give a distribution over the power set of the dice values. For example, in the case of **medium**, we can say that the set $\{2, 3, 4, 5\}$ will be chosen with probability 0.2 and $\{3, 4\}$ with probability 0.8. We call this distribution a mass assignment and write it as:

$$\text{MA}_{\textbf{medium}} = \{3, 4\} : 0.8, \{2, 3, 4, 5\} : 0.2$$

A mass assignment over S is a probability distribution over the power set of S, namely S.

Similarly the mass assignments for **small** and **large** are:

$$\text{MA}_{\textbf{small}} = \{1\} : 0.2, \{1, 2\} : 0.6, \{1, 2, 3\} : 0.2$$
$$\text{MA}_{\textbf{large}} = \{6\} : 0.2, \{5, 6\} : 0.6, \{4, 5, 6\} : 0.2$$

The probabilities associated with the subsets, focal elements, are called masses.

These mass assignments are also called random sets and basic probability assignments in the literature. The reason for giving them a new name is to distinguish the theory of mass assignments from that of the theory of random sets and also the Dempster Shafer Theory.

The mass assignments above correspond to families of distributions. For example, we can distribute the masses associated with each subset among the elements of that subset in many ways to obtain a resulting probability distribution over the dice values.

If we wish to obtain a single distribution, how should we distribute these masses? To be totally unbiased we should distribute the masses according to the prior for the dice values. Since the dice is assumed to be fair we distribute the masses equally among the elements of their corresponding subsets of dice values. Thus for **medium** we distribute 0.8 equally among 3 and 4 and the mass 0.2 equally among 2, 3, 4, and 5. We therefore obtain the distribution for **medium**:

$$\text{lpd}_{\textbf{medium}} = 2 : 0.05, 3 : 0.4 + 0.05 = 0.45, 4 : 0.4 + 0.05 = 0.45, 5 : 0.05$$

We call this the 'least prejudiced distribution'. The least prejudiced distribution for **small** and **large** are similarly:

lpd_{small} = 1 : 0.2 + 0.3 + 0.0667 = 0.5667, 2 : 0.3 + 0.0667 = 0.3667, 3 : 0.0667
lpd_{large} = 4 : 0.0667, 5 : 0.3667, 6 ; 0.5667

Corresponding to any fuzzy set there is a least prejudiced distribution. This distribution is fundamental to our approach to soft computing or computing with words where the words are represented by fuzzy sets. With this interpretation, probability theory can be used for inference purposes in a simple way. Using the prior in this way is like using a local entropy maximisation to distribute the masses. We do this for each subset separately.

An algebra of mass assignments can be developed by introducing such concepts as the meet, join of two mass assignments, the compliment of a mass assignment and a restriction of a mass assignment. This has been discussed in Baldwin [1-4] and will not be discussed further in this paper. We can also define such concepts as point and interval semantic unifications. These provide point values and intervals for $Pr(X$ is $\mathbf{f}$ | X is $\mathbf{g})$ where $\mathbf{f}$ and $\mathbf{g}$ are two fuzzy sets defined on the same universe of discourse. They can be continuous or discrete. These are derived directly from the mass assignments of $\mathbf{f}$ and $\mathbf{g}$ and take into account the prior distribution for the variable X.

2.1   Fuzzy Sets from Data

In this section we will describe how we can construct fuzzy sets from data. This is important in data mining and more generally in machine learning methods. We can find a fuzzy set from any probability distribution by choosing the fuzzy set such that its least prejudiced distribution is equal to the given distribution. This is the method we use to extract fuzzy sets directly from data. Given values for a particular feature we can determine a frequency distribution and from this determine the corresponding fuzzy set. This can be done for both discrete and continuous fuzzy sets. In the case of continuous fuzzy sets smoothing is required to get a good representative fuzzy set which generalises well.

2.2   Transformation to Word Spaces

Suppose F is a continuous attribute. We cover the range of F with fuzzy sets. We consider both trapezoidal and triangular fuzzy sets.

- Using trapezoidal fuzzy sets, the fuzzy sets can be as:

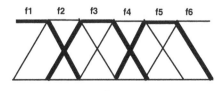

Consider F = **f**. This value can be written as a fuzzy set in terms of the fuzzy set labels {**fi**}. We call the fuzzy set labels words. Consider that the value of F is f, then we have:

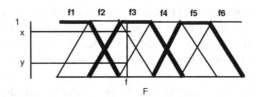

f = **f3** / 1 + **f2** / x + f4 / y ; where y < x < 1.
The mass assignment for f is
M_f = **f3** : 1-x, {**f2, f3**} : x-y, {**f2, f3, f4**} : y
so that the least prejudiced distribution is
lpd_f = **f2** : 1/2(x-y) + 1/3(y) = 1/2(x) - 1/6(y)

  f3 : (1-x) + 1/2(x-y) + 1/3(y) = 1 -1/2(x) - 1/6(y)

  f4 : 1/3(y)

We can therefore associate 1/2(x) - 1/6(y) of f to **f2**

        1 -1/2(x) - 1/6(y) of f to **f3**

        1/3(y) of f to f**4**

We can overlap the fuzzy sets as in:

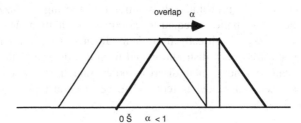

An overlap of 1 corresponds to the case above.

With any overlap a similar calculation to that above can be done to provide the distribution of the example value among the different fuzzy set words.

- Using a complete set of mutually exclusive triangular fuzzy sets:

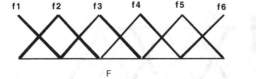

membership values for
any value F will sum to 1

Any value of the feature F, namely f, can be written in terms of a fuzzy set of the fuzzy sets words **fi**. Only at most two fuzzy words will be used for each precise value f:

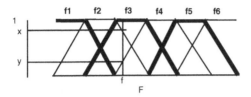

$f = \mathbf{f3} / x + \mathbf{f2} / y$; where x > y
This is not a normalised fuzzy set.
The mass assignment for f is
$M_f = \mathbf{f3} : x\text{-}y, \{\mathbf{f2}, \mathbf{f3}\} : y, \emptyset : 1\text{-}x$
We can obtain a normalised fuzzy set in two ways:

(a)   Redistribute the mass y associated with $\emptyset$ equally among **f2** and **f3**. This gives the modified mass assignment
$M'_f =$ $\{\mathbf{f3}\} : (x\text{-}y) + 1/2(y), \{\mathbf{f2}, \mathbf{f3}\} : y, \{\mathbf{f2}\} : 1/2(y)$
which gives the least prejudiced distribution
$lpd_f =$ $\mathbf{f2} : y$
$\mathbf{f3} : x$
The distribution is given by the membership values in the corresponding fuzzy sets.

(b)   Redistribute the mass y associated with $\emptyset$ among $\{\mathbf{f3}\}$ and $\{\mathbf{f2}, \mathbf{f3}\}$ in the same proportions as the masses for these,
i.e. we add y (x-y)/x to $\{\mathbf{f3}\}$ and y y/x to $\{\mathbf{f2}, \mathbf{f3}\}$.
This gives the modified mass assignment
$M'_f =$ $\{\mathbf{f3}\} : (x\text{-}y) + y(x\text{-}y) / x = (x\text{-}y)(x+y) / x = (x\text{-}y) / x$

$\{\mathbf{f2}, \mathbf{f3}\} : y + y^2 / x = y(x + y) / x = y / x$
giving the least prejudiced distribution
$lpdf = \mathbf{f2} : y / 2x, \mathbf{f3} : \{(x\text{-}y)/x\} + y / 2x = 1 - (y / 2x)$
This is the same result as if we had converted the mass assignment M_f to a least prejudiced distribution ignoring completely the mass of y on $\emptyset$ and then normalising the resulting distribution.
IF $M_f = \mathbf{f3} : x\text{-}y, \{\mathbf{f2}, \mathbf{f3}\} : y, \emptyset : 1\text{-}x$
then the least prejudiced distribution ignoring the $\emptyset$ mass is
$\mathbf{f2} : 1/2(y), \mathbf{f3} : x - 1/2(y)$
and normalising this gives the result above.
This approach is easily generalised to the case where we only know a fuzzy set value **f** for the attribute F.

3   Two Viewpoints for Machine Learning

Consider a classification problem in which objects with attributes $\{A1, \ldots, An\}$ are to be classified with class labels $\{C1, \ldots, Cm\}$. A training set of examples Tr is given and also a test set Ts. The attribute domains are covered with words given by trapezoidal or triangular fuzzy sets as described previously. Each object in Tr of a given class Ci can be allocated as a distribution over the word cells of the multidimensional attribute word space. The object will have values for each of the attributes. These values are distributed over the set of words associated with that space. Suppose that associated with the domain of attribute Ak we have the set of words $\{w_{ki}\}$ then the value of Ak will give a distribution over $\{w_{ki}\}$. This will be the case whether the value of the attribute is a precise value or fuzzy set defined on the domain of Ak. We repeat this for values of each of the attributes. We multiply these distributions to obtain a distribution over the word space associated with $A1 \times A2 \ldots \times An$, B say. This provides a count of the proportions of this object in the multidimensional word cells. We repeat with all the examples in Tr for class Ck. If the example has a fuzzy representation for its classification over the set of class labels then this fuzzy set is converted to a distribution over the classes and that proportion belonging to class k is distributed over the word space as just described. We can therefore deal with examples with fuzzy classifications as well as pure classifications. This is important for prediction type problems in which the classes are fuzzy sets on the prediction space. A predicted value for an example in Tr would have a fuzzy set representation over the class labels.

The examples in Tr provide us with a distribution over B for each class. We have effectively Pr(Ck | multidimensional word cell) for all k and all word cells. These distributions can be represented as extended Fril [5-9].

Alternatively, the distribution over the multidimensional word space can be converted to a discrete fuzzy set **F** as described above and the rule for classification Ck is:

Classification is Ck IFF attribute word values belong to **F**

This is an equivalence rule which can be expressed directly in Fril.

These two viewpoints are equivalent from Fril point of view since the inference methods of Fril are based on probability theory and the mass assignment theory is used to give this interpretation. For example, if for a new example, it has a distribution over B which has a fuzzy set representation of **F'**, then Pr(**F** | **F'**) is determined using semantic unification. Both **F** and **F'** are discrete fuzzy sets defined over B. This represents the probability of the body being true. This probability is passed to the head of the rule since we are using an equivalence rule.

The same result is obtained from the extended Fril rule.

In the case of prediction, the classes Ck will be words on the output space. The extended Fril rules, one for each classification, will, for a new case, provide a probability distribution, $\{\alpha k\}$ over the $\{Ck\}$. The defuzzified predicted point value is then the weighted sum $\sum_k \alpha_k \omega_k$ where ω_k is the expected value of the least prejudiced distribution of the fuzzy set associated with the word representing class Ck.

This has no difficulties for low-dimensional problems, but we have the problem of the curse of dimensionality. As we have more attributes to consider we have an exponential growth in the computation. We can get the most efficient extended Fril rule by using a mass assignment ID3 approach as discussed below, although this more efficient decision tree may introduce a bias as far as the generalisation to examples in Tx is concerned. This is the case because some branches in the decision tree are not present in order to represent the correct classifications in the training set Tr. These might, however, be of value for cases in Tx. This is less likely to occur when using fuzzy sets than for the case when only crisp sets are used.

In this section we will discuss ways of dealing with the curse of dimensionality that breaks the problem into sub-problems of lower dimension. The solution of the lower dimensional problems are then fused together. The most extreme form of this is to consider each of the attributes separately. Thus in this approach we find a classification rule with respect to each attribute, namely:

Class is Ck from attribute Ai point of view IFF attribute Ai belongs to **Fki**

where **Fki** is a discrete fuzzy set over the words associated with attribute Ai.

We could also use the conditional probabilities $Pr(w_{ki} \mid$ class k) in an extended Fril rule:

Class is Ck from attribute Ai point of view
with { probability $Pr(w_{ki} \mid$ class K) IFF attribute Ak is w_{ki} }$_{all\ k}$

Thus for a given new example we will use these rules to determine a distribution over the classes from each attribute point of view.

How do we fuse these view points together? Two obvious schemes are apparent.

- Conjunctive fusion

In this case we multiply the probabilities of the various view points for a given classification. This is equivalent to using the conjunctive fuzzy rule:

Class is Ck IFF attribute A1 belongs to **Fk1** and attribute A2 belongs to **Fk2** and ...
Attribute An belongs to **Fkn**.

- Evidential fusion

In this case we take a weighted average of the supports for class k from the different view points. This is equivalent to using the Fril evidential logic rule:

Class is Ck   IFF   A1 belongs to **Fk1** with weight wk1

A2 belongs to **Fk2** with weight wk2

.

.

.

An belongs to **Fkn** with weight wkn

These two approaches with each attribute taken separately was used as the basic method in the Fril data browser. It has some relationship to using naïve Bayes for classification.

The weights in the above evidential logic rule are determined using mass assignment discrimination analysis. If, for example, Fkr has no overlap with Fkj, for all j, j $\neq$ r, then wkr = 1 and all the other weights would equal 0. If there is complete overlap, then wkr would be 0. By taking the semantic unifications of Pr(Fkr | Fkj) for j $\neq$ r into account we can determine a good weight for wr. This is described in Baldwin [1, 2, 10, 11].

We can extend these approaches to higher dimensional sub-sets than that of single dimensions. The problem is what sub-sets should we choose. We can use overlapping subsets of attributes. Groups of attributes can be chosen and each one used separately. The solutions are fused as above for the one-dimensional case. *Ad hoc* methods which have some intuitive appeal have been used to select groupings of attributes for this purpose.

The discrimination method for assessing the importance of an attribute can be used with a genetic programming approach to choose combinations of features where the combinations can be algebraic and relational. This approach requires further investigation but forms an important aspect of our mass assignment inductive logic approach. The genetic programming makes the search for combined attributes more efficient in the various search methods of inductive logic programming to obtain good rules.

4   Mass Assignment ID3, Belief Networks and Other Applications

In both these approaches to machine learning conditional probabilities must be assessed with respect to the specific architectures of the problem. In order to determine these conditional probabilities when attribute values are transformed to a word space where the words are represented by fuzzy sets, we must use the modified counting procedure discussed above. This will provide us with estimates of the required probabilities.

In the case of the ID3 approach the constructed architecture is a decision tree. Each node has an associated attribute of the database or more generally a compound feature. This is selected by information theoretic considerations first given by Quinlan. The branches from the node correspond to the word values for the attribute or feature. For example, if the attribute is temperature, then we might select word values {**low, me-**

dium, high} for the values of this attribute. The fuzzy sets for these words are triangular or trapezoidal. A tuple in the database of the learning set of examples will have a value for this attribute. Suppose this is θ which can be a precise value or a fuzzy set on the temperature space. The value θ is transformed to the temperature word space and represented as a distribution:

$$\theta = \text{low} : \theta_{\text{low}}, \text{medium} : \theta_{\text{med}}, \text{high} : \theta_{\text{high}}$$

by the method discussed above. If the fuzzy sets are triangular and mutually exclusive then:

$$\theta_{\text{low}} = \Pr(\textbf{low} \mid \theta), \theta_{\text{med}} = \Pr(\textbf{medium} \mid \theta), \theta_{\text{high}} = \Pr(\textbf{high} \mid \theta)$$

We therefore pass the proportion θ_{low} of this tuple along the branch with label **low**, θ_{high} along the branch with label **medium** and θ_{high} along the branch with label **high**. The tuple in the database at this node may already have a proportion allocated to it. If it is the starting node then the proportion will be 1.

Each tuple of the database at the node is passed, in this way, to the nodes at the end of each of the branches. These children nodes will have databases with new proportions allocated to them. For the new nodes the probability distribution over the classifications can be determined. If one class has a higher probability associated with it than some specified value, then we do not expand this node. If this is not the case, then the node is expanded by choosing the next appropriate attribute or feature according to information theory considerations, as before.

In this way the decision tree is grown and the only difference from the normal ID3 method [12] is the use of the modified counting procedure to determine the proportions of tuples passed along each branch. This added computation is trivial and, in fact, because fewer branches will generally be required when using the fuzzy divisions of the continuous variables or fuzzy groupings of discrete variables, the overall computation can be reduced from the normal ID3 approach. The calculation of the entropy for determining which appropriate attribute to choose next also requires the modified counting procedure.

Several tricks can be used to merge branches when deriving the tree to give a simplified tree. This is called forward pruning. The normal method of post pruning of ID3 can also be used to provide further simplification to the decision tree. For the final nodes, the distribution over the classes can be determined. We thus have $\Pr(Ci \mid \text{branch})$ for all Ci for a given node. Thus we have for a given class, say Ci, the conditional probabilities {$\Pr(Ci \mid \text{branch } k)$ for all k} where branch k is made up of a conjunction of branches from the starting node which corresponds to a conjunction of words, one for each attribute. These can be represented as Fril extended rules. We thus obtain a Fril extended rule for each class.

The class distribution for a new case can be determined by using these Fril extended rules, one for each class and the inference methods of Fril.

The same approach as we have used to find the conditional probabilities for the ID3 approach can be used to find the conditional probabilities for Bayesian belief network architectures from databases. The variables in a belief network can take a discrete set of values. We can deal with continuous variables by allowing the variable to take word values expressed by fuzzy sets. Also discrete variables can have word values corresponding to fuzzy sets defined on the set of values of the discrete sets. This extension to the fuzzy case will allow for more simple computations to determine the joint distribution since we are finding the joint distribution over the multidimensional word space. Variables will take values corresponding to these word labels. Once the conditional probability tables have been constructed using the modified counting procedure above, the same approaches for inference can be used as is used at present with Belief Networks [13-15]. The arguments for the use of fuzzy defined words rather than crisp intervals or exact groupings are as we have already explained for classification. We get better interpolation between similar cases and reduced computation.

The same approach can be used for back propagation neural nets when we have to consider continuous variables or discrete variables with many possible values. In this case, the value of the input variable is distributed over the words and this distribution becomes the input to the neural net. This will provide an automatic scaling and also provide natural interpolation and smoothing of statistical fluctuations. It does, of course, increase the number of inputs substantially. The mass assignment approach to computing with words also has application to the radial basis functions approach of neural computing. The fuzzy set derived from the least prejudiced distribution over the multidimensional word space can be used to estimate the radial basis function for a given cluster. More work is required to develop these ideas.

5   Summarising Data

Another important area of application is summarising data. Humans looking at data presented in the form of a database can often see relationships between the attributes. We would like the computer to find such relationships and form a knowledge base representing the relevant summary of the database. We can rewrite the database in terms of the word values of the attributes rather than using the original values. There are fewer possible tuples for a set of attributes when using word values expressed by fuzzy sets. The tuples of the original database would be transformed to the new word attribute values database. Each tuple of the original database would be distributed over several in the new one. The new database would be smaller and have proportions associated with each tuple. It is much easier to find the desired relationships using this new database. Methods of predicate invention and search methods associated with inductive logic programming could be used to discover interesting relationships in the data [16].

We can build up a knowledge base from different data sources and use this to make more general inferences.

In this section we will give some examples of more general rules and show how the mass assignment theory can be used to process them. These rules can be thought of as natural language type statements which summarise data in a database. Consider the following summary and query:

88   Jim F. Baldwin

Summary from large database of student performances
A good project student will do well in most subjects, above average in several and poor in at most only a few subjects
What is the % score of a good project student?

where:

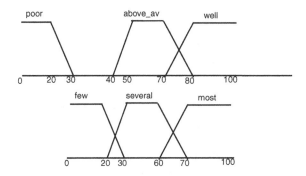

The result of using a mass-assignment, least-prejudiced distribution approach to calculating **av** is:

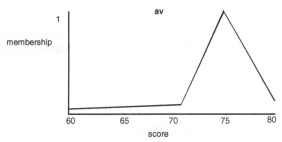

The solution to our query is a fuzzy set. If the user wishes for a point value, we must defuzzify this fuzzy set by deriving the expected value of the least prejudiced distribution of this fuzzy set.

This problem is an example of a class of such problems which we can associate with databases. If we use the extension principle of fuzzy logic [17] for these problems, we have to solve complex nonlinear mathematical programming problems. The use of the least prejudiced distribution approach avoids this complexity. We would argue that using these more complex forms of linguistic statements to summarise a database can still lead to excessive computation. We would prefer to use Fril rules which are probabilistic conditional logic programming rules in which predicate variables can be instantiated to fuzzy sets. The conditional probabilities associated with the rules provide an approximation to the fuzzy quantifiers used above. This simplification leads to much easier computation without losing too much accuracy.

6   User Modelling for Intelligent Software Assistants

Intelligent software assistants require a model of the user in order to make sensible and relevant decisions. The user model with the relevant IA knowledge base is used by the IA to predict the human responses and the human needs, to provide time and information management, to suggest to the user things to do and to help the user in general to be more efficient. We are also assuming that we have a multi-modal interface between user and computer. This allows the IA to make inferences with respect to individual viewpoints of these modalities. The IA will then fuse these inferences into a final inference. Two important problems arise from this. The first one is concerned with the knowledge representation of the user model, how we build the model, and how we use the model with the other IA knowledge bases to make inferences and decisions. The second is concerned with the fusion problem.

It is important to recognise that we will only have sparse information about a particular user and while this will build up over time, we should not expect to be able to use learning methods which require large amounts of data to provide the user model.

How can we make inference when we have only sparse data?

In human terms we do this all the time. We meet someone and make decisions about that person with reference to a set of prototypical persons which we have built up over time observing many people. We should have data for building up clusters of types of persons, types of behaviour, etc, and these clusters will form our prototypes. These prototypes can be built in many ways — databases of individuals, the user can provide his/her understanding of prototypes, etc. For this discussion we will assume that we have a collection of prototypical people.

We must have some form of representation for these prototypes. There are several possible forms of knowledge representation. We can form clusters of people with respect to certain behavioural and descriptive characteristics. A basic question is how do we represent these clusters. One approach would be to represent each person in the cluster as a point vector and to find the average vector for the cluster and this would represent our prototype for the cluster. This would lead to a form of case-base reasoning in which, when we are presented with the user, we would match the user to the nearest prototype vector. We will consider this to be too simplistic from two points of view. Firstly, the vector form of representation is attribute based and we would like to consider relationships between concepts in addition to basic attributes. Secondly, we would prefer a fuller representation of the cluster than a single point. We can achieve both these demands with the use of conceptual graphs [18]. In this way we can represent the cluster both as a whole and as relationships between attributes. To illustrate the difference, consider a cluster of almost perfect circles. One way of representing this cluster would be to take a prototypical circle with radius r and centre c. The vector (r, c) would then represent the prototypical case. We could accept an almost perfect circle as a member of this cluster if its average radius and centre lie close to r and c. A second way of representing the cluster would be to say that the radius must be some fuzzy set **f** and the centre have co-ordinates (**gx, gy**) where **gx** and **gy** are two fuzzy sets. The fuzzy sets **f**, **gx** and **gy** define a family of circles with varying membership. This fuzzy circle would be our cluster of acceptable circles. If a new almost perfect circle lay in this fuzzy circle, we would accept it as belonging to the cluster. It is this second approach which we will consider in the rest of the paper. We can also think of important relationships with respect to this example. For example, consider the two concepts: maximum diameter and minimum diameter — these are attributes which can be given values for any almost perfect circle in the cluster. The difference between these values will have a maximum magnitude for the allowed cases. We can then say that for any almost perfect circle the difference in the maximum and minimum diameters must be **g** where **g** is a fuzzy number. This defines a relationship between the two attributes.

We will recap on the main argument so far. We cluster people into clusters of similar behaviours and characteristics. Each cluster will then be represented by a form of knowledge representation which will use fuzzy sets and allow for the range of examples in each cluster to be represented with all the appropriate relationships between the attributes recorded. The form of knowledge representation we will use is conceptual graphs. This is a special formulation of semantic nets which overcomes some of the difficulties, such as the 'isa' problem, which were found in early uses of semantic nets. Each cluster represents a prototype and this will be used to make inference for a new person who matches the prototype closely. This form of reasoning will be inductive or even analogical and will have no truth guarantee. The computer will gain new insights into the user by recognising that the user behaves in a similar manner to a given prototypical person and assuming that a similar behaviour will be expected from the user as that given by the prototypical person. Since a prototypical person is in fact a range of people, we will select at random a precise person and use this to draw inference. The match of the user to the cluster prototype will in general only be partial and we will only take account of what is necessary to answer the question of interest. Missing information which will include the answer to the question of interest will come from the cluster graph.

Conceptual graphs are bi-nodal directed graphs with concept and relational nodes. The concept nodes have a name and an instantiation. For example, the concept height can be represented by the node:

$$\boxed{\text{HEIGHT : tall}}$$

Height is the name of the concept and it has a field which can be instantiated to a value, a set of values, or a fuzzy set. In this case we have given the instantiation the value tall which is a fuzzy set on the height space.

Relational nodes connect with concept nodes and are given names to represent the relationship. For example:

Contains is the relational node. BOX and DIAMOND are concept nodes with particular identifiers or instantiations. This is also an example of a conceptual graph.

A more interesting conceptual graph is:

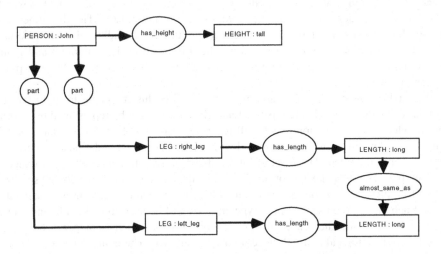

Every English sentence can be represented with a conceptual graph and to every conceptual graph there is an English sentence. For example the above graph corresponds to the sentence:

John is a tall person with long legs of almost the same length.

This provides us with another reason why conceptual graphs are a useful form of knowledge representation for us. We have a link with natural language — this natural language link is useful for human/computer.

In this section we will discuss the preliminary ideas for inference with respect to a user with reference to the conceptual graph prototypes. We will assume that for a given context we have conceptual graph prototypes derived from the study of people within this same context and we also have a relevant conceptual graph for the specific user formed by previous observations of his/her behaviour. Let the prototype graphs be P1, ..., Pn and the specific user graph be S.

A question is being asked by the computer about what action to take for the specific user. If the user was one of the prototypes then the answer would be given by part of the graph. Let these answers be sub-graphs denoted by A1, ..., An respectively.

The computer will use S in conjunction with P1, ..., Pn to provide an answer A for the specific user. How can we infer A from the various graphs?

The question itself can be represented by a graph with empty referent fields of the concepts. This graph is important because it indicates what concepts are important in deriving the answer. We do not need all of each of the graphs P1, ..., Pn to obtain A1, ..., An. Let the question graph be represented by Q.

We will match Q to each of P1, ..., Pn — this will correspond to a maximal join — all nodes in Q should match the corresponding nodes in each of P1, ..., Pn. In matching the unknown referent fields, the concepts in Q will be given appropriate instantiations for the matchings with P1, ..., Pn. These matchings will be highlighted and also the sub-graph corresponding to the answer will be highlighted for each of P1, ..., Pn. The non-highlighted nodes of each of P1, ..., Pn will then be stripped from these graphs to obtain graphs P'1, ..., P'n.

The graph S corresponding to the specific user is also treated in this way — Q is mapped on to S and S is stripped of non-highlighted nodes. S will not contain the sub-graph corresponding to the answer. If it did we would not be inferring from the prototype graphs but from S directly. S could contain a sub-part of the answer sub-graph in which case this would also be highlighted. S is then stripped of non-highlighted nodes to give S'.

The answer A is now formed from P'1, ..., P'n and S' in some way. S' will not map completely on to any of P'1, ..., P'n. We form the maximal joins of S' with P'1, ..., P'n to obtain P"1, ..., P"n. These maximal joins will not be complete joins and some measure of completeness will be used to give a support for how well S' matches each of P'1, ..., P'n. Let these supports be given by s1, ..., sn. The answer graphs A"1, ..., A"n are now selected. These will not be the same as A1, ..., An since further instantiations may have occurred in order to provide the various matches. If S contains part of the answer sub-graph then this will further instantiate A1, ..., An. Nodes in Ai may be instantiated because of instantiations in other parts of A'i during the matching process with S'.

We now have a set of answer graphs A"1, ..., A"n with respective supports s1, ..., sn. If the support is zero then we simply reject the corresponding graph completely. There are various schemes to fuse the answer graphs together taking into account their supports. We will call these combining schemes. Rather than define *ad hoc* combining schemes we should learn the best combining scheme for a given question. We may though not have enough data for this purpose and so we must have some default combining scheme.

If the answer graphs have the same structure, then we can take weighted averages of them where the averaging is done on the referents of the concepts and in general would correspond to taking a weighted average of fuzzy sets. This presents no problems. The graphs may have different structures and then some unioning of graphs will be necessary. This takes us into new areas of research and we will not give more details at this time.

The answer will be the graph A and this will contain the necessary information for the computer to take appropriate action for the user. How well this is received by the user will be noted or induced and this can be used to modify the combining scheme for future use. For example, if the user refused to accept the action, then the computer may ask the user what his choice would be and the combining scheme could be adjusted to provide the user's preferred choice. The dialogue between the user and the computer can be done in simplified natural language since conceptual graphs match into natural language sentences quite easily.

7   Conclusions

We have indicated many important areas of application of the modified counting procedure to machine learning, a fuzzy version of ID3 and Belief Networks for data mining, neural networks, linguistic summarisation of database relationships, linguistic analysis using fuzzy quantifiers and user modelling for intelligent human/computer interfaces.

The modified counting procedure allows the transformation from the original attribute cross-product space to a new multidimensional word space in which each word is a fuzzy set. This transformation allows continuous and discrete variables to be represented by fuzzy labels which we have called words. The use of fuzzy words gives greater accuracy because natural interpolation is invoked, greater compression because of the more efficient representation, and a natural smoothing of noisy data.

This extension of methods that use crisp intervals to the corresponding methods using fuzzy intervals is simple. The fuzzy labels can be treated as symbolic labels with existing methods of classical analysis provided the modified counting procedure is used in the appropriate places.

The modified counting procedure is derived using the voting model semantic of fuzzy sets and the mass assignment theory.

The use of fuzzy sets in the broad area of intelligent knowledge base systems and machine learning has been given. Other applications to intelligent systems along similar lines can be created. This provides an exciting future for the use of fuzzy sets in the field of artificial intelligence. There is no conflict with the probabilistic approach, nor any conflict with existing acceptable methods.

References

1.   Baldwin, J. F.: 'Evidential Reasoning under Probabilistic and Fuzzy Uncertainties', in 'An Introduction to Fuzzy Logic and Applications in Intelligent Systems', eds. Yager R. R. and Zadeh L. A., Kluwer Academic Publishers, pp. 297-335 (1991).
2.   Baldwin, J. F.: 'A New Approach to Inference Under Uncertainty for Knowledge Based systems', in 'Symbolic and Quantitative Approaches to Uncertainty', eds. Kruse R. and Siegel P., Springer-Verlag, Lecture Notes in Computer science 548, pp. 107-115 (1991).
3.   Baldwin, J. F.: 'A Calculus For Mass Assignments In Evidential Reasoning', in 'Advances in the Dempster-Shafer Theory of Evidence', eds. Fedrizzi M., Kacprzyk J. and Yager R. R., John Wiley (1992).

4. Baldwin, J. F.: 'The Management of Fuzzy and Probabilistic Uncertainties for Knowledge Based Systems', in 'Encyclopedia of AI', ed. Shapiro S. A., John Wiley (2nd Ed.), pp. 528-537 (1992).

5. Baldwin, J. F.: 'Support Logic Programming', in 'Fuzzy Sets - Theory and Applications', eds. Jones A. et al, D. Reidel, pp. 133-170 (1986).

6. Baldwin, J. F.: 'Fuzzy Reasoning in Fril for Fuzzy Control and other Knowledge-based Applications', Asia-Pacific Engineering Journal, Vol. 3, pp. 59-81 (1993).

7. Baldwin, J. F.: 'Knowledge from Data using Fril and Fuzzy Methods', in 'Fuzzy Logic in AI', ed. Baldwin J. F., John Wiley, pp. 33-76 (1996).

8. Baldwin, J. F., Martin, T. P. and Pilsworth, B. W.: 'Fril - Fuzzy and Evidential Reasoning in AI', Research Studies Press (John Wiley) (1995).

9. Baldwin, J. F., Martin, T. P. and Pilsworth, B. W.: 'Fril Manual (Version 4.0)', Fril Systems Ltd, Bristol Business Centre, Maggs House, Queens Road, Bristol, BS8 1QX, UK, pp. 1-697 (1998).

10. Baldwin, J. F. and Martin, T. P.: 'Refining Knowledge from Uncertain Relations – a Fuzzy Data Browser based on Fuzzy Object-Oriented Programming in Fril', Proc. 4th IEEE International Conference on Fuzzy Systems, Yokohama, Japan, pp. 27-34 (1995).

11. Baldwin, J. F. and Martin, T. P.: 'A Fuzzy Data Browser in Fril', in 'Fuzzy Logic in AI', ed. Baldwin J.F. , John Wiley, pp. 101-124 (1996).

12. Quinlan, J. R.: 'C4.5:Programs for Machine Learning', Morgan Kaufmann (1993).

13. Pearl, J.: 'Probabilistic reasoning in Intelligent Systems: Networks of Plausible Inference', Morgan Kaufmann (1988).

14. Neopolitan, R.: 'Probabilistic Reasoning in Expert Systems: Theory and Algorithms', John Wiley (1990).

15. Jenson, F.: 'An Introduction to Bayesian Networks', Springer-Verlag (1996).

16. Muggleton, S: 'Inductive Logic Programming', Academic Press (1992).

17. Zadeh, L.: 'Fuzzy Logic and Approximate Reasoning', Synrhese, Vol. 30, (1978).

18. Sowa, J. F.: 'Conceptual Structures - Information Processing in Mind and Machine', Addison Wesley (1984).

Problems and Prospects in Fuzzy Data Analysis

Rudolf Kruse[1], Christian Borgelt[1], and Detlef Nauck[2]

[1] Otto-von-Guericke University of Magdeburg, Faculty of Computer Science
(FIN-IWS)
Universitaetsplatz 2, D-39106 Magdeburg, Germany
{rudolf.kruse,christian.borgelt}@cs.uni-magdeburg.de
[2] Intelligent Systems Research Group, BT Labs
Adastral Park, Martlesham Heath, Ipswich IP5 3RE, United Kingdom
detlef.nauck@bt.com

Abstract. In meeting the challenges that resulted from the explosion of
collected, stored, and transferred data, *Knowledge Discovery in
Databases* or *Data Mining* has emerged as a new research area. However,
the approaches studied in this area have mainly been oriented towards
highly structured and precise data. In addition, the goal to obtain understandable results is often neglected. Therefore we suggest concentrating
on *Information Mining*, i.e. the analysis of heterogeneous information
sources with the main aim of producing comprehensible results. Since
the aim of fuzzy technology has always been to model linguistic information and to achieve understandable solutions, we expect it to play an
important role in information mining.

1 Introduction: A View of Information Mining

Due to modern information technology, which produces ever more powerful computers every year, it is possible today to collect, store, transfer, and combine huge
amounts of data at very low costs. Thus an ever-increasing number of companies
and scientific and governmental institutions can afford to build up large archives
of documents and other data like numbers, tables, images, and sounds. However,
exploiting the information contained in these archives in an intelligent way turns
out to be fairly difficult. In contrast to the abundance of data there is a lack of
tools that can transform this data into useful information and knowledge. Although a user often has a vague understanding of the data and its meaning—he
can usually formulate hypotheses and guess dependencies— he rarely knows:

- where to find the "interesting" or "relevant" pieces of information;
- whether these pieces of information support his hypotheses and models;
- whether (other) interesting phenomena are hidden in the data,
- which methods are best suited to find the needed pieces of information in a
  fast and reliable way;
- how the data can be translated into human notions that are appropriate for
  the context in which it is needed.

B. Azvine et al. (Eds.): Intelligent Systems and Soft Computing, LNAI 1804, pp. 95–   , 2000.
© Springer-Verlag Berlin Heidelberg 2000

In reply to these challenges a new area of research has emerged, which has been named "Knowledge Discovery in Databases" or "Data Mining". Although the standard definition of knowledge discovery and data mining [ ] only speaks of discovery in *data*, thus not restricting the type and the organization of the data to work on, it has to be admitted that research up to now concentrated on highly structured data. Usually a minimal requirement is relational data. Most methods (e.g. classical methods like decision trees and neural networks) even demand as input a single uniform table, i.e. a set of tuples of attribute values. It is obvious, however, that this paradigm is hardly adequate for mining image or sound data or even textual descriptions, since it is inappropriate to see such data as, say, tuples of picture elements. Although such data can often be treated successfully by transforming it into structured tables using feature extraction, it is not hard to see that methods are needed which yield, for example, descriptions of what an image depicts, and other methods which can make use of such descriptions, e.g. for retrieval purposes.

Another important point to be made is the following: the fact that pure neural networks are often seen as data mining methods, although their learning result (matrices of numbers) is hardly interpretable, shows that in contrast to the standard definition the goal of *understandable* patterns is often neglected. Of course, there are applications where comprehensible results are not needed and, for example, the prediction accuracy of a classifier is the only criterion of success. Therefore interpretable results should not be seen as a *conditio sine qua non*. However, our own experience—gathered as part of several cooperative ventures with industry—is that modern technologies are accepted more readily, if the methods applied are easy to understand and the results can be checked against human intuition. In addition, if we want to gain insight into a domain, training, for instance, a neural network is not of much help.

Therefore we suggest concentrating on *information mining*, which we see as an extension of data mining and which can be defined in analogy to the KDD definition given in Fayyad et al [ ] as follows:

Information mining is the non-trivial process of identifying valid, novel, potentially useful, and *understandable* patterns in *heterogeneous information sources*.

The term *information* is thus meant to indicate two things: in the first place, it points out that the heterogeneous sources to mine can already provide *information*, understood as expert background knowledge, textual descriptions, images and sounds, etc, and not only raw data. Secondly, it emphasizes that the results must be *comprehensible* ("must provide a user with information"), so that a user can check their plausibility and can get insight into the domain from which the data comes.

For research this results in the challenges:

- to develop theories and scalable techniques that can extract knowledge from large, dynamic, multi-relational, and multi-medial information sources,
- to close the semantic gap between structured data and human notions and concepts, i.e. to be able to translate computer representations into human notions and concepts and vice versa.

The goal of fuzzy systems has always been to model human expert knowledge and to produce systems that are easy to understand. Therefore we expect fuzzy systems technology to play a prominent role in the quest to meet these challenges. In the following we try to point out how fuzzy techniques can help with information mining.

2   Strengths of Fuzzy Set Models

Although there is still some philosophical discussion going on as to whether a (symbolic) language is necessary for consciousness and thinking abilities, it is undisputed that language is humans' most effective tool to structure their experience and to model their environment. Therefore, in order to represent the background knowledge of human experts and to arrive at understandable data mining results, it is absolutely necessary to model linguistic terms and do what Zadeh so pointedly called *computing with words* [ ].

A fundamental property of linguistic terms is their inherent vagueness, i.e. they have "fuzzy" boundaries: for each linguistic term there usually are some phenomena to which it can clearly be applied and some others, which cannot be described using this term. But in between these phenomena there lies a "penumbra" of phenomena for which it is not definite whether the term is applicable or not. Well-known examples include the terms *pile of sand* (which is the basis of the classic *sorites* paradox) and *bald*. In both cases no precise number of grains of sand or hairs, respectively, can be given which separates the situations in which the terms are applicable from those in which they are not.

The reason for this inherent vagueness is that for practical purposes full precision is not necessary and may even be a waste of resources. To quote an example by Wittgenstein [ ], the request "Please stay around here!" is, of course, inexact. It would be more precise to draw a line on the ground, or, because the line has a certain width and thus would still not be fully exact, to use a colour boundary. But this precision would be entirely pointless, since the inexact request can be expected to work very well.

Fuzzy set theory provides excellent means to model the "fuzzy" boundaries of linguistic terms by introducing gradual memberships. In contrast to classical set theory, in which an object or a case either is a member of a given set (defined, e.g. by some property) or not, fuzzy set theory makes it possible that an object or a case belongs to a set only to a certain degree, thus modelling the penumbra of the linguistic term describing the property that defines the set.

Interpretations of membership degrees include *similarity*, *preference*, and *uncertainty*: they can state how similar an object or case is to a prototypical one, they can indicate preferences between suboptimal solutions to a problem, or they can model uncertainty about the true situation, if this situation is described in imprecise terms. Drawing on Wittgenstein's example as an illustration, we may say that the locations "around here" are (for example, with respect to the person being in sight or calling distance) sufficiently similar to "here", so that the request works well. Or we may say that it would be preferred, if the person stayed exactly "here", but some deviation from "here" would still be acceptable. Finally, if we tell someone to stay "around here" and then go away, we are uncertain about the exact location this person is in at a given moment. It is obvious that all of these interpretations are needed in applications and thus it is not surprising that they have all proven useful for solving practical problems. They also turned out to be worth considering when non-linguistic, but imprecise, i.e. set-valued information has to be modelled.

In general, due to their closeness to human reasoning, solutions obtained using fuzzy approaches are easy to understand and to apply. Due to these strengths, fuzzy systems are the method of choice, if linguistic, vague, or imprecise information has to be modelled.

3   Fuzzy Set Methods in Data Mining

The research in knowledge discovery in databases and data mining has led to a large number of suggestions for a general model of the knowledge discovery process. A recent suggestion for such a model, which can be expected to have considerable impact, since it is backed by several large companies like NCR and DaimlerChrysler, is the CRISP-DM model (CRoss Industry Standard Process for Data Mining) [ ].

The basic structure of this process model is depicted in Fig. . The circle indicates that data mining is essentially a circular process, in which the evaluation of the results can trigger a re-execution of the data preparation and model generation steps. In this process, fuzzy set methods can profitably be applied in several phases.

The *business understanding* and *data understanding* phases are usually strongly human centred and only little automation can be achieved here. These phases serve mainly to define the goals of the knowledge-discovery project, to estimate its potential benefit, and to identify and collect the necessary data. In addition, background domain knowledge and meta knowledge about the data is gathered. In these phases, fuzzy set methods can be used to formulate, for instance, the background domain knowledge in vague terms, but still in a form that can be used in a subsequent modelling phase. Furthermore, fuzzy database queries are useful to find the data needed and to check whether it may be useful to take additional, related data into account.

In the *data preparation* step, the gathered data is cleaned, transformed, and maybe properly scaled, to produce the input for the modelling techniques. In

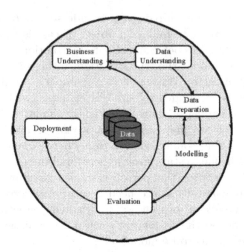

Fig. 1. The CRISP-DM Model.

this step fuzzy methods may, for example, be used to detect outliers, e.g. by *fuzzy clustering* the data [,] and then finding those data points that are far away from the cluster prototypes.

The *modelling* phase, in which models are constructed from the data in order, for instance, to predict future developments or to build classifiers, can, of course, benefit most from fuzzy data analysis approaches. These approaches can be divided into two classes. The first class, *fuzzy data* analysis [ ], consists of approaches that analyse fuzzy data—data derived from imprecise measurement instruments or from the descriptions of human domain experts. An example from our own research is the induction of *possibilistic graphical models* [ ] from data which complements the induction of the well-known probabilistic graphical models. The second class, fuzzy *data analysis* [ ], consists of methods that use fuzzy techniques to structure and analyze crisp data, for instance, *fuzzy clustering* for data segmentation and rule generation and *neuro-fuzzy systems* for rule generation.

In the *evaluation* phase, in which the results are tested and their quality is assessed, the usefulness of fuzzy modelling methods becomes most obvious. Since they yield interpretable systems, they can easily be checked for plausibility against the intuition and expectations of human experts. In addition, the results can provide new insights into the domain under consideration, in contrast to, e.g. pure neural networks, which are black boxes.

To illustrate the usefulness of fuzzy data analysis approaches, in the following sections we discuss the topics generating fuzzy rules from data and learning possibilistic graphical models in a little more detail.

4   Rule Generation with Neuro-Fuzzy-Systems

In order to use fuzzy systems in data analysis, it must be possible to induce fuzzy rules from data. To describe a fuzzy system completely we need to determine a rule base (structure) and fuzzy partitions (parameters) for all variables. The data driven induction of fuzzy systems by simple heuristics based on local computations is usually called *neuro-fuzzy* [ ]. If we apply such techniques, we must be aware of the trade-off between precision and interpretability. A fuzzy solution is not only judged for its accuracy, but also—if not especially—for its simplicity and readability. The user of the fuzzy system must be able to comprehend the rule base.

Important points for the interpretability of a fuzzy system are that:

- there are only few fuzzy rules in the rule base;
- there are only few variables used in each rule;
- the variables are partitioned by few meaningful fuzzy sets;
- no linguistic label is represented by more than one fuzzy set.

There are several ways to induce the structure of a fuzzy system. Cluster-oriented and hyperbox-oriented approaches to fuzzy rule learning create rules and fuzzy sets at the same time. Structure-oriented approaches need initial fuzzy partitions to create a rule base [ ].

Cluster-oriented rule learning approaches are based on fuzzy cluster analysis [,], i.e. the learning process is unsupervised. Hyperbox-oriented approaches use a supervised learning algorithm that tries to cover the training data by overlapping hyperboxes [ ]. Fuzzy rules are created in both approaches by projection of clusters or hyperboxes. The main problem of both approaches is that each generated fuzzy rule uses individual membership functions and thus the rule base is hard to interpret. Cluster-oriented approaches additionally suffer from a loss of information and can only determine an appropriate number of rules, if they are iterated with different fixed rule base sizes.

Structure-oriented approaches avoid all these drawbacks, because they do not search for (hyperellipsoidal or hyperrectangular) clusters in the data space. By providing (initial) fuzzy sets before fuzzy rules are created the data space is structured by a multidimensional fuzzy grid. A rule base is created by selecting those grid cells that contain data. This can be done in a single pass through the training data. This way of learning fuzzy rules was suggested in Wang and Mendel [ ]. Extended versions were used in the neuro-fuzzy classification system NEFCLASS [ ]. NEFCLASS uses a performance measure for the detected fuzzy rules. Thus the size of the rule base can be determined automatically by adding rules ordered by their performance until all training data is covered. The performance measure is also used to compute the best consequent for each rule.

The number of fuzzy rules can also be restricted by including only the best rules in the rule base. It is also possible to use pruning methods to reduce the number of rules and the number of variables used by the rules. In order to obtain meaningful fuzzy partitions, it is better to create rule bases by structure-oriented learning than by cluster-oriented or by hyperbox-oriented rule learning.

The latter two approaches create individual fuzzy sets for each rule and thus provide less interpretable solutions. Structure-oriented methods allow the user to provide appropriate fuzzy partitions in advance such that all rules share the same fuzzy sets. Thus the induced rule base can be interpreted well.

After the rule base of a fuzzy system has been generated, we must usually train the membership function in order to improve the performance. In NEF-CLASS, for example, the fuzzy sets are tuned by a simple backpropagation-like procedure. The algorithm does not use gradient-descent, because the degree of fulfilment of a fuzzy rule is determined by the minimum, and non-continuous membership function may be used. Instead a simple heuristics is used that results in shifting the fuzzy sets and in enlarging or reducing their support.

The main idea of NEFCLASS is to create comprehensible fuzzy classifiers, by ensuring that fuzzy sets cannot be modified arbitrarily during learning. Constraints can be applied in order to make sure that the fuzzy sets still fit their linguistic labels after learning. For the sake of interpretability we do not want adjacent fuzzy sets to exchange positions, we want the fuzzy sets to overlap appropriately, etc.

We will not describe more details of learning fuzzy rules here, but refer to the paper on "NEFCLASS-J – A Java based Soft Computing Tool" in this volume. In the next section we discuss some aspects of information fusion that can be implemented by neuro-fuzzy systems.

5   Information Fusion with Neuro-Fuzzy Models

If neuro-fuzzy methods are used in information mining, it is useful to consider their capabilities in fusing information from different sources. Information fusion refers to the acquisition, processing, exploitation, and merging of information originating from multiple sources to provide a better insight and understanding of the phenomena under consideration. There are several levels of information fusion. Fusion may take place at the level of data acquisition, data pre-processing, data or knowledge representation, or at the model or decision making level. On lower levels where raw data is involved, the term (sensor) *data fusion* is preferred. Some aspects of information fusion can be implemented by NEFCLASS. For a conceptual and comparative study of fusion strategies in various calculi of uncertainty see Gebhardt and Kruse [ ] and Dubois et al [ ].

If a fuzzy classifier is created based on a supervised learning problem, then the most common way is to provide a data set, where each pattern is labelled—ideally with its correct class. That means we assume that each pattern belongs to one class only. Sometimes it is not possible to determine this class correctly due to a lack of information. Instead of a crisp classification it would also be possible to label each pattern with a vector of membership degrees. This requires that a vague classification is obtained in some way for the training patterns, e.g. by partially contradicting expert opinions.

Training patterns with fuzzy classifications are one way to implement information fusion with neuro-fuzzy systems. If we assume that a group of n experts

provide partially contradicting classifications for a set of training data we can
fuse the expert opinions into fuzzy sets that describe the classification for each
training pattern. According to the context model, we can view the experts as
different observation contexts [ ]. The training then reflects fusion of expert
opinions on data set level.

Due to the capabilities of its learning algorithms NEFCLASS can handle such
training data in the process of creating a fuzzy classifier. However, it does not
implement fusion on data set level itself. For information fusion in neuro-fuzzy
environments like NEFCLASS we usually consider three operator schemes:

$$\text{fuse}(R, R') \quad : \quad \text{fuse two rule sets } R \text{ and } R',$$
$$\text{induce}(D) \quad : \quad \text{induce a rule set from a given data set } D,$$
$$\text{revise}(R, D) \quad : \quad \text{revise a rule set in the light of a data set } D.$$

An aspect of information fusion that is implemented by NEFCLASS is to
integrate expert knowledge in form of a set of fuzzy rules R and knowledge
induced from a data set D:

$$\text{fuse}(R, \text{induce}(D)).$$

If expert knowledge about the classification problem is available, then the rule
base of the fuzzy classifier can be initialized with suitable fuzzy rules before rule
learning is invoked to complete the rule base. If the algorithm creates a rule from
data that contradicts with an expert rule then we can, for example:

– always prefer expert rule;
– always prefer the learned rule; or
– select the rule with the higher performance value.

In NEFCLASS we determine the performance of all rules over the training data
and in case of contradiction the better rule prevails. This reflects fusion of expert
opinions and knowledge obtained from observations. Note that providing a rule
base and tuning it, e.g. by modifying membership functions, is not information
fusion but knowledge revision or update:

$$\text{revise}(R, D).$$

In this case the rule base is seen as prior knowledge and the tuned rule base is
posterior knowledge. This approach is also known in Bayesian statistics, where
a given prior probability distribution is revised by additional evidence to a posterior distribution [,]. Since NEFCLASS is mainly used to train a fuzzy rule
base it usually performs

$$\text{revise}(\text{fuse}(R, \text{induce}(D)))$$

if an expert's rule base is given in advance.

Because NEFCLASS is able to resolve conflicts between rules based on rule
performance, it is also able to fuse expert opinions on fuzzy rule level:

$$\text{fuse}(R, R').$$

Rule bases R and R' from different experts can be entered into the system. They will then be fused into one rule base and contradictions are resolved automatically by deleting from each pair of contradicting rules the rule with lower performance.

After all contradictions between expert rules and rules learned from data were resolved, usually not all rules can be included into the rule base, because its size is limited by some criterion. In this case we must decide whether:

– to include expert rules in any case; or
– to include rules by descending performances values.

The decision depends on the trust we have in the expert's knowledge and in the training data. A mixed approach can be used, e.g. include the best expert rules and then use the best learned rules to complete the rule base.

A similar decision must be made, when the rule base is pruned after training, i.e. is it acceptable to remove an expert rule during pruning, or must such rules remain in the rule base. In NEFCLASS expert rules and rules induced from data are not treated differently.

An example of information fusion in neuro-fuzzy system with an application to stock index prediction can be found in Siekmann et al [ ].

6   Dependency Analysis with Graphical Models

Since reasoning in multi-dimensional domains tends to be infeasible in the domains as a whole—and the more so, if uncertainty and imprecision are involved—decomposition techniques, that reduce the reasoning process to computations in lower-dimensional subspaces, have become very popular. In the field of graphical modelling, *decomposition* is based on dependence and independence relations between the attributes or variables that are used to describe the domain under consideration. The structure of these dependence and independence relations are represented as a graph (hence the name graphical models), in which each node stands for an attribute and each edge for a direct dependence between two attributes. The precise set of dependence and (conditional) independence statements that hold in the modeled domain can be read from the graph using simple graph theoretic criteria, for instance, d-separation, if the graph is a directed one, or simple separation, if the graph is undirected.

The conditional independence graph (as it is also called) is, however, only the *qualitative* or *structural component* of a graphical model. To do reasoning, it has to be enhanced by a *quantitative component* that provides confidence information about the different points of the underlying domain. This information can often be represented as a distribution function on the underlying domain, for example, a probability distribution, a possibility distribution, a mass distribution, etc. With respect to this quantitative component, the conditional independence graph describes a *factorization* of the distribution function on the domain as a whole into conditional or marginal distribution functions on lower-dimensional subspaces.

Graphical models make reasoning much more efficient, because propagating the evidential information about the values of some attributes to the unobserved ones and computing the marginal distributions for the unobserved attributes can be implemented by locally communicating node and edge processors in the conditional independence graph.

For some time the standard approach to construct a graphical model has been to let a human domain expert specify the dependency structure of the considered domain. This provided the conditional independence graph. Then the human domain expert had to estimate the necessary conditional or marginal distribution functions, which then formed the quantitative component of the graphical model. This approach, however, can be tedious and time consuming, especially, if the domain under consideration is large. In addition, it may be impossible to carry it out, if no or only vague knowledge is available about the dependence and independence relations that hold in the domain to be modelled. Therefore recent research has concentrated on learning graphical models from databases of sample cases.

Due to the origin of graphical modelling research in probabilistic reasoning, the most widely known methods are, of course, learning algorithms for Bayesian or Markov networks. However, these approaches—as probabilistic approaches do in general—suffer from certain deficiencies, if imprecise information, understood as set-valued data, has to be taken into account. For this reason recently possibilistic graphical models also gained some attention [ ], for which learning algorithms have been developed in analogy to the probabilistic case. These methods can be used to do dependency analysis, even if the data to analyse is highly imprecise, and can thus offer interesting perspectives for future research.

We have implemented these methods as a plug-in for the well-known data mining tool *Clementine* (ISL/SPSS). Its probabilistic version is currently used at DaimlerChrysler for fault analysis.

7   Possibilistic Graphical Models

A *possibility distribution* π on a universe of discourse Ω is a mapping from Ω into the unit interval, i.e. $\pi : \Omega \to [0, 1]$, see Zadeh [ ] and Dubois and Prade [ ]. From an intuitive point of view, $\pi(\omega)$ quantifies the degree of possibility that $\omega = \omega_0$ is true, where ω_0 is the actual state of the world: $\pi(\omega) = 0$ means that $\omega = \omega_0$ is impossible, $\pi(\omega) = 1$ means that $\omega = \omega_0$ is possible without any restrictions, and $\pi(\omega) \in (0, 1)$ means that $\omega = \omega_0$ is possible only with restrictions, i.e. that there is evidence that supports $\omega = \omega_0$ as well as evidence that contradicts $\omega = \omega_0$.

Several suggestions have been made for semantics of a *theory of possibility* as a framework for reasoning with uncertain and imprecise data. The interpretation of a degree of possibility we prefer is based on the context model [,]. In this model possibility distributions are seen as *information-compressed* representations of (not necessarily nested) random sets and a degree of possibility as the one-point coverage of a random set [ ].

To be more precise: Let ω_0 be the actual, but unknown state of a domain of interest, which is contained in a set Ω of possible states. Let $(C, 2^C, P)$, $C = \{c_1, c_2, \ldots, c_m\}$, be a finite probability space and $\gamma : C \to 2^\Omega$ a set-valued mapping. C is seen as a set of contexts that have to be distinguished for a set-valued specification of ω_0. The contexts are supposed to describe different physical and observation-related frame conditions. $P(\{c\})$ is the (subjective) probability of the (occurrence or selection of the) context c.

A set $\gamma(c)$ is assumed to be the *most specific correct set-valued specification* of ω_0, which is implied by the frame conditions that characterize the context c. By "most specific set-valued specification" we mean that $\omega_0 \in \gamma(c)$ is guaranteed to be true for $\gamma(c)$, but is not guaranteed for any proper subset of $\gamma(c)$. The resulting *random set* $\Gamma = (\gamma, P)$ is an imperfect (i.e. imprecise *and* uncertain) specification of ω_0. Let π_Γ denote the *one-point coverage* of Γ (the *possibility distribution induced by* Γ), which is defined as

$$\pi_\Gamma : \Omega \to [0, 1], \quad \pi_\Gamma(\omega) = P\left(\{c \in C \mid \omega \in \gamma(c)\}\right).$$

In a complete model the contexts in C must be specified in detail to make the relationships between all contexts c_j and their corresponding specifications $\gamma(c_j)$ explicit. But if the contexts are unknown or ignored, then $\pi_\Gamma(\omega)$ is the total mass of all contexts c that provide a specification $\gamma(c)$ in which ω_0 is contained, and this quantifies the *possibility of truth* of the statement "$\omega = \omega_0$" [,].

That in this interpretation a possibility distribution represents uncertain *and* imprecise knowledge can be understood best by comparing it to a probability distribution and to a relation. A probability distribution covers *uncertain*, but *precise* knowledge. This becomes obvious, if one notices that a possibility distribution in the interpretation described above reduces to a probability distribution, if $\forall c_j \in C : |\gamma(c_j)| = 1$, i.e. if for all contexts the specification of ω_0 is precise. On the other hand, a relation represents *imprecise*, but *certain* knowledge about dependencies between attributes. Thus, not surprisingly, a relation can also be seen as a special case of a possibility distribution, namely if there is only one context. Hence the context-dependent specifications are responsible for the imprecision, the contexts for the uncertainty in the imperfect knowledge expressed by a possibility distribution.

Although well-known for a couple of years [ ], a unique concept of possibilistic independence has not been fixed yet. In our opinion, the problem is that possibility theory is a calculus for uncertain *and* imprecise reasoning, the first of which is related to probability theory, the latter to relational theory (see above). But these two theories employ different notions of independence, namely stochastic independence and lossless join decomposability. Stochastic independence is an *uncertainty-based* type of independence, whereas lossless join decomposability is an *imprecision-based* type of independence. Since possibility theory addresses both kinds of imperfect knowledge, notions of possibilistic independence can be uncertainty-based or imprecision-based.

With respect to this consideration two definitions of possibilistic independence have been justified [ ], namely uncertainty-based possibilistic independence, which is derived from *Dempster's rule of conditioning* [ ] adapted to possibility measures, and imprecision-based possibilistic independence, which coincides with the well-known concept of *possibilistic non-interactivity* [ ]. The latter can be seen as a generalization of lossless join decomposability to the possibilistic setting, since it treats each α-cut of a possibility distribution like a relation.

Because of its consistency with the *extension principle* [ ], we confine ourselves to possibilistic non-interactivity. As a concept of possibilistic independence it can be defined as follows: let X, Y, and Z be three disjoint subsets of variables in V. Then X is called *conditionally independent* of Y given Z with respect to π, abbreviated $X \perp\!\!\!\perp_\pi Y \mid Z$, iff

$$\forall \omega \in \Omega : \quad \pi(\omega_{X \cup Y} \mid \omega_Z) = \min\{\pi(\omega_X \mid \omega_Z), \pi(\omega_Y \mid \omega_Z)\}$$

whenever $\pi(\omega_Z) > 0$, where $\pi(\cdot \mid \cdot)$ is a non-normalized conditional possibility distribution, i.e.

$$\pi(\omega_X \mid \omega_Z) = \max\{\pi(\omega') \mid \omega' \in \Omega \wedge \operatorname{proj}_X^V(\omega) = \omega_X \wedge \operatorname{proj}_Z^V(\omega) = \omega_Z\}.$$

Both mentioned types of possibilistic independence satisfy the *semi-graphoid axioms* [,]. Possibilistic independence based on Dempster's rule in addition satisfies the intersection axiom and thus can be used within the framework of the valuation-based systems already mentioned above [ ]. However, the intersection axiom is related to uncertainty-based independence. Relational independence does not satisfy this axiom, and therefore it cannot be satisfied by possibilistic non-interactivity as a more general type of imprecision-based independence.

Similar to probabilistic networks, a possibilistic network can be seen as a decomposition of a multi-variate possibility distribution. The factorization formulae can be derived from the corresponding probabilistic factorization formulae (for Markov networks) by replacing the product by the minimum.

Just as for probabilistic networks, it is possible in principle to estimate the quality of a given possibilistic network by exploiting its factorization property. For each $\omega \in \Omega$ the degree of possibility computed from the network is compared to the degree of possibility derived from the database to learn from. But again this approach can be costly.

Contrary to probabilistic networks, the induction of possibilistic networks from data has been studied much less extensively. A first result, which consists in an algorithm that is closely related to the $K2$ algorithm for the induction of Bayesian networks, was presented in Gebhardt and Kruse [ ]. Instead of the Bayesian evaluation measure used in $K2$, it relies on a measure derived from the *nonspecificity* of a possibility distribution. Roughly speaking, the notion of nonspecificity plays the same role in possibility theory that the notion of *entropy* plays in probability theory. Based on the connection of the imprecision part of a possibility distribution to relations, the nonspecificity of a possibility distribution can also be seen as a generalization of *Hartley information* [ ] to the possibilistic setting.

In Gebhardt and Kruse [ ] a rigid foundation of a learning algorithm for possibilistic networks is given. It starts from a comparison of the nonspecificity of a given multi-variate possibility distribution to the distribution represented by a possibilistic network, thus measuring the loss of specificity, if the multi-variate possibility distribution is represented by the network. In order to arrive at an efficient algorithm, an approximation for this loss of specificity is derived, which can be computed locally on the hyperedges of the network. As the search method a generalization of the optimum weight spanning tree algorithm to hypergraphs is used. Several other heuristic local evaluation measures, which can be used with different search methods, are presented in Borgelt and Kruse [,].

It should be emphasized, that, as already discussed above, an essential advantage of possibilistic networks over probabilistic ones is their ability to deal with imprecision, i.e. multi-valued, information. When learning possibilistic networks from data, this leads to the convenient situation that missing values in an observation or a set of values for an attribute, all of which have to be considered possible, do not pose any problems.

8   Concluding Remarks

In knowledge discovery and data mining as it is, there is a tendency to focus on purely data-driven approaches in a first step. More model-based approaches are only used in the refinement phases (which in industry are often not necessary, because the first successful approach wins—and the winner takes all). However, to arrive at truly useful results, we must take background knowledge and, in general, non-numeric information into account and we must concentrate on comprehensible models.

The complexity of the learning task, obviously, leads to a problem: when learning from information, one must choose between (often quantitative) methods that achieve good performance and (often qualitative) models that explain what is going on to a user. This is another good example of Zadeh's principle of the incompatibility between precision and meaning. Of course, precision and high performance are important goals. However, in the most successful fuzzy applications in industry such as intelligent control and pattern classification, the introduction of fuzzy sets was motivated by the need for more human-friendly computerized devices that help a user to formulate his knowledge and to clarify, to process, to retrieve and to exploit the available information in a most simple way. In order to achieve this user-friendliness, often certain (limited) reductions in performance and solution quality are accepted.

So the question is: what is a good solution from the point of view of a user in the field of information mining? Of course, correctness, completeness, and efficiency are important, but in order to manage systems that are more and more complex, there is a constantly growing demand to keep the solutions conceptually simple and understandable. This calls for a formal theory of utility in which the simplicity of a system is taken into account. Unfortunately such a theory is extremely hard to come by, because for complex domains it is difficult to measure the degree of simplicity and it is even more difficult to assess the gain achieved by making a system simpler. Nevertheless, this is a lasting challenge for the fuzzy community to meet.

References

1. Fayyad U., Piatetsky-Shapiro G., Smyth P. and Uthurusamy R., Eds.: 'Advances in Knowledge Discovery and Data Mining'. Cambridge, MA, USA, AAAI Press / MIT Press (1996).
2. Zadeh L.: 'Fuzzy logic = computing with words'. IEEE Transactions on Fuzzy Systems, Vol. 4, pp. 103–111 (1996).
3. Wittgenstein L.: 'Philosophical Investigations'. Englewood Cliffs, NJ, USA, Prentice Hall (1973 (first published 1952)).
4. Chapman P., Clinton J., Khabaza T., Reinartz T. and Wirth R. 'The crisp-dm process model', (1999). Available from http://www.ncr.dk/CRISP/.
5. Bezdek J., Keller J., Krishnapuram R. and Pal N.: 'Fuzzy Models and Algorithms for Pattern Recognition and Image Processing'. The Handbooks on Fuzzy Sets. Norwell MA, USA, Kluwer (1998).   ,
6. Höppner F., Klawonn F., Kruse R. and Runkler T.: 'Fuzzy Cluster Analysis'. Chichester, England, J. Wiley & Sons (1999).   ,
7. Kruse R. and Meyer K.: 'Statistics with Vague Data'. Dordrecht, Netherlands, Reidel (1987).
8. Borgelt C., Gebhardt J. and Kruse R.: 'Chapter f1.2: Inference methods'. In 'Handbook of Fuzzy Computation', E. Ruspini, P. Bonissone, and W. Pedrycz, Eds. Institute of Physics Publishing Ltd., Bristol, United Kingdom (1998).   ,
9. Bandemer H. and Näther W.: 'Fuzzy Data Analysis'. Dordrecht, Netherlands, Kluwer (1992).
10. Nauck D., Klawonn F. and Kruse R.: 'Foundations of Neuro-Fuzzy Systems'. Chichester, England, J. Wiley & Sons (1997).
11. Nauck D. and Kruse R.: 'Chapter d.2: Neuro-fuzzy systems'. In 'Handbook of Fuzzy Computation', P. B. E. Ruspini and W. Pedrycz, Eds. Institute of Physics Publishing Ltd., Bristol, UK (1998).
12. Berthold M. and Huber K.: 'Constructing fuzzy graphs from examples'. Int. J. Intelligent Data Analysis, Vol. 3(1), pp. 37–51 (1999).
13. Wang L.-X. and Mendel J.: 'Generating fuzzy rules by learning from examples'. IEEE Trans. Syst., Man, Cybern., Vol. 22, pp. 1414–1227 (1992).
14. Gebhardt J. and Kruse R.: 'Parallel combination of information sources'. In 'Handbook of Defeasible Reasoning and Uncertainty Management Systems. Vol. 3: Belief Change', D. Gabbay and P. Smets, Eds. Kluwer, Dordrecht, Netherlands, pp. 329–375 (1998).
15. Dubois D., Prade H. and Yager R.: 'Merging fuzzy information'. In 'Approximate Reasoning and Fuzzy Information Systems', D. D. J.C. Bezdek and H. Prade, Eds. Kluwer, Dordrecht, Netherlands, pp. 335–402 (1999).
16. Kruse R., Gebhardt J. and Klawonn F.: 'Foundations of Fuzzy Systems'. Chichester, England, J. Wiley & Sons (1994).   ,
17. Cooke R.: 'Experts in Uncertainty: Opinion and Subjectivity Probability in Science'. New York, NY, Oxford University Press (1991).
18. Fisher D. and Lenz H.: 'Learning from Data.'. No. 112 in Lecture Notes in Statistics. New York, NY, Springer (1996).

19. Siekmann S., Gebhardt J. and Kruse R.: 'Information fusion in the context of stock index prediction'. In 'Proc. ECSQARU'99' (London, UK) (1999).
20. Zadeh L.: 'Fuzzy sets as a basis for a theory of possibility'. Fuzzy Sets and Systems, Vol. 1, pp. 3–28 (1978).
21. Dubois D. and Prade H.: 'Possibility Theory'. New York, NY, Plenum Press (1988).
22. Gebhardt J. and Kruse R.: 'The context model — an integrating view of vagueness and uncertainty'. Int. Journal of Approximate Reasoning, Vol. 9, pp. 283–314 (1993).
23. Nguyen H.: 'Using random sets'. Information Science, Vol. 34, pp. 265–274 (1984).
24. Gebhardt J. and Kruse R.: 'Possinfer — a software tool for possibilistic inference'. In 'Fuzzy Set Methods in Information Engineering: A Guided Tour of Applications', H. P. D. Dubois and R. Yager, Eds. Wiley, New York, NY, pp. 407–418 (1996).
25. Hisdal E.: 'Conditional possibilities, independence, and noninteraction'. Fuzzy Sets and Systems, Vol. 1, pp. 283–297 (1978).
26. de Campos L., Gebhardt J. and Kruse R.: 'Syntactic and semantic approaches to possibilistic independence'. Technical report, University of Granada Spain, and University of Braunschweig, Germany (1995).
27. Shafer G.: 'A Mathematical Theory of Evidence'. Princeton, NJ, Princeton University Press (1976).
28. Zadeh L.: 'The concept of a linguistic variable and its application to approximate reasoning'. Information Sciences, Vol. 9, pp. 43–80 (1975).
29. Dawid A.: 'Conditional independence in statistical theory'. SIAM Journal on Computing, Vol. 41, pp. 1–31 (1979).
30. Pearl J. and Paz A.: 'Graphoids: a graph based logic for reasoning about relevance relations'. In 'Advances in Artificial Intelligence 2', B. B. et al, Ed. North Holland, Amsterdam, Netherlands, pp. 357–363 (1987).
31. Shafer G. and Shenoy P.: 'Local computations in hypertrees'. Working paper 201, School of Business, University of Kansas, Lawrence, KS (1988).
32. Gebhardt J. and Kruse R.: 'Learning possibilistic networks from data'. In 'Proc. 5th Int. Workshop on Artificial Intelligence and Statistics' (Fort Lauderdale, FL), pp. 233–244 (1995).
33. Hartley R.: 'Transmission of information'. The Bell Systems Technical Journal, Vol. 7, pp. 535–563 (1928).
34. Gebhardt J. and Kruse R.: 'Tightest hypertree decompositions of multivariate possibility distributions'. In 'Proc. Int. Conf. on Information Processing and Management of Uncertainty in Knowledge-based Systems (IPMU'96)' (Granada, Spain), pp. 923–927 (1996).
35. Borgelt C. and Kruse R.: 'Evaluation measures for learning probabilistic and possibilistic networks'. In 'Proc. 6th IEEE Int. Conf. on Fuzzy Systems' (Barcelona, Spain), pp. 669–676 (1997).
36. Borgelt C. and Kruse R.: 'Some experimental results on learning probabilistic and possibilistic networks with different evaluation measures'. In 'Proc. 1st Int. J. Conf. on Qualitative and Quantitative Practical Reasoning, ECSQARU-FAPR'97' (Bad Honnef, Germany), pp. 71–85 (1997).

Soft Agent Computing: Towards Enhancing Agent Technology with Soft Computing

Abe Mamdani, Arash G. Sichanie, and Jeremy Pitt

Intelligent & Interactive Systems(IIS), Department of Electrical & Electronic Engineering
Imperial College of Science, Technology & Medicine
Exhibition Road, London, SW7 2BZ, UK
{e.mamdani,a.sichanie,j.pitt}@ic.ac.uk

Abstract. Soft Agent Computing (SAC) is a new branch of computational intelligence which draws together the ideas of soft computing with the agent paradigm. It is believed this union will deliver technology which inherits the benefits of both and thereby provide solutions which have some of the features of human cognition and the intuitive, system level, abstraction of agent technology. Notwithstanding the attraction of SAC it is recognised that there are many deep technical and philosophical issues yet to be solved. In this paper, we investigate a number of these issues from two different perspectives, agent characteristics and architectural. Then we present different abstraction layers of a SAC architecture and propose and describe a practical SAC system, based on the Beliefs-Desires-Intentions model. Finally, various aspects to be considered when building SAC systems are discussed and a number of potential research areas for further research are recommended.

1 Introduction

Three main thrusts in the recent Intelligent Systems research activities are: elements of computation intelligence, agent technology and technological solutions for certain business process applications, The strengths and weaknesses of traditional AI when applied to a spectrum of application domains are well known to the research community. Researchers have become interested in the claims being made by the so-called soft computing community. Further study was required to provide a succinct account of the field and investigate ways in which soft computing can be made to enrich agent technology. The reason for this interest in soft computing is the recognition that as the complexity of the global information society continues to rise humans will need cognitive assistance to deal with their own creation. Additionally there is also the recognition that notwithstanding the long-term work of the HCI community, modern IT systems remain low on user friendliness. These twin requirements of cognitive assistance and adoption to human modes of thought have guided the study in this paper.

B. Azvine et al. (Eds.): Intelligent Systems and Soft Computing, LNAI 1804, pp. 110-135, 2000.
© Springer-Verlag Berlin Heidelberg 2000

To explore the benefits of utilising soft computing techniques in the agent paradigm, the desirable characteristics of agent systems as well as the acclaimed capabilities of soft computing techniques are investigated as the first stage of our study. Section 2 of this paper represents the essential background required for such recognition where the capabilities of soft computing techniques and the objectives of agent systems are outlined and a succinct account of the motivations and major achievements of each is presented individually. We approach Soft Agent Computing from two different perspectives. The first view studies the acclaimed attributes of agent systems and investigates the suitability of soft techniques for building a system with such attributes (SAC behaviour). The second view describes the architectural aspects of SAC which is inclusive of soft computing components and the agent paradigm (SAC structure). Sections 3.1 and 3.2 describe the first and second views respectively. Section 3.1 describes the 'softening' of agent attributes (this is explained at the beginning of the section) and Section 3.2 describes an abstract architecture for SAC. Section 3 also includes definitions for the terminology used for SAC throughout this paper. Section 4 is where a practical SAC system based on the Beliefs-Desires-Intentions model is presented and different implementation issues are discussed. Sections 3 and 4 contain the main technical content of this paper.

2   Agent Technology and Soft Computing

In this section a background of agent technology and soft computing is presented. The issues involved in each of these concepts together with its capabilities to resolve relative problems and achieve desired objectives are discussed individually.

2.1   Agent Technology

There are many definitions and taxonomies of agents, e.g. Wooldridge and Jennings [1] and Nwana [2]. We believe that any definition of an agent is likely to depend on the application or context of use. However, the agent *metaphor* is extremely appropriate in the design of complex interactive and distributed systems, and so here we discuss our working assumptions about 'agenthood', which serve as a rationale for soft agents below. At the highest level of abstraction, we require that an agent be an identifiable software or hardware unit that exhibits some 'intelligence', to which a user delegates responsibility for a task, and the agent is accountable for and answerable to the user for that task. At the lowest level of abstraction, a software agent is an embedded process that encapsulates some notion of state, communicates with other processes by message passing, and can perceive/affect its environment by means of sensors/actuators (where both environment and sensing can be implemented in software).

The agent process will also require an ontology, grounded in the application domain, an AI component, for reasoning about the domain, and a more or less anthropomorphic shell, for user interaction. In particular, a user delegates responsibility for a task to the agent (process). The agent may then operate autonomously, or it may seek feedback from the user to guide operation. Therefore an agent is always accountable or answerable to a human user. In a user-agent system, the agent provides assistance to the user, by taking actions in order to complete a task and taking responsibility for completing the task, while the task itself is delegated by the user and may be something that the user could or would ordinarily do for him/herself. In a multi-agent system, each agent is a concurrently executing embedded process, which has a separate identifiable functionality, takes actions to achieve that functionality, and is responsible for realising that functionality. A user agent can be said to exhibit 'intelligence' if it acts so as to maximise its expected utility (this idea comes from the economic theory of rational agency). Agents in a multi-agent system can be said to exhibit 'intelligence' if they show emergent behaviour (i.e. they co-operate to achieve collectively goals that they could not achieve individually).

Agent computing can be viewed from two major perspectives: agent attributes and agent architectures. Agent attributes refer to the characteristics or properties that an agent-based system is capable of exhibiting. These depend upon the requirements of the application domain.

Some of the desirable agent attributes that are well recognised in agency are: *Reactivity* (perceives its environment and responds in a timely fashion to changes in the environment), *Autonomy* (operates without being contingent on human direction, is responsible for most of its own decision making, has some control over its own actions and internal state), *Proactivity* (exhibits goal-directed behaviour, can take initiatives), *Continuity* (is a continuously running process rather than a one-off computation), *Interactivity* (communicates with other agents in some well-defined language, communicates with user(s) through appropriate interface), *Adaptivity* (changes its behaviour based on its previous experience, new or altered requirements, changes in the environment), *Mobility* (ability to transport itself from one machine to another across a network), *Robustness* (the ability to deal with unexpected messages without crashing or ignoring the message), *Rationality* (will act so as to achieve its goals, won't act so as not to achieve them), *Character* (believable 'personality' and emotional state), *Orientation* (benevolence, do what is required, won't stop others doing what is required without good cause), *Veracity* (always tells truth) and *Reflectivity* (exhibits self-awareness by introspection of its own internal state which is used to inform action).

Agent architecture relates to a structure for implementation of agent-based systems. This structure forms the kernel of an autonomous agent. Many agent architectures have been proposed and discussed. The most common taxonomy groups the agent architectures into three main categories: reactive architectures, deliberative architectures and interactive architectures [3]. However, the boundaries between these are not quite sharp. An agent could exhibit a selective set of the mentioned attributes and still not necessarily fall into any of those categories. It should be clear that an agent internal architecture, will exhibit certain (agent) attributes that are a product of the architecture and are necessary to meet the application requirements.

2.2   Soft Computing

The term 'Soft Computing' itself was coined by Zadeh [4], and considered to be an extension of fuzzy logic by merging it with neural networks and evolutionary computing. A concise definition of soft computing is: "… a term that describes a collection of techniques capable of dealing with imprecise, uncertain, or vague information" [4]. Under this definition, soft computing is not a single technology or methodology, rather it is a partnership. According to Azvine et al [5], its partners circa 1996 are fuzzy logic, neuro-computing, genetic computing and probabilistic reasoning, which subsumes evidential reasoning, chaotic systems, belief networks and part of machine learning.

Soft computing aims to expand the range of computer applications to the demands of the real world by allowing decision-making models that are open, and allow for incomplete, uncertain and vague information, but nevertheless avoid inconsistencies and ambiguities. This aim is supported by the fact that there are techniques available, (though in some cases they need to be researched further) for handling uncertainty, incompleteness, vagueness, adaptation and for dealing with open co-operating systems.

For a while AI offered an alternative paradigm that gave the impression that a human-like software may also be better able to deal with real-world problems. However, in the first place, tight specifications have become such an expected norm within the computing world (educational and market-place) that it requires immense vision to specify soft aspects of computing. Secondly, by widely adopting mathematical logic, the AI world has made hard computing a virtue. The result is that it is the human who is required to adapt to hard computing rather than the computing research community taking up the challenge to provide the means to offer 'real-world computing'.

In actual fact, techniques exist that can permit computers to be used in a less precisely defined fashion. Many of these techniques are at the fringes of the field of AI and operations research. Non-determinism is at the heart of agent-based systems. Coupled with that, the use of uncertainty techniques, imprecise and fuzzy representation of information, advanced search techniques such as genetic algorithms, neural-network-based learning and adaptation, etc, all serve to enhance what may be termed soft computing. So far each of these techniques has been studied in isolation. We feel that soft computing emerges from the coming together of several of these techniques in a single application.

2.3   Summary

In this section we presented an introduction to agent metaphor and soft computing. The agent metaphor has highlighted agent attributes and architectures and the collection of *ad hoc* techniques which comprise, to some people, soft computing, were discussed. Recently, work on agent-based architectures also shows that it is possible to produce complex systems that have loosely coupled agents in a distributed environment, which will inevitably behave in a non-deterministic way. Non-determinism, uncertainty, vagueness, adaptability are some of the features that form an essential part of a soft computing capability. It is therefore appropriate to investigate the conjunction of agent-based computing and soft computing as a methodology for developing complex systems that have to be embedded in vague environments. In the next section, we will show how *post hoc* application of these techniques to agent attributes and architecture leads naturally to the notion of, and a methodology for, soft agent computing.

3   Soft Agent Computing

In this section, first we define a set of desired attributes (called *soft* attributes) that soft agents should exhibit. Subsequently, we propose a general architecture for soft agents and discuss the relative issues.

A soft agent will still have 'intelligence', responsibility for a task, and accountability to a user. It will also still need:

- an ontology, grounded in at least the particular application domain;
- an algorithmic computing component, for reasoning about tasks in the application domain;
- an anthropomorphic shell, for user interaction and understanding.

However, in a soft agent, either the ontology can be soft, e.g. access can be based on soft pattern matches (e.g. fuzzy matching and the best fit in a semantic network), and/or the algorithmic computing component is, or includes, a soft computing technique, and/or the anthropomorphic shell can include 'computing with words' [6] or multi-modal interaction (including speech, facial and gesture recognition and output). The soft computing techniques play the major role in the proposed algorithmic computing component; however, the classical AI components could also be included as part of this component. Greater generality overall would improve the cost understanding capability.

3.1   Soft Agent Attributes

The term *softening* here refers to parameterising and applying one or a number of soft computing techniques to an aspect of agent paradigm. If a soft computing technique is utilised in any of the algorithmic computing components of an agent besides or instead of classical AI components, this means softening some or all of its attributes. Desirable agent attributes were presented in section 2.1. Note though that some of these attributes cannot be softened, and some are intrinsically (by nature) soft. For example, the following attributes cannot be softened: continuity, autonomy, and mobility; and the following attributes are arguably intrinsically soft: reflectivity, character (soft techniques used to develop character), and orientation (veracity is contingent).

The remaining attributes of agency, reactivity, proactivity, interactivity, adaptivity, robustness, and rationality, can be softened. There are various ways of softening agent attributes. In the following paragraphs, we present our approach including the benefits that these practices could result in.

Soft Reactivity   The field of reactive planning is based on the idea that a planning system need not worry about unexpected developments in its environment: it only has to execute whatever action it deems necessary given its own current state. Reactive agent architectures therefore avoid the complexities of planning in dynamic, inaccessible or incomplete environments. For an embedded agent, which only has incomplete knowledge of its environment, there may be no provably correct action (e.g. by logical inference), but nevertheless a requirement that 'something must be done' will exist. An agent can exhibit soft reactivity either if it simplifies the environment and treats it as a finite state machine, but the reasoning behind taking actions is based on a soft computing technique; or, more interestingly, if it takes actions based on a 'best guess' about the actual state of environment, i.e. it only has a partial knowledge of that environment. This implies a need to reason with uncertainty and incompleteness. Soft computing techniques provide the appropriate decision-making capability (akin to human uses of 'intuition', 'gut reaction', etc, to supplement logical thought processes) and the ability to grade decisions. Zadeh's theory of fuzzy decision making and the usual tools for assigning a 'degree of belief' to elements of an agent's knowledge, such as probability theory, are among techniques suitable for this purpose. The application of fuzzy logic in agent planning (softening plans) is discussed in the later sections of this paper.

Furthermore, some form of sensitivity analysis provides a handle on confidence level management, and, for little extra overhead, a mechanism for learning which is less crude than reinforcement learning. Thus the advantages of softening reactivity are that it should encourage autonomy and adaptivity, through a refinement of decision-making facilities and growing confidence in the reliability of those decisions.

Soft Pro-activity   A soft agent may have an incomplete or under-specified representation of a user's goals, or it may soften a user's 'hard' goals. This latter is the approach taken to co-operative answering from computerised databases [7], where users' queries are relaxed in an attempt to provide more and more relevant information, in the way that a human respondent would. Fuzzy logic has been used in such applications, for example, Bosc and Pivert [8] describe SQLf, a fuzzy extension of the database query language SQL, which is used to support imprecise database queries. Soft pro-active agents need not only reason about users' goals, they may also reason about their plans as well. There are many activities where people do not invent new methods to find a solution to their problem, but apply typical methods that can be described as a certain sequence of actions, usually formalised in AI as a 'script' [9]. To perform an action, some preconditions may have to be satisfied, and for some actions, a pre-condition might be to 'know' some information. Such pre-conditions are called epistemic pre-conditions.

A soft agent that is providing assistance to a user (i.e. a user agent) can store plan descriptions based on a model of the user's plans and goals (could include imprecise and incomplete data). If requests for information can be matched to epistemic pre-conditions presented by soft variables (e.g. Zadeh's fuzzy matching), the agent can calculate the likelihood that the user's intention is to perform that plan, and act (pro-act) accordingly. For example, a query about air-line ticket prices could be matched with an epistemic pre-condition for buying a ticket for a flight. A soft agent being pro-active would reason about the likelihood of the match and seek to provide further information beyond just the ticket prices.

Any human providing co-operative assistance tries to help the 'user' to a set of goals which may not actually be 'known' by the user (or imprecise and without complete description). So, in general, pro-active behaviour, which is intended to be co-operative, has soft nature. The advantage of softening proactivity is that the agent can exhibit a more co-operative and human-like behaviour, and be able to build and use more general user models. A user trying to combine and customise services from a set of multiple service providers in order to establish his/her own value-added service would be greatly helped by such an agent.

Soft Interactivity There are two possibilities for soft interactivity: either agent-agent interaction can be softened, or user-agent interaction can be softened. We will consider each in turn. Firstly, for agent-agent interaction, consider Fig. 1. This shows two schematic agents: they communicate by passing messages according to an agreed format (a protocol for speech acts), and they decide which message to send next based on decisions made by the negotiation module, and this, in conjunction with the ontology of the application, will determine the content of a message.

There are three ways this scenario can be softened. Firstly, in negotiation, the negotiation strategy may be softened by being based on a soft computing technique; secondly, the protocol can be softened, so that message exchange can be more arbitrary, and thirdly, the negotiable content may be softened. The protocol can be presented as a finite state diagram in which the decisions made upon transfers from one state to the others could be based on a soft computing technique (e.g. fuzzy reasoning). Such a decision is made on the basis of the imprecise and incomplete state variables presented by soft values (e.g. granulised). The content may be softened in two ways: either the service level agreement (à la ADEPT, see O'Brien and Wiegand [10]) can be stated in fuzzy terms (e.g. quickly, occasionally, frequently), or the ontological content can be fuzzy and needs somehow to be matched.

Soft interactivity between user and agent involves softening the user-agent interface via the anthropomorphic shell, as mentioned above. This means replacing the existing crisp dialogue systems used for agent interaction (e.g. the form-based dialogue for softbots [11]) and replacing it with a dialogue style which could include Zadeh's 'computing with words' [6] or multi-modal interaction (including speech, facial and gesture recognition). Output from the agent could be softened in a similar fashion.

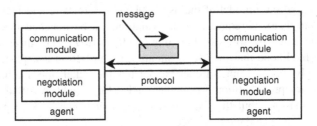

Fig. 1. Agent-agent interaction

By softening the communication protocols between agents, conversations become inherently non-deterministic. By converting tight constraint into a more flexible form (soft) on the possible range of agent responses, we put less tight constraints on the agent's commitments or how they are delivered. The problem of verifiability and enforcement caused by abandoning tight constraint protocols seem relaxed in soft constraint versions. As a result of these, an extended range of behaviour, which also enhances autonomy, could emerge to provide localised responsibility. The main advantage of soft interactivity is that increased responsibility coupled with increased freedom to communicate encourages emergent behaviour. 'Crisp' contract-net protocols could now be supplemented by the agent equivalent of 'off-line discussions', which influence the 'public' negotiation.

Soft Adaptivity   Adaptivity might be taken to imply softness, but changes in behaviour can be programmed based on 'crisp' methods, for example reinforcement learning in a maze-learning (physical) agent. In AI, work on adjusting previously constructed plans (i.e. scripts) to meet novel situations is called adaptive planning [12], and this can, for example, be based on case-based reasoning [13]. However, adaptive agents can adapt their behaviour based on either incomplete knowledge or soft computing techniques. For example, consider the user-agent system shown in Fig. 2.

Here, the user agent is providing 'on-line' support to the user for using the application: note that it is specifically *not* an interface or layer between the user and application, it is there to assist the user in his/her use of the application. There are three ways the agent could acquire the appropriate knowledge to provide this support: either it could be programmed by the user, it could be knowledge-based, or it could use machine learning techniques. The first two are crisp, and indeed relatively inflexible. In the machine learning approach, the agent can learn by:

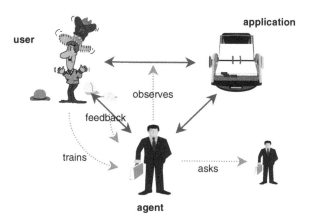

Fig. 2.   Human-Agent-Application interaction

- observing the user;
- indirect user feedback;
- training by the user;
- asking other agents.

The mechanisms by which these learning methods could be applied could all be based on soft computing.

This assists with the development of soft reactivity and proactivity and anticipates truly adaptive behaviour. The perceived benefit of soft adaptivity is the acknowledgement that soft computing biologically inspired learning techniques seem potentially more suited to learning than 'crisp' techniques, although we would not rule out either approach.

Soft Robustness   Although 'soft robustness' might appear to be a contradiction in terms, for an agent it means the ability to deal with unexpected inputs 'sensibly'. In open agent systems, an agent has to be able to deal with any situation. Soft robustness provides a more positive, pro-active form of exception handing that transcends 'on error goto' or 'return to sender', i.e. the agent endeavours to do something constructive with an incoming message which is not fully understood. Some of this behaviour is only possible with good agent adaptivity, and the ability to absorb history information gained from previous states (soft computing learning techniques, e.g. neural networks) offers a more refined means of managing state behaviour. The advantage of softening this attribute is to encourage homogeneity in open agent systems: new agents and new messages can be absorbed seamlessly. For an incoming message that is not understood, for example, this means handling it by referral back to the sender for clarification, or forwarding to higher authority, a more appropriate recipient, or the user. The mechanism by which the decision on where to send the message is made can be soft, for example based on an analysis of the content of the message and evaluation against a soft ontology.

Soft Rationality This is, in our view, the most critical attribute to soften, and the hardest. Some definitions of rationality in agents state that an agent is rational if and only if it seeks to maximise its expected utility. The fundamental idea of decision theory is that an agent is rational if and only if it chooses an action that yields the highest expected utility, *averaged over all the possible outcomes of the action*. This is closer to what we might consider soft rationality. Soft computing extensions to decision theory (e.g. fuzzy decision theory) provides an appropriate tool for such applications where the environment includes fuzzy variables. A soft agent might not act so as to achieve its goals and maximise its expected utility. In fact, in a multi-soft-agent system which is trying to achieve pareto-optimality (i.e. the 'minimisation of unhappiness'), an agent may act so as to achieve the highest expected utility of the collective system, even if this means that its individual contribution to that utility is less than it might have yielded had it acted to try to achieve its highest expected utility. This is a move towards achieving 'ethical' behaviour for an agent, and a system of ethics implies the ability to act sub-optimally. Sub-optimal behaviour, compromises, and concessions are critical for emergent behaviour and optimality for the community (i.e. pareto-optimality).

Examples of such systems include queuing systems or resource management systems. For instance, imagine a number of agents generating e-mail messages whose contents can range from short text messages to long multimedia displays. The agents might have the individual goal of getting their messages out as quickly as possible, but collectively the overall goal of minimising total delay. Agents could then negotiate over the position of their messages in the queue, and indeed one agent trying to send a long message could let another agent send a short message before it, even if it arrived in the queue later (the argument being, naturally, that it is better overall for the long message to be a little delayed than for the short to be delayed a lot).

These situations arise naturally in human endeavour, for example from sharing sweets in the playground to check-out queues in supermarkets. They arise equally in automated manufacturing and production (e.g. car assembly scheduling), but the mechanics of negotiation in such situations are complex, subtle, and with conventional methods, possibly beyond implementation [14]. We believe the obvious benefits of self-configuring, self-optimising systems of rational agents are considerable and soft-computing approaches seem appropriate in providing the required assistance towards making soft rationality viable.

3.2   Soft Agent Architectures

The object-oriented approach is one of the most effective and common approaches for controlling some of the problems created by increasing connectivity and consumer demands which are powered an unprecedented growth in software volume and complexity [15]. Software agent technology is not excluded from the mentioned problems and it is often considered as the next highest layer of abstraction. Therefore, by careful choice in the building blocks and their inter-relationships, it should be possible to construct a soft agent architecture which has general applicability. Modelling languages, such as Unified Modelling Language (UML), can be used as an extension to the object-oriented approach for specifying, visualising, constructing, and documenting the artefacts of soft agent software systems. These languages provide extensibility and specialisation mechanisms to extend the core concepts. They are independent of particular programming languages and development processes and provide a formal basis for understanding the modelling language.

Using the above architectural methodology we consider a major class of agent architectures. Two other classes are derived from this major class which we will discuss shortly. One class uses incompleteness and imprecision internally but presents a crisp interface to the world at large, and the other is a more complex class, which lives in a totally incomplete and imprecise world. The later class is by far the more exciting technology but the ontological issues are formidable.

Naturally a soft agent will have a hybrid structure. The degree to which techniques and design philosophies are utilised from different AI paradigms will be much greater than for their 'hard' cousins. We consider the soft agent to be a part of a multi-agent system, and therefore naturally a Distributed Computing Environment is required.

We recognise that designers of soft agent systems must be watchful of the following:

- ensuring that the number and variety of *ad hoc* (or unprincipled) designs is kept within manageable bounds (portfolio considerations);
- attempting to define the application areas in broad, coherent classes so that common solutions are feasible (containment of variety);
- from the outset beginning to develop a theory to guide the selection of design principles (design elegance).

In addition, the soft components and the anthropomorphic features that distinguish SAC will impose their own set of problems, some of which are addressed in the next section. Firstly, the logical location of soft elements will need to be determined very carefully, otherwise the resulting systems could be characterised as only having a *soft veneer with a brittle core*. Secondly, the anthropomorphic features of SAC pose a new set of challenges, which the agent software community is not as well prepared to solve as it is for the issues outlined above. As Watt [16] points out: "There is a psychological price to be paid for the anthropomorphism built into many (interface) agents. Just because an agent has a human name, looks human, or speaks like a human, it does not mean that people will interact with them as if they are human; the behaviour of the agent has to live up to this expectation, and, if it fails, there is a kind of 'anthropomorphic dissonance' which undermines the collaboration ..."

Therefore the problems and challenges which face the constructor of an SAC architecture are somewhat formidable. Also it must be kept in mind that by architecture we mean a set of definitions, inter-relationships and design methodologies which guide the construction of a usable system. The completion of this significant task is to a degree described in the next section and outlines are provided to guide further research.

The precise internal construction of each soft agent would depend on the function to be carried out and any (extended along the soft dimension) from the agent taxonomy of Franklin and Graesser [17] or the typography of Nwana and Ndumu [18] or the classification of Smith [19] could be appropriate.

The following short section describes the SAC architecture which covers the range of the bifurcation mentioned above. We defined one major branch of collaborative agents. Then a number of branched architectures are discussed in terms of their internal and external standings.

Collaborative Soft Agent In this section we would like firstly to define common soft agent infrastructure (CSAI). CSAI is a distributed computing environment with a number of domain-independent agent platforms. The collaborative agent situation is complicated by the fact that Agents can collaborate with others on the same CSAI, (see Fig. 4) or with agents located on other CSAIs (see Fig. 5). It is assumed that within any particular CSAI the soft paradigm is extent. Such an assumption may not pertain in early SAC systems.

Fig. 3 depicts the internal architecture of the collaborative soft agent (SA). Note that, in the figure, CtS/StC (crisp to soft or soft to crisp) converters layer, and modules provide an interface between agencies and between each agency and other (non-agent) IT artefacts.

The agent communicates with a human through the psychological layer. One of the roles of the psychological layer would be to infer mood, attentiveness, etc, from the visual input and correlate with the text/speech communications from the user. The interface to a human user may include vision as well as text/speech. All items within the kernel execute their functions in the soft computing paradigm. In the next section we discuss whether fuzzy logic, or Zadeh's [6] computing with words, neurocomputing or other techniques are chosen for this core soft capability.

At the present stage in SAC it is considered a safe option to retain a crisp representation for the knowledge base of role-specific information. This knowledge base will also provide the strictly limited world model needed by a collaborative agent. All of the specific agent software conducts its inference, etc, within the SAC paradigm.

A consequence of this is that the soft knowledge base will be a complex entity. Semantic networks, neural networks or fuzzy rule bases are candidate solutions.

The crisp/soft and soft/crisp converters which interface to the IT world (for instance databases, Internet) and other agencies would have to be device and domain dependent. This follows from the fact that current IT languages and protocols are very brittle: miss a time-out by a few milliseconds and the channel is disconnected; launch a request to WWW with only one character/position incorrect and the connection fails, etc.

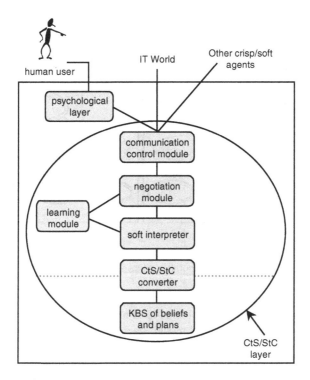

Fig. 3. Collaborative soft agent: internal architecture

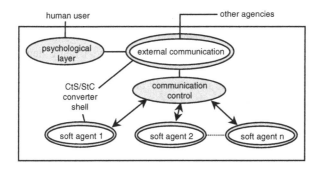

Fig. 4. Collaborative agent: agency view

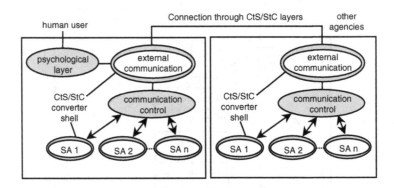

Fig. 5. Collaborative agent — top level view

The crisp/soft converter between the soft knowledge base (SKA) and any underlying agent domain could also be problematic. It may be necessary to condense the SKA and agent domain into a soft world model. Each agency can be expanded in the manner depicted in Fig. 4.

Note here that it is assumed that each variety of agent within the agency will need a role-specific KB. Whether this is contained in each agent as a soft component or crisp as shown above is discussed in the next section. Since the role-specific KB of each agent could be of relatively low complexity, intuition suggests it should be integrated with the task execution model. It is possible that the psychological layer may have to be task specific.

All communication, collaboration and co-operation between agents and agencies are conducted within the soft paradigm. Only communications with other IT artefacts not enjoying a soft approach require a crisp-to-soft converter. The negotiation module which conducts negotiations between collaborative soft agents can be softened so that the negotiation strategy is soft, the information model being negotiated over is soft (i.e. a soft ontology), and the negotiation protocol used between agents can also be softened. This is softening the interactivity attribute. The resource management module and enactment engine can also be softened, for example to deal with promises, sub-contracts, etc. This is softening the rationality, reactivity, pro-activity and adaptivity attributes.

3.3   Soft Agent Computing — Towards a Methodology

Soft Agent Computing should not be defined as a set of techniques which include agents as well as soft computing techniques, which are combined into some hybrid melange, and applications sought. Instead, the application should be well defined, the agent architecture and attributes should be developed, the overall system should be inspected for areas where there is vagueness, and then it should be decided which soft computing technique, or technique(s) are best applied, and how. In particular, the soft computing dimension should be subsumed this way into an emerging software design methodology involving process-oriented design (rather than object-oriented design), with the real possibility of delivering machine intelligence for the control of complex systems.

The principal guidelines that emerge from this initial study for soft agent computing are:

- the choice of where and how to use soft computing techniques is highly dependent on the application and ontology used — this should not be viewed as delay commitment to technique and should be dealt with when close to the problem;
- progressive (incremental) development of soft agent computing is necessary and important;
- soft-crisp and crisp-soft converters are a key requirement since they guarantee proper function of the soft computing techniques in solving problems;
- soft agent computing offers meta-rules for agent behaviour determined by the composition of their soft attributes.

4   Soft Agents in Practice

In the previous sections, we theoretically introduced the benefits that can be gained by integrating the agent paradigm and soft computing and subsequently presented an abstract architecture for such integration. Furthermore, major designing issues were discussed and some guiding principles were proposed. Nevertheless, various practical approaches to the design and implementation of such systems according to the proposed ideas are feasible. In order to illustrate how the outlined notions can be practically utilised in agent paradigms, in this section of the paper we briefly introduce our approach in designing and developing a prototype SAC system. The presentation includes the basic functioning principles and the architecture of such a system. Soft Agent Computing system (SAC) are being designed and developed at the Intelligent and Interactive Systems research group of the Imperial College. However, here only the design issues related to the proposed system are described in order to demonstrate how the union of soft computing and agent paradigm can be realised in practice. A more detailed description of the SAC architecture will be presented somewhere else.

One of the motivations for presenting the SAC architecture here is to help with the realisation of the soft agent computing notion. A major step towards developing soft agents is to find the logical location of the soft elements in the agent paradigm, particularly in agent architecture. Naturally, there are many ways of achieving this aim. One of the feasible approaches could be outlined in line with the following procedure:

1) investigate the current crisp agent architectures;
2) select an appropriate architecture;
3) apply soft techniques.

The investigation and selection are based on a set of criteria explained in the following section. After selection, the strengths and the weaknesses of the chosen architecture are highlighted. Then by viewing soft computing as a toolbox of practical implementation techniques, these techniques are applied to the specific weakness areas identified in the agent paradigms. The usefulness of soft techniques can only be assessed by experimenting with them on specific problems. Achieving the desired attributes (soft attributes) outlined in the previous sections is our main aim. In the following sub-sections we first describe our investigation for finding an appropriate architecture, justify our selection and then present the SAC architecture.

4.1   Current Agent Architectures (Non-Soft)

A number of various agent architectures have been implemented and are being researched at present. Although most of these architectures use various terminologies, they are all in principle trying to achieve a set of commonly agreed goals. Note that although we only soften one particular architecture (in our case the most popular one) this can easily be extended to other architectures.

We are developing the SAC architecture as the next step in the evolution of pragmatic BDI-based agent architectures. Our approach to agent architectural theories and design has been to start with a BDI-theoretic core followed by incremental improvements based upon incorporation or modification based on the soft computing research of others and our own ongoing research and experience. SAC combines what we believe to be the best aspects of several leading-edge intelligent agent frameworks, including the original BDI (beliefs, desires, intentions) theories and specification of the Procedural Reasoning System (PRS) of Georgeff and Lansky [20], Rao [21], and others, the Structured Circuit Semantics (SCS) representation of Lee and Durfee [22], and the Act plan interlingua of Myers and Wilkins [23, 24] and others. In addition, SAC draws upon pragmatics garnered from the PRS implementations of the University of Michigan (called UMPRS) [25, 26] and SRI International (called PRS-CL) [27].

Starting with a BDI-theoretic 'kernel' allows us to reap the benefits of a large body of research on the theory and implementation of, in particular, the Procedural Reasoning System (PRS). Explicit modelling of the concepts of beliefs, goals (desires), and intentions within an agent architecture provides a number of advantages, including facilitating the use of declarative representations for each of these concepts. This is where fuzzy logic and Lotfi Zadeh's 'computing with words' can be very useful. The use of declarative representations in turn facilitates automated generation, manipulation, and even communication of these soft representations. Other advantages of starting with a PRS-based BDI architecture include a sound model of goal-driven and data-driven task achievement, meta-level reasoning, and procedurally specified behaviour. Although capabilities are not a central attribute of BDI theories, implemented architectures typically include explicit, declarative modelling of the capabilities of the agent in the form of plans and primitive actions.

Alternative agent architectures provide some, but not all of the advantages of the BDI-based PRS framework. Many 'agent' architectures such as Aglets and Java Agent Template (JAT) from IBM and Agent Tcl [28] from Dartmouth, have little or no explicit representations of any of the mentalistic attributes of beliefs, intentions, capabilities, or even goals (often argued to be the key feature of agency).

Furthermore, programmers encode the behaviour of these agents almost completely through low-level hardcoding. Each of these agents provides specialised functionality in some focus area (e.g. ARA and Agent Tcl are specialised to provide mobility capabilities), but do not otherwise provide what we consider a complete reasoning architecture.

Agent architectures such as SOAR [29] and AOP-based (Agent-Oriented Programming) [30] architectures such as Agent-0 [31], PLACA [32] all provide significantly more complete representation and reasoning frameworks than those mentioned in the preceding paragraph. SOAR implements a unified theory of cognition (Newell 1990) and provides a wide range of desired agent architecture capabilities, including integrated execution, means-ends planning, meta-level reasoning, and learning. The primary disadvantage of SOAR is its highly unintuitive and constrained rule-based behaviour representation and reasoning cycle.

It would require a significant overhaul of SOAR to improve the procedural expressiveness of its rule representation. The AOP-based architectures provide explicit internal representations of mentalistic concepts such as beliefs and commitments, but they emphasise social interaction capabilities over individual capabilities (even though PLACA does extend the AOP paradigm to include generative planning capabilities).

In addition to these primarily monolithic agent architectures, there are a number of multi-level agent architectures such as TouringMachines [34], Atlantis [35], and InteRRap [3].

Agent architectures of this style vary widely in their theoretical foundation, internal representations, architectural components, and particular emphasis on specific representational or behavioural issues or application domain. One common problem with multi-layer architectures is that they require a specialised programming language for each layer (e.g. reactive layer language, scheduling layer language, planning layer language, co-ordination layer language).

None of these architectures provides as mature or cohesive a theoretical basis as that provided by the BDI theories and PRS specification. Both the BDI theories and PRS specification have their limitations too, of course, but we believe they provide a much stronger starting point.

In the next two subsections, first we describe how soft elements can be applied to various logical locations of an agent with Beliefs, Desires, Plans, Intentions and Actions, and then we present the two scenarios from the ongoing research in which a Soft Agent (SA) is implemented.

4.2   SAC Architecture Based on BDI

SAC is composed of four primary components: a world model, a plan library, a soft interpreter and intention mechanism. This is illustrated in Fig. 6. The illustrated architecture is configured for a specific application and ontology (i.e. an Intelligent Personal Assistant; however, here we would like to place emphasis on the architectural issues rather than the application).

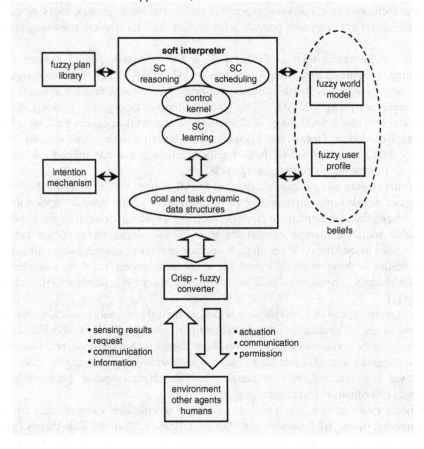

Fig. 6. SAC architecture

The *world model* is a fuzzy database that, together with the user profile, represents the beliefs of the agent. The SAC World Model holds the facts that represent the current state of the world as it is known by the agent. Information that might be kept there includes state variables, sensory information, conclusions from deduction or inferencing, modelling information about other agents, etc. It also keeps information about the *user profile* such as user habits, interests, likes and dislikes, etc. Each world model entry is a simple proposition of the form:

relation_name Fuzzy_arg1 Fuzzy_arg2 ... Fuzzy_argN;

The ordering, semantics, and typing of the arguments is unconstrained however; in our experiment we used fuzzy sets to represent some of the arguments. A fuzzy Java class is created to represent fuzzy set arguments, manage membership functions and perform fuzzy reasoning. A membership function should be assigned for each argument. For example, *Systems resources* is a relation with three fuzzy arguments, each of which represent one of the factors of the system resources required for executing a task:

System_resources CPU Available_Memory Network_Traffic

and one possible instance could be:

System_resources Low Low Medium

The member function for *CPU* fuzzy set is shown in Fig. 7.

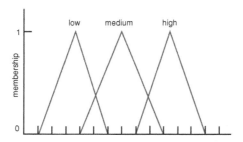

Fig. 7. Membership function for CPU

World model relation's arguments could also be strings, floating point numbers, integer numbers, and native Java objects.

The SAC execution semantics and behaviour are a combination of those of UMPRS and SCS. Changes to the world model or the posting of new goals triggers reasoning to search for plans that might be applied to the current situation. Two problems might appear here. For each goal there might be a number of plans available in the plan library, or there might not be any plans available for a specific goal. In the former case, the SAC soft interpreter forms a list of applicable plans and selects one plan from the list, based on a soft computing technique, in here, fuzzy reasoning. However, there are also other alternative options available (e.g. a neural network which is trained to find the best plan using a number of agent parameters, an evolutionary computation element which searches the best possible plan for a goal). In the latter case, there might be two possible situations — firstly the agent has a plan which is not completely tailored to the goal but can be used to achieve the goal to some degrees. In this case fuzzy matching is used to match the best suited plan. In the second case, where the agent does not have any near enough plans to achieve a goal or partly achieve the goal, the SAC will ask another SAC for a suitable plan. After the selection procedure the soft interpreter intends the plan (i.e. commits itself to execution of the instantiated plan). The intended plans are added into the intention tree, which is a part-intention mechanism. At every single moment there might be a number of committed plans in the intention tree. This raises another problem, which is more difficult to deal with, and that is the question of which plan to execute. Some of the PRS implementations use a static intention graph in order to sort the plans in order. Some others execute the first intention found with the highest utility (i.e. as if there was an SCS DO_BEST over all top-level goals). We use a soft technique to select the best plan for execution.

The *plan library* is a collection of plans that the agent can use to achieve its goals. A soft technique could be used as a plan selection strategy. Each plan has an invocation and a context condition as in PRS [20]. Both of these conditions should be satisfied for a plan to be selected. Crisp conditions limit the flexibility of plans. On the other hand fuzzy conditions could increase the flexibility of plans by making them applicable to a wider set of goals. In addition, each plan may include an explicitly or implicitly defined soft technique for utility calculation, which is used to influence selection of certain procedures over others through the default utility-based meta-level soft reasoning mechanism of SAC, similar to the use of utility functions in JAM [36].

The *soft interpreter* is the agent's 'brain' that uses a collection of soft tools (e.g. fuzzy logic) to reason about what the agent should do and when and how to do it. Among its components there is a reasoner and a scheduler. The scheduler is in charge of scheduling user and system tasks. It also assists the intention mechanism. Fuzzy scheduling principles are used in which a representation of flexible temporal constraints is made. Agent temporal constraints such as task starting date, release date and due date are subject to preference. These requirements are modelled by a fuzzy number and relevant membership functions are used. Besides the main function outlined above, inside the soft interpreter, there are a number of other lightweight declarative procedures that the agent interleaves between plan steps in order to perform functionality outside of the scope of SAC's normal goal/plan-based reasoning (e.g. to manage the dynamic goal/task data structures — one example of its task is to buffer incoming messages). The SAC interpreter is responsible for selecting and executing plans based upon the intentions, plans, goals, and beliefs about the current situation. Associated with the interpreter is the intention mechanism, a run-time stack (stacked based upon subgoaling) of goals with and without instantiated plans. A SAC agent may have a large number of alternative plans for accomplishing any single goal and the SAC interpreter uses fuzzy reasoning to reason about all of the alternative combinations of plans, goals, and variable bindings (based on goal arguments and beliefs) before selecting the best alternative given the particular situation. The agent checks all the plans that can be applied to a goal to make sure they are relevant to the current situation. Those plans that are applicable are collected into what is called the applicable plan list (APL).

If generation of an APL results in one or more entries, the agent possibly enters into meta-level reasoning, i.e. it reasons about how to decide which of the APL elements to intend to its intention structure. The agent could again use soft techniques to perform this decision-making, so that meta-level reasoning about its meta-level reasoning may ensue. Meta-level reasoning also becomes active when there are no plans for a specific goal, or when the goal is not known for the agent.

5   Conclusions and Further Work

In this paper, we discussed the benefits and various approaches in integrating soft computing and agent technology for high-performance intelligent systems. The objectives of this integration and the resulting benefits were also discussed in detail. SAC is a framework to test and experiment with the benefits of applying soft techniques to the agent paradigm. The logical locations of soft techniques in a BDI agent with PRS implementation is also presented in the paper. We believe the architectural outlines proposed in this paper will greatly help with practical implementations of SAC. We have also shown how a practical SAC architecture could exhibit soft reactivity and soft pro-activity. As a part of our conclusion, we would like to outline a number of points ensuing from this research. As far as the target application areas are concerned, with a field of enquiry potentially so large and complex as soft agent computing, it will be important from the outset to identify and define the application domains to be targeted. One potential application domain, which is under investigation at the present, is intelligent personal assistant, which will involve interaction between the technical, commercial and strategic arms of an enterprise. In design and implementation frameworks for building soft agent computing, it is essential to have a thorough and methodological approach. Since the agent technology is poised for a major market thrust, a structured engineering approach is essential. Therefore the following areas of SAC will require significant attention.

Design Methodology This will need to include how to translate application requirements into a system specification. Such an activity is difficult enough for traditional software but is significantly complicated by the 'soft' components.

Systems Architecture Much has been written on the need for an architectural approach to software systems (e.g. RACE I: Network Management Architectures). For our purposes we can define an architecture as a system of definitions of entities and the specification of protocols and relationships between those entities necessary to ensure a sound system design. Some initial ideas have been presented in the previous sections but a great deal more work needs to be carried out.

Interagent Dynamics As the absolute number and variety of agents grows, the dynamics of their interaction between themselves, with extant IT artefacts and with humans, will need close attention. The fear is that since agents have an element of autonomy agent systems could become unstable. It will need to be determined whether the introduction of a soft computing element into the agent make-up will enhance or dampen this potential unstable tendency of agent systems.

Soft Computing Components Since the range of techniques available for the soft element of SAC solutions is potentially very large (there is a great deal of research going on using many different combinations and forms of soft computing techniques), it appears necessary to curb the excesses of designer originality (to avoid diversion from the main research aim outlined in this paper), at least in the earlier years. In constructing the selection of soft computing components it will, of course, be essential to take close account of the applications targeted.

Run Time Environments The selection of the hardware platform, operating system, APIs, etc, should not pose especially new or difficult problems for SAC solutions. But, and this could be important especially during the research and development phase, designers will need to keep in mind the delivery system. As an extreme example there would be severe problems in specifying a 100,000 node neural network as the soft component in a time critical application that was required to run on low-end PCs. Since the scope of SAC solutions is very wide ranging, from simple interface agents to large-scale collaborative agents, platform issues will need to be addressed early in the R&D cycle.

Specific Soft Computing Issues These issues arise out of the introduction of soft computing components into agent technology. Since the prime motivation for SAC is to make IT technology more intuitive, able to exploit imprecision and incompleteness and thereby be more approachable by people who are not IT specialists, it is to be expected that new problems will arise. These will include the following issues and will need significant study and development before SAC solutions will gain ready acceptance.

Human-Soft Agent Interaction Even if only partial success is forthcoming in the early SAC research programme it is most likely that soft agents will exhibit anthropomorphic features to a much greater extent than today's traditional or standard agent software. This could well mean that the non-IT professional user could easily be lulled into a false sense of security. They may bestow on SAC systems levels of intelligence, knowledge and capability that early systems will not possess. Therefore both the marketing and the human-SAC interface will need to present a careful and succinct account of just what the soft agent is capable of undertaking and where its 'boundary of capability' lies.

Ontology The extraction, storing and utilisation of knowledge is at the very heart of the AI tradition — and these ontological issues are no less (and maybe even more) critical for SAC. If software systems are to exploit imprecision and incompleteness and deal satisfactorily with human vagueness then their knowledge bases need to be rich, well structured and cross indexed at least for the cognitive domain in which they operate. Put bluntly, this is an immense task. There are a number of routes to possible universal solutions including work by Lenat [37], Brooks [38] and Aleksander [39]. But what characterises these research programmes is that immediate low-cost solutions will not be at hand in the short time frames necessary for SAC implementation.

Therefore there will be a need to develop *ad hoc* ontologies for each domain being addressed. In order that work on application ontologies does not collapse into a fragmented set of 'one-off' solutions it will be necessary to set in place a portfolio-wide guiding principle. Such an action would ensure that in the absence of a 'universal' ontology at least a measure of coherence could be achieved across the SAC portfolio.

Communication Languages Inextricably linked with the ontological issues is that of intra-agent and human-agent communication. A great deal of work has been carried out world-wide on agent communication languages (ACL). Following the ideas set down in the paper by Nwana [2] and Wooldridge [14] it seems that a suitable way forward would be to enhance a standard ACL (FIPA or KQML being obvious choices [40] with the semantics and protocols, etc, necessary for a soft agent to address a target application domain. Although this approach is by no means novel it does have the merit of being both practical — in the sense that it will lead to rapid commercial exploitation — and forward looking. The latter pertains since KQML has the possibility of becoming a *de facto* global standard. However, even in this most practical of ways forward, the 'welding-in' of fuzziness and imprecision to the ACL will be a difficult technical task. But by grounding the endeavour in a real application the range of soft attributes will be limited in scope and the promise of a commercial application of SAC will be close at hand.

Issues concerning human-soft agent communication are perhaps even more difficult. As noted previously the fear is that increasingly anthropomorphic software will generate user expectations that cannot be fulfilled at this stage in the development of computational intelligence. What seems certain is that the soft agent interface must exhibit far more human-like characteristics than today's HCIs. Accordingly it is recommended that work ongoing by Watt [16] be simultaneously extended both in theoretical scope and also narrowed to a particular BT application. Such a two-pronged approach should bring rewards in the short and medium term.

Agent Etiquette Even for standard agents which do not exhibit well-developed anthropomorphic characteristics there is a growing body of opinion [41] that etiquette, or a codified system of behaviour, is necessary. Therefore it must be the case that SAC systems will have an even greater need for a well-defined code of behaviour, otherwise severe human-soft agent misunderstandings are likely to occur frequently.

It is likely that the very exploitation of a soft approach will raise the problems of agent etiquette up a level. Since today's (hard) agents do not have well-developed anthropomorphic interfaces users are unlikely to expect them to exhibit any degree of morality or sensitivity to the human condition. But if the 'psychological agent' layer of Watt [16] is introduced, as recommended above, these issues become a major feature of the SAC interface.

Acknowledgements

This work was carried out under BT Contract Agreement ML720676 and follow-up studentship. We would particularly like to thank Nader Azarmi, Behnam Azvine, Hyacinth Nwana for the opportunity to undertake this work, and for their encouragement and interesting comments while executing it. We would also like to thank Wayne Wobcke for his comments on an earlier version of this paper.

References

1. Wooldridge N. and Jennings N.: 'Intelligent Agents: Theory and Practice', The Knowledge Engineering Review, Vol. 10, No. 2, pp. 115–152 (1995).
2. Nwana H.: 'Software Agents: An Overview', The Knowledge Engineering Review, Vol. 11, No. 3 (1996).
3. Muller J. P. and Pischel M.: 'Integrating Agent Interaction into a Planner-Reactor Achitecture', Proceedings of the 1994 Distributed AI Workshop, pp. 250-264, Lake Quinalt, WA (1994).
4. Zadeh L. A.: 'Fuzzy Logic, Neural Networks and Soft Computing', Comm of ACM, Vol. 37, No 3, pp. 77-84 (March 1994).
5. Azvine B., Azarmi N. and Tsui K.: 'Soft Computing: A Tool for Building Intelligent Systems', BT Technol J, Vol. 14, No. 4, pp. 37–45 (1996).
6. Zadeh L. A.: 'The Roles of Fuzzy Logic and Soft Computing in the Conception: Design and Deployment of Intelligent Systems', BT Technol J, Vol. 14, No. 4, pp. 32–36 (1996).
7. Demolombe R.: 'Co-operative Answering from Computerised databases', CEC Project GOAL Deliverable D4, Department of Computing, Imperial College (1993).
8. Bosc P. and Pivert O.: 'About Equivalencies in SQLf, A relational Language Supporting Imprecise Querying', Proc. IFES'91 (1991).
9. Allen J and Litman D.: 'Plans, Goals, and Natural Language', Technical Report, University of Rochester (1986).
10. O'Brien P. and Wiegand M.: 'Agents of Change in Business Process Management', BT Technol J, Vol. 14, No. 4, pp. 133–140 (1996).
11. Etzioni X. and Weld O.: 'A Softbot Interface to the Internet', Intelligent Agents, CACM, Vol. 37, No.7 (1994).
12. Alterman R.: 'Adaptive Planning', Cognitive Science, Vol. 12, pp. 393–422 (1988).
13. Hammond K.: 'Case-based Planning: Viewing Planning as a Memory Task', Academic Press (1989).
14. Wooldridge N.: 'Agents and Scheduling', Proc. PAAM'96 (1996).
15. Booch G.: 'Coming of Age in an Object-Oriented World', IEEE Software (November 1994).
16. Watt S.: 'Artificial Societies and Psychological Agents', BT Technol J, Vol. 14, No. 4, pp. 89–97 (1996).
17. Franklin S. and Graesser A.: 'Is it an Agent, or just a Program?: A Taxonomy for Autonomous Agents', Proc. Third International Workshop on Agent Theories, Architectures, and Languages, Springer-Verlag (1996).
18. Nwana H. and Ndumu D.: 'An Introduction to Agent Technology', BT Technol J, Vol. 14, No. 4, pp. 55–67 (1996).

19. Smith R.: 'Invited Lecture', PAAM'96 (1996).
20. Georgeff M. and Lansky A. L.: 'Reactive Reasoning and Planning', Proceedings of the Sixth National Conference on Artificial Intelligence, pp. 677-682, Seattle, Washington (1987).
21. Rao A. S. and Georgeff M. P.: 'Modeling Rational Agents Within a BDI-architecture', Proceedings of the Second International Conference on Principles of Knowledge Representation and Reasoning, Morgan Kaufmann Publishers, San Mateo, CA (1991).
22. Lee J. and Durfee E.H.: 'Structured Circuit Semantics for Reactive Plan Execution Systems', Proceedings of the Twelfth National Conference on Artificial Intelligence, pp. 1232-1237 (1994).
23. Wilkins D. E. and Myers K. L.: 'A Common Knowledge Representation for Plan Generation and Reactive Execution', Journal of Logic and Computation, Vol. 5, No. 6, pp. 731-761 (1995).
24. Myers K. L. and Wilkins D. E.: 'The Act Formalism, Version 2.2', SRI International Artificial Intelligence Center Technical Report, Menlo Park, CA (1997).
25. Huber M. J., Lee J., Kenny P., and Durfee E.H.: 'UM-PRS Programmer and User Guide', The University of Michigan, Ann Arbor MI 48109 (1993) [see http://members. home.net/marcush/IRS].
26. Lee J., Huber M. J., Durfee E. H., and Kenny P. G.: 'UM-PRS: An Implementation of the Procedural Reasoning System for Multirobot Applications', Conference on Intelligent Robotics in Field, Factory, Service, and Space (CIRFFSS'94), pp. 842-849, Houston, Texas (1994).
27. Myers K. L.: 'User Guide for the Procedural Reasoning System', SRI International AI Center Technical Report, SRI International, Menlo Park, CA (1997).
28. Gray R. S, Kotz D., Cybenko G., and Rus D.: 'Agent Tcl', in 'Mobile Agents', eds, Cockayne W. and Zyda M., Manning Publishing (1997).
29. Laird J. E., Newell A., and Rosenbloom P. S.: 'SOAR: An Architecture for General Intelligence', AI Journal, pp. 1-64 (1987).
30. Shoham Y.: 'Agent-oriented Programming', Artificial Intelligence, Vol. 60, No. 1, pp. 51-92. (1993).
31. Shoham Y.: 'AGENT0: A Simple Agent Language and Its Interpreter', Proceedings of the Ninth National Conference on Artificial Intelligence, pp. 704-709, Anaheim, California (1991).
32. Thomas R. S.: 'The PLACA Agent Programming Language', in 'Intelligent Agents - Theories, Architectures, and Languages', eds, Wooldridge M. and Jennings N. R., pp. 356-370, Springer-Verlag (1995).
33. Newell A.: 'Unified Theories of Cognition', Harvard University Press, (1990).
34. Ferguson I. A.: 'TouringMachines: An Architecture for Dynamic, Rational Mobile Agents', Ph.D. Thesis, University of Cambridge, UK (1992).
35. Gat E.: 'Integrating Planning and Acting in a Heterogeneous Asynchronous Architecture for Controlling Real-World Mobile Robots', Proceedings of the Tenth National Conference on Artificial Intelligence, pp. 809-817, San Jose, CA (1992).
36. Huber M. J.: 'A BDI-theoretic Mobile Agent Architecture', Proceedings of the Third International Conference on Autonomous Agents (Agents'99), Seattle, WA (May 1999).
37. Lenat D. and Guha R.: 'Building Large Knowledge-Based Systems: Representation and Inference in the CYC Project', Addison-Wesley (1990).
38. Brooks R.: 'A Robust Layered Control System for a Mobile Robot', IEEE Journal of Robotics and Automation, Vol. 2, pp. 14-23 (1986).

39. Aleksander I., Evans R. G and Sales N. J: 'Towards intentional neural systems: Experiments with MAGNUS', Proc.IEE Fourth Intl. Conf. on Artificial Neural Networks, Cambridge, UK (1995).
40. Fritzson R., Finin T. McKay D. and McEntire R.: 'KQML - A Language and Protocol for Knowledge and Information Exchange', 13th International Distributed AI Workshop, Seattle (1994).
41. Eichmann D.: 'Ethical Web Agents', 2nd WWW Conference (1996).

NEFCLASS-J
– A JAVA-Based Soft Computing Tool

Detlef Nauck[1] and Rudolf Kruse[2]

[1] Intelligent Systems Research Group, BT Labs
Adastral Park, Martlesham Heath, Ipswich IP5 3RE, United Kingdom
`detlef.nauck@bt.com`
[2] University of Magdeburg, Faculty of Computer Science (FIN-IWS)
Universitaetsplatz 2, D-39106 Magdeburg, Germany
`rudolf.kruse@cs.uni-magdeburg.de`

Abstract. Neuro-fuzzy classification systems offer means to obtain fuzzy classification rules by a learning algorithm. It is usually no problem to find a suitable fuzzy classifier by learning from data; however, it can be hard to obtain a classifier that can be interpreted conveniently. There is usually a trade-off between accuracy and readability. In this paper we discuss NEFCLASS – our neuro-fuzzy approach for classification problems – and its most recent JAVA implementation NEFCLASS-J. We show how a comprehensible fuzzy classifier can be obtained by a learning process and how automatic strategies for pruning rules and variables from a trained classifier can enhance its interpretability.

1 Introduction

The term *soft computing* was coined by the father of fuzzy logic, Lotfi A. Zadeh [ ]. In contrast to *hard computing* that is based on using crisp numbers or symbols, the principal aim of soft computing is to exploit the tolerance of uncertainty and vagueness in the area of cognitive reasoning. This can lead to considerable reduction in complexity when real-world problems have to be solved. Soft computing provides easy to handle, robust, and low-priced solutions in many areas of application. In addition soft computing solutions based on fuzzy systems, for instance, are often much simpler to understand and to maintain.

The notion of soft computing subsumes several approaches like fuzzy systems, neural networks, evolutionary computation and various methods of probabilistic reasoning, and especially the combinations of these methods, like, for example, neuro-fuzzy systems.

In this paper we discuss one aspect of soft computing: neuro-fuzzy systems. Neuro-fuzzy systems are usually described as combinations of neural networks and fuzzy systems. However, this description is far too "fuzzy". We prefer to think of neuro-fuzzy approaches as a special way to learn fuzzy systems from data. Our interpretation is described by the following five points [ ].

– A neuro-fuzzy system is a fuzzy system trained by a (heuristical) learning algorithm (usually) derived from neural networks.

B. Azvine et al. (Eds.): Intelligent Systems and Soft Computing, LNAI 1804, pp. 139– , 2000.
© Springer-Verlag Berlin Heidelberg 2000

- A neuro-fuzzy system can be represented by a feed-forward neural network architecture. However, this is not a prerequisite to training, it is merely a convenience to visualise the structure and the flow of data.
- A neuro-fuzzy system can always be interpreted in terms of fuzzy if-then rules.
- A neuro-fuzzy system's training procedure takes the semantics of the underlying fuzzy model into account to preserve the linguistic interpretability of the model.
- A neuro-fuzzy system performs (special cases of) function approximation. It has nothing to do with fuzzy logic in the narrow sense, i.e. generalised logical rules.

Modern neuro-fuzzy systems are often represented as multilayer feedforward neural networks [, , , , ,]. In addition, there are also combinations of fuzzy techniques with other neural network architectures, for example self-organising feature maps [,], or fuzzy associative memories [ ]. Some approaches refrain from representing a fuzzy system in a network architecture. They just apply a learning procedure to the parameters of the fuzzy system, or explicitly use a neural network to determine them. There are several different approaches which have much in common, but differ in implementational aspects. For an overview on neuro-fuzzy systems see for example [, ,].

In this paper we discuss neuro-fuzzy modelling in the area of classification. Classification of customer data, for instance, is an important data analysis problem for modern companies. It is for example important to know if a customer may be interested in a certain mailing, if certain services should be offered to him, or if there is a danger that he might cancel a contract.

Classical approaches to classification usually use statistical methods like discriminant analysis. But statistical approaches are often based on assumptions that do not hold for real world data and the results can be hard to interpret. The readability of a solution, however, is often very important for its acceptance and application.

It is also possible to use a fuzzy system for classification. A fuzzy classifier is based on linguistic (fuzzy) rules like, for example,

> **if**   income is *high* **and** *age* is *approximately 40* **and**
> ... **and** residence area is *middle class*
> **then** customer belongs to class *A*,

where the vague expressions like *high, approximately 40*, etc, are represented by fuzzy sets.

What is the advantage of having another method for classification? A fuzzy classifier is not a replacement for methods like statistics or other forms of machine learning and it does not yield better results. Fuzzy classification offers a different way of achieving the same goal. If a decision is made for a fuzzy classifier usually the following advantages are considered:

- vague knowledge can be used;
- the classifier is interpretable in form of linguistic rules;
- from an applicational point of view the classifier is easy to implement, to use and to understand.

It is necessary to stress that fuzzy classifiers that use rules like the one given above are only useful, if direct dependencies of features to class informations are to be modelled. It is implicitly assumed that the features themselves are independent of each other. If more complex domains must be modelled, where dependencies or conditional independencies between all variables of a given problem have to be explicitly represented, then graphical models (dependency networks) like, for instance, Bayesian networks [,] or possibilistic networks [,] should be preferred. Fuzzy classifiers can be viewed as an alternative to neural networks, regression models, or nearest-neighbour classifiers, if the above-mentioned advantages are of interest.

Neuro-fuzzy classification systems offer means to obtain fuzzy classification rules by a learning algorithm. It is usually no problem to find a suitable fuzzy classifier by learning from data, however, it can be hard to obtain a classifier that can be interpreted conveniently. In this paper we discuss NEFCLASS [ ], a **ne**uro-fuzzy approach for **clas**sification. NEFCLASS especially aims at obtaining interpretable results, because it constrains the learning algorithm and allows the user to interactively influence the training process. The interpretability of the learning result can be improved by interactive strategies for pruning rules and variables from a trained classifier.

2   Building Fuzzy Classifiers

We consider the task to assign a pattern which is a vector $\mathbf{x} = (x_1, \ldots, x_n) \in \mathbb{R}^n$ to a class C which is a subset of $\mathbb{R}^n$. We want to solve this task by learning fuzzy classification rules from a set of labelled training data, where each pattern of the training set is assigned to the class it most likely belongs to. The fuzzy rules used to classify the data are of the form:

$R :$ **if** x_1 is μ_1 **and** x_2 is μ_2 **and** $\ldots$ **and** x_n is μ_n **then** the pattern $(x_1, x_2, \ldots, x_n)$ belongs to class C_i, where $\mu_1, \ldots, \mu_n$ are fuzzy sets.

Such a rule is evaluated by determining the degree of membership of each feature $x_i \in \mathbb{R}$ to the respective fuzzy set $\mu_i : \mathbb{R} \rightarrow [0, 1]$ in the antecedent of the rule. The degrees of membership are combined by the minimum that is used to implement the operator "and". The resulting number from $[0, 1]$ indicates the degree of membership to the class $C_i \subseteq \mathbb{R}^n$ specified in the consequent of the rule. This way a pattern can belong to several classes with different degrees of membership.

The task of the NEFCLASS approach is to discover these rules and to learn the shape of the membership functions to determine the correct class or category of a given input pattern. The patterns' feature values are described by linguistic terms (like *big, small,* etc) which are represented by fuzzy sets. The complete classifier consists of a number of linguistic rules (fuzzy rules).

The main goal of NEFCLASS is to create a readable classifier that also provides an acceptable accuracy. However, the user has to be aware that readability and accuracy usually do not go together. An interpretable fuzzy system should display the following features:

- few meaningful fuzzy rules with few variables in their antecedents;
- few meaningful fuzzy sets for each variable;
- there are no rule weights [ ];
- identical linguistic terms are represented by identical fuzzy sets;
- only normal fuzzy sets are used, or even better fuzzy numbers or fuzzy intervals [ ].

These features pose a lot of restrictions on how a fuzzy system can be created from training data. If a high performance of the fuzzy system is the main goal, then it is necessary to fit the system to the data very accurately. This approach, however, usually yields fuzzy systems that do not display the above-mentioned features [ ] and are in fact black-box models. A user has therefore to decide what is more important – accuracy or readability. NEFCLASS provides means to ensure the readability of the solution by giving the user complete control over the learning process. It should also be stressed that interpretable solutions can usually not be obtained without the user's co-operation. The user must decide whether the solution's readability is sufficient or not, and must be ready to influence the learning process when necessary. NEFCLASS must be seen as a tool that *supports* users in finding readable fuzzy classifiers. It is *not* an automatic classifier creator where data is fed in and a solution pops out. It is necessary that the user *works* with the tool (with *work* being the operative word).

For this reason it is necessary that NEFCLASS uses only very fast learning strategies to give users the possibility to interact with the tool. Therefore NEFCLASS does not induce fuzzy classification rules by searching for clusters, but by selecting rules from a grid (Fig.). By specifying initial fuzzy sets for each feature the data space is structured, i.e. we provide a certain granularity for the feature space. Rules are found in this structure by finding places that contain data. Afterwards the fuzzy sets are tuned to enhance the performance of the rule base. The learning algorithm operates only on single dimensions, and it does not need to handle the high-dimensional features space simultaneously. It is therefore a much simpler and faster approach like, for instance, cluster analysis approaches that create fuzzy rules from data by searching for hyper-ellipsoidal [ ] or hyper-rectangular clusters [,].

In fuzzy clustering approaches [,] fuzzy rules are constructed by projecting clusters onto the single dimensions [ ]. In the case of hyper-ellipsoidal clusters the projection causes a loss of information (see Fig.) which is avoided, when hyper-rectangular clusters are used [ ]. However, in both cases the induced fuzzy rules are sometimes not easy to interpret. NEFCLASS modifies the fuzzy sets directly, and can therefore use constraints to make sure that the induced fuzzy rules can be interpreted well.

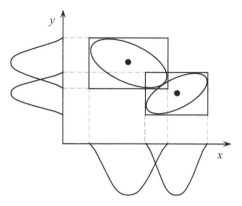

Fig. 1. If fuzzy rules are created by projecting ellipsoidal cluster a loss of information occurs – the resulting rule is only equivalent to an encompassing hyper-box

3   The Architecture of the NEFCLASS Model

A NEFCLASS model is a fuzzy classifier represented as a 3-layer feedforward architecture that is derived from a generic fuzzy perceptron [ ] (Fig.).

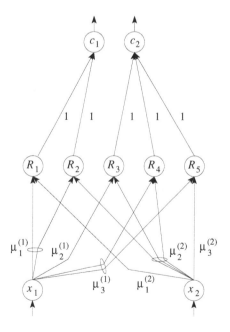

Fig. 2. The architecture of the NEFCLASS model

The first layer U_1 contains the input units representing the pattern features. The activation a_x of a unit $x \in U_1$ is usually equal to its external input. However, it can be different, if the input unit does some kind of preprocessing (normalisation, etc). The hidden layer U_2 holds k rule units representing k fuzzy rules, and the third layer U_3 consists of output units, one for each class. The activation of a rule unit $R \in U_2$, and the activation of an output unit $c \in U_3$ when a pattern **p** is propagated are computed by:

$$a_R^{(p)} = \min_{x \in U_1} \{W(x, R)(a_x^{(p)})\},$$

$$a_c^{(p)} = \max_{R \in U_2} \{a_R^{(p)}\},$$

or alternatively: $a_c^{(p)} = \sum_{\{R | R \in U_2 \wedge W(R,c) > 0\}} \dfrac{W(R, c) \cdot a_R^{(p)}}{W(R, c)},$

where $W(x, R)$ is the *fuzzy weight* on the connection from input unit x to rule unit R. $W(R, c)$ is the weight on the connection from rule unit R to output unit c. For semantical reasons all these weights are fixed at 1, if a connections exists, or at 0, if no connection exists [ ].

Alternatively, the output activation can be computed by a weighted sum instead of a maximum operation. This can be selected in accordance to the application problem. Instead of min and max, other t-norms and t-conorms can be used.

The rule base is an approximation of an (unknown) function $\varphi : \mathbb{R}^n \to \{0, 1\}^m$ that represents the classification task where $\varphi(\mathbf{x}) = (c_1, \ldots, c_m)$ such that $c_i = 1$ and $c_j = 0$ ($j \in \{1, \ldots, m\}, j \neq i$), i.e. **x** belongs to class C_i. Because of the mathematics involved the rule base actually does not approximate φ but the function $\varphi' : \mathbb{R}^n \to [0, 1]^m$. We will get $\varphi(\mathbf{x})$ by $\varphi(\mathbf{x}) = \psi(\varphi'(\mathbf{x}))$, where ψ reflects the interpretation of the classification result obtained from a NEFCLASS system. In our case we will map the highest component of each vector **c** to 1 and its other components to 0 to determine the most likely class of a pattern (winner takes all). The information provided by the output vector can be additionally used to indicate overlapping of classes, or to reject certain classifications, for example, if a pattern is mapped to two classes with equal degrees of membership.

To represent a fuzzy classifier in the form of a feedforward network has some advantages. For example, it is obvious that NEFCASS uses *shared weights* on some of the connections (in Fig.   this is shown by ellipses drawn around the connections). This way we make sure, that for each linguistic value (e.g. "x_1 is *positive big*") there is only one representation as a fuzzy set. It cannot happen that two fuzzy sets that are identical at the beginning of the learning process develop differently, and so the semantics of the rule base encoded in the structure of the network is not affected [ ]. Connections that share a weight always come from the same input unit. In Fig.   the hidden nodes R_2 and R_4 represent the rules

$$R_2: \text{if } x_1 \text{ is } \mu_2^{(1)} \text{ and } x_2 \text{ is } \mu_2^{(2)} \text{ then pattern belongs to class } C_1$$
$$R_4: \text{if } x_1 \text{ is } \mu_3^{(1)} \text{ and } x_2 \text{ is } \mu_2^{(2)} \text{ then pattern belongs to class } C_2$$

Both rules use "x_2 is $\mu_2^{(2)}$" in their antecedents. NEFCLASS makes sure that the representation of the fuzzy set $\mu_2^{(2)}$ is identical in both rules. The graph representation of the classifier visualizes the data flow through the model, both for learning (backward path) and classification (forward path). It is more easy to compare NEFCLASS to other fuzzy classification approaches, when the representation as a feedforward network is chosen.

This is the reason that graphical representations of neuro-fuzzy approaches are still predominant in the literature. However, it should be noted that this kind of representation is not a prerequisite for applying a learning procedure, it is merely a convenience.

The fuzzy sets and the linguistic rules which perform the classification, and define the structure of the resulting NEFCLASS model, are obtained from a set of examples by learning. The following section briefly describes the idea of the learning algorithm.

4   Learning Techniques in NEFCLASS-J

A NEFCLASS system can be built from partial knowledge about the patterns, and can then be refined by learning, or it can be created from scratch by learning. A user has to define a number of initial fuzzy sets partitioning the domains of the input features.

The previously published learning algorithm for NEFCLASS was not able to cope with missing values and symbolic data. Also the number of rules had to be given in advance and pruning required user interaction [,]. The new learning algorithm that is implemented in NEFCLASS-J [,] provides the following functionalities:

- fuzzy rule learning;
- automatic determination of the number of rules;
- prior knowledge can be used;
- constrained fuzzy set training;
- training different types of membership functions (triangular, trapezoidal, bell-shaped, discrete);
- online or batch learning;
- treatment of missing values;
- using both numeric *and* symbolic data;
- automatic pruning strategies;
- automatic cross-validation.

Real world data often has missing values and data analysis software must deal with it. Usually fill-in strategies are used that replace missing values, for example, with a mean value, or the EM algorithm for learning is applied. NEFCLASS deals with missing values by assuming that any value may be possible in such a case.

Symbolic information is also very often contained in real world data and it is often transformed to artificial metric scales. However, it would be useful to be able to create fuzzy rules from data that contains symbolic variables without converting them. NEFCLASS-J can deal with symbolic data by using so-called *mixed* fuzzy rules [ ].

In learning fuzzy rule bases the number of fuzzy rules must often be given in advance. Neuro-fuzzy approaches that automatically determine the number of rules [ ] can create strongly overlapping rules that can be hard to interpret. Another way is to partition the variables by membership functions and to use all rules that cover some training data [ ]. This usually leads to large rule bases. The previous version of NEFCLASS reduced the number of rules by selection procedures, but the user had to specify a maximum number of rules. NEFCLASS-J now tries to find a minimal number of the best fuzzy rules that cover all training data. The new pruning strategies of NEFCLASS-J also support this approach, by identifying rules that can be removed from the rule base, if they cover only a small amount of data that is also sufficiently covered by other rules.

In the following we briefly discuss the steps of the learning algorithm. For details please refer to Nauck [,]. To create a fuzzy classifier with NEFCLASS-J the following includes the following steps.

1. Set up an initial fuzzy partition for each variable, thus creating a grid structure of overlapping hyperboxes in the data space. Each hyperbox is a potential fuzzy rule.
2. Select the best k fuzzy rules from the grid structure. This is done by selecting each hyperbox that contains data and ranking them according to their performance. The value of k is either determined automatically such that all training patterns are covered by a rule, or the user sets a maximum value for k.
3. Iteratively process all patterns of the training set and use the classification error in a backpropagation-like algorithm to update the parameters of the membership functions.
4. Start the automatic pruning process in order to delete superfluous variables and to reduce the size of the rule base.
5. If desired, repeat the process on subsets of the training data (cross-validation).

NEFCLASS-J at first creates an initial rule base consisting of all rules that are supported by the training data. The maximum number of rules is bound from above by:

$$\min\left\{ \left|\tilde{\mathcal{L}}\right|, \ \prod_{i}^{n} q_i \right\}$$

where $\left|\tilde{\mathcal{L}}\right|$ is the cardinality of the training data set and q_i is the number of fuzzy sets provided for variable x_i. Usually the number of rules will be much smaller, because we can expect most training data to have a clustered structure.

Rule learning is a very fast procedure and requires two cycles through the training set. In the first cycle all antecedents are identified, and in the second cycle the best consequent for each antecedent is determined and performance values for the rules are computed. We use μ_r to denote the antecedent of rule R_r. With $\mu_r(\mathbf{p}) = \min\{\mu_r^{(1)}(x_1), \ldots, \mu_r^{(n)}(x_n)\}$ we denote the degree of fulfilment of a rule given input pattern $\mathbf{p}$. The consequent is a class label c_r. Let class$(\mathbf{p})$ denote the class of $\mathbf{p}$. The performance of a rule $R_r = (\mu_r, c_r)$ is defined as:

$$\text{perf}_r = \frac{1}{|\tilde{\mathcal{L}}|} \sum_{\substack{(\mathbf{p},\mathbf{t})\in\tilde{\mathcal{L}} \\ \text{class}(\mathbf{p})=c_r}} \mu_r(\mathbf{p}) \cdot t_{c_r} - \sum_{\substack{(\mathbf{p},\mathbf{t})\in\tilde{\mathcal{L}} \\ \text{class}(\mathbf{p})\neq c_r}} \mu_r(\mathbf{p}) \cdot (1 - t_{c_r}).$$

For the performance $-1 \leq \text{perf}_r \leq 1$ holds, where $\text{perf}_r = 1$, if all training patterns are correctly classified by the rule and each training pattern $\mathbf{p}$ is assigned to exactly one class by its target vector $\mathbf{t}$. If a rule classifies all patterns perfectly wrong, $\text{perf}_r = -1$ holds. For $\text{perf}_r = 0$ the rule either covers no patterns or causes as many errors as correct classifications.

The goal of the rule learning algorithm is to construct a rule base consisting only of rules with large positive performance values. The final rule base can be created by one of two evaluation procedures - *best* or *best per class* selection. The first option orders the rules by their performance and selects the best rules. This can result in a rule base that does not cover all classes, if the number of rules is fixed. The second selection scheme avoids this by selecting an equal number of rules for each class according to the performance values.

The problem of rule learning is to specify a suitable rule base size. The algorithm can automatically determine the size of the rule base by continuing to select rules by one of the two selection schemes until all training patterns are covered by at least one rule. If the rule base becomes too large by this approach, it can be reduced by applying the automatic pruning strategies after training the membership functions.

After the rule base has been determined, the algorithm begins to train the membership functions in order to increase the performance of the whole classifier. The training process is based on backpropagating the output error, but without performing gradient descent. This is not possible, because the t-norm used to compute the degree of fulfilment and the membership function may not be differentiable. Instead simple and computationally efficient heuristics are used to shift the fuzzy sets and to enlarge or reduce their supports depending on the error [ ]. The training of the membership functions is usually constrained in order to obtain interpretable fuzzy sets. Depending on the demands of the user, the modifications must meet one or more of several constraints, for example:

- a membership function must not pass one of its neighbours;
- membership functions must be symmetrical;
- degrees of membership must add up to 1 for each value (i.e. membership functions intersect at a degree of membership of 0.5).

The goal of applying NEFCLASS is to find a comprehensible classifier. However, a good interpretation of the learning result cannot always be guaranteed, especially for high-dimensional problems. Because interpretation is one reason for using a fuzzy classifier in the first place, there is a need to enhance the learning algorithms of a neuro-fuzzy system with pruning techniques for simplifying the obtained result.

Pruning is based on a simple greedy algorithm that does not need to compute complex test values as it is sometimes necessary in neural network pruning methods. NEFCLASS-J uses four heuristic strategies that were already defined for previous implementations [,], but now pruning is done in an automatic fashion without the necessity of user interaction. The pruning strategies are given in the following list.

1. Pruning by correlation: the variable that has the smallest influence on the classification is deleted. To identify this variable statistical measures like correlations and χ^2 tests or information theoretic measures like information gain can be used.
2. Pruning by classification frequency: the rule that yields the largest degree of fulfilment in the least number of cases is deleted.
3. Pruning by redundancy: the linguistic term that yields the minimal degree of membership in an active rule in the least number of cases is deleted.
4. Pruning by fuzziness: the fuzzy set with the largest support is identified and all terms that use this fuzzy set are removed from the antecedents of all rules.

After each pruning step the membership functions are trained again. Each of these four pruning strategies is iterated until a pruning step fails. Then the next pruning strategy is selected. If the rule base becomes inconsistent during pruning (which may happen in steps (1), (2), (4)) the inconsistencies are automatically resolved by deleting contradictory rules or generalisations/specialisations of rules according to their performance values until the rule base is consistent again. Pruning will not remove the last rule for a class. A pruning step fails, if the error has increased after training the membership functions, or if the rule base cannot be made consistent again. In this case the pruning step is undone.

The learning algorithm is visualised by Fig. . The first part of Fig. shows how rules are selected from a grid structure in feature space that is given by the fuzzy sets of the individual variables. The second part of the figure displays the situation after the learning algorithm for the membership functions was applied to improve the classification result.

5   Using NEFCLASS-J

In this section we show how NEFCLASS-J can be used to obtain a classifier from data by using the Iris data set [ ] and the Wisconsin Breast Cancer (WBC) data set [ ].

NEFCLASS-J is a JAVA application that implements the NEFCLASS approach and provides a graphical user interface (Fig.). The tool provides a rule editor that can be used to modify the rule base manually or to provide prior

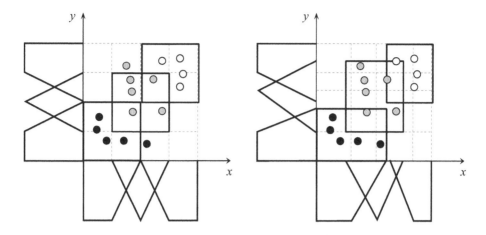

Fig. 3. NEFCLASS selects rules from a grid structure (left) and modifies membership functions in order to improve the classification result (right)

knowledge. The rule base can be written to a text file. During the training process the user can observe a plot of the classification error and the changes in the membership functions. The learning process can be interrupted at any time in order to modify learning parameters. The classification result is given both in the form of a confusion matrix and as a result file where each case is classified. The software can be run on any platform for which a JAVA runtime environment is available. NEFCLASS-J is available from http://fuzzy.cs.uni-magdeburg.de.

In the following subsections we discuss three examples. First we show how NEFCLASS-J creates a classifier when the training data contains missing values. Then we briefly show how a small rule base can be obtained by pruning. These two experiments use the Iris data. The last experiment uses the WBC data set to show how NEFCLASS-J handles data that contains symbolical and numerical features.

5.1   Example 1 – Missing Values

Missing values are common in many practical settings. It is not always possible to observe all features of a pattern. This can be due to high costs, faulty sensors, errors in recording, etc. If a feature is sometimes measured and sometimes not, we can use the cases for which it has been measured to learn to predict its values when it is not. In decision tree learning, for example, the probability distribution of the feature is used when a value is missing [ ]. Another approach to learning in the presence of unobserved variables is the EM algorithm (estimation and maximisation) [,]. The EM algorithm searches for a maximum likelihood hypothesis by repeatedly re-estimating the expected values of the unobserved variables given the current hypothesis, then recalculating the maximum likelihood hypothesis using these expected values [ ].

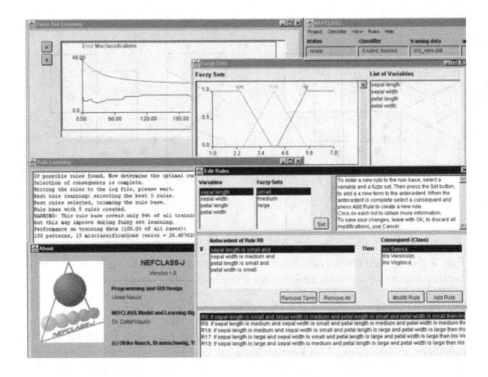

Fig. 4. Overview of the graphical user interface of NEFCLASS-J

Other approaches to deal with missing data [38] are:

− to use only cases with complete data;
− to delete cases and/or variables with missing data with excessive levels;
− to use imputation methods that replace missing values with a constant, the mean, a value computed by regression, etc.

For NEFCLASS we use the following simple strategy. If a feature is missing, we do not make any assumptions about its value but assume that any value may be possible. Based on this assumption we do not want to restrict the application of a fuzzy rule to a pattern with missing features. This means a missing value will not influence the computation of the degree of fulfilment of a rule. This can be done by assigning 1.0 as the degree of membership to the missing feature [39], i.e. a missing value has a degree of membership of 1.0 with any fuzzy set. A pattern where all features are missing would then fulfil any rule of the fuzzy rule base with a degree of 1.0, i.e. any class would be possible for such a pattern. We denote a pattern with missing values by $\mathbf{p} = (\mathbf{x}, ?)$. According to Berthold and Huber [39] we compute the degree of fulfilment μ_r of some rule R_r by:

$$\mu_r(\mathbf{x}, ?) = \min_{x_i} \{\mu_r^{(i)}(x_i), 1\} = \min_{x_i} \{\mu_r^{(i)}(x_i)\}.$$

In NEFCLASS we must consider three stages where missing values must be considered:

1. learning fuzzy rules;
2. training membership functions;
3. classification of patterns.

Item (3) was just considered above. Berthold and Huber [ ] suggested to complete an input pattern with missing values by using the fuzzy rule base of the classifier during training. We will not use this approach here, because it cannot be used for rule learning and we want to use the same technique in all three stages.

Rule learning in NEFCLASS consists of three steps:

1. determine all possible antecedents;
2. create an initial rule base by finding an appropriate consequent for each antecedent;
3. select a final rule base from the initial rule base by computing the performance of each rule.

Step (1) is implemented by the Wang/Mendel approach [ ]. This means antecedents are created by selecting hyperboxes from a structured data space (structure-oriented approach [ ]). If we encounter a missing value, any fuzzy set can be included in the antecedent for the corresponding variable. Therefore we create all combinations of fuzzy sets that are possible for the current training pattern.

Example: Consider the situation in Fig. . We use three fuzzy sets to partition each variable. If we obtain the input pattern $(x_0, ?)$ as shown in Fig. we can assign the fuzzy set *large* to the first feature, because it yields the largest degree of membership for x_0. As the value for y is missing, any fuzzy set is possible for y. Therefore we create the antecedents (x is *large* and y is *small*), (x is *large* and y is *medium*), and (x is *large* and y is *large*). In step (2) of the rule-learning algorithm appropriate consequents will be determined for these antecedents, depending on all training patterns. In step (3) the rules with the highest performance will be selected.

After a rule base was created, the membership functions are trained by NEFCLASS. If a missing value is encountered, then for the corresponding fuzzy set simply no training signal will be generated from this pattern.

As a simple example to demonstrate the capabilities of handling missing values we used the Iris data set. The Iris data is a well-known benchmark for classification approaches, although it represents a very simple classification problem. The data set consists of 150 patterns with 4 features. There are 3 classes (iris setosa, iris virginica and iris versicolour) that each contain 50 patterns. The first and second class are linearly separable to each other, and the second and third class slightly overlap.

The results are given in Table . For the first experiment we randomly deleted one feature in 30 randomly selected cases. For the second experiment we randomly deleted 85 values from 70 randomly selected cases in the data set, i.e. now there are also cases where more than one feature is missing.

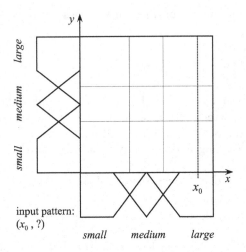

Fig. 5. Rule learning with missing values: three rules are created by the pattern $(x_0, ?)$, because for y three fuzzy sets are possible

Table 1. Results for the Iris data with different numbers of missing values

missing values	rules	error training	error test
0	9	3	2
30	6	4	2
85	7	4	5

For learning, the data set was randomly split in two stratified samples each containing 75 patterns. One sample was used for training and the other for validation. The rule-learning procedure automatically determined the number of rules (see Section   ) and continued to train the membership functions until no further improvement on the validation set was observed (stop training method). As we can see in Table   the number of classification errors slightly increases with the number of missing values.

5.2   Example 2 – Rule Learning and Pruning

To illustrate automatic rule learning and pruning we again use the Iris data set (no missing values). Like in Section   we use one half of the data for training and the other half for validation. For this experiment we chose to partition each variable by three trapezoidal fuzzy sets *small, medium, large*, where *small* and *large* are only half trapezoids attached to the boundaries of the domains.

Automatic rule learning with *best per class* selection creates a rule base with nine rules. After training the membership functions for 100 cycles with batch learning (offline learning) we obtain five errors on the training set and six errors on the validation set.

The pruning algorithm starts with pruning by correlation and removes x_2, x_1 and x_3 in the first three steps resulting in rule bases of six, four and three rules respectively. The final rule base causes four errors on the training set and two errors on the validation set and uses just variable x_4 (petal width):

R_1: if x_4 is *small* then Iris setosa
R_2: if x_4 is *medium* then Iris versicolor
R_3: if x_4 is *large* then Iris virginica

The membership functions of x_4 are given in Fig. .

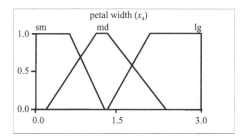

Fig. 6. Fuzzy sets for petal width

5.3   Example 3 – Numerical and Symbolical Data

To illustrate how NEFCLASS-J can handle training data that contains symbolical and numerical features we use the WBC data set, which is a breast cancer database that was provided by W.H. Wolberg from the University of Wisconsin Hospitals, Madison [ ]. The data set contains 699 cases and 16 of these cases have missing values. Although the NEFCLASS-J can handle data with missing values (compare Section   ), we deleted those cases, because other approaches with which we compare our result (see Table) cannot handle missing values.

Each case is represented by an identification number and nine attributes (x_1: clump thickness, x_2: uniformity of cell size, x_3: uniformity of cell shape, x_4: marginal adhesion, x_5: single epithelial cell size, x_6: bare nuclei, x_7: bland chromatin, x_8: normal nucleoli, x_9: mitoses). All attributes are from the domain $\{1, \ldots, 10\}$. Each case belongs to one of two classes (benign: 458 cases, or malignant: 241 cases). The values of all nine variables are actually from an ordinal scale. Classifiers usually simply treat them as metric values and good classification results can be obtained this way (see Table).

To test the learning algorithm we chose to interpret variables x_3 and x_6 as symbolical (categorical) variables and the rest as metric variables. We chose x_3

Table 2. The confusion matrix of the final classifier obtained by NEFCLASS-J

			Predicted Class					
	malign		benign		not classified		sum	
malign	222	(32.50%)	17	(2.49%)	0	(0.00%)	239	(34.99%)
benign	12	(1.76%)	432	(63.25%)	0	(0.00%)	444	(65.01%)
sum	234	(34.26%)	449	(65.74%)	0	(0.00%)	683	(100.00%)

correct: 654 (95.75%), misclassified: 29 (4.25%), error: 58.32.

and x_6 because these two variables are usually considered as influential by other classification approaches applied to the WBC data.

For training we used 10-fold cross validation, and let the tool select the best two rules per class during rule learning. For each metric variable two initial membership functions were given (half trapezoids). The fuzzy sets for the symbolical variables were created during rule learning [ ]. The fuzzy sets were trained until the error on the validation set could not be further decreased, but not longer than 300 cycles.

The final classifier contains only two rules using one or two variables:

1. if x_2 (uniformity of cell size) is *small* and
   x_6 (bare nuclei) is $term_1^{(6)}$ then *benign*;
2. if x_2 (uniformity of cell size) is *large* then *malign*.

The membership functions after training are shown in Fig. . The (discrete) fuzzy set for the symbolical variable x_6 is drawn as a histogram. Its exact representation is:

$$term_1^{(6)} = \{(1, 1.0), (2, 0.99), (3, 0.75), (4, 0.63),$$
$$(5, 0.68), (6, 0.0), (7, 0.14), (8, 0.02),$$
$$(9, 0.0), (10, 0.22)\}.$$

This classifier causes 29 misclassifications (4.25%) on the *training data* (see Table), i.e. its classification rate is 95.75%. The error estimation for *unseen data* obtained from cross validation yields 3.95% ± 1.88% misclassifications, i.e. an estimated classification rate of 96.05% ± 1.88% (99% confidence interval). This error estimation must be interpreted this way: a classifier that is obtained by the described learning procedure and using the described parameters and training data is estimated to produce an error of 3.95% ± 1.88% on unseen data.

The final rule base was also discovered in three of the validation cycles. Altogether seven different rule bases were discovered during validation (nine rule bases with two rules, one rule base with three rules). However, most of the other rule bases were very similar and differed only in additionally using the other symbolical variable x_3, using x_3 instead of x_2, or using just x_2.

Table compares the result obtained with NEFCLASS-J (last entry) to results obtained with other approaches including a previous release of NEFCLASS

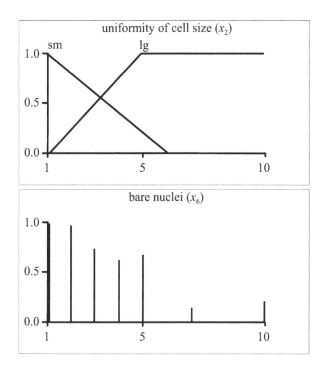

Fig. 7. Membership functions for the metric variable x_2 and the symbolical variable x_6 after training

for Unix workstations (NEFCLASS-X [ ]) The classification performance on unseen data is very good and the classifier is very compact. The error estimates given in column "Validation" of Table   are either obtained from 1-leave-out cross validation, 10-fold cross validation, or from testing the solution once by holding out 50% of the data for a test set.

6   Application of NEFCLASS-J

NEFCLASS-J can be applied in every domain, where a classifier is needed, and where certain properties of the classifier are of interest:

– comprehensibility (instead of a black box model);
– simplicity and tolerance for vagueness (instead of a very accurate but complex model);
– low cost (instead of a long identification process for complex models).

The problem that is to be solved by NEFCLASS-J should have the following characteristics:

– direct dependency between input variables and classification, i.e. it is sufficient to assume independency between the inputs;

Table 3. Comparing the NEFCLASS learning outcome for the WBC data set to some other approaches. Numbers in () are mean values from cross validation. The column "Error" contains an estimated error for unseen data

Model	Tool	Remarks	Error	Validation
Discriminant Analysis	SPSS	linear model 9 variables	3.95%	1-leave-out
Multilayer Perceptron	SNNS	4 hidden units, RProp	5.18%	50% test set
Decision Tree	C4.5	31 (24.4) nodes, pruned	4.9%	10-fold
Rules from Decision Tree	C4.5rules	8 (7.5) rules using 1–3 variables	4.6%	10-fold
NEFCLASS (metric variables)	NEFCLASS-X (Unix version)	2 (2.1) rules using 5–6 variables	4.94%	10-fold
NEFCLASS (2 symbolical variables)	NEFCLASS-J (Java version)	2 (2.1) rules using 1–3 variables	3.95%	10-fold

- there is no deep knowledge about the distribution of the data or the dependency of the variables;
- the problem is of low dimensionality (approximately less then 20 input variables);
- it is more important to obtain a rough solution fast, than to find a very accurate solution in a long process.

For medical problems, symptoms or test results can be used to classify patients. Especially for medical applications it is important to stress that there is usually no desire for automatic classification. It is more important to support the decision-making process of the physician and to provide further information. A classifier build with NEFCLASS-J can do this. The physician can easily check the classifier for plausibility. He or she can verify why a certain classification result was obtained for a certain patient, by checking the degree of fulfilment of the individual fuzzy rules. Instead of a simple classification the physician also gets a description of the patient in terms of the fuzzy rules that are active for this patient. An example in the area of breast cancer diagnosis is discussed in Nauck and Kruse [,].

In stock market analysis there is often a lot of vague expert knowledge available from brokers. NEFCLASS-J is especially suitable in environments, where prior knowledge exists, because such knowledge can be conveniently integrated into the classifier before training. This is usually not the case for other classification methods like statistics, neural networks, etc. In Siekmann et al [ ] another neuro-fuzzy model researched by our group in cooperation with Siemens AG is described. It was applied to the prediction of the daily German stock market index DAX, and refined prior expert knowledge by training. The applied neuro-fuzzy model differs from NEFCLASS in using an architecture that was especially designed to be implemented in the neural network simulation environment SENN.

For insurance companies the classification of customers is very important, e.g. to realize cross-selling strategies or to do risk assessment. In an ongoing industrial project we apply NEFCLASS-J to determine customers that are about to cancel their contract and customers who should be offered new contracts. In this setting we also research the possibility to build meta-models with NEFCLASS-J.

Insurance companies often send customer records to local representatives in order to contact the customers and offer them additional contracts. To reduce the costs involved in this process it is important to identify customers very accurately. However, the sales personal likes to know, why certain selected people are considered to be promising new customers. If there are a lot of misclassified records, the sales personal tends to generalise these errors to all selected records and looses motivation to further contact the selected persons. If the sales persons receive also a simple linguistic description why the records they obtained were selected, they can check the description for plausibility and can verify the customer data against it. If a customer record fits the linguistic description only to some extent, this can be used as an explanation for an unsuccessful contact to the respective customer. The sales person has also the possibility to rank the customer records according to their correspondence with the model, in order to contact the most promising customers first.

NEFCLASS-J can be used to provide a simple linguistic description of the classification result, but another more accurate classifier may be used to actually process the customer data, if the performance of the simple descriptive model obtained by NEFCLASS-J turns out to be not sufficient.

In this case a second less accurate but more readable classifier obtained by NEFCLASS-J functions a (simplified) meta-model for the first classifier which is actually used as a model for the customer data. The first (very accurate) classifier can be realized by any approach, e.g. statistics or neural networks. But of course it can also be realized with NEFCLASS-J by using more membership functions and more rules to obtain a more accurate (but less readable) classifier.

7 Conclusions

We have discussed our neuro-fuzzy model NEFCLASS and its implementation NEFCLASS-J. The tool supports a user to obtain a readable fuzzy classifier by learning from data. In addition to the learning strategies the tool allows to simplify a rule base by several interactive pruning methods. The example that we discussed above shows that a neuro-fuzzy approach is mainly suitable as a development tool. It cannot do all the work, the user still has to make an effort to obtain a sufficiently interpretable solution. The user must decide if the obtained classifier is sufficient for his or her purposes. While the user works with the tool he or she gains some knowledge about the data. This knowledge can be used to restart the training process to obtain more suitable solutions – classifiers that are either more comprehensible or more accurate – depending on the demands of the user. An accurate **and** interpretable fuzzy classifier can usually not simply be found by an automatic learning process. The price for readability has to be paid for by a loss in accuracy.

The learning and pruning strategies of NEFCLASS are simple and fast heuristics, and they are not supposed to function as an automatic process to create a fuzzy system. The user must be able to supervise and interpret the learning procedure in all its stages. The NEFCLASS-J software provides this functionality. The software tool and the data that was used by us to obtain the results presented in this paper, can be found at http://fuzzy.cs.uni-magdeburg.de.

References

1. Zadeh L. A.: 'Soft computing and fuzzy logic'. IEEE Software, Vol. 11(6), pp. 48–56 (1994).
2. Nauck D., Klawonn F. and Kruse R.: 'Foundations of Neuro-Fuzzy Systems'. Chichester, Wiley (1997).   ,   ,   ,
3. Berenji H. R. and Khedkar P.: 'Learning and tuning fuzzy logic controllers through reinforcements'. IEEE Trans. Neural Networks, Vol. 3, pp. 724–740 (1992).
4. Buckley J. J. and Hayashi Y.: 'Fuzzy neural networks: A survey'. Fuzzy Sets and Systems, Vol. 66, pp. 1–13 (1994).
5. Buckley J. J. and Hayashi Y.: 'Neural networks for fuzzy systems'. Fuzzy Sets and Systems, Vol. 71, pp. 265–276 (1995).
6. Halgamuge S. K. and Glesner M.: 'Neural networks in designing fuzzy systems for real world applications'. Fuzzy Sets and Systems, Vol. 65, pp. 1–12 (1994).
7. Jang J. S. R.: 'ANFIS: Adaptive-network-based fuzzy inference systems'. IEEE Trans. Systems, Man & Cybernetics, Vol. 23, pp. 665–685 (1993).
8. Tschichold Gürman N.: 'Generation and improvement of fuzzy classifiers with incremental learning using fuzzy rulenet'. In 'Applied Computing 1995. Proc. 1995 ACM Symposium on Applied Computing, Nashville, Feb. 26–28', K. M. George, J. H. Carrol, E. Deaton, D. Oppenheim, and J. Hightower, Eds. (New York: ACM Press), pp. 466–470 (1995).
9. Bezdek J. C., Tsao E. C.-K. and Pal N. R.: 'Fuzzy Kohonen clustering networks'. In 'Proc. IEEE Int. Conf. on Fuzzy Systems 1992' (San Diego, CA), pp. 1035–1043 (1992).
10. Vuorimaa P.: 'Fuzzy self-organizing map'. Fuzzy Sets and Systems, Vol. 66, pp. 223–231 (1994).
11. Kosko B.: 'Neural Networks and Fuzzy Systems. A Dynamical Systems Approach to Machine Intelligence'. Englewood Cliffs, NJ, Prentice Hall (1992).
12. Lin C.-T. and Lee C. S. G.: 'Neural Fuzzy Systems. A Neuro-Fuzzy Synergism to Intelligent Systems'. New York, Prentice Hall (1996).
13. Kruse R., Schwecke E. and Heinsohn J.: 'Uncertainty and Vagueness in Knowledge-Based Systems: Numerical Methods'. Berlin, Springer-Verlag (1991).
14. Pearl J.: 'Probabilistic Reasoning in Intelligent Systems. Networks of Plausible Inference'. San Francisco, Morgan Kaufmann (1988).
15. Gebhardt J. and Kruse R.: 'Learning possibilistic networks from data'. In 'Proc. of Fifth Int. Workshop on Artificial Intelligence and Statistics' (Fort Lauderdale, Florida), pp. 233–244 (1994).
16. Kruse R., Gebhardt J. and Klawonn F.: 'Foundations of Fuzzy Systems'. Chichester, Wiley (1994).   ,

17. Nauck D. and Kruse R.: 'A neuro-fuzzy method to learn fuzzy classification rules from data'. Fuzzy Sets and Systems, Vol. 89, pp. 277–288 (1997).   ,

18. Nauck D. and Kruse R.: 'How the learning of rule weights affects the interpretability of fuzzy systems'. In 'Proc. IEEE Int. Conf. on Fuzzy Systems 1998' (Anchorage), pp. 1235–1240 (1998).   ,

19. Bersini H. and Bontempi G.: 'Now comes the time to defuzzify neuro-fuzzy models'. Fuzzy Sets and Systems, Vol. 90, pp. 161–170 (1997).

20. Klawonn F. and Kruse R.: 'Constructing a fuzzy controller from data'. Fuzzy Sets and Systems, Vol. 85, pp. 177–193 (1997).

21. Abe S. and Lan M.-S.: 'A method for fuzzy rules extraction directly from numerical data and its application to pattern classification'. IEEE Trans. Fuzzy Systems, Vol. 3(1), pp. 18–28 (1995).

22. Abe S., Lan M.-S. and Thawonmas R.: 'Tuning of a fuzzy classifier derived from data'. Int. J. Approximate Reasoning, Vol. 14(1), pp. 1–24 (1996).

23. Bezdek J. C.: 'Pattern Recognition with Fuzzy Objective Function Algorithms'. New York, Plenum Press (1981).

24. Bezdek J. C. and Pal S. K., Eds.: 'Fuzzy Models for Pattern Recognition'. New York, IEEE Press (1992).

25. Tschichold Gürman N.: 'The neural network model rulenet and its application to mobile robot navigation'. Fuzzy Sets and Systems, Vol. 85, pp. 287–303 (1997).

26. Nauck D. and Kruse R.: 'New learning strategies for NEFCLASS'. In 'Proc. Seventh International Fuzzy Systems Association World Congress IFSA'97', M. Mares, R. Mesiar, V. Novak, J. Ramik, and A. Stupnanova, Eds., Vol. IV (Prague: Academia), pp. 50–55 (1997).   ,   ,

27. Nauck D. and Kruse R.: 'NEFCLASS-X – a soft computing tool to build readable fuzzy classifiers'. BT Technology Journal, Vol. 16(3), pp. 180–190 (1998).   ,

28. Nauck D., Nauck U. and Kruse R.: 'NEFCLASS for JAVA – new learning algorithms'. In 'Proc. 18th International Conf. of the North American Fuzzy Information Processing Society (NAFIPS99)' (New York, NY: IEEE), pp. 472–476 (1999).

29. Nauck U.: 'Design and implementation of a neuro-fuzzy data analysis tool in Java'. Master's thesis, Technical University of Braunschweig, Braunschweig, (1999).

30. Nauck D.: 'Using symbolic data in neuro-fuzzy classification'. In 'Proc. 18th International Conf. of the North American Fuzzy Information Processing Society (NAFIPS99)' (New York, NY: IEEE), pp. 536–540 (1999).   ,

31. Wang L.-X. and Mendel J. M.: 'Generating fuzzy rules by learning from examples'. IEEE Trans. Syst., Man, Cybern., Vol. 22(6), pp. 1414–1427 (1992).   ,

32. Nauck D.: 'Data Analysis with Neuro-Fuzzy Methods'. Madgeburg, University of Magdeburg (1999).

33. Fisher R.: 'The use of multiple measurements in taxonomic problems'. Annual Eugenics, Vol. 7(Part II), pp. 179–188 (1936).

34. Wolberg W. and Mangasarian O.: 'Multisurface method of pattern separation for medical diagnosis applied to breast cytology'. Proc. National Academy of Sciences, Vol. 87, pp. 9193–9196 (1990).   ,

35. Quinlan J.: 'C4.5: Programs for Machine Learning'. San Mateo, CA, Morgan Kaufman (1993).

36. Dempster A., Laird N. and Rubin D.: 'Maximum likelihood from incomplete data via the EM algorithm'. Journal of the Royal Statistic Society, Series B, Vol. 39, pp. 1–38 (1977).

37. Mitchell T. M.: 'Machine Learning'. New York, NY, McGraw-Hill (1997).
38. Hair J. F., Anderson R. E., Tatham R. L. and Black W. C.: 'Multivariate Data Analysis', fifth edition ed. Upper Saddle River, NJ, Prentice-Hall (1998).
39. Berthold M. and Huber K.-P.: 'Tolerating missing values in a fuzzy environment'. In 'Proc. Seventh International Fuzzy Systems Association World Congress IFSA'97', M. Mares, R. Mesiar, V. Novak, J. Ramik, and A. Stupnanova, Eds., Vol. I (Prague: Academia), pp. 359–362 (1997).
40. Nauck D. and Kruse R.: 'Neuro-fuzzy systems'. In 'Handbook of Fuzzy Computation', E. Ruspini, P. Bonissone, and W. Pedrycz, Eds. Institute of Physics Publishing Ltd., Philadelphia, PA, Ch. D.2 (1998).
41. Nauck D. and Kruse R.: 'What are neuro-fuzzy classifiers?'. In 'Proc. Seventh International Fuzzy Systems Association World Congress IFSA'97', M. Mares, R. Mesiar, V. Novak, J. Ramik, and A. Stupnanova, Eds., Vol. III (Prague: Academia), pp. 228–233 (1997).
42. Siekmann S., Kruse R., Neuneier R. and Zimmermann H. G.: 'Advanced neuro-fuzzy techniques applied to the german stock index dax'. In 'Proc. Second European Workshop on Fuzzy Decision Analysis and Neural Networks for Management, Planning, and Optimization (EFDAN'97)' (Dortmund), pp. 170–179 (1997).

Soft Computing for Intelligent Knowledge-Based Systems

Trevor P. Martin and Jim F. Baldwin

Advanced Computing Research Centre and Department of Engineering Mathematics
University of Bristol
{trevor.martin,jim.baldwin}@bristol.ac.uk

Abstract. Knowledge-based systems are founded on the idea that knowledge should be declarative, so that it can be easily read, understood, and altered by a human user as well as by a machine. Logic fulfils these criteria, and logic programming has been widely used for implementing knowledge-based systems. One major shortcoming of logic programming is the lack of a mechanism to deal with the uncertainty inherent in many knowledge-based systems. Soft computing is a key technology for the management of uncertainty, although so far its major successes have been centred on fuzzy control rather than higher-level information management. This paper outlines some of the issues related to the area of soft computing in knowledge-based systems, and suggests some simple problems to test the capabilities of software. Fril is discussed as an implementation language for knowledge-based systems involving uncertainty, and some of its applications are outlined.

1   Introduction

Soft computing encompasses a range of techniques, generally grouped together as fuzzy logic, neural network theory and probabilistic reasoning — the distinguishing feature being a tolerance of imprecision, uncertainty and partial truth [1]. In commercial terms, the major successes of soft computing so far have been in fuzzy control and to a lesser extent in classification tasks using neural nets. Soft computing is promoted as a key technology in the information age, providing tools capable of containing the information explosion at a manageable level for humans. Raw data is often not in a form which a human can easily understand. Large volume data from fields such as medicine, science and engineering, finance and economics, marketing, social welfare, education, advertising, law, the arts, etc, is available. We store it in large databases, hoping that it will be useful. To be useful we must be able to discover relationships between the attributes of the database, and find rules to predict values of one attribute when others are known. A database may not have all its entries correct, there may be errors, or values may not be known exactly. We require a human/computer partnership

B. Azvine et al. (Eds.): Intelligent Systems and Soft Computing, LNAI 1804, pp. 161-187, 2000.

where the human is the interested party and the computer has the appropriate software to assist [2]. We suggest that fuzzy logic needs to move on from relatively low-level control tasks into this field of intelligent assistance in information processing [3-5]. For example, Dubois, Prade and Yager [6] identify information clarification, information retrieval, and information exploitation as areas in which fuzzy methods can be used. The general area of soft computing is applicable to these problems.

Typically in soft computing, software is developed as a research solution for a specific problem or group of problems. The complementary nature of the techniques within soft computing often makes it difficult to compare methods. As the use of soft computing increases we will find more users wanting to take software 'off the shelf' and apply it to their own specific problem. Such users may understand the basic theory underlying the software, but should not have to devote a large effort to evaluating and comparing different software packages. There is a need to know the capabilities and limitations of available software.

Ideally a library of demonstrator problems will enable an end user to evaluate soft computing tools by finding a problem similar to his own, determine whether or not a particular software package can handle the problem, and also see how easy it is to express the problem using the software. Thus the purpose of a benchmarking suite would be to compare capabilities, with run-time performance very much as a secondary measure.

This paper is divided into four sections, answering the questions identified above:

- an outline of issues related to soft computing in knowledge-based systems;
- some simple problems to test the capabilities of soft computing tools;
- discussion of some available software for creating knowledge-based systems involving uncertainty, focusing on Fril;
- some successful applications of Fril.

2   Uncertainty in Knowledge-Based Systems

At a high level, we can regard software as a black box taking input data, performing some sort of processing, and returning output data. We are interested in uncertainty in one or more of these stages — in the input data, in the output data, or in the processing stage. A knowledge-based system imposes constraints on the processing involved — it must be understandable at some level by a human with expertise in the field addressed by the software, i.e. the program should be *declarative* in nature, so that the processing can be understood without reference to the effect of a program on a computer. For many, this requirement leads straight to the use of logic (or a logic-based approach) for knowledge representation; however, we argue that pure logic is too restrictive and needs to be augmented with a mechanism for handling uncertainty.

2.1   The Need for Uncertainty in Knowledge-Based Systems

Knowledge-based systems attempt to capture some aspect of human intelligence and reasoning, and almost inevitably involve uncertainty. Two types of uncertainty are important, those depicted by probability and fuzzy set theories. Fuzzy set theory is not an alternative to probability theory and the two theories are not competing. These two theories are in fact related by the mass assignment framework [7, 8]. A normalised fuzzy set on X induces a possibility distribution over X which defines a family of probability distributions over X. This family of probability distributions can be represented as a mass assignment which is a probability distribution over the power set of X. Modification to this understanding must be made in the case of un-normalised fuzzy sets, when a degree of inconsistency is present.

We define a fuzzy set in terms of membership values, but what are these values and how can we estimate them? These are important questions and are equivalent to asking how we can interpret a fuzzy set. Mass assignment theory uses a voting model to interpret a fuzzy set.

We can appreciate the need for fuzziness even though we do not understand it. Fuzziness is a human phenomenon and has little, if anything, to do with the real world. Humans need to label objects, give description to situations, generalise from one situation to similar ones. If we defined a car precisely we would need to update the definition when a new model came out. A fuzzy understanding of the concept 'car' allows us to appreciate that an object which is similar in most important respects is a car. Fuzziness is necessary for generalisation; most inferences made by people are inductive rather than deductive. Understanding the concept of a car does not mean giving a precise specification and functionality of each and every part. We choose a set of general features and relations between these features which are important for giving the name 'car' to several examples. These features and relations will apply to other cases of 'car' and the differences will be lost in the abstractions of the semantics of the features and relations. There will nevertheless be difficult cases for which a decision seems borderline. In these cases we may wish to simply say we cannot make a decision. Fuzzy set theory expects one to be able to give a degree of applicability and therefore have some measure of closeness of match. This assumes there can be degrees of possibility and not just possible and impossible.

Another reason why we use fuzzy labels is one of complexity. We simplify our understanding of the relationship between concepts by using fuzzy labels. We might conclude that 'most tall people wear large shoes'. This description is very economic and easy to handle. We could replace it with numerous, more precise statements but would probably find the more complex description too difficult to handle. This is the reason for the success of fuzzy control. A few fuzzy rules give the required breadth of description without losing the accuracy required to make reasonable decisions.

We will accept that the need for fuzzy set theory arises because our natural language contains words that cannot be given precise definition. We need to classify, to divide reality into parts, to partition the set of values a variable can take into broad categories. This necessarily introduces fuzzy boundaries and we use fuzzy sets for the classifications.

2.2   Uncertainty in Input and/or Output Data

Fuzzy sets are proposed as a way of expressing natural language constructs using uncertain data values. At some level we must be able to say exactly what is meant by a fuzzy set as an item of uncertain data. In a fuzzy controller, it is not necessary for an end user to know anything about the fuzzy sets; however, it should be clear to the designer what membership functions mean. Frequently an 'intuitive' meaning is proposed, e.g. water temperatures can be 'hot' or 'cold', etc. Bezdek [9] suggests that membership functions should be "adjusted for maximum utility in a given situation." However, this leaves membership functions with no objective meaning — they are simply parameters to make the software function correctly. For a fuzzy knowledge-based system to be meaningful to a human, the membership functions should have an interpretation which is independent of the machine operation, i.e. one which does not require the software to be executed in order to determine its 'meaning'. Probabilistic representations of uncertain data have a strictly defined interpretation, although eliciting the actual numbers may be difficult. We are not concerned with the details of specific approaches here — the point is that, in a knowledge-based system, we should be able to determine exactly what is meant by the representation of uncertainty in input or output values.

Even without allowing vagueness, it may be difficult to represent imprecise information such as "John's height is between 1.6 and 1.7 metres" or "Bill's car is a Porsche or a Jaguar". The information is expressible in logic; however, computer-based implementations typically assume that information is known completely or not at all. The problem is compounded when one allows vague values — "John is of medium height" or "Bill drives an expensive car".

This form of uncertainty can be modelled using a possibility distribution, either continuous or discrete depending on the underlying domain. However, it is not sufficient merely to extend a programming framework by allowing fuzzy attribute values (or any other uncertain attribute values) — one must also be able to say what is *meant* by such values, without reference to computer operation. We must also distinguish between the notions of conjunctive and disjunctive possibility distributions (see also Baldwin, Martin and Pilsworth [10], Dubois and Prade [11], and Yager [12].

2.3   Uncertainty in the Processing Stage

Regarding software as a black box, transforming input to outputs, is not altogether satisfactory. A neural net, for example, may perform a complicated transformation of inputs which is not meaningful to the human user, and so is best regarded as a black box. This is a weakness of the neural net approach — how can a user be expected to trust the output of the software if he has no idea what is going on within the system. The degree to which a user needs to (or indeed can) understand the internal workings of a general software package is open to debate; however, some form of transparency is essential for a knowledge-based system, as the ability to explain an answer is a key feature. We must therefore demand a semantics for the processing of the data, in the same way as we demand a semantics for the data — and this should also be understandable without reference to the operations performed by a computer.

3   Logic Programming for Knowledge-Based Systems

In the 40-something years of its history as a practical discipline, artificial intelligence (AI) has followed a very different path from mainstream computing. While the early 'conventional' high-level languages concentrated largely on numerical computation, AI programmers were more concerned with manipulating symbols, as embodied by the development of LISP. In a sense we have now reached a point of confluence, where many parts of the AI community recognise the need for numerical as well as symbolic processing, and where symbolic computation probably accounts for the majority of computer use through document preparation and dissemination using word processors, Internet, etc. In addition, AI techniques such as expert systems, intelligent help, deductive databases, grammar, speech and image processing, are becoming part of mainstream computing.

One of the main reasons for AI's early focus on symbolic computation was the notion that AI programs should be *declarative*, i.e. a program should be open to interpretation as a theory as well as being executable as a series of instructions on a computer. LISP was based on Church's lambda calculus; in the 1970s, the idea of logic programming [12, 13] became popular — receiving a particular boost when it was chosen as the basis for the Japanese Fifth Generation project in the early 1980s. A pure logic program can be interpreted as a logic theory, or as a sequence of instructions to be executed. Soundness and completeness results can be proved for logic programs, and equivalence of programs can be used to transform code to enhance efficiency without losing 'accuracy'.

A program clause Ci:

$$Ai \leftarrow Bi1, Bi2, Bi3, \dots Bin$$

is regarded both as a logical axiom and as a procedure definition. A query:

$$\leftarrow G1, G2, G3, \dots Gm$$

is regarded both as a logic theorem to be proved from the axioms and as a sequence of procedure calls to be made. An execution step involves unifying a goal Gi with the head of some clause Ci, so that the new goal statement is:

$$\leftarrow (G1, G2, \dots Gi\text{-}1, Bi1, Bi2, Bi3, \dots Bin, Gi+1, \dots Gm) \Theta$$

where Θ is the unifier for Ai and Gi. Computation terminates when an empty goal statement is produced.

Logic programming deals with axioms whose content is irrelevant — only form is important. However, in order to relate such a program to the real world, one must choose an interpretation, i.e. a mapping between the different symbols in the program and some universe of discourse, U. Each predicate (for example) then defines a relation on U, each constant symbol corresponds to an element in the universe, etc. One can go further and define a set of domains Di as subsets of the universe of objects U:

$$\forall i: Di \subseteq U$$

Domains may be discrete or continuous, and finite or infinite. A predicate then defines a relation, i.e. a subset of the Cartesian product of two or more domains:

$$Ri \subseteq Di1 \times Di2 \times \ldots \times Din$$

where n is the arity of the relation Ri. The relation may be defined by extension, i.e. a set of facts, by intension, i.e. rules, or by a mixture of both. The extension of all relations is the set of logical consequences of the program.

Logic programming (as represented by Prolog) is well-suited to the implementation of knowledge-based systems. Its declarative leanings facilitate the split into knowledge bases and inference strategy; its well-defined control strategy means that a depth-first inference mechanism is available without any effort, and other inference mechanisms can be programmed straightforwardly; its meta-programming features mean that explanation and more advanced features such as on-line adaptation are also relatively easy to program. Of course, logic programming is not the only solution — functional programming also has an elegant mathematical foundation, and procedural languages such as C have been used to implement knowledge-based systems. One could argue that since computers interpret binary code, high-level programming languages are unnecessary, and all programs should be written in machine code. However, few people would accept this view since the structures in high-level programming languages enable a convenient representation of algorithms and data. In a similar vein, our view is that logic programming provides the most convenient framework for knowledge-based systems — knowledge-bases can be represented in a declarative, human-readable form and the general programming capabilities allow sophisticated inference strategies and other tools to be written.

3.1   Uncertainty in Logic Programming

In order to use logic programs to create knowledge-based systems involving uncertainty, we must extend the logic programming framework to express and process uncertainty. In this section, we outline the extensions necessary.

3.2   Uncertainty in Attribute Values

This form of uncertainty can be modelled using a possibility distribution, either continuous or discrete depending on the underlying domain. An attribute value is then either an element of the relevant domain or a fuzzy subset of the domain, and a relation is:

$$Ri \subseteq \{(a_{i1}, a_{i2}, ..., a_{in}) \mid a_{ij} \in Dij \lor a_{ij} \subseteq_f Dij, 1 \bullet j \bullet n\}$$

(a_{ij} are attribute values and $\subseteq_f$ denotes fuzzy subset).

The statement:

"the dice score was *high*"

where *high* represents the fuzzy set $\{4{:}0.6, 5{:}0.9, 6{:}1\}$ should allow us to state that:

> the dice score was 4 (with degree C4)
OR the dice score was 5 (with degree C5)
OR the dice score was 6 (with degree C6)

where the term 'degree' is deliberately unspecified, but is a numerically based value on a scale where 0 represents falsity and 1 represents truth.

We note finally that the disjunctive interpretation extends the expressiveness of the framework. The conjunctive interpretation, "John speaks French and English and German" is easily restated as the conjunction "John speaks French" AND "John speaks English" AND "John speaks German". However, the disjunctive interpretation, "John speaks exactly one language out of French, English, and German" is more difficult to represent using Horn clauses.

3.3   Uncertainty in Queries

The use of uncertain queries is related to the notion of uncertainty in attribute values. Instead of having to define crisp conditions for a database query, e.g. "find all sales staff who have sold more than 100 units a month for each of the last 6 months", one can use more natural but vague conditions such as "find all sales staff who have *consistently* sold *large quantities* in the *last few months*" where the italicised terms are defined on the appropriate domains. This reduces the problem of queries cutting out near misses, e.g. the salesman who sells 99 units a month in the example above.

Allowing uncertainty in queries and attributes leads to an inference problem — we need to match the uncertain terms in some way. There are four cases to examine (see also Dubois, Lang, and Prade [11]). Consider a set D of facts and rules, and a query Q:

(i)   Q is a crisp query, D contains complete information. In this case, it is a simple matter to establish whether Q is true or false by determining whether or not it is a logical consequence of D. For a simple example, let D contain the fact that John's height is 6ft and Q1 be the statement "John's height is 6ft" and Q2 the statement "John's height is 5ft". Clearly Q1 is true and Q2 is false. This is the situation handled by classical logic.

(ii)   Q is a fuzzy query, i.e. it contains a vague predicate or quantifier, and D contains complete information. In this case, we may not be able to derive Q from D with complete certainty. Using a similar example to that given above, let D contain the fact that John's height is 5ft 10in and Q be the statement "John is tall". A numerical estimate can be attached to the conclusion Q, as we cannot say that Q is definitely true or false.

An alternative approach is to disallow any fuzzy statements and insist on a crisp definition of predicates ('tall' in this instance). This has the disadvantage that some terms in the formal language used to represent knowledge may not have the same meaning as the same terms used in everyday language, e.g. 'tall' could be defined to be any height over 6ft.

(iii)   Q is a crisp statement, D contains incomplete information. In this case, Q is definitely true or false but it may not be possible to determine which, due to lack of information. For example, let D contain the fact that John's height is 6ft or 5ft 11in, and Q be the statement "John's height is 6ft". The database does not contain sufficient information to establish the truth of Q, but it can give information on the possibility or probability that Q could be true.

(iv)   Q is a fuzzy statement, D contains incomplete information, e.g. D contains statements "Bill is average height", "John is several centimetres taller then Bill" and Q is the statement "John is tall". This is the most complex situation and is considered further below.

3.4   Uncertainty in Relations

A crisp relation is a subset of the Cartesian product of two or more domains:

$$Ri \subseteq Di1 \times Di2 \times \ldots \times Din$$

where n is the arity of the relation Ri. A logic program computes tuples in a relation, i.e. tuples which satisfy some logical condition. As suggested above, modelling uncertainty in the system forces us to allow for the possibility that tuples do not completely satisfy a predicate, for example, let us take the relation:

$$Fluent\text{-}Speaker \subseteq Person \times Language$$

and consider the tuples (John, English), (John, French), (John, Spanish). If John is a native English speaker, and knows no French, then the first two tuples respectively belong and do not belong to the relation. However, if John knows a little Spanish then the final tuple lies between these two extremes. Again, one can attach a numerical value between 0 and 1 to show where the tuple lies in the range between false and true — but it must be clear what this number actually means.

One could argue that there is an equivalence between uncertainty in one attribute value of a tuple in a binary relation and an uncertain monadic relation. For example, the data that John is *young* could be modelled using a binary relation:

$$\text{Age} \subseteq \text{Person} \times \text{N}_{130}$$

where N_{130} is the set of natural numbers less than 130. Then (John, *young*) would be a tuple in the relation Age with an appropriate definition for the fuzzy set *young*.

Alternatively, we could use monadic relations, Young, MiddleAged, Old, etc:

$$\text{Young} \subseteq_f \text{Person}, \quad \text{MiddleAged} \subseteq_f \text{Person}, \quad \text{etc}$$

where $\subseteq_f$ indicates fuzzy subsethood and the tuple (John) may have uncertainty as to the degree of membership in Young, MiddleAged, etc. It is important to know whether these are equivalent representations — particularly for the knowledge engineer when designing the system. We note that the binary relation form allows crisp and uncertain data to be stored (e.g. both "Mary is 29" and John is *young*) without loss of data; furthermore, it allows more flexibility in queries (e.g. "find people whose age is *around 40*") with the vague term *about 40* defined at query time.

More generally in a logic program, clauses may be conditional. A numerical value between 0 and 1 indicates that there is uncertainty attached to the rule — we must again be clear what exactly is represented by this uncertainty.

3.5   Uncertainty in Inference

Uncertainty in inference has been touched on in the preceding sub-sections. Equality is the first logical concept that must be extended, as it is no longer sufficient to look for simple syntactic equality. In logic programming terms, this means we must extend the notion of unification in some way [14]. Since unification is the fundamental operation of logic programming, this extension is only a realistic alternative if it can be made efficient — see Baldwin, Lawry and Martin [15] for example.

The main problem with adding uncertainty to a logic programming system is determining how to combine the numerical uncertainty associated with clauses used in a proof. Probability is the best defined and longest established numerical treatment of uncertainty, yet still hits problems when combined with logic. We can illustrate the problem with a simple example:

A box contains coloured objects which are either red or blue and either cubes or spheres. It is known that 60% of the objects are red, and that 30% are cubes. Let:

p denote object is red   and   q denote object is a cube

then we know $\Pr(p) = 0.6$ and $\Pr(q) = 0.3$, but can say almost nothing about $\Pr(p \wedge q)$.

Let us now assume further information is available, namely 60% are red cubes, 15% are red spheres, 12% are blue cubes, 13% are blue spheres:

$$Pr\,(p \wedge q) = 0.6$$
$$Pr\,(p \wedge \neg q) = 0.15$$
$$Pr\,(\neg p \wedge q) = 0.12$$
$$Pr\,(\neg p \wedge \neg q) = 0.13$$

Now we want to express the uncertain rule that if an object is red then it is probably a cube. The logic formula $p \supset q$ is true in 85% of cases, but the conditional probability $Pr(q|p) = 0.8$. Does uncertainty attached to a rule have a logical or a statistical basis? To further complicate the situation, a programmer may want to represent a rule obtained from an unreliable expert. In a logic programming environment, we must ensure that the programmer is aware of the interpretation of uncertainty embodied in the system. Of course, when the numbers are interpreted as *degrees of truth* it may be easier to retain truth-functionality.

Integrating the uncertainty-handling mechanism into the system also presents a choice. We can regard a logic program as a split:

Program = Logic + Control,

and we have the possibilities:

Uncertain program = Logic + Control + Uncertainty

or:

Uncertain Program = Uncertain Logic + Control

In other words, we can either extend the logical basis of the system, for example Lee [16] defined a fuzzy resolution method, or we can separate the calculation of uncertainty from the inference process. A proof of the conclusion is found; a separate mechanism considers the uncertainty attached to the clauses used in the proof, and calculates the resultant uncertainty. This is the mechanism used in Fril (see Section 4).

3.6   Fusion of Uncertain Conclusions

In logic programming, we are generally content to find a single solution to a query. Given a binary predicate p we might ask "are there values X and Y such that p(X, Y) holds?" — strictly speaking, a yes/no answer is all that is required, although instantiations for X and Y are also helpful in many cases. Because of the execution strategy used, Prolog systems will by default return answers one at a time (including duplicate answers). This is not adequate for a system where answers may be qualified by uncertainty. It is possible that a particular solution can be derived in more than one way from the program clauses — each proof path having a different calculation of uncertainty and hence a different final value. If two proof paths lead to the conclusion p(a,b) with uncertainty values c1 and c2, how should we combine these into an overall value? This is referred to as the problem of fusion.

Clearly any fusion function f which combines uncertainty values should satisfy end point criteria such as:

$$f(\text{True, True}) = \text{True,} \qquad\qquad f(\text{False, False}) = \text{False,}$$

and be commutative and associative:

$$f(x, y) = f(y, x) \quad f(x, f(y, z)) = f(f(x, y), z)$$

A related problem arises from treating rules individually. Consider universes U_Y = {a, b, c, d, e}, U_X = {c1, c2, c3} and two rules:

Y = {a, b} IF X = c1
Y = {c, d} IF X = c2

with an input X = {c1, c2}.

The first rule gives Y = {a, b, c, d, e}, the second gives Y = {a, b, c, d, e}, and intersecting gives Y = {a, b, c, d, e}.

Logically it follows that we can use other rules from which the correct solution can be inferred. From the above example, the following rule is valid:

Y = {a, b, c, d} IF X = {c1, c2}

so that we can infer:

Y = {a, b, c, d} which is more accurate than the inferences from individual rules.

4   Mass Assignment Theory and Fril

We outline the methods used in Fril to cope with the problems discussed above. Fril is founded on the theory of mass assignments, which unites fuzzy and probabilistic uncertainty in a single framework. It is covered in Baldwin [8], and Baldwin, Martin and Pilsworth [10] and we only summarise the essential points here for completeness.

4.1   Essentials of Mass Assignment Theory

Mass assignment theory gives a semantics of fuzzy sets using a voting model involving human voters. Consider a dice and a representative set of people labelled 1 to 10.

Each person is asked to accept or reject the dice score of x as **small**. They can believe x is a borderline case but they have to make a binary decision to accept or reject. We take the membership of x in the fuzzy set **small** to be the proportion of persons who accept x as **small**.

Thus we know that everyone accepted 1 as small, 90% of persons accepted 2 as small and 30% of persons accepted 3 as small. We only know the proportions who accepted each score and not the complete voting pattern of each person. We assume that anyone who accepted x as being small will accept also any score lower than x of being small. With this assumption we can write down the voting pattern:

1	2	3	4	5	6	7	8	9	10	persons
1	1	1	1	1	1	1	1	1	1	everyone accepts 1
2	2	2	2	2	2	2	2	2		90% accept 2
3	3	3								30% accept 3

Therefore 1 person accepts $\{1\}$, 6 persons accept $\{1, 2\}$ and 3 persons accept $\{1, 2, 3\}$ as being the possible sets of scores when told the dice is small. If a member is drawn at random then the probability distribution for the set of scores this person will accept is:

$$\{1\} : 0.1, \{1, 2\}: 0.6, \{1, 2, 3\} : 0.3$$

This is a probability distribution on the power set of dice scores, known as a mass assignment and written as:

$$m_{small} = \{1\} : 0.1, \{1, 2\}: 0.6, \{1, 2, 3\} : 0.3$$

It is, of course, a random set [17] and also a basic probability assignment of Shafer Dempster theory [18]. We give it the name of mass assignment because we use it in a different way to Shafer Dempster. The mass assignment corresponds to a family of distributions on the set of dice scores. Each mass associated with a set of more than one element can be divided in some way among the elements of the set. This leads to a distribution over dice scores and there are an infinite number of ways in which this can be done. The least prejudiced distribution divides the masses among the elements of the set associated with them according to the prior for the dice scores.

The converse of this problem is: given the dice value is **small,** what is the distribution over possible dice scores for the dice value. This is only a small modification from the following non-fuzzy case. If the dice score is even then we would say that the scores 2, 4, and 6 were equally likely for a fair dice. In this case we put a mass of 1 with the set $\{2, 4, 6\}$ and split the mass equally among the elements of the set of possible scores. The only difference between this and our fuzzy case is that the mass assignment came from a fuzzy set rather than a crisp set. It also makes sense to ask for the probability that the dice value will be in a certain set given that the dice value is in some other set. For example, we can ask what is the probability that the dice value will be $\{1 \text{ or } 2\}$ given that it is even:

$$\Pr(\{\text{dice value in } \{1, 2\} \mid \text{dice value is even}) = 1/3$$

Similarly we can ask for the probability of the dice value being *about_2* when we know it is *small* where *about_2* is a fuzzy set defined by:

about_2 = 1 / 0.4 + 2 / 1 + 3 / 0.4

with mass assignment m_{about_2} = {2} : 0.6, {1, 2, 3} : 0.4

We can see the equivalent of this in tabular form in Fig. 1.We can use a mass assignment with the least prejudiced distribution to obtain a point value probability. The continuous case can be treated either analytically or by mean of a discrete sampling approach.

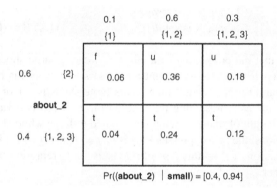

Fig. 1. Tabular form of the probability of the dice being *about_2* when it is *small*.

4.2   Fril

Fril extends logic programming (Prolog) by allowing fuzzy sets as fundamental data objects, and associating support pairs with clauses. A support pair is an interval containing a point-value probability. The probabilistic fuzzy rules [8, 19, 20] of Fril represent our theory for the way the variables of our application relate to one another. We do not restrict ourselves to simple flat IF ... THEN rules normally associated with fuzzy control. The rules are logic programming clauses in which the variables associated with predicates can be instantiated to any term, including fuzzy sets, and conditional probabilistic intervals can be associated with each rule. These have various interpretations dependent on the type of rule but in all cases represent an interval containing the conditional probability of the head of the rule given some instantiation of the rule body.

In addition to the normal logic programming style of execution, Fril allows three types of rules involving uncertainty:

1.   the basic rule, for example:

> ((suitability X for sports stadium Y is *high*)
>   (access X from parts of city is *easy*)
>   (cost_to_build Y at X is *fairly_cheap*)) : (0.9 1)

which states that there is a high probability (0.9 - 1) that any place X is highly suitable to build a sports stadium Y if X is easily accessed and Y can be built fairly cheaply at X — italicised words represent fuzzy sets;

2.   the extended rule, for example:

> ((shoe_size man X is *large*)
>   (((height X is *tall*))
>   ((height X is *average*))
>   ((height X is *small*)))) :   (0.8 1) (0.5 0.6) (0 0.1)

which states that the probability of a tall man wearing large shoes is at least 0.8, the probability that an average height man wears large shoes is between 0.5 and 0.6, the probability that a small man wears large shoes is 0.1 or less — we can think of the rule as representing the relationship between two variables, S (shoe size) and H (height of man), S being instantiated to large while H has three possible instantiations; the rule expresses Pr(S is *large* | H is hi) where hi is a particular fuzzy instantiation of H — this type of rule is useful to represent fuzzy causal nets and many other types of applications;

3.   the evidential logic rule, for example:

> (suitability_as_secretary person X is *good*)
>   (evlog *most*   (
>   (readability of X is *high*)   0.1
>   (neatness X is *fairly_good*)   0.2
>   (qualifications X are *applicable*)   0.1
>   (concentration X is *long*)   0.3
>   (typing_skills X is *very_good*)   0.2
>   (shorthand X is *adequate*) 0.1)) : ((1 1)(0 0))

which says that a person's suitability as a secretary is good if most of the weighted features in the body of the rule are satisfied, the term *most* being a fuzzy set chosen to provide optimism for those persons who satisfy the criteria well and pessimism for those who satisfy the criteria badly — the italicised words are fuzzy sets defined in the program, while the satisfaction of features such as (qualifications X are applicable) is determined from another rule; the weights associated with the features can be optimised if a database of examples is provided [10, 21].

The three Fril rules are of the form:

< <u>head</u> > IF < <u>body</u> > : <<u>list of support pairs</u> >

The list of support pairs provide intervals containing conditional probabilities of some instantiation of the head given some instantiation of the body. A generalised Jeffrey's rule for support pairs is the basic inference rule of Fril, and mass assignment theory is used where necessary to combine fuzzy and probabilistic uncertainty. Full details are given in Baldwin [8] and Martin and Pilsworth [10].

4.3   Fuzzy Sets in Fril

Fril allows uncertainty in attribute values to be represented by fuzzy sets. The fuzzy sets may defined on an underlying domain which may in turn have a prior distribution defined over it. Fril allows fuzzy sets to represent uncertain values and extends the unification mechanism to cope with this. Additionally, we can interpret continuous fuzzy subsets as fuzzy numbers and perform simple arithmetic on them.

4.4   Execution

Logic programs are executed by posing a query, which is answered by determining whether that query (or some instance of it) is a logical consequence of the clauses in the knowledge base. Execution is a search over an *and-or* tree. Execution of a support logic program is also a search over the *and-or* tree, with additional computation defined by mass assignment theory to calculate supports associated with each solution. The entire *and-or* tree is searched so that all proof paths may be taken into account. Fril is implemented as a compiler for the abstract Fril machine [22], which is a modification of the Warren Abstract Machine [23] used in most Prolog compilers. This yields a highly efficient support logic programming system. Clauses (possibly involving supports and fuzzy sets) are compiled into sequences of abstract machine instructions, which can be executed by a software emulator or by a hardware implementation of the abstract machine [10, 15, 24, 25].

5   Applications of Fril

Fril has been applied to a wide range of problems. We list a few below.

5.1   Fuzzy Data Browser

In many large databases, information may be incomplete or uncertain. Even where everything is known, the volume of data can obscure important relationships within the data. Rules derived from the data can illuminate relationships, and represent fuzzy data compression since the database can be approximately reconstructed from the rules.

The Fril data browser can be used to form rules which predict the value of an attribute in one tuple from known values of other attributes in that tuple, plus the attribute values in other 'similar' tuples. The database is partitioned into fuzzy subsets containing similar values of the variable under consideration; each rule then uses fuzzy sets to summarise values of other variables in that partition. In this way, rules which are meaningful to a human expert can be generated. The user can also suggest relationships in the data, and test them — for example, a supermarket manager might like to know how well the statement "most customers who buy expensive wine often buy exotic cheeses at the same time" matches transaction data for his store. Applications of the data browser include:

- image classification, deriving and applying rules to categorise regions of a partitioned image into classes such as vegetation, road, building, vehicle, etc [26];

- generating rules for hand-written character recognition [27];

- learning rules to classify odours into categories such as *unpleasant, strong, very acidic,* using signals from conductive polymer sensors [28-30];

- classifying faces as male or female, given a set of 18 measurements referring to features such as thickness of eyebrows, distance from bottom of nose to top of mouth, etc [2];

- predicting values and detecting empirical relationships in a database of measurement from geological experiments [29];

- monitoring data from an aircraft black-box flight recorder, to detect anomalous readings — these either indicate that a piece of equipment is malfunctioning, or that measurements are being reported incorrectly, monitoring data from an aircraft black-box flight recorder, where it is necessary to detect anomalous readings which can either indicate that a piece of equipment is malfunctioning, or that measurements are being reported incorrectly;

- classifying underwater sounds, where the browser must generate rules which can be understood by humans — this application has achieved very high success rates (up to 92%), outstripping the performance of a standard neural net package, yet retaining the transparency of the rule-based approach, while the neural net, in contrast, provides no explanation or insight into the classification process [31];

- detecting changes in satellite images, using fuzzy rules derived from examples — the system is intended to monitor an area and discover changes related to building construction or demolition, and, during testing, the system detected a small change involving re-roofing houses which had previously not been noticed.

5.2   Fuzzy Control Module

A fuzzy control module has been written in Fril, giving a choice of inference strategies, (support logic, Mamdani, Lukasiewicz, Kleene-Dienes), aggregation operators (intersection, dempster, union) and defuzzification methods (expected value, centroid, maximum membership). Unlike many systems, a hierarchy of rules can be used. Fril is particularly suited to investigating higher-level control problems, where (for example) an expert might know that one control strategy is appropriate in one set of circumstances, but a different strategy is needed in different circumstances. This high-level expert knowledge is easy to model in Fril.

5.3   Intelligent Manual

The MUNVAR project funded by the CEC identified a need for an intelligent interface to technical literature. The specific case chosen as a demonstrator was a study [32] by the Swedish Nuclear Inspectorate into techniques of assessing the safety of nuclear waste repositories. This study documented methods that could be used, and analysed their validity at a hypothetical site. The document is intended to give guidance to waste management companies preparing a safety assessment for a specific site.

Initial objectives were that the system should be able to:

- trace back from a conclusion to the information justifying that conclusion;
- find the modelling approach used for a given subproblem;
- aid in examining the consequences of changing the modelling approach;
- handle the uncertainty inherent in different modelling approaches, ranging from uncertainties in experimentally determined values through to determining whether a particular modelling approach is valid.

Subsequent development of this work has focused on a loosely coupled package involving Fril which handles knowledge-based aspects and Mathematica which deals with mathematical modelling. The system has been applied to target motion analysis (UK Defence Research Agency) and management of uncertain engineering data (Intera Ltd).

5.4   Aircrew Modelling

The Defence and Avionics Division of Cray Systems Ltd used Fril to produce a modelling tool for representing the behaviour of aircrew in helicopter and fixed wing operations [33]. The tool is used to produce models of aircrew behaviour that can run within a simulation environment to aid the assessment of pilot workload on specific missions and examine the workload effects of various avionics and decision support aids in the cockpit. It is also to be used for modelling aircraft in combat simulations.

The model represents the three fundamental tasks of the aircrew: data perception, situation assessment and decisions about the actions to be taken. It also provides a mechanism for representing memory characteristics of the aircrew. A fourth activity, within the model, evaluates the extent of any factors that may affect the performance of the aircrew, (so-called 'affectors'). These include physical affectors such as aircraft vibration, g-forces, temperature, cockpit pressure and psychological affectors such as fear, work overload, etc.

The behaviour and reasoning characteristics of the aircrew model, written in Fril, are accessed from an Ada simulation framework via C data structures and control routines. For example, the data perception task determines what instruments or other data the aircrew would examine as a result of an event, and obtains that data, if available, from the simulation framework. This perceived data is passed on to the situation assessment task which determines the state of the aircraft within its current context and its ability to fulfil its mission. Using this perceived situation, the aircrew model decides what actions should be performed to optimise the success of the mission, addressing any outstanding problems.

Fril lends itself ideally to the modelling of such a task by its ability to combine rule-based reasoning with the qualitative analysis capabilities afforded by support logic and fuzzy sets. The uncertainty handling mechanism proves particularly useful in the evaluation of affectors and in representing the degree to which the resultant effects should be applied to the conscious tasks of the aircrew classification and case-based reasoning.

5.5   Orthodontic Expert System

An expert system for planning orthodontic treatment [34, 35] was originally developed at the University of Bristol in collaboration with practitioners at the Bristol Dental Hospital. Recently this work was extended and the system is commercially available from Team Management Systems Ltd [36].

Orthodontics concerns management of the growth and development of teeth to prevent or correct such problems as overcrowding or misalignment. The development of the system involved analysing the decision-making processes used by orthodontists, to identify possible methods of emulating the process by computer. This resulted in a knowledge representation which used fuzzy sets since orthodontic reasoning routinely involves the manipulation of vague or uncertain concepts.

The expert system has been tested extensively using a number of general dental practitioners entering a sample of cases. The system's recommendations have been shown to be comparable to the recommendations of a consultant orthodontist when assessed by peer review in a blind trial.

5.6   Design/Assessment of Composite Materials

CODEX [37] is an expert system for the design and assessment of composite plates and struts, being developed by the University of Bristol and the Civil Aircraft Division of British Aerospace.

Due to the orthotropic macro-mechanical behaviour of advanced fibre-reinforced composites, layers of material are bonded with fibres in different orientations to give all-round strength. Optimisation of the amount of material with respect to weight, cost, stiffness, strength and other less quantifiable factors is central. The computer system aids users in the design of plates and struts, and allows assessment of the relative merits of previous designs based on such criteria. The plate or strut designs obtained can be compared by using a set of rules representing different design criteria. The relative importance of the rules can be set by the user, and an overall assessment for a design is derived using Fril.

5.7   Administration of Money Market Services

CAMES (Client Administration Expert System) uses conceptual graphs for knowledge representation [38]. This application concerns the administration of money market services and was developed for commercial exploitation by Reuters Ltd in 1989. Reuters developed the system in Fril using a conceptual graph tool-kit provided by Fril Systems Ltd.

6   Other Fuzzy and Possibility-Based Approaches

We briefly mention some other systems which have been implemented for knowledge-based systems under uncertainty. We have ignored the numerous *proposals* for systems to deal with uncertainty in knowledge-based systems, and concentrate only on those which have been implemented as practical, usable systems. We also focus on logic programming and related systems, ignoring the so-called fuzzy development environments which are targeted on simple fuzzy control applications. Although it can be argued that a fuzzy controller is a knowledge-based system — it has a rule-base, an inference procedure, and mechanisms for handling data fusion and conflict — our view is that such systems are little more than sophisticated interpolation algorithms, and cannot easily deal with issues such as:

- hierarchical and recursive rules;
- explanation of results;
- theoretical understanding of the results.

In addition to the logic programming systems, brief comments on production systems extended with fuzzy capabilities are included. These are similar in capability and scope of application to the logic programming formalism. A major disadvantage compared to logic programming is the complex control strategy and the difficulty in defining recursive rules — while not insurmountable, this is considerably less elegant than the natural way in which recursion can be expressed and controlled in a Prolog-like system.

6.1   FProlog

Fril version 1 was developed in the late 1970s following Baldwin's work on fuzzy relations, and version 2 followed in the early 1980s. Both were true relational languages. In order to add a procedural capability, a fuzzy Prolog interpreter [10] was written and integrated with the relational system. The interpreter could also function as a stand-alone fuzzy Prolog system. It allowed fuzzy relations to be defined, with a membership value giving the degree of truth of the tuple. Standard fuzzy operators (such as min/max) were used to compute truth values for conjunctions, etc, and to combine truth values arising from different proof paths for the same conclusion. Uncertainty was not allowed for rules, although it was possible to circumvent this by programming appropriate calculations. Uncertainty in attribute values was also modelled by programming rather than as a fundamental part of the language; hence no modification to the unification algorithm was needed. Recursive rules were possible, although, as no uncertainty was attached to rules, this adds little to the uncertainty modelling aspects of the language.

6.2   Fuzzy Prolog

Mukaidono has worked on fuzzy logic programming for a considerable time [39, 40], his most recent contribution being a fuzzy Prolog-based on Lukasiewicz implication (LbFP), summarised in Martin and Arcelli Fontana [41]. In LbFP, uncertain attribute values are not allowed as fundamental objects, although it is possible to simulate their effect using programming techniques. No changes to the unification algorithm are therefore necessary. Facts and rules are augmented with truth values in the interval [0, 1] where 1 represents truth and 0 represents unknown or meaningless (this is related to standard Prolog where failure to prove is only equivalent to proof of falsity under the assumptions of negation by failure). The truth values with a rule body are combined using min/max/1-x for conjunction, disjunction, and negation respectively. The max operator is also used to combine truth values from different proof paths for the same solution. LbFP is formulated in terms of tree resolution rather than the more usual linear resolution.

Mukaidono and Yasui consider a number of implication operators, concluding that Lukasiewicz implication is the most appropriate for their needs. In particular, it can be used for recursive rules such as:

X+1 is a small number if X is a small number (with some degree of truth m < 1)

Given the base case that 0 is definitely a small number, Mukaidono and Yasui require that ∞ has membership zero in the set of small numbers defined by the extension of this rule. They note that many candidate implication operators can be ruled out because they do not reach zero in this limit — indeed, some do not decrease at all.

6.3   f-PROLOG

Li and Liu [42] defined a fuzzy Prolog in a manner reminiscent of the FProlog system discussed above. Their extensions were:

(i)   in allowing uncertain rules, P :-[f]- Q1, Q2, ..., Qn

           where P, Qi are logic atoms and the conclusion P holds with the product of f
           and the minimum truth value associated with the body goals, Qi

(ii)   in specifying a minimum threshold for a query to be satisfied, e.g. find a
           solution with truth value > 0.8.

6.4   Prolog-ELF

Prolog-ELF [43] was a product of the early Fifth Generation research programme. It augmented clauses with a truth value in the interval [0, 1], which were either assigned at compile time or (possibly) computed at runtime. The system is based on Lee's fuzzy resolution method [16], and clauses are written in the form:

    +P -Q -R #

to emphasise that resolution is being used. The standard min/max/1-x operations are used for conjunction, disjunction, and negation; in line with Lee, truth values of positive literals are required to be in the interval [0.5, 1]. Multiple proof paths are combined using max, and no uncertainty is allowed in attribute values.

6.5   Fuzzy Production Systems

We finally mention some fuzzy production systems. In many respects, these are close to fuzzy logic programming systems as they use rules augmented by uncertainty, and may also allow uncertain data values. The main difference is one of interpretation — in production systems, rules are interpreted only procedurally, as condition/action pairs. Production systems may adopt forward or backward chaining execution mechanisms, and generally examine all rules rather than the fixed search strategy usually found in logic programming. This may be a disadvantage when predictability of program behaviour is considered.

FLOPS [44][1] is a fuzzy extension to the OPS-5 production system. Data values may be discrete or continuous fuzzy sets. Continuous fuzzy sets must have Gaussian membership functions, and can model fuzzy numbers including arithmetic operations. Rules and facts are qualified by 'confidence values' which are integers in the range 0-1000; a min-max calculus is used to compute confidence values of results.

7   Benchmarking Problems

We list some simple problems to illustrate different capabilities of knowledge-based systems involving uncertainty. The neural-net and machine-learning communities are already well advanced on this route with a number of Web sites (see http://www.ics.uci.edu/~mlearn/MLRepository.html and links contained there); similarly, there are several well-known fuzzy control problems such as the inverted pendulum, truck reversal, etc. We concentrate here on knowledge-based systems. This is not intended to be anything like a comprehensive list, but is a starting point to stimulate further contributions. The problems are not intended to be computationally difficult, but rather to illustrate the concepts which can be expressed within a particular framework or system.

7.1   Fuzziness and Probability

You are told that a fair dice is thrown and the value is *small* where *small* is a fuzzy set defined as :

small = 1 : 1 + 2 : 0.9 + 3 : 0.4   where the notation element : membership is used

Can we derive the distribution Pr(dice is i | dice is *small*)?
What if the dice is weighted, with prior:

1 / 0.1, 2 / 0.2, 3 / 0.3, 4 / 0.2, 5 / 0.1, 6 / 0.1   where the notation element/ probability is used

What is Pr(dice is *about_2* | dice is *small*) where *about_2* is a fuzzy set defined as:

about_2 = 1 : 0.3 + 2 : 1 + 3 : 0.3

(see Baldwin and Martin [45] for details of the mass assignment solution to this problem)

---

[1]See also http://users.aol.com/fuzzysys/

7.2 Probability, Fuzziness and Arithmetic

Two fair dice are thrown, the value of dice 1 is *small* (defined above) and the value of dice 2 is *large*, where *large* is:

$$large = 4 : 0.3 + 5 : 1 + 6 : 1$$

1. What is the total score?

2. If dice 1 is biased as above, what is the total?

3. John is of *average height* and Bill is several centimetres taller than John (with suitable definitions for *average height* and *several* centimetres). What is the height of Bill ? Is he *tall* (given a suitable definition of tall)?

4. Take three approximate values given by the continuous fuzzy subsets of the real line:

    F1 = [-1:0 1:1 3:0],   F2 = [2:0 3:1 4:0], and F3 = [1:0 2:1 3:0], with linear interpolation between the points

    Calculate the following quantities:

    (i) the sum F1 + F3, and difference F1 - F3   (ii) the product F1 * F3,
    (iii) F2 * (F1 + F3) (iv) (F2 * F1) + (F2 * F3)   (v) (F1 - F3)^2

7.3   Some Simple Database Problems

1. Take a small database of Name $\times$ Nationality $\times$ Height — say 200 tuples, almost all having Nationality = Swedish and height satisfying the definition of *tall* from the previous example. From this database, is it true so say that most Swedes are tall?

    Throw away the data and replace it with the summary "Most Swedes are tall". From this summary, what is the average height of Swedes? (see also Zadeh [5]).

2. Take a small database of Name $\times$ Subject $\times$ Exam mark. Find the names of good project students, where a good project student is defined as one with mostly good exam scores, at least a few excellent marks, and very few or no poor marks. Appropriate definitions to be used for:

    "good", "excellent", and "poor"on the domain of exam marks
    "mostly", "at least a few", and "very few or no" on the domain of proportions
    [0, 1]

7.4   Machine Learning/Knowledge Discovery in Databases

There are several collections of datasets suitable for testing software which implements some form of learning. The majority of this data is numerical and consists of relatively large datasets, i.e. a size suitable for statistical treatment as well as neural net and other machine learning approaches. It would be useful to extend this body of data in two ways:

- to include symbolic data as well as numeric;
- to test generalisation from small data sets as well as interpolative reasoning in large datasets.

As an example, consider the following problem from Baldwin[46].

A mask is randomly dropped on to the grid shown in Fig. 2 and moved until at least one pixel is found. Patterns for good L and bad L are shown. Not all of these patterns are discriminatory, and some occur twice as frequently as the corresponding pattern in the other classification. It is known that errors in transmission can occur so that the third row of patterns (unknown classification) can occur; we assume that only one pixel is affected in the case of an error. Given any one of the patterns, classify the object as a good L or a bad L.

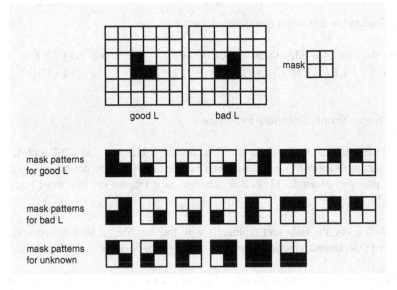

Fig. 2. Mask problem [46]

7.5   Other Problems

Clearly the list above is a small sample of the total required. Other areas that should be addressed include:

- sensor processing — pattern recognition, vision, speech/sound recognition, olfactive sensors;
- fuzzy control problems such as inverted pendulum, truck reversal, air conditioning;
- pre-processing data — clustering, classifying, removal of noise;
- longer inference chains involving uncertain rules;
- data fusion — how to combine different sources and resolve conflicts.

8   Conclusions

Knowledge-based systems involving uncertainty should be able to provide a semantics for their representation of uncertainty in data and inference. As Bezdek [47] said, we should "...think about how we use terms such as 'intelligent system'," and "... discourage the use of seductive semantics in algorithmic descriptions and encourage the use of strict verifiable definitions of computational properties". Some simple problems have been outlined as demonstrators for the capabilities of knowledge-based systems using soft computing techniques. Collaboration from software providers (both commercial and academic) and researchers in a range of application areas will be needed to make progress towards a complete benchmarking suite for the capabilities of soft computing tools.

It is perhaps worth emphasising that the early expert system success stories such as Mycin and Prospector included treatment of uncertainty, and arguably succeeded because of this. The role of uncertainty in knowledge-based systems is crucial, and logic programming is one of the main approaches to actually building knowledge-based systems, as opposed to discussing and philosophising about them. In this paper, we have outlined the extensions to logic programming necessary to handle uncertainty, concentrating on the practical rather than theoretical aspects. In particular, the Fril approach to the problem has been discussed, together with some other fuzzy Prolog systems.

There is still work to do in the field, but the combination of logical inference and uncertainty management techniques have much to offer in the implementation of intelligent information systems.

References

1. Zadeh, L. A.: 'The Roles of Fuzzy Logic and Soft Computing in the Conception, Design, and Deployment of Intelligent Systems', in 'Software Agents and Soft Computing: Concepts and Applications', eds, Nwana H. S. and Azarmi N., Springer. (LNCS 1198) pp. 183-190 (1997).
2. Baldwin, J. F. and Martin, T. P.: 'A Fuzzy Data Browser in Fril', in 'Fuzzy Logic in AI', ed, Baldwin J. F., John Wiley, pp. 101-124 (1996).
3. Baldwin, J. F. and Martin, T. P.: 'From Fuzzy Databases to an Intelligent Manual using Fril', J. Intelligent Information Systems, Vol. 2, pp. 365-395 (1993).

4.   Baldwin, J. F. and Martin, T. P.: 'The Intelligent Manual in Fril', Proc. EUFIT93 - First European Congress on Fuzzy and Intelligent Technologies, Aachen, Germany, pp. 624-630 (1993).
5.   Zadeh, L. A.: 'Fuzzy Logic = Computing with Words,' IEEE Transactions on Fuzzy Systems, Vol. 4, pp. 103-111 (1996).
6.   Dubois, D., Prade, H. and Yager, R. R.: 'Information Engineering and Fuzzy Logic', Proc. FUZZ-IEEE 96, New Orleans, pp. 1525-1531 (1996).
7.   Baldwin, J. F.: 'A Calculus For Mass Assignments In Evidential Reasoning', in 'Advances in the Dempster-Shafer Theory of Evidence', eds, Fedrizzi M., Kacprzyk J. and Yager R. R., John Wiley (1992).
8.   Baldwin. J. F.: 'The Management of Fuzzy and Probabilistic Uncertainities for Knowledge Based Systems', in 'Encyclopedia of AI', ed, Shapiro S. A., John Wiley. (2nd ed) pp. 528-537 (1992).
9.   Bezdek, J. C.: 'Fuzzy Models', IEEE Trans. Fuzzy Systems, Vol. 1, No. 1, pp. 1-5 (1993).
10. Baldwin, J. F., Martin, T. P. and Pilsworth, B. W.: 'FRIL - Fuzzy and Evidential Reasoning in AI', Research Studies Press (John Wiley) (1995).
11. Dubois, D. and Prade, H.: 'Fuzzy sets in approximate reasoning 1 - inference with possibility distributions', Fuzzy Sets and Systems, Vol. 40, pp. 143-202 (1991).
12. Kowalski, R.: 'Logic for Problem Solving', Elsevier (1997).
13. Robinson, J. A.: 'A Machine Oriented Logic based on the Resolution Principle', ACM, Vol. 12, pp. 23-41 (1965).
14. Virtanen, H. E.: 'Linguistic Logic Programming', in 'Logic Programming and Soft Computing', eds, Martin T.P. and Arcelli Fontana F., RSP/Wiley, pp. 91-110 (1998).
15. Baldwin, J. F., Lawry, J. and Martin, T. P.: 'Efficient Algorithms for Semantic Unification', Proc. Information Processing and the Management of Uncertainty, Spain, pp. 527-532 (1996).
16. Lee, R. C. T.: 'Fuzzy Logic and the Resolution Principle', JACM, Vol. 19, pp. 109-119 (1972).
17. Nguyen, H. T.: 'On Random Sets and Belief Functions', J. Math. Anal. & Appl., Vol. 65, pp. 531-542 (1978).
18. Shafer, G.: 'A Mathematical Theory of Evidence', Princeton University Press (1976).
19. Baldwin, J. F.: 'Evidential Reasoning under Probabilistic and Fuzzy Uncertainties', in 'An Introduction to Fuzzy Logic and Applications in Intelligent Systems', eds, Yager R. R. and Zadeh L. A., Kluwer Academic Publishers, pp. 297-335 (1991).
20. Baldwin, J. F.: 'A New Approach to Inference Under Uncertainty for Knowledge Based systems', in 'Symbolic and Quantitative Approaches to Uncertainty', eds, Kruse R. and Siegel P., Springer-Verlag, LNCS548, pp. 107-115 (1991).
21. Baldwin, J. F.: 'Fuzzy Sets, Fuzzy Clustering, and Fuzzy Rules in AI', in 'Fuzzy Logic in AI', ed, Ralescu A. L., Springer Verlag, pp. 10-23 (1993).
22. Baldwin, J. F. and Martin. T. P.: 'An Abstract Mechanism for Handling Uncertainty', in 'Uncertainty in Knowledge Bases', eds, Bouchon-Meunier B., Yager R. R. and Zadeh L. A., Springer Verlag, pp. 126-135 (1991).
23. Warren, D. H. D.: 'An Abstract Prolog Instruction Set', SRI International, Menlo Park, CA (1983).
24. Baldwin, J. F. and Martin, T. P.: 'An Abstract Mechanism for Handling Uncertainty', Proc. Inf Processing and the Management of Uncertainty, Paris, pp. 333-336 (1990).
25. Baldwin, J. F. and Martin, T. P.: 'Fast Operations on Fuzzy Sets in the Abstract Fril Machine', Proc. First IEEE International Conference on Fuzzy Systems, San Diego, CA, pp. 803-810. (1992).

26. Baldwin, J. F., Martin, T. P. and Shanahan, J. G.: 'Modelling with Words using Cartesian Granule Features', Proc. FUZZ-IEEE-97, Barcelona, Spain, pp. 1295-1300 (1997).

27. Baldwin, J. F., Martin, T. P. and Stylianidis, O.: '...', (1998).

28. Baldwin, J. F., et al.: 'Machine recognition of odours in FRIL', in 'New Applications in Fuzzy Logic' (to appear), ed, Baldwin J. F. (1998).

29. Baldwin, J. F. and Martin, T. P.: 'Fuzzy Modelling in an Intelligent Data Browser', Proc. 4th IEEE International Conference on Fuzzy Systems, Yokohama, Japan, pp. 1885-1890 (1995).

30. Baldwin, J. F., Martin, T. P. and McCoy, S. A.: 'Incremental Learning in a Fril-based Odour Classifier', Proc. EUFIT-98, Aachen, Germany (1998).

31. Baldwin, J. F., Gooch, R. M. and Martin, T. P.: 'Fuzzy Processing of Hydrophone Sounds', Fuzzy Sets and Systems, Vol. 77, No. 1, pp. 35-48 (1996).

32. SKI: 'Project-90', Technical Report 91:23, Statens Kärnkraftinspektion, Stockholm, Sweden (1991).

33. Monk, M. R. M. and Swabey, M.: 'Simulation of Aircrew Behaviour for System Integration using Knowledge-Based Programming', Proc. Modelling and Simulation: ESM93, Lyons, France, 459-463 (1993).

34. Sims Williams, J. H., Brown, I. D. and Matthewman, A.: 'An Orthodontic Expert System', Fuzzy Sets and Systems, Vol. 30, pp. 121-133 (1989).

35. Sims Williams, J. H., et al.: 'A Computer Controlled Expert System for Orthodontic Advice', British Dental Journal, Vol. 163, pp. 161-166 (1987).

36. Mackin, N. and Stephens, C. D.: 'Developing and Testing a Fuzzy Expert System - an Example in Orthodontics', Proc. Fuzzy Logic - Applications and Future Directions, London, pp. 61-69 (1997).

37. Wu, C. M. L., Webber, J. P. H. and Morton, S. K.: 'A knowledge-based expert system for laminated composite strut design', Aeronautical Journal, Vol. 95, pp. 1-20 (1991).

38. Smith, B.: 'CAMES - Expert System Administration of Money Market Services', Proc. Conceptual Graphs Workshop, European Conference on AI (1990).

39. Mukaidono M., Shen, Z. L. and Ding, L.: 'Fundamentals of Fuzzy Prolog', Int. J. Approximate Reasoning, Vol. 3, pp. 179-193 (1989).

40. Mukaidono, M. and Yasui, M.: 'Postulates and Proposals of Fuzzy Prolog', Proc. EUFIT 94, Germany, pp. 1080-1086 (1994).

41. Martin, T. P. and Arcelli Fontana, F., (eds): 'Logic Programming and Soft Computing: Uncertainty in A.I.', Research Studies Press/John Wiley (1998).

42. Li, D. and Liu, D.: 'A Fuzzy PROLOG Database System', Research Studies Press (John Wiley) (1990).

43. Ishizuka, M. and Kanai, N.: 'PROLOG-ELF incorporating Fuzzy Logic', New Generation Computing, Vol. 4, pp. 479-486 (1985).

44. Budkley, J. J., Siler, W. and Tucker, D.: 'FLOPS - a Fuzzy Expert Systems', Fuzzy Sets and Systems, Vol. 20, pp. 1-16 (1986).

45. Baldwin, J. F. and Martin, T. P.: 'Basic Concepts of a Fuzzy Logic Data Browser with Applications', in 'Software Agents and Soft Computing: Concepts and Applications', eds, Nwana H. S. and Azarmi N., Springer (LNAI 1198), pp. 211-241 (1997).

46. Baldwin, J. F.: 'Knowledge from Data using Fril and Fuzzy Methods', in 'Fuzzy Logic in AI', ed, Baldwin J. F., John Wiley, pp. 33-76 (1996).

47. Bezdek, J. C.: 'What is Computational Intelligence?' in 'Computational Intelligence - Imitating Life', eds, Zurada J. M., Marks R. J. II and Robinson C. J., IEEE Press. pp. 1-12 (1994).

Advanced Fuzzy Clustering and Decision Tree Plug-Ins for DataEngine™

Christian Borgelt and Heiko Timm

Otto-von-Guericke University of Magdeburg
Faculty of Computer Science (FIN-IWS)
Universitätsplatz 2, D-39106 Magdeburg, Germany

{christian.borgelt,heiko.timm}@cs.uni-magdeburg.de

Abstract. Although a large variety of data analysis tools are available on the market today, none of them is perfect; they all have their strengths and weaknesses. In such a situation it is important that a user can enhance the capabilities of a data analysis tool by his or her own favourite methods in order to compensate for shortcomings of the shipped version. However, only few commercial products offer such a possibility. A rare exception is DataEngine™, which is provided with a well-documented interface for user-defined function blocks (plug-ins). In this paper we describe three plug-ins we implemented for this well-known tool: An *advanced fuzzy clustering plug-in* that extends the fuzzy c-means algorithm (which is a built-in feature of DataEngine™) by other, more flexible algorithms, a *decision tree classifier plug-in* that overcomes the serious drawback that DataEngine™ lacks a native module for this highly important technique, and finally a *naive Bayes classifier plug-in* that makes available an old and time-tested statistical classification method.

1 Introduction

The rapidly growing amount of data that is collected and stored nowadays has created a need for intelligent and easy to use data analysis software, since we are already far beyond the point up to which a "manual" analysis is possible. Several companies have responded to this need and as a consequence a variety of tools and software packages, each with its own strengths and weaknesses, is available today. In this paper we concentrate on one of them, namely DataEngine™ , a data analysis tool that is strongly oriented towards soft computing methods [ ]. Of course, it also offers basic statistical techniques, but its main strengths are fuzzy logic based methods (fuzzy rule bases, fuzzy c-means clustering) and artificial neural networks (multi-layer perceptrons, (fuzzy) Kohonen feature maps). For an impression of this program, see Fig. , which shows its main window.

An important strength of DataEngine™ is that it is equipped with what may be called a "graphical programming interface", although it is not the only

---

[1] DataEngine™ is distributed by Management Intelligenter Technologien GmbH, Aachen, Germany. It is available for MS Windows 95/98™ and MS Windows NT™.

B. Azvine et al. (Eds.): Intelligent Systems and Soft Computing, LNAI 1804, pp. 188– , 2000.
© Springer-Verlag Berlin Heidelberg 2000

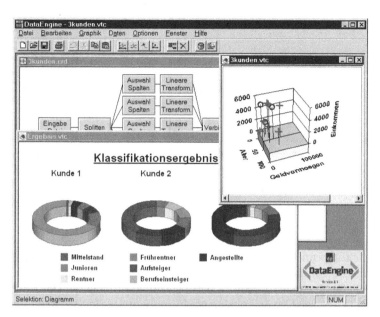

Fig. 1. DataEngine™ main window with some example visualizations. In the background there is a so-called "card" specifying a data flow.

tool on the market that uses such an interface. This interface allows a user to specify a data flow in a kind of graphical macro language that consists of function blocks, each of which—depending on its type—aggregates, modifies, analyses, or visualizes the data or constructs a model. The basic version of DataEngine™ offers a rich variety of techniques in the form of function blocks, including data access (flat files or ODBC), data preprocessing, descriptive statistics, 2D and 3D visualizations, training and executing neural networks etc. Examples of the visualization capabilities of Data Engine™are shown in Fig. .

An example of a so-called "card", i.e. a workspace in which a data flow can be specified graphically, is shown on the left in Fig. . It describes the data flow for the induction, pruning, and testing of a decision tree. On the left there are two function blocks labelled "Eingabe Datei" which provide access to data files, the upper to the training, the lower to the test data. The function block to the right of the upper input block (labelled "Splitten") splits the data flow, so that the same input data can be fed into several function blocks. The two topmost function blocks in the middle column induce ("Ent.baum lernen") and prune ("Ent.baum stutzen") a decision tree on the data, the other two ("Ent.baum ausführen") execute the pruned decision tree on the training and the test data.

---

[2] Unfortunately we only have a German version of DataEngine™, so all function blocks are labelled in German.

[3] These decision tree functions blocks are part of the plug-in described in section .

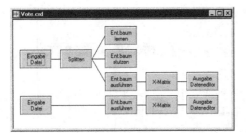 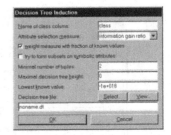

Fig. 2. A so-called "card" of DataEngine™ (left), i.e. a workspace in which a data flow can be specified with a graphical macro language consisting of function blocks, and the configuration dialog of a function block (right).

(That it is the pruned decision tree that is executed cannot be read directly from this card, though, because it is passed via a file. DataEngine™ does not offer an explicit facility to pass models between function blocks.) The result of each execution is analysed by computing confusion matrices ("X-Matrix"), which are then displayed in a data editor ("Ausgabe Dateneditor"). Each function block is equipped with a so-called configuration dialogue, in which parameters of the block can be entered. As an example the configuration dialogue of the decision tree induction function block is shown on the right in Fig. .

Despite the rich variety of methods it offers, DataEngine™, like any other data analysis tool, is far from perfect. Fortunately—and this is a rare exception—a user need not be content with the capabilities of the shipped version, but can compensate detected shortcomings by enhancing the program with so-called *user-defined function blocks* or *plug-ins*. DataEngine™ supports a well-documented interface for Microsoft Visual C/C++™, Borland C/C++™ and Borland Delphi™ (other languages are also possible, provided a MS Windows™ dynamic link library can be created) via which the data tables of DataEngine™ can be accessed and processed with any user-defined method. We have made extensive use of this interface: up to now we have implemented three plug-ins to overcome weaknesses of the original product or to extend its capabilities.

The first plug-in is a fuzzy clustering module [ ], where *clustering* is the process of finding groups of similar cases or objects in a given dataset. The term "fuzzy" indicates that the grouping is not crisp, i.e. the cases or objects are not assigned to one (and only one) cluster each, but may belong (with different degrees) to more than one cluster. In many applications such a "softening" of the boundaries between clusters leads to better results.

Although DataEngine™ is equipped with a built-in fuzzy clustering module, it is rather limited in this respect, since it only offers the standard fuzzy c-means algorithm. However, there are several other fuzzy clustering algorithms that are much more flexible with respect to the shape and the size of the clusters. In order to make these algorithms more widely available we implemented these methods as a plug-in. This plug-in can be obtained from the MIT GmbH, which distributes it under the name "Advanced Fuzzy Clustering".

The other two plug-ins are classifiers. A *classifier* is a program which automatically classifies a case or an object, i.e. assigns it according to its features to one of several given classes. For example, if the cases are patients in a hospital, the attributes are properties of the patients (e.g. sex, age, etc) and their symptoms (e.g. fever, high blood pressure, etc), the classes may be diseases or drugs to administer. The automatic induction of a classifier from a dataset of sample cases is a very frequent task in applications.

The best-known type of classifier is, of course, the decision tree. However, although a decision tree induction module cannot be dispensed with in data analysis—several data analysis tools even rely exclusively on this comprehensible and often highly successful method—DataEngine™ lacks a native module for this type of classifier. In order to overcome this serious drawback, we implemented the well-known top-down induction method for decision trees [ ]. The "DecisionXpert" plug-in, which is offered by the MIT GmbH as an add-on for DataEngine™, is based on this implementation.

The second classifier plug-in uses the old and time-tested naive Bayes approach of classical statistics to construct a classifier and to classify new cases [ ]. Although it is not a technique a data analysis tool is obliged to offer (like decision trees), it is often a convenient alternative to other classification techniques, since it is a very efficient method and yields classifiers that are, like decision trees, easily comprehensible.

The following sections each describe one plug-in: the advanced fuzzy clustering plug-in is discussed in section , the decision tree plug-in in section , and the naive Bayes classifier plug-in in section . Each section first introduces the basic theory underlying the implemented methods and then describes the function blocks of the plug-in. We tried to make these sections as self-contained as possible so that any of them can be read independently of any other.

2   The Fuzzy Clustering Plug-In

The terms "classification" and "to classify" are ambiguous. With respect to classifiers like decision trees, they are used to describe the process of assigning a class from a *predefined* set to an object or case under consideration. In classical statistics, however, these terms usually have a different meaning: they are used to describe the process of dividing a dataset of sample cases into groups of similar cases, with the groups *not* predefined, but to be found by the classification algorithm. This process is also called classification, because the groups to be found are usually (and confusingly) called *classes*. To avoid the confusion that may result from this ambiguity, the latter process, i.e. dividing a dataset into groups of similar cases, is often called *clustering* or *cluster analysis*, thus replacing the ambiguous term *class* with the less ambiguous *cluster*. Nevertheless a reader should keep in mind that in this section "to classify" has a different meaning than in the following ones (except where explicitly indicated otherwise).

Cluster analysis is, as already mentioned, a technique to classify data, i.e. to divide a given dataset of sample cases into a set of classes or *clusters*. The goal is to divide the dataset in such a way that two cases from the same cluster are as similar as possible and two cases from different clusters are as dissimilar as possible. Thus one tries to model the human ability to group similar objects or cases into classes and categories.

In classical cluster analysis [ ] each case or object is assigned to exactly one cluster, i.e. classical cluster analysis yields a crisp partitioning of a dataset with "sharp" boundaries between the clusters. It is therefore also called *crisp cluster analysis*. A crisp partitioning of the dataset, however, though often indisputably successful, is not always appropriate. If the "clouds" formed by the data points corresponding to the cases or objects under consideration are not clearly separated by regions bare of any data points, but if, in contrast, in the joint domain of the attributes there are only regions of higher and lesser data point density, then the boundaries between the clusters can only be drawn with a certain amount of arbitrariness. Due to this arbitrariness it may be doubted, at least for data points close to the boundaries, whether a definite assignment to one class is justified.

An intuitive approach to deal with such situations is to make it possible that a data point belongs in part to one cluster, in part to a second etc. *Fuzzy cluster analysis* does just this: it relaxes the requirement that a data point must be assigned to exactly one cluster by allowing gradual memberships, thus offering the opportunity to deal with data points that do not belong definitely to one cluster [,]. In general, the performance of fuzzy clustering algorithms is superior to that of the corresponding crisp clustering algorithms [ ].

2.1   Fuzzy C-Means Algorithm

A widely used fuzzy clustering algorithm is the fuzzy c-means algorithm (*FCM*) [ ] that is a built-in function of DataEngine™. This algorithm divides a given dataset $X = \{x_1, \ldots, x_n\} \subseteq \mathbb{R}^p$ into C clusters by minimizing the objective function

$$J(X, U, \beta) = \sum_{i=1}^{c} \sum_{j=1}^{n} u_{ij}^m d^2(\beta_i, x_j) \tag{1}$$

subject to

$$\sum_{j=1}^{n} u_{ij} > 0 \quad \text{for all } i \in \{1, \ldots, c\} \tag{2}$$

$$\sum_{i=1}^{c} u_{ij} = 1 \quad \text{for all } j \in \{1, \ldots, n\} \tag{3}$$

where $u_{ij} \in [0, 1]$ is the membership degree of datum x_j to cluster i, $\beta_i = (c_i)$ is the the prototype of cluster i, c_i is the centre of cluster i, and $d(\beta_i, x_j)$ is the distance between datum x_j and prototype β_i. The $c \times n$ matrix $U = [u_{ij}]$ is also

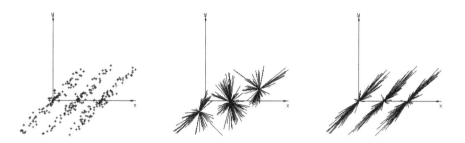

Fig. 3. Dataset 1 (left) and clustering results with the fuzzy c-means algorithm (middle) and the Gustafson-Kessel algorithm (right) for three clusters.

called the fuzzy partition matrix and the parameter m is called the fuzzifier. Usually $m = 2$ is chosen.

Constraint ( ) guarantees that no cluster is empty and constraint ( ) ensures that the sum of the membership degrees for each datum equals 1. Fuzzy clustering algorithms which satisfy these constraints are also called *probabilistic clustering algorithms*, since the membership degrees for one datum formally resemble the probabilities of its being a member of the different cluster.

The fuzzy c-means algorithm divides a given dataset X into c clusters of equal size and shape. The shape of the clusters depends on the distance function $d^2(c_i, x_j)$. With the Euclidean distance, the most common choice, it divides a dataset into c spherical clusters.

Although the fuzzy c-means algorithm is widely used, it fails for some classification tasks, as can be seen in Figs.   and . If the shape of the clusters is not spherical or if the clusters differ considerably in their size, the result of the fuzzy c-means algorithm is often not very intuitive and only poorly fits the data. Another problem of the fuzzy c-means algorithm is its sensitivity to noise and outliers. This sensitivity is caused by restriction ( ), which equips every datum with the same weight and thus the same influence on the classification result.

To amend these problems we have implemented several fuzzy clustering algorithms that can be seen as extensions of the fuzzy c-means method. These algorithms divide a given dataset into clusters of different size and shape and are less sensitive to noise and outliers.

2.2   Possibilistic Clustering Algorithms

In applications it is a common requirement that the algorithms used should be robust. With respect to noise and outliers, this means that the performance of the algorithms should not deteriorate drastically due to noise or outliers [ ]. Unfortunately, due to restriction ( ) the fuzzy c-means algorithm is sensitive to noise and outliers and thus not an ideal of robustness.

Fig. 4. Dataset 2 (left) and clustering results with the fuzzy c-means algorithm (middle) and the Gustafson-Kessel algorithm (right) for four clusters.

One approach to reduce this sensitivity is to use an extra cluster for noise and outliers [,]. Another approach is to remove restriction ( ) so that it becomes possible that data that resembles noise or outliers can have a low membership degree to all clusters. This approach is usually called *possibilistic clustering*. To avoid the trivial solution, i.e. $u_{ij} = 0$ for all $i \in \{1, \ldots, c\}$, $j \in \{1, \ldots, n\}$, the objective function of a possibilistic clustering algorithm has to be modified to:

$$J(X, U, \beta) = \sum_{i=1}^{c} \sum_{j=1}^{n} u_{ij}^m d^2(\beta_i, x_j) + \sum_{i=1}^{c} \eta_i \sum_{j=1}^{n} (1 - u_{ij})^m \qquad (4)$$

where $\eta_i > 0$. The first term minimizes the weighted distances and the second term avoids the trivial solution. A fuzzy clustering algorithm that minimizes the above function subject to constraint ( ) is called a *possibilistic clustering algorithm*, since the membership degrees for a datum resemble the possibility (in the sense of possibility theory) of its being a member of the different clusters.

Minimizing the objective function ( ) with respect to the membership degrees leads to the following equation for updating the membership degrees u_{ij} [ ]:

$$u_{ij} = \frac{1}{1 + \left(\dfrac{d^2(x_j, \beta_i)}{\eta_i} \right)^{\frac{1}{m-1}}}. \qquad (5)$$

Equation ( ) shows that η_i determines the distance at which the membership degree equals 0.5. If $d^2(x_j, \beta_i)$ equals η_i, the membership degree is 0.5. So it is useful to choose η_i for each cluster separately [ ]. η_i can be determined, for instance, by computing the fuzzy intra cluster distance ( )

$$\eta_i = \frac{K}{N_i} \sum_{j=1}^{n} u_{ij}^m d^2(x_j, \beta_i) \qquad (6)$$

where $N_i = \sum_{j=1}^{n} (u_{ij})^m$. Usually $K = 1$ is chosen. In contrast to probabilistic clustering algorithm it is recommended to choose $m = 1.5$ [ ].

The fundamental difference between a probabilistic clustering algorithm and a possibilistic clustering algorithm is that a probabilistic clustering algorithm is primarily a partitioning algorithm while a possibilistic clustering algorithm is a mode-seeking algorithm, i.e. is, a possibilistic clustering algorithm partitions a data set into c clusters, regardless of how many clusters are actually present. In contrast, each component generated by a possibilistic clustering algorithm corresponds to a dense region in the data set, i.e. if the actual number of clusters is smaller than c, some clusters might be detected twice, and if the number of clusters is higher than c, often some clusters go undetected. To avoid some clusters being detected twice while other clusters go undetected, it is recommended to initialize a possibilistic clustering algorithm with the results of the corresponding probabilistic version if the data set is not too noisy [ ].

The possibilistic fuzzy c-means algorithm has been successfully used in several applications and it often helps to deal with noisy data [,]. However, if the data is too noisy, the above initialization fails. In that case the user has to be very careful with the choice of η_i and the initialization of the possibilistic clustering algorithm [, ,]. As an attempt to improve the possibilistic clustering algorithm, a mixed fuzzy-possibilistic version has been suggested [ ].

2.3   The Gustafson-Kessel Algorithm and the FMLE

In contrast to the fuzzy c-means algorithm the Gustafson-Kessel algorithm (GK) searches for clusters of different shape [ ]. To determine the shape of the clusters the algorithm computes for each cluster a separate norm matrix A_i, $A_i = (\det C_i)^{\frac{1}{n}} C_i^{-1}$. These norm matrices are updated together with the centres of the corresponding clusters. Therefore the prototypes of the clusters are a pair (c_i, C_i), where c_i is the centre of the cluster and C_i is the covariance matrix, which defines the shapes of the clusters.

In a fashion similar to the fuzzy c-means algorithm, the Gustafson-Kessel computes the distance to the prototypes as:

$$d^2(x_j, \beta_i) = (\det C_i)^{\frac{1}{n}} (x_j - c_i)^T C_i^{-1} (x_j - c_i). \tag{7}$$

To minimize the objective function with respect to the prototypes, the prototypes are updated according to the following equations [ ]:

$$c_i = \frac{1}{N_i} \sum_{j=1}^{n} u_{ij}^m x_j, \tag{8}$$

$$C_i = \frac{1}{N_i} \sum_{j=1}^{n} u_{ij}^m (x_j - c_i)(x_j - c_i)^T. \tag{9}$$

The Gustafson-Kessel algorithm is a simple fuzzy clustering algorithm to detect ellipsoidal clusters with approximately the same size but different shapes.

Another modification of the fuzzy c-means algorithm is the fuzzy maximum likelihood estimation algorithm ($FMLE$) [ ]. This algorithm divides a given data set into clusters of different shape and different size. The idea of the FMLE algorithm is to interpret the data set as a p-dimensional normal distribution. Therefore the distance of a datum to a cluster is inversely proportional to the posterior possibility that a datum x_{ij} is the realization of the ith normal distribution. Therefore the distance between a datum x_j and a cluster c_i is computed as:

$$d^2(x_j, \beta_i) = d_{ij}^2 = \frac{(det(C_i))^{\frac{1}{2}}}{P_i} \exp\left(\frac{(x_j - c_i)C_i^{-1}(x_j - c_i)^T}{2}\right). \qquad (10)$$

2.4   Simplified Versions of the GK and the FMLE

The Gustafson-Kessel and the FMLE algorithm both extend the fuzzy c-means algorithm by computing covariance matrices for each cluster. Since the covariance matrices decode norms which transform spherical clusters to ellipses or ellipsoids, the Gustafson-Kessel and the FMLE algorithm are able to detect clusters of different shape.

The idea of the simplified versions of the Gustafson-Kessel and the FMLE algorithm is to use only diagonal matrices instead of positive definite symmetric matrices as the Gustafson-Kessel or the FMLE algorithm [ ], i.e. the algorithms search only for clusters that are axis parallel. This has the advantage that it is not necessary to invert matrices and to compute determinants. Therefore these algorithms have a lower computational complexity than the Gustafson-Kessel and the FMLE algorithm. These axis-parallel variants are an interesting compromise between the flexibility of the original versions and the low computational costs of the fuzzy c-means algorithm.

In addition, these algorithms are especially suited for fuzzy rule generation, i.e. for extracting descriptive rules from a data set by classifying the inputs. Since for each rule each input variable has its own interval, the clusters have to describe rectangles, which can be approximated well by axis-parallel clusters.

2.5   The DataEngine™ Plug-In

We have implemented the fuzzy clustering algorithms described in this section as a plug-in for DataEngine™. The plug-in consists of five function blocks:

Fuzzy Cluster Analysis — Several fuzzy clustering algorithms
This function block contains the main functionality of the plug-in. It contains the fuzzy clustering algorithms and executes them on the given dataset. In the configuration dialogue the algorithm, the number of clusters, and several parameters of the algorithm can be specified. Its input is unclassified data and its output is the classified data and their membership degrees to the clusters that can be used as input for other function blocks. In addition, the prototypes of the clusters are stored in a user-specified file. The prototypes can be used by other function blocks of the plug-in, for instance, as a classifier.

Classification — Classify a dataset

This function block classifies a dataset with respect to clusters that have been determined with the above function block. The cluster prototypes are read from the file to which they were saved by the first function block.

Validity Measures — Evaluation of a clustering

This function block is used to assess the quality of a computed classification. Several different validity measures can be chosen.

Parameter Extraction — Extract cluster parameters

This function block extracts the parameters of the clusters. Depending on the algorithm, the centre and the covariance matrix of each cluster are extracted.

Labelling — Labelling of a classification

With this function block labels (i.e. names) can be assigned to the clusters. This can be done automatically based on labelled data or manually.

3   The Decision Tree Plug-In

Decision trees are classifiers which—as the name already indicates—have a tree-like structure. To each leaf a class, to each inner node an attribute is assigned. There can be several leaves associated with the same class and several inner nodes associated with the same attribute. The descendants of the inner nodes are reached via edges, to each of which a value of the attribute associated with the node is assigned. Each leaf represents a decision "The case considered belongs to class c.", where c is the class associated with the leaf. Each inner node corresponds to an instruction "Test attribute A and follow the edge to which the observed value is assigned!", where A is the attribute associated with the node. A case is classified by starting at the root of the tree and executing the instructions in the inner nodes until a leaf is reached, which then states a class.

From the above description it is obvious that decision trees are very simple to use. Unfortunately, it is not quite as simple to construct them manually. Especially if the number of possible test attributes is large and the available knowledge about the underlying relations between the classes and the test attributes is vague, manual construction can be tedious and time consuming. However, if a database of sample cases is available, one can try an automatic induction [, ,]. The usual approach is a top-down process (TDIDT — top-down induction of decision trees), which uses a "divide and conquer" principle together with a greedy selection of test attributes according to the value ascribed to them by an evaluation measure. In section   we illustrate this approach using a simple (artificial) medical example.

Since the success of the induction algorithm depends heavily on the attribute selection measure used, in section   we list a large variety of such measures. However, limits of space prevent us from discussing in detail the ideas underlying them. Which of these measures yields the best results cannot be stated in general,

Table 1. Patient data consisting of a set of descriptive attributes together with an effective drug (effective with respect to some unspecified disease).

No	Sex	Age	Blood Pressure	Drug
1	male	20	normal	A
2	female	73	normal	B
3	female	37	high	A
4	male	33	low	B
5	female	48	high	A
6	male	29	normal	A
7	female	52	normal	B
8	male	42	low	B
9	male	61	normal	B
10	female	30	normal	A
11	female	26	low	B
12	male	54	high	A

but depends on the application. Therefore all of these measures can be selected for the decision tree induction function block of the DataEngine™ plug-in we describe in section   . In addition to the induction function block, this plug-in consists of function blocks for pruning a decision tree, for executing a decision tree to classify a set of cases and for computing a confusion matrix (which is useful to assess the quality of a learned classifier).

3.1 Induction of Decision Trees

As already remarked above, the induction of decision trees from data rests on a "divide and conquer" principle together with a greedy selection of the attributes to test: from a given set of classified case descriptions the conditional frequency distributions of the classes, given the attributes used in the case descriptions, are computed. These distributions are evaluated using some measure and the attribute yielding the best value is selected as the next test attribute. This is the greedy part of the algorithm. Then the case descriptions are divided according to the values of the chosen test attribute and the procedure is applied recursively to the resulting subsets. This is the "divide and conquer" part of the algorithm. The recursion stops, if either all cases of a subset belong to the same class, or no attribute yields an improvement of the classification, or there are no attributes left for a test. We illustrate this procedure with a simple example and state the induction algorithm in pseudo-code.

A Simple Example. Table   shows the features of twelve patients—sex, age, and a qualitative statement of the blood pressure—together with a drug, which for the patient has been effective in the treatment of some unspecified disease.

If we neglect the features of the patients, the effective drug can be predicted only with a rate of success of 50%, since drug A as well as drug B were effective in six cases. Because such a situation is unfavourable for future treatments, we try to induce a decision tree, which will (hopefully) allow us to derive the effective drug from the features of a patient.

To this end we consider all conditional distributions of the effective drugs given the available features (see table   ). It is obvious that the patient's sex is without any influence, since for male as well as for female patients both drugs were effective in half of the cases (thus being politically correct, i.e. here non-sexist). The patient's age yields a better result: below forty years of age drug A has been effective in four out of six cases. Over forty years of age the same holds for drug B. Hence, the success rate is 67%. However, testing the blood pressure yields an even better result: if it is high, drug A, if it is low, drug B is the correct drug. Only if the blood pressure is normal, the prediction is not improved. The overall success rate is 75%.

Since the blood pressure allows us to determine the effective drug with the highest rate of success, it is chosen as the first test attribute and placed at the root of the decision tree. The case descriptions of the table are divided according to the values they contain for this attribute. The effective drug is definite for patients with low or high blood pressure, and thus these cases need not be considered further. For the patients with normal blood pressure we test again the conditional distribution of the effective drug given the patient's sex and age (see Table   ). The patients' sex allows us to determine the correct drug for patients with normal blood pressure with a success rate of 67%. However, dividing the patients in those younger than forty and those older, perfectly separates the cases in which drug A was effective from those in which drug B was effective. Therefore the age is chosen as a second test attribute and thus a reliable method to determine the effective drug has been found. The corresponding decision tree, which can be read directly from Table   (right), is shown in Fig. .

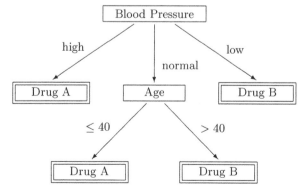

Fig. 5. The induced decision tree for the effective drug.

Table 2. The conditional distributions of the effective drug given the sex (left), the age (middle, divided into "less than 40" and "over 40") and the blood pressure (right).

No	Sex	Drug
1	male	A
6	male	A
12	male	A
4	male	B
8	male	B
9	male	B
3	female	A
5	female	A
10	female	A
2	female	B
7	female	B
11	female	B

No	Age	Drug
1	20	A
11	26	B
6	29	A
10	30	A
4	33	B
3	37	A
8	42	B
5	48	A
7	52	B
12	54	A
9	61	B
2	73	B

No	Blood Pressure	Drug
3	high	A
5	high	A
12	high	A
1	normal	A
6	normal	A
10	normal	A
2	normal	B
7	normal	B
9	normal	B
4	low	B
8	low	B
11	low	B

Table 3. The second order conditional distributions of the effective drug given the blood pressure and the sex (left) and the blood pressure and the age (right, divided into "less than 40" and "over 40").

No	Blood Pressure	Sex	Drug
3	high		A
5	high		A
12	high		A
1	normal	male	A
6	normal	male	A
9	normal	male	B
2	normal	female	B
7	normal	female	B
10	normal	female	A
4	low		B
8	low		B
11	low		B

No	Blood Pressure	Age	Drug
3	high		A
5	high		A
12	high		A
1	normal	20	A
6	normal	29	A
10	normal	30	A
7	normal	52	B
9	normal	61	B
2	normal	73	B
11	low		B
4	low		B
8	low		B

```
function grow_tree (S : set of cases) : node;
begin
    best_v := WORTHLESS;
    for all untested attributes A do
        compute frequencies N_{ij}, N_{i.}, N_{.j}
            for 1 ≤ i ≤ n_C and 1 ≤ j ≤ n_A;
        compute value v of a selection measure
            using N_{ij}, N_{i.}, N_{.j};
        if v > best_v
        then best_v := v;
            best_A := A;
        end;
    end
    if best_v = WORTHLESS
    then create leaf node n;
        assign majority class of S to n;
    else create test node n;
        assign test on attribute best_A to n;
        for all a ∈ dom(best_A) do
            n.child[a] := grow_tree(S|_{best_A=a});
        end;
    end;
    return n;
end;   (* grow_tree() *)
```

Fig. 6. The TDIDT (top-down induction of decision trees) algorithm.

The Induction Algorithm. The general algorithm to induce a decision tree from data is shown in Fig.   in a pseudo-code similar to Pascal. In the first part of the algorithm for each attribute the frequency distribution of its values and the classes is determined. From this distribution the value of an evaluation measure is computed. The attribute with the highest value is stored in the variable $best\_A$. This is a crucial step in the algorithm, since a wrong assessment of the attributes and thus a bad choice for the test attribute can severely diminish the classifier's performance. (More about evaluation measures can be found in section   .) In the second part of the algorithm either a leaf or a test node is created — depending on the outcome of the first part. If a test node is created, the case descriptions are divided according to their value for the chosen test attribute and for each resulting subset the function grow_tree is called recursively.

To simplify the algorithm we assumed in this description that all attributes have a finite number of symbolic values. Integer or real-valued attributes can be processed by sorting the occurring values and choosing a cut value for each pair of consecutive values (e.g. the arithmetic mean of the two values). Using this cut value an (artificial) symbolic attribute with values "greater than cut value" and "less than cut value" is created. The best cut value, i.e. the one whose corresponding symbolic attribute is rated best by the chosen evaluation measure, is selected to represent the numeric attribute.

During the recursive descent already tested symbolic attributes are marked, since another test of these attributes is obviously pointless: dividing the cases leads to all cases having the same value for a tested attribute in the deeper levels of the recursion. Integer and real-valued attributes, however, are not marked, since deeper down in the recursion a different cut value may be chosen and thus the range of values may be subdivided further.

After a decision tree has been induced, it is often pruned in order to simplify it and to reduce possible overfitting to random properties of the training data. However, reasons of space prevent us from studying this step in detail.

3.2   Attribute Selection Measures

As already indicated at the beginning of this section and substantiated by the description of the general induction algorithm in the preceding section, the success of the induction of a decision tree from data depends to a high degree on the attribute selection measure used. Several years of research, not only in decision tree induction but also in the closely related area of inducing Bayesian networks from data, has led to a large variety of evaluation measures, which draw from a substantial set of ideas to assess the quality of an attribute. Unfortunately, limits of space prevent us from discussing in detail these measures and the ideas underlying them. Hence we only give a list:

- information gain I_{gain} (mutual information/cross entropy) [, ,]
- information gain ratio I_{gr} [,]
- symmetric information gain ratio I_{sgr} [ ]
- Gini index [,]
- symmetric Gini index [ ]
- modified Gini index [ ]
- relief measure [,]
- χ^2 measure
- weight of evidence [ ]
- relevance [ ]
- K2 metric [,]
- BDeu metric [,]
- minimum description length with relative frequency coding l_{rel} [ ]
- minimum description length with absolute frequencies coding l_{abs} [ ]
  (closely related to the K2 metric)
- stochastic complexity [,]
- specificity gain S_{gain} [,]
- (symmetric) specificity gain ratio S_{gr} [ ]

It may be worth noting that the K2 metric and the BDeu metric were originally developed for learning Bayesian networks and that the specificity measures are based not on probability or information theory but on possibility theory—an alternative theory for reasoning with imperfect knowledge that is closely connected to fuzzy set theory. A reader who is interested in more detailed information about the measures listed above may consult [ ] or [ ].

Unfortunately, no general rule can be given as to which measure should be chosen. Although some measures (e.g. the information gain ratio and the minimum description length measures) perform slightly better on average, all have their strengths and weaknesses. For each measure there are specific situations in which it performs best and hence it can pay to try several measures.

3.3   The DataEngine™ Plug-In

We have implemented a powerful decision tree induction algorithm as a plug-in for DataEngine™ in order to improve this esteemed tool even further. This plug-in consists of four function blocks:

grow — grow a decision tree
This function block receives as input a table of classified sample cases and grows a decision tree. The data types of the table columns (either symbolic or numeric) can be stated in the unit fields of the table columns, which can also be used to instruct the algorithm to ignore certain columns. Although tables passed to user-defined functions blocks may not contain unknown values, this function block provides a facility to specify which table fields should be considered as unknown: in the configuration dialogue one may enter a value for the lowest known value. All values below this value are considered to be unknown. In addition the configuration dialogue lets you choose the attribute selection measure (see the preceding section for a list), whether the measure should be weighted with the fraction of known values (to take into account the lesser utility of rarely known attributes), whether the algorithm should try to form subsets on symbolic attributes, a maximal height for the decision tree to be learned, and the name of a file into which the learned decision tree should be saved.

prune — prune a learned decision tree
This function block receives as input a learned decision tree stored in a file and a table of classified sample cases, which may or may not be the table from which the decision tree was learned. It prunes the decision tree using the table applying one of two pruning methods (either pessimistic pruning or confidence level pruning), which are governed by a parameter that can be entered in the configuration dialogue. In addition, the configuration dialogue lets you enter a maximal height for the pruned tree, and (to be able to deal with unknown values, see above) a lowest known value. The pruned decision tree is written to another file, whose name can also be specified in the configuration dialogue.

exec — execute a learned decision tree
This function block receives as input a learned (and maybe pruned) decision tree stored in a file and a table of cases. It executes the decision tree for each case in the table and adds to it a new column containing the class predicted by the decision tree. The configuration dialogue lets you enter the name of the new column and (as described for the two blocks above) a lowest known value.

xmat — compute a confusion matrix

This function block receives as input a table. Its configuration dialogue lets you enter the names of two columns for which a confusion matrix shall be determined. It generates a table containing the confusion matrix (either with absolute or relative numbers) and the sums over lines and columns (excluding the diagonal elements). These sums are the number of confusions or misclassifications, if one column contains the correct classification, the other the prediction of a classifier.

All function blocks that deal directly with decision trees, i.e. the blocks *grow*, *prune*, and *exec* also comprise a decision tree viewer which lets you navigate through a learned decision tree using the well-known MS Windows™ tree view control (used, for example, in the MS Windows™ explorer to visualize the hierarchic file system). Hence you need not accept the learned classifier as a black box (as is usually the case for, for example, neural networks), but you can inspect how an induced decision tree arrives at its results.

4   The Naive Bayes Classifier Plug-In

Naive Bayes classifiers [, , ,] are an old and well-known type of classifiers which use a probabilistic approach to assign the classes, i.e. they try to compute the conditional probabilities of the different classes given the values of other attributes and predict the class with the highest conditional probability. Since it is usually impossible to store or even to estimate these conditional probabilities, they exploit Bayes rule and a set of conditional independence statements to simplify the task. A detailed description is given in section   .

Due to the strong independence assumptions, but also because some attributes may not be able to contribute to the classification accuracy, it is not always advisable to use all available attributes. With all attributes a naive Bayes classifier is more complicated than necessary and sometimes even yields results that can be improved upon by using fewer attributes. Therefore a naive Bayes classifier should be simplified. Two very simple methods to reduce the number of attributes are discussed in section   .

In section   we describe the plug-in we implemented for DataEngine™. This plug-in consists of three function blocks: one to induce (and simplify) a naive Bayes classifier, one to classify new data, and one to compute a confusion matrix to evaluate the quality of the induced classifier. The latter function block is the same as the function block *xmat* of the decision tree plug-in.

4.1   Naive Bayes Classifiers

As already mentioned above, naive Bayes classifiers use a probabilistic approach to classify data: they try to compute conditional class probabilities and then predict the most probable class. To be more precise, let C denote a class attribute with a finite domain of m classes, i.e. $\mathrm{dom}(C) = \{c_1, \ldots, c_m\}$, and let $U = \{A_1, \ldots, A_n\}$ be a set of other attributes used to describe a case or an object of the universe of discourse. These other attributes may be symbolic, i.e. $\mathrm{dom}(A_j) = \{a_1^{(j)}, \ldots, a_{m_j}^{(j)}\}$, or numeric, i.e. $\mathrm{dom}(A_j) = \mathbb{R}$. For simplicity, we always use the notation $a_{i_j}^{(j)}$ for a value of an attribute A_j, independent of whether it is a symbolic or a numeric one. With this notation, a case or an object can be described by an instantiation $\omega = (a_{i_1}^{(1)}, \ldots, a_{i_n}^{(n)})$ of the attributes $A_1, \ldots, A_n$ and thus the universe of discourse is $\Omega = \mathrm{dom}(A_1) \times \ldots \times \mathrm{dom}(A_n)$.

For a given instantiation ω, a naive Bayes classifier tries to compute the conditional probability

$$P(C = c_i \mid \omega) = P\left(C = c_i \;\middle|\; \bigwedge_{j=1}^{n} A_j = a_{i_j}^{(j)}\right)$$

for all c_i and then predicts the class for which this probability is highest. Of course, it is usually impossible to store all of these conditional probabilities explicitly, so that a simple lookup would be all that is needed to find the most probable class. If there are numeric attributes, this is obvious (some parameterized function is needed then). But even if all attributes are symbolic, such an approach most often is infeasible: a class (or a class probability distribution) has to be stored for each point of the Cartesian product of the attribute domains, whose size grows exponentially with the number of attributes. To circumvent this problem, naive Bayes classifiers exploit—as their name already indicates— Bayes rule and a set of conditional independence assumptions. With Bayes rule the conditional probabilities are inverted, i.e. naive Bayes classifiers consider :

$$P\left(C = c_i \;\middle|\; \bigwedge_{j=1}^{n} A_j = a_{i_j}^{(j)}\right) = \frac{f\left(\bigwedge_{j=1}^{n} A_j = a_{i_j}^{(j)} \;\middle|\; C = c_i\right) \cdot P(C = c_i)}{f\left(\bigwedge_{j=1}^{n} A_j = a_{i_j}^{(j)}\right)}.$$

Of course, for this inversion to be possible, the probability density function $f\left(\bigwedge_{A_j \in U} A_j = a_{i_j}^{(j)}\right)$ must be strictly positive.

There are two observations to be made about the inversion carried out above. In the first place, the denominator of the fraction on the right can be neglected, since for a given case or object to be classified, it is fixed and therefore does not have any influence on the class ranking (which is all we are interested in). In addition, its influence can always be restored by normalizing the class distribution, i.e. we can exploit:

$$f\left(\bigwedge_{j=1}^{n} A_j = a_{i_j}^{(j)}\right) = \sum_{i=1}^{m} f\left(\bigwedge_{j=1}^{n} A_j = a_{i_j}^{(j)} \;\middle|\; C = c_i\right) \cdot P(C = c_i).$$

---

[4] To be able to use this notation for numeric attributes, one simply has to choose an appropriate uncountably infinite index set $\mathcal{I}_j$, from which the index i_j is to be taken.

[5] For simplicity, we always use a probability density function f, although this is strictly correct only, if there is at least one numeric attribute. If all attributes are symbolic, this should be a probability P. The only exception is the class attribute, since it necessarily has a finite domain.

It follows that we only need to consider:

$$P\left(C = c_i \mid \bigwedge_{j=1}^{n} A_j = a_{i_j}^{(j)}\right) = \frac{P(C = c_i)}{S} f\left(\bigwedge_{j=1}^{n} A_j = a_{i_j}^{(j)} \mid C = c_i\right),$$

where S is a normalization constant.

Secondly, we can see that just inverting the probabilities does not buy us anything, since the probability space is just as large as it was before the inversion. However, here the second ingredient of naive Bayes classifiers, which is responsible for the "naive" in their name, comes in, namely the conditional independence assumptions. To exploit them, we first apply the chain rule of probability:

$$P\left(C = c_i \mid \bigwedge_{j=1}^{n} A_j = a_{i_j}^{(j)}\right)$$
$$= \frac{P(C = c_i)}{S} \prod_{k=1}^{n} f\left(A_k = a_{i_k}^{(k)} \mid \bigwedge_{j=1}^{k-1} A_j = a_{i_j}^{(j)}, C = c_i\right).$$

Now we make the crucial assumption that given the value of the class attribute, any attribute A_j is independent of any other. That is, we assume that knowing the class is enough to determine the probability (density) for a value $a_{i_j}^{(j)}$, i.e., that we need not know the values of any other attributes. Of course, this is a pretty strong assumption, which is very likely to fail. However, it considerably simplifies the formula stated above, since with it we can cancel all attributes A_j appearing in the conditions:

$$P\left(C = c_i \mid \bigwedge_{j=1}^{n} A_j = a_{i_j}^{(j)}\right) = \frac{P(C = c_i)}{S} \prod_{j=1}^{n} f\left(A_j = a_{i_j}^{(j)} \mid C = c_i\right).$$

This is the fundamental formula underlying naive Bayes classifiers. For a symbolic attribute A_j the conditional probabilities $P(A_j = a_{i_j}^{(j)} \mid C = c_i)$ are stored as a simple conditional probability table. This is feasible now, since there is only one condition and hence only $m \cdot m_j$ probabilities have to be stored. For numeric attributes it is usually assumed that the probability density is a Gaussian function (a normal distribution) and hence only the expected values $\mu_j(c_i)$ and the variances $\sigma_j^2(c_i)$ need to be stored in this case.

It should be noted that naive Bayes classifiers can be seen as a special type of probabilistic networks, or, to be more precise, of Bayesian networks [ ]. Due to the strong independence assumptions underlying them, the corresponding network has a very simple structure: it is star-like with the class attribute being the source of all edges (see Fig.).

---

[6] Strictly speaking, the constant S is dependent on the instantiation $(a_{i_1}^{(1)}, \ldots, a_{i_n}^{(n)})$. However, as already said above, when classifying a given case or object, this instantiation is fixed and hence we need to consider only one value S.

[7] Actually only $m \cdot (m_j - 1)$ probabilities are really necessary. Since the probabilities have to add up to one, one value can be discarded from each conditional distribution. However, in implementations it is usually much easier to store all probabilities.

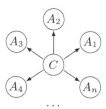

Fig. 7. A naive Bayes classifier is a Bayesian network with a star-like structure.

Naive Bayes classifiers can easily be induced from a dataset of preclassified sample cases. All one has to do is to estimate the conditional probabilities/probability densities $f(A_j = a_{i_j}^{(j)} \mid C = c_i)$ using, for instance, maximum likelihood estimation. For symbolic attributes, this yields:

$$\hat{P}(A_j = a_{i_j}^{(j)} \mid C = c_i) = \frac{\#(A_j = a_{i_j}^{(j)}, C = c_i)}{\#(C = c_i)},$$

where $\#(C = c_i)$ is the number of sample cases that belong to the class c_i and $\#(A_j = a_{i_j}^{(j)}, C = c_i)$ is the number of sample cases belonging to class c_i and having the value $a_{i_j}^{(j)}$ for the attribute A_j. To ensure that the probability is strictly positive (see above), it is assumed that there is at least one example for each class in the dataset. Otherwise the class is simply removed from the domain of the class attribute. If an attribute value does not occur given some class, its probability is either set to $\frac{1}{2N}$, where N is the number of sample cases, or a uniform prior of, for example, $\frac{1}{N}$ is always added to the estimated distribution, which is then renormalized (Laplace correction). For a numeric attribute A_j the standard maximum likelihood estimation functions

$$\hat{\mu}_j(c_i) = \frac{1}{\#(C = c_i)} \sum_{k=1}^{\#(C=c_i)} a_{i_j(k)}^{(j)}$$

for the expected value, where $a_{i_j(k)}^{(j)}$ is the value of the attribute A_j in the k-th sample case belonging to class c_i, and

$$\hat{\sigma}_j^2(c_i) = \frac{1}{\#(C = c_i)} \sum_{k=1}^{\#(C=c_i)} \left(a_{i_j(k)}^{(j)} - \hat{\mu}_j(c_i) \right)^2$$

for the variance can be used.

As an illustrative example, let us take a look at the well-known iris data [ ]. The problem is to predict the iris type (iris setosa, iris versicolor, or iris virginica) from measurements of the sepal length and width and the petal length and width. Due to the limited number of dimensions of a sheet of paper we confine ourselves to the latter two measures. The naive Bayes classifier induced from

Table 4. A naive Bayes classifier for the iris data. The normal distributions are described by stating $\hat{\mu} \pm \hat{\sigma}$.

iris type	setosa	versicolor	virginica
prior prob.	0.333	0.333	0.333
petal length	1.46 ± 0.17	4.26 ± 0.46	5.55 ± 0.55
petal width	0.24 ± 0.11	1.33 ± 0.20	2.03 ± 0.27

these two measures and all 150 cases is shown in Table . It is easy to see from this table how different petal lengths and widths provide evidence for the different types of iris flowers. The conditional probability density functions used by this naive Bayes classifier to predict the iris type are shown graphically in Fig. . The ellipses are the 2σ-boundaries of the (bivariate) normal distributions. As a consequence of the strong conditional independence assumptions, these ellipses are axis-parallel: the normal distributions are estimated separately for each dimension and no covariance is taken into account.

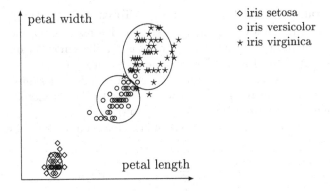

Fig. 8. Naive Bayes density functions for the iris data. The ellipses are the 2σ-boundaries of the probability density functions.

4.2   Classifier Simplification

A naive Bayes classifier makes strong independence assumptions (see above). It is not surprising that these assumptions are likely to fail. If they fail, the classifier may be worse than necessary. In addition, some attributes may not contribute to the classification accuracy, making the classifier more complicated than necessary. To cope with these problems, simplification methods may be used, for instance, simple greedy attribute selection. With this procedure one can hope to find a subset of attributes for which the strong assumptions hold at least approximately.

We consider here two very simple, but effective, attribute selection methods: the first method starts with a classifier that simply predicts the majority class and does not use any attribute information. Then attributes are added one by one. In each step that attribute is selected which, if added, leads to the smallest number of misclassifications on the training data. The process stops when adding any of the remaining attributes does not reduce the number of errors.

The second method is a reversal of the first. It starts with a classifier that uses all available attributes and then removes attributes step by step. In each step that attribute is selected which, if removed, leads to the smallest number of misclassifications on the training data. The process stops when removing any of the remaining attributes leads to a larger number of errors.

4.3 The DataEngine™ Plug-In

We have implemented a naive Bayes classifier as a plug-in DataEngine™ in order to improve the capabilities of this tool. It consists of three function blocks:

nbi — naive Bayes classifier induction

This function block receives as input a table of classified sample cases and induces a naive Bayes classifier. The data types of the table columns (either symbolic or numeric) can be stated in the unit fields of the table columns, which can also be used to instruct the algorithm to ignore certain columns. Although tables passed to user-defined functions blocks may not contain unknown values, this function block provides, as the decision tree function blocks, a facility to specify which table fields should be considered as unknown: in the configuration dialogue you may enter a value for the lowest known value. All values below this value are considered to be unknown. In addition, the configuration dialogue lets you choose a simplification method and you can specify the Laplace correction to be used (as a multiple of the standard value $\frac{1}{n}$, where n is the number of tuples from which the classifier is induced) and the name of a file into which the induced naive Bayes classifier should be saved.

nbc — naive Bayes classification

This function block receives as input an induced naive Bayes classifier stored in a file and a table of cases. It executes the naive Bayes classifier for each tuple in the table and adds to it a new column containing the class predicted by the classifier. The configuration dialogue lets you enter the name of the classification column, the Laplace correction to be used (again as a multiple of the standard value $\frac{1}{n}$, where n is the number of tuples from which the classifier was induced), and (just as described for the block above) a lowest known value. In addition you can request an additional column into which a confidence value is written for each classified tuple. This confidence value is the probability of the predicted class as computed by the classifier.

xmat — compute a confusion matrix
This function blocks is identical to the one with the same name in the decision tree plug-in, see section   .

All function block dealing directly with naive Bayes classifiers (*nbi* and *nbc*) also comprise a viewer which lets you inspect the constructed naive Bayes classifier using the well-known MS Windows tree view control (used, for example, in the MS Windows explorer to visualize the hierarchic file system). Hence you need not accept the classifier as a black box (as is usually the case for, for example, neural networks), but you can inspect what evidence it exploits to arrive at its results.

5 Conclusions

None of the data analysis tools available today is perfect, but with some tools a user has to be content with the capabilities supplied by the programmers, without a chance of ever overcoming the restrictions and weaknesses of the shipped version. Some, though very few tools, however, with DataEngine™ among them, offer the possibility for user-specific extensions. In this paper we described how we exploited the DataEngine™ interface for user-defined function blocks to implement three plug-ins that overcome weaknesses of the original product and extend its capabilities. The fact that two of the plug-ins have become commercial products that are sold now by the makers of DataEngine™ as add-ons to their basic tool shows that it can pay for a software company to produce open and extensible systems, although it takes considerable effort to do so.

References

1. Nürnberger A. and Timm H.: 'Or software: Dataengine'. OR Spektrum, Vol. 21, pp. 305–313 (1999).
2. Timm H.: 'A fuzzy cluster analysis plug-in for dataengine'. In 'Proc. 2nd Data Analysis Symposium' (Aachen) (1998).
3. Borgelt C.: 'A decision tree plug-in for dataengine'. In 'Proc. 2nd Data Analysis Symposium' (Aachen) (1998).
4. Borgelt C.: 'A naive bayes classifier plug-in for dataengine'. In 'Proc. 2nd Data Analysis Symposium' (Aachen) (1999).
5. Berry M. and Linoff G.: 'Data Mining Techniques — For Marketing, Sales and Customer Support'. Chichester, England, J. Wiley & Sons (1997).
6. Bezdek J.: 'Pattern Recognition with Fuzzy Objective Function Algorithms'. New York, NY, Plenum (1981).
7. Bezdek J. and Pal S.: 'Fuzzy Models for Pattern Recognition — Methods that Search for Structures in Data'. Piscataway, NJ, IEEE Press (1992).
8. Davé R. and Krishnapuram R.: 'Robust clustering methods: A unified view'. IEEE Trans. on Fuzzy Systems, Vol. 5, pp. 270–293 (1997).   ,
9. Davé R.: 'Characterization and detection of noise in clustering'. Pattern Recognition Letters, Vol. 12, pp. 657–664 (1991).

10. Krishnapuram R. and Keller J.: 'A possibilistic approach to clustering'. IEEE Transactions on Fuzzy Systems, Vol. 1, pp. 98–110 (1993).
11. Krishnapuram R. and Keller J.: 'The possibilistic c-means algorithm: Insights and recommendations'. IEEE Trans. on Fuzzy Systems, Vol. 4, pp. 385–393 (1996).
12. Nasroui O. and Krishnapuram R.: 'Crisp interpretations of fuzzy and possibilistic clustering algorithm'. In 'Proc. 3rd European Congress on Fuzzy and Intelligent Technologies (EUFIT'95, Aachen, Germany)' (Aachen: Verlag Mainz), pp. 1312–1318 (1994).
13. Barni M., Capellini V. and Mecocci A.: 'Comments on "a possibilistic approach to clustering"'. IEEE Transactions on Fuzzy Systems, Vol. 4, pp. 393–396 (1996).

14. Pal N., Pal K. and Bezdek J.: 'A mixed c-means clustering model'. In 'Proc. 6th IEEE Int. Conf. on Fuzzy Systems (FUZZ-IEEE'97, Barcelona, Spain)' (Piscataway, NJ: IEEE Press), pp. 11–21 (1997).
15. Gustafson E. and Kessel W.: 'Fuzzy clustering with a fuzzy covariance matrix'. In 'Proc. IEEE Conf. on Decision and Control (CDC'79, San Diego, CA)' (Piscataway, NJ: IEEE Press), pp. 761–766 (1979).
16. Höppner F., Klawonn F., Kruse R. and Runkler T.: 'Fuzzy Cluster Analysis'. Chichester, J. Wiley & Sons (1999).
17. Gath I. and Geva A.: 'Unsupervised optimal fuzzy clustering'. IEEE Trans. on Pattern Analysis and Machine Intelligence (PAMI), Vol. 11, pp. 773–781 (1989).

18. Breiman L., Friedman J., Olshen R. and Stone C.: 'Classification and Regression Trees'. Belmont, CA, Wadsworth International (1984).
19. Quinlan J.: 'Induction of decision trees'. Machine Learning, Vol. 1, pp. 81–106 (1986).
20. Quinlan J.: 'C4.5: Programs for Machine Learning'. San Mateo, CA, Morgan Kaufman (1993).
21. Kullback S. and Leibler R.: 'On information and sufficiency'. Ann. Math. Statistics, Vol. 22, pp. 79–86 (1951).
22. Chow C. and Liu C.: 'Approximating discrete probability distributions with dependence trees'. IEEE Trans. on Information Theory, Vol. 14(3), pp. 462–467 (1968).

23. Lopez de Mantaras R.: 'A distance-based attribute selection measure for decision tree induction'. Machine Learning, Vol. 6, pp. 81–92 (1991).
24. Wehenkel L.: 'On uncertainty measures used for decision tree induction'. In 'Proc. Int. Conf. on Information Processing and Management of Uncertainty in Knowledge-based Systems (IPMU'96)' (Granada, Spain), pp. 413–417 (1996).
25. Zhou X. and Dillon T.: 'A statistical-heuristic feature selection criterion for decision tree induction'. IEEE Trans. on Pattern Analysis and Machine Intelligence (PAMI), Vol. 13, pp. 834–841 (1991).
26. Kononenko I.: 'Estimating attributes: Analysis and extensions of relief'. In 'Proc. 7th Europ. Conf. on Machine Learning (ECML'94)' (New York, NY: Springer) (1994).
27. Kira K. and Rendell L.: 'A practical approach to feature selection'. In 'Proc. 9th Int. Conf. on Machine Learning (ICML'92)' (San Franscisco, CA: Morgan Kaufman), pp. 250–256 (1992).
28. Kononenko I.: 'On biases in estimating multi-valued attributes'. In 'Proc. 1st Int. Conf. on Knowledge Discovery and Data Mining (KDD'95, Montreal, Canada)' (Menlo Park, CA: AAAI Press), pp. 1034–1040 (1995).

29. Baim P.: 'A method for attribute selection in inductive learning systems'. IEEE Trans. on Pattern Analysis and Machine Intelligence (PAMI), Vol. 10, pp. 888–896 (1988).

30. Cooper G. and Herskovits E.: 'A Bayesian Method for the Induction of Probabilistic Networks from Data'. Machine Learning. Dordrecht, Kluwer (1992).

31. Heckerman D., Geiger D. and Chickering D.: 'Learning bayesian networks: The combination of knowledge and statistical data'. Machine Learning, Vol. 20, pp. 197–243 (1995).

32. Buntine W.: 'Theory refinement on bayesian networks'. In 'Proc. 7th Conf. on Uncertainty in Artificial Intelligence' (Los Angeles, CA: Morgan Kaufman), pp. 52–60 (1991).

33. Krichevsky R. and Trofimov V.: 'The performance of universal coding'. IEEE Trans. on Information Theory, Vol. 27(2), pp. 199–207 (1983).

34. Rissanen J.: 'Stochastic complexity'. Journal of the Royal Statistical Society (Series B), Vol. 49, pp. 223–239 (1987).

35. Gebhardt J. and Kruse R.: 'Tightest hypertree decompositions of multivariate possibility distributions'. In 'Proc. Int. Conf. on Information Processing and Management of Uncertainty in Knowledge-based Systems (IPMU'96)' (Granada, Spain), pp. 923–927 (1996).

36. Borgelt C. and Kruse R.: 'Evaluation measures for learning probabilistic and possibilistic networks'. In 'Proc. 6th IEEE Int. Conf. on Fuzzy Systems (FUZZ-IEEE'97, Barcelona, Spain)' (Piscataway, NJ: IEEE Press), pp. 1034–1038 (1997).

37. Borgelt C. and Kruse R.: 'Attributauswahlmaße für die induktion von entscheidungsbäumen: Ein überblick'. In 'Data Mining: Theoretische Aspekte und Anwendungen', G. Nakhaeizadeh, Ed. Physica-Verlag, Heidelberg, pp. 77–98 (1998).

38. Good I.: 'The Estimation of Probabilities: An Essay on Modern Bayesian Methods'. Cambridge, MA, MIT Press (1965).

39. Duda R. and Hart P.: 'Pattern Classification and Scene Analysis'. New York, NY, J. Wiley & Sons (1973).

40. Langley P., Iba W. and Thompson K.: 'An analysis of bayesian classifiers'. In 'Proc. 10th Nat. Conf. on Artificial Intelligence (AAAI'92, San Jose, CA, USA)' (Menlo Park and Cambridge, CA: AAAI Press and MIT Press), pp. 223–228 (1992).

41. Langley P. and Sage S.: 'Induction of selective bayesian classifiers'. In 'Proc. 10th Conf. on Uncertainty in Artificial Intelligence (UAI'94, Seattle, WA, USA)' (San Mateo, CA: Morgan Kaufmann), pp. 399–406 (1994).

42. Pearl J.: 'Probabilistic Reasoning in Intelligent Systems: Networks of Plausible Inference (2nd edition)'. San Mateo, CA, Morgan Kaufman (1992).

43. Fisher R.: 'The use of multiple measurements in taxonomic problems'. Annals of Eugenics, Vol. 7(2), pp. 179–188 (1936).

The Intelligent Assistant: An Overview

Behnam Azvine, David Djian, Kwok Ching Tsui, and Wayne Wobcke

Intelligent Systems Research Group, BT Labs
Adastral Park, Martlesham Heath, Ipswich IP5 3RE, United Kingdom
{ben.azvine,david.djian,kc.tsui}@bt.com, wobckew@info.bt.co.uk

Abstract. The Intelligent Assistant (IA) is an integrated system of intelligent software agents that helps the user with communication, information and time management. The IA includes specialist assistants for e-mail prioritization and telephone call filtering (communication management), Web search and Yellow Pages® lookup (information management), and calendar scheduling (time management). Each such assistant is designed to have a model of the user and a learning module for acquiring user preferences. In addition, the IA includes a toolbar providing a graphical interface to the system, a multimodal interface for accepting spoken commands and tracking the user's activity, and a co-ordinator responsible for managing communication from the system to the user and for initiating system activities on the user's behalf. A primary design objective of the IA is that its operation is as transparent as possible, to enable the user to control the system as far as is practicable without incurring a heavy overhead when creating and modifying the system's behaviour. Hence each specialist assistant is designed to represent its user model in a way that is intuitively understandable to non-technical users, and is configured to adaptively modify its user model through time to accommodate the user's changing preferences. However, in contrast to adaptive interface agents built under the behaviour-based paradigm, the assistants in the IA embrace complex AI representations and machine learning techniques to accomplish more sophisticated behaviour.

1 Motivation

Intelligent software assistants have become a major business opportunity in view of the rapid developments in Internet and Network Computing and the need for computers to better "understand" their users in order to customise and prioritise information and communication.

The market for such systems is large and growing. For example, it is predicted that by 2005 there will be 0.5 billion mobile phone users and 1 billion Internet users. Information and communication overload is already a common problem for computer users, so the scale of this problem is only likely to increase in the future. Software assistants that can ease the burden on users by filtering

---

[1] Yellow Pages® is a registered trade mark of British Telecommunications plc in the United Kingdom.

B. Azvine et al. (Eds.): Intelligent Systems and Soft Computing, LNAI 1804, pp. 215– , 2000.
© Springer-Verlag Berlin Heidelberg 2000

unwanted communication and searching for and delivering the right information at the right time will alleviate these problems for the user, and provide differentiation in a competitive market-place for the business. As software assistants make computers more user friendly by hiding the complexity of the underlying computational processes (as noted by Maes [ ]), the increased usability of the systems may expand the potential market for these services, making the problem of information overload even more critical. Thus the general motivation for the IA is to address the problems of information and communication overload in a way that is personalized to the preferences of an individual user.

Intelligent assistants are basically designed for use in any situation where the combination of human and current computer technology is either too slow, too expensive or under strain. The development of ever more complex systems creates a real need for computers that better "understand" their users and which are capable of more "personalized" service.

Internal representations or models of the user, the environment and the world play an important part in the architecture of intelligent systems [ ]. Real-world problems are typically ill-defined, difficult to model and with large-scale solution spaces [ ]. In these cases precise models are impractical, too expensive or non-existent. Therefore there is a need for approximate modelling techniques capable of handling imperfect and sometimes conflicting information. Soft computing (SC) offers a framework for integrating such techniques.

Learning and adaptation are important features of SC techniques. Fuzzy and probabilistic techniques can be used as the basic mechanism for implementing the reflexive and deliberative functions necessary for building intelligent systems. Approximate reasoning is required in the user model where the information from the user is incomplete, uncertain or vague. Neuro-fuzzy techniques provide us with powerful and efficient neural network learning algorithms to learn interpretable fuzzy rules and automatically adjust their parameters [ ].

The IA is designed to aid the user in aspects of communication, information and time management. The system is organized as an integrated collection of software agents that communicate with one another through message passing. The IA includes specialist assistants for telephone call filtering (the Telephone Assistant), e-mail prioritization (the E-mail Assistant), Web search (the Web Assistant), Yellow Pages lookup (the YPA), and agenda management (the Diary Assistant). The IA also has a number of agents that support the specialist assistants: the Toolbar provides a graphical interface to the IA, the Speech Assistant enables the system to process spoken commands, the Co-ordinator manages communication from the system to the user and initiates actions on the user's behalf, the Profile Assistant maintains a generic user model used by the information management assistants, and the Database Assistant maintains information such as contact details for the user's acquaintances.

By a *software agent*, we mean a system that performs tasks on behalf of its user to help the user accomplish goals: the user thus delegates some responsibility for achieving these goals to the agent. This *delegation* sense of agency contrasts with the definition of an agent based on some notion of *rationality*, under which (usually) a system has, or is ascribed, beliefs, desires and intentions, or (alternatively) is designed to achieve "optimum" performance in some operating environment (see Russell and Norvig [ ] for a general description of agents in Artificial Intelligence, and Nwana [ ] for an extensive survey of software agents as well as a discussion on the terminology).

The personal assistant metaphor was promoted by Maes [ ] as characterizing a class of software agent that learned from the user as he/she performed a repetitive task over a period of time. The idea was that a system could adapt its behaviour to the user's habits by "looking over the shoulder" of the user, and hence could improve its performance with only minimal intervention. Some early systems were also known as *interface agents* because they typically provided a single point of contact between a user and a single software system such as a mail handler or calendar system. The systems described in Maes [ ] used a combination of memory-based reasoning and reinforcement learning, and were thus aligned with the "behaviour-based" approach to AI favoured by Maes [ ].

Another influential metaphor in software engineering is the tool metaphor, under which the system is akin to a tool the user can employ to help perform some task. The user should thus feel in control of the system at all times. In contrast to Maes's personal assistants, two central principles followed by Malone, Lai and Grant [ ] are that systems should be semi-formal and radically tailorable. By *semi-formal*, it is meant that the system should blur the boundary between its internal formal representations and a more intuitively understandable "semi-formal" user's picture of the system's operation. By *radically tailorable*, it is meant that the user should be able to manipulate the system's models and thus tailor its behaviour to meet his/her own individual needs. Although the tool metaphor may seem to preclude delegation of a task to a software agent, our view is that delegation is allowable when the user is confident that the agent's actions will accord with his/her expectations, thus maintaining a sense of user control over the system as well as some autonomy of the agent.

The IA combines both these metaphors to provide a system that is at once under the user's control (as a tool) but which is also adaptive (adjusting its behaviour over time by observing the user's actions), c.f. Azvine and Wobcke [ ]. The main reasons for adopting this hybrid design approach are as follows:

- simple learning techniques such as those used by interface agents are often slow to learn appropriate behaviour; a way for the user to define acceptable initial behaviour is therefore desirable from the usability point of view as well as to bootstrap the learning (*hence semi-formal representations*);
- the behaviour of the IA assistants is complex and so the potential for the learning to lead to incorrect behaviour is increased: it is important that the user understands and feels in control of the system if he/she is to delegate responsibility to it (*hence radical tailorability*);
- the individual assistants need to learn complex behaviour: simple adaptation techniques are not always applicable (*hence complex AI representations and machine learning approaches*);

– it is important to minimize the amount of user intervention and to accommodate the user's changing preferences over time (*hence adaptivity*).

Of course, the effectiveness of the IA (and of any personal assistant) depends to a large extent on striking the right balance between the time saved by the system adapting to the user's habits and preferences to suggest helpful actions and the time lost from user intervention necessary to modify unhelpful behaviour resulting from learning an incorrect model.

The assistants in the IA use a variety of techniques appropriate to the tasks being performed. The Telephone and E-mail Assistants use Bayesian network models of user priorities and preferences. The Telephone Assistant maintains a set of priorities of the user's acquaintances, and uses these in conjunction with the caller's telephone number to determine the importance of an incoming call. The E-mail Assistant computes the importance of each incoming message based on its sender, recipients, size and content (the subject field). Both assistants continually adapt their behaviour as the user's priorities change, and the models are adjustable by the user at any time.

The Web Assistant and the YPA use a profile of the user's interests (maintained by a Profile Assistant) to augment search queries with the aim of producing more relevant information. The user profile is represented as a hierarchical structure of clusters of keywords [ ], and is computed from recently read e-mails, Web pages, and various other sources. The YPA includes a back-end database computed from the Yellow Pages semi-display advertisements, and a front end consisting of a natural language query interface with a dialogue management component. WordNet is used to help refine queries by searching for synonyms and hypernyms of query terms when an initial query fails. The YPA also exploits the explicit structure of the Yellow Pages (such as classifications and cross references) to improve the search results. The profile is fully available to the user and can be modified at any time.

The Diary Assistant schedules tasks based on preferences for task times and durations supplied by the user using simple natural language terms, such as *morning* and *late afternoon*, which are interpreted using fuzzy functions. There are two modes of search for constructing schedules: *global* search is used when allocating time slots to a number of tasks, while *local* search is used when adding or changing a single task in a schedule. The local search algorithm uses an iterative improvement strategy based on the heuristic of minimizing changes to task sequences. The user model consists of the meaning of these fuzzy terms and the preference functions for different types of task. At present these are fixed, but in future work we intend to investigate techniques for learning these functions.

The organization of the remainder of this paper is based on the components of the IA. We begin with a discussion of related work on software agents. Then we describe the components of the IA in more detail. We first describe the main user interface (the Toolbar and Multimodal User Interface), then the Coordinator, before focusing on communication management (the Telephone and E-mail Assistants), information management (the Web and YPA Assistants), and time management (the Diary Assistant). We conclude with a simple scenario illustrating the interaction between the various assistants to create an integrated intelligent personal assistant.

2   Related Work

There have been numerous personal assistants described in the literature; all that we know are designed for helping the user perform a single task. Perhaps the earliest reference to interfaces as agents is the UCEgo question answering component of the Unix Consultant described by Chin [ ]. This system attempted to infer the user's goals and answer questions appropriately. Maes [ ] describes interface agents for a mail handler and a calendar system. In each case, the system used memory-based reasoning and reinforcement learning to predict the user's response in a very specific situation, such as determining the right folder for storing mail or whether to accept, decline or request renegotiation of a proposed meeting time. Part of the rationale for the IA project is to extend the approach to more difficult tasks which require more sophisticated user models and more complex learning algorithms.

Another strand of related work stems from the learning apprentice metaphor. One learning apprentice system in a domain partially overlapping that of the IA is the CAP system described by Dent *et al.* [ ]. This system aimed to learn rules for preferred meeting times, locations, etc, by observing a single user over a period of time. CAP used a machine learning classification algorithm, ID3, although neural networks were also tried. One major problem with such a system is that the learning takes a long time to determine useful rules, and it is assumed that the user's preferences are static throughout this learning period.

A more complex task requiring a system of software agents is the visitor hosting task, in which a schedule of meetings for a visitor to the host's institution is to be found that satisfies the constraints and preferences of the people who match the visitor's interests. An early such system was described by Kautz *et al.* [ ]. In this system, user agents communicated via e-mail with a task agent (the visitor bot) to collect preferences, and a standard software package was used to determine the final schedule. A more detailed architecture for a similar application was specified by Sycara and Zeng [ ]. They proposed the TCA (Task Control Architecture) in which multiple task agents were connected to multiple interface agents and multiple information agents. In contrast to the system of Kautz *et al.*, this system emphasized the planning and co-ordination requirements of the task, and the aim was to produce a generic architecture applicable to a number of problems. Another application using an agent architecture that emphasized the planning capabilities of individual agents was used for information retrieval from multiple sources, see Oates *et al.* [ ]. The main task agent was based on the DECAF architecture of Decker *et al.* [ ].

What distinguishes the IA from all these earlier systems is that there is no single task that the IA is performing. The system consists of a number of specialist assistants each of which performs a task for which the user can delegate some responsibility to the agent. Each assistant is designed to have its own user model, its own learning algorithm, and its own preferred interface. This multiplicity of assistants necessitates a simple interface to the overall system. Thus techniques for multimodal user interfaces such as those developed by Wahlster [ ] are used in the IA. The IA includes a module for interpreting speech commands and a vision system used for inferring the user's presence and current activity. A similar type of multimodal interface is integrated with the Open Agent Architecture, see Moran *et al.* [ ].

Another need resulting from the multiplicity of assistants is that the communications from different assistants to the user must be co-ordinated, so as to avoid overload from many assistants vying for the attention of the user at the same time. The IA includes a special Co-ordinator which maintains information about the user's current and future activities so that communications from an assistant that cannot be delivered when the agent requests can be scheduled for an appropriate time. In addition, the Co-ordinator can enable the IA to proactively respond to the user's goals (corresponding to tasks in the user's diary) by initiating requests that enlist the services of the specialist assistants, for example to conduct a Web search for information related to a forthcoming presentation. The Co-ordinator uses a rational agent architecture based on the PRS system of Georgeff and Lansky [ ], extended to enable scheduling and simple rescheduling of system events. Thus the sense of co-ordination used for the IA is somewhat different from other senses used in the literature, which tend to involve commitments between multiple planning agents, c.f. Jennings [ ]. It is closer to the sense of co-ordination in Sycara and Zeng [ ], extended to handle multiple autonomous agents (in their visitor hosting system, only one agent, an interface agent, communicates with any one user). We sometimes refer to our notion of co-ordination as orchestration, as the Co-ordinator plays a role analogous to the conductor of an orchestra.

3   User Interface

The Toolbar, shown in Fig. , is the primary interface between the user and the IA. Although individual assistants typically have their own interface, the purpose of having a toolbar is to keep screen space usage to a minimum, leaving more space on the screen for other applications. The agents corresponding to the icons in Fig. are the Co-ordinator, the E-mail Assistant, the Telephone Assistant, the Database Assistant, the Web Assistant, the YPA, the Speech Assistant, the Diary Assistant, and the Profile Assistant. The border of the E-mail Assistant icon is flashing, indicating that the assistant has information it wants to convey to the user, e.g. the arrival of high priority mail.

The Toolbar serves four major functions:

- notification of events that happen in an assistant;
- control of windows that belong to the assistants;
- control of the system and virtual clock time (for demonstration purposes);
- provision of an alarm clock service.

Fig. 1. Toolbar Interface to the IA

The Toolbar is sensitive to the movement of the mouse. When the mouse is moved across any button, the name of the assistant the button represents is shown as a bubble, as illustrated in Fig. 1, where the mouse has been moved over the icon for the Database Assistant. Its purpose is to provide an easy reference to the user, especially in the early stages of using the IA when he/she may not be familiar with the icons used to represent the assistants.

A second interface to the IA is the Multimodal User Interface (MMUI). The idea of the multimodal user interface is to exploit multiple channels of communication between the user and the application. Common channels of communication include keyboard, mouse, graphical display and the limited use of sound, such as beeps. The MMUI of the IA also employs vision and speech as well as making use of the keyboard to infer information about the user's activities.

In a distributed multi-agent system such as the IA, the MMUI is seen as a service provider to the other assistants. It is up to the subscribers of these services to decide how the information is interpreted and used. For example, the Telephone Assistant may be set to refuse any phone call if the user is not at his/her desk. However, the Web Assistant will not be interested in this presence information when initiating a search request: this only matters when the assistant wants to contact the user.

Speech services in the IA are run in a client/server mode. The Speech Assistant is run as a server and all IA assistants can run a client that connects to the server and configures a recognizer with its own specific vocabulary and grammar. The system used is the Stap system developed at BT Laboratories [20]. Multiple Stap speech recognizers are run in parallel. When a speech utterance is received, it is dispatched to all recognizers, which then try to find the best match from their own grammar and vocabulary. A simple voting system is used to select the best result from those recognizers that have returned a meaningful output, i.e. not *silence* or *not recognized*.

Visual input has been used in some other applications such as the Smart Work Manager, described more fully in Tsui and Azvine [21] in this volume. The vision system predicts the user's focus of attention using an artificial neural network. Vision information is used in the IA to predict the user's presence and activity, as also described in Tsui and Azvine [21].

An aspect of the multimodal interface that is also demonstrated in the Smart Work Manager is the fusion of information from different sources, e.g. speech and visual input. The goal is to help resolve the command interpreter resolve references in ambiguous commands such as *phone him* using the context supplied by the vision system.

4   Co-ordinator

The individual assistants in the IA are all autonomous; they each perform an activity to help the user repeatedly achieve goals, and they each have their own special interface to the user. Co-ordination is therefore necessary firstly to avoid overloading the user with information from multiple assistants at the same time—this type of co-ordination essentially involves managing communication from the assistants to the user. A more interesting aspect of co-ordination involves proactive behaviour—this refers to the system itself performing tasks on behalf of the user that require the action of more than one assistant (comprising simple plans of action). An important aspect of both types of co-ordination is the performance of actions at appropriate times. As a simple example, a reminder of a meeting should be given at a time close to the meeting and at a time when the user is likely to be available to receive the reminder. The reminder also has a deadline (the start time of the meeting) after which attempting the action is useless. Thus temporal reasoning is central to achieving co-ordination.

The IA achieves both forms of co-ordination through the action of a special Co-ordinator, responsible for maintaining information about the user's state and future activities, and for scheduling its own future actions and (some of) the activities of the other assistants. To avoid communication overload, the Co-ordinator has a simple user interface, shown in Fig. , recording information about whether the user is:

- accepting phone calls;
- accepting e-mails;
- accepting interruptions (from any assistant).

This information is updated automatically using information from the Diary Assistant (each entry in the diary has a flag indicating whether or not the task is interruptible), and is used by the other assistants in determining whether or not to perform an action. For example, the Telephone Assistant uses this information directly when responding to an incoming call, checking the user's state before allowing the phone to ring. The state can also be updated directly from the user interface: if the user sets the state to interruptible, the state switches to accepting phone calls and e-mails automatically (and similarly when setting the state to non-interruptible, the state is set to refusing phone calls and e-mails).

The Co-ordinator is distinguished as the only agent in the IA capable of scheduling future tasks. This part of the Co-ordinator is built on a belief-desire-intention agent architecture which is an extension of the PRS system of Georgeff and Lansky [ ]. The beliefs of the Co-ordinator are facts about the user state and the future actions of the user as supplied by the Diary Assistant. The goals of the Co-ordinator correspond to (some of) the user's tasks, also determined using information from the Diary Assistant. For each goal, the Co-ordinator schedules system tasks (creates intentions) using a plan template related to the goal type taken from an existing plan library, and subsequently executes the system tasks at the determined time. For example, a reminder to a meeting is scheduled for a time 5 minutes before the user becomes unreachable from

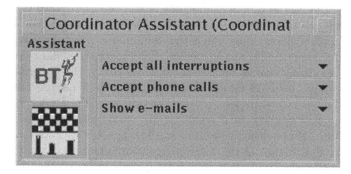

Fig. 2. Co-ordinator Interface

that point until the start of the meeting—the action's deadline). The user is currently notified of any notifications through the Toolbar: the Co-ordinator's icon flashes, a beep is emitted, and the message appears in the Co-ordinator's interface window (Fig. 2). However, other means of communication, such as a mobile phone, could also be used for notification: all that is needed is the technical capability for the IA to initiate phone calls and the use of speech synthesis to generate a voice message.

The Co-ordinator must maintain the timeliness of its scheduled actions. This sometimes means that tasks need to be rescheduled when the user task (goal) time is changed in the diary. For example, when the user changes the time of a meeting, the Co-ordinator must reschedule the reminder to the meeting. In the present implementation, this is done by simply deleting the goal and all its associated tasks (upon notification of the change from the diary), creating a new goal corresponding to the new time and then scheduling new tasks in response to the new goal. Another need for rescheduling occurs when the time comes for an action to be executed which involves notifying the user (such as issuing a reminder) but the user is not reachable for some reason (the Co-ordinator's model of the user's tasks is not necessarily complete). In this case, the notification is rescheduled for the next time the user is known to be reachable according to the presently available information (unless this time is past the task's deadline, in which case the goal is dropped).

The Co-ordinator is also capable of initiating actions to satisfy the user's implicit goals. These are typically commonly recurring goals such as reading e-mails, which we therefore call *recurrent goals*. To assist in scheduling such actions, the Co-ordinator also has a user model consisting of the preferred times for performing these common actions. The times are expressed using fuzzy terms, so an example fact in such a model is 'likes to read daily e-mail in late afternoon'. At a particular time each day (presently 11:00 p.m.), the Co-ordinator sets up internal goals corresponding to such tasks, e.g. *read daily e-mails*. However, the action corresponding to this goal is not to schedule a reminder to read daily e-mail, but rather to schedule a time at which the reminder will be scheduled.

When determining the time for later scheduling, the user model is consulted so that (in this case), the scheduling action is performed some time before "late afternoon". Then at that time, the actual reminder is scheduled, and eventually, the reminder issued. The reason behind this "meta-scheduling" is that when the initial recurrent goal is generated (at 11:00 p.m.), the Co-ordinator is not assumed to have accurate information about the user's day, so scheduling the reminder then would be useless (or else the time of the reminder would require rescheduling in the event of a conflict). To avoid this, a scheduling event is scheduled for a time when the system can be expected to have more complete information. Full details of the internal agent architecture of the Co-ordinator are given in Wobcke [ ] in this volume.

5   Telephone Assistant

The Telephone Assistant (TA) handles incoming telephone calls on behalf of the user, the aim being to minimize disruption caused by frequent calls. For each incoming call, the TA determines whether to interrupt the user (before the phone rings) based on the importance of the caller and on various contextual factors such as the frequency of recent calls from that caller and the presence of a related entry in the diary (e.g. a meeting with the caller). When deciding to interrupt the user, the TA displays a panel indicating that a call has arrived; the user then has the option of accepting or declining to answer the call. The TA uses this feedback to learn an overall priority model for how the user weights the different factors in deciding whether or not to answer a call.

The main difficulty in defining a decision process for the TA is that this mechanism must be:

- *flexible* in order to take into account the uncertainty in the knowledge the system has of the real world, so that a call is *likely* to be urgent, rather than *is* urgent;
- *adaptable* to a change of requirements over time as the result of the user's priorities changing, for instance when a new project starts or when an old one finishes.

For these reasons, the Telephone and E-mail Assistants (see below) use Bayesian networks to represent both their user models and their internal decision models.

The user model of the TA is a Bayesian network giving a priority for each of the user's acquaintances; a representation of such a model is shown in Fig. . In the figure, the names of callers whose calls are always answered are coloured green, while those who are rejected are coloured red (although note that due to contextual factors, these callers sometimes get through). An important point is that the user does not need to know conditional probability to understand and manipulate the model. All that matters is the intuition that higher priorities mean a greater likelihood of the caller being let through by the TA. Indeed, the actual numbers on the priorities do not matter either; all that matters is that the overall behaviour of the TA accords with the user's expectations.

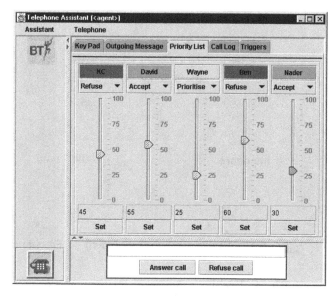

Fig. 3. Telephone Assistant User Model

The internal decision model of the TA is also represented as a Bayesian network (not accessible to the user), shown in Fig. 4.

Nodes in the graph correspond to discrete random variables, and arrows represent dependencies used for computation rather than causal links. The TA defines the context of an interruption as represented in the input nodes of the network as follows:

- Caller: the caller's name as derived from their phone number (obtained using the Database Assistant);
- Frequency: how often this number has called recently (obtained from the TA call log);
- Diary (type): the next type of activity, if any, relating to the caller (obtained from the Diary Assistant);
- Diary (soon): how soon before the activity relating to the caller in Diary (type) will occur (obtained from the Diary Assistant).

Note the distinction between features relating to urgency and features relating to importance. Urgency here refers to the timeliness of a call, importance refers to the usefulness of the information likely to be obtained from a call.

The TA makes extensive use of the services of the other assistants. The messages sent and received by the TA are summarized in Fig. 5. Notification messages are received from the Speech Assistant where the message contains a command to execute. Currently, the commands supported are:

- phone Ben;
- phone him.

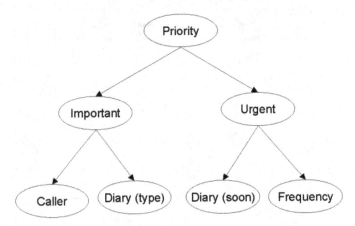

Fig. 4. Telephone Assistant Decision Model

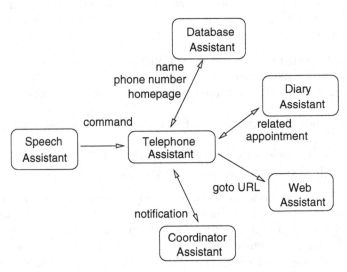

Fig. 5. Telephone Assistant Interactions

The Database Assistant is used to identify an incoming caller, and to provide a URL corresponding to the caller's home page; the TA can ask the Web Assistant to display this Web page while the user decides whether to answer a call. As described above, the TA requests information from the Diary Assistant about entries related to the caller in the diary. Finally, the TA requests permission from the Co-ordinator to interrupt the user as a final filter on high priority incoming phone calls. The TA can also initiate a call when the user clicks on a contact's name, using the Database Assistant to perform the translation between name and phone number. The Telephone Assistant is further described in Djian [ ] in this volume.

6   E-Mail Assistant

The purpose of the E-mail Assistant (EA) is to filter incoming e-mail messages for the user. Based on the sender, recipients, size and content of the message (the subject field), the system determines a suggested time that the message should be read (*now, today, this week, this month,* or *never*).

As in the Telephone Assistant, the EA uses Bayesian networks to represent its internal decision model. For the sender, the input nodes to the network are similar to the TA caller priority model. For the recipient, the input nodes are whether the message was sent to the user alone, to others or to a distribution list. For size, the input nodes are whether the message is small, medium or large (note that the message could satisfy a number of these conditions to greater or lesser degree). Finally, for the content, the Profile Assistant is used to match the subject field to the user's profile. If there is a match, the priority of the message is increased. This makes the behaviour of the E-mail Assistant tailored to the preferences of the individual user.

The main interface to the E-mail Assistant is shown in Fig. . The tabs at the top of the panel indicate the various folders containing already prioritized mail. Current messages are indicated by coloured envelopes at the bottom of the display (red for messages suggested to be read now, orange for today, yellow for this week, white for this month, black for never). Clicking on an envelope results in the corresponding message being displayed, and at this point, the user can enter feedback concerning the appropriate folder in which this message should have been filed. This information is used by the EA to learn the weightings on the various factors contributing to the system's suggestions. The user can also request the EA to file all currently unread mail according to its recommendations.

Fig.   shows the messages sent and received by the E-mail Assistant. Currently, the EA only handles notification messages from the Speech Assistant. Speech commands can also be typed in a window accessed from the EA main menu. The speech commands supported by the EA are:

- new mail;
- compose mail.

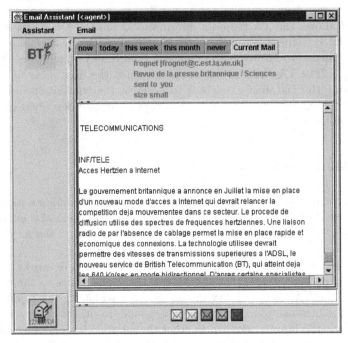

Fig. 6. E-mail Assistant Interface

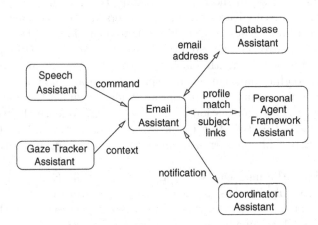

Fig. 7. E-mail Assistant Interactions

The various services that the EA requires from the other assistants are as follows. As for the Telephone Assistant, the Database Assistant provides the contact details of the senders of e-mails. The EA also requests permission from the Co-ordinator to interrupt the user when a high priority (read now) message arrives. When the user composes an outgoing message, the Profile Assistant can also provide hyper-links (URLs) to documents which are relevant to the e-mail. Once the user has typed the subject keywords, the EA sends a query to the Profile Assistant and relevant links are displayed in an applet.

Details of the E-mail Assistant are given in Djian [ ] in this volume.

7   Web Assistant

The Web Assistant (WA) provides an interface between the IA and the World Wide Web; it centralizes all the Web search requests in the IA. A component of the WA is a Web browser available as freeware on the Internet that can parse simple HTML files and present results in the same way as commercial Web browsers. This gives the WA the facility to display Web pages in response to requests from other assistants.

When a search request arrives, the WA spawns a thread to deal with the search. As a result, the WA is capable of handling multiple search requests at the same time. The WA is capable of handling search requests initiated both by the user and by the Co-ordinator in response to a user task (in this case, the search keywords are determined by the Co-ordinator from the task description in the diary). The WA then connects to the World Wide Web and formats the result of the search for presentation. It employs a meta-search engine (MetaCrawler) which interacts with several common search engines to perform the actual search. However, before a request is passed to MetaCrawler, the WA tries to augment the keyword(s) using information from the user's profile of interests (obtained from the Profile Assistant) and using an online thesaurus (WordNet).

All search requests are handled as follows:

1. keyword expansion;
2. for each expanded query, contact MetaCrawler to perform search (with 10 second turnaround constraint);
3. combine search results for presentation.

The objective of keyword expansion is to enhance the search to provide more relevant information to the user. Although efficient search engines and meta-search engines are widely available, there are few restrictions on performing multiple searches in terms of turnaround time. The idea is that when a keyword is entered, it is likely that this word represents an area new to the user. However, it is equally likely that the user implicitly wants to find information within an area of his/her current interests. By augmenting the search by keyword expansion, the WA is more likely to satisfy the user's requirements. This is particularly useful as computer users increasingly entrust software agents to look for information on the Internet.

Fig.   shows part of the information used by the Web Assistant for keyword expansion: (a) part of the common knowledge, (b) subcategories of the word 'computer', and (c) hypernyms of 'computer'.

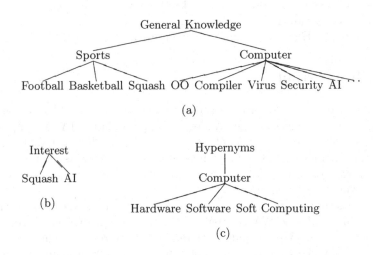

Fig. 8. Information used for Keyword Expansion

For each keyword entered in a request, the hypernym (the more general category to which a word belongs) of the keyword is mapped to the user's interests. If matching hypernyms are found, new queries are formed in addition to the original query. Then the subcategories for the matched hypernyms are used to form more additional queries. As a result of these two procedures, the number of queries is often increased many times.

As an example, suppose the user asks a query on 'security'. Based on the user's interest in Artificial Intelligence, the query is first expanded to 'computer security'. The subcategories of 'computer' in the profile are then used to expand the query to 'hardware security', 'software security', and 'Soft Computing security'. All these queries, five in total, are sent to MetaCrawler.

The result page for the above query on 'security' is shown in Fig. . The first part of the Web page contains contains the keywords and the expanded keywords, linked to the corresponding anchors containing the search results. For each of the Web pages returned by MetaCrawler, a post-processing method strips out any extraneous information to give a condensed Web page, which is then inserted into the appropriate position in the result page. The user is notified through the Toolbar when the search results are ready.

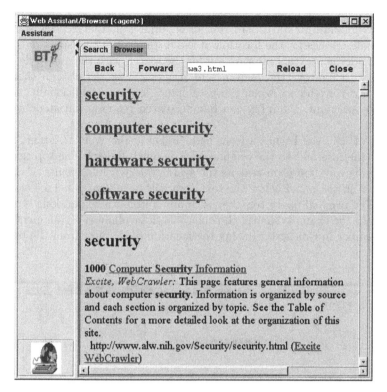

Fig. 9. Web Assistant Result Page

8   YPA

The YPA provides a natural language query interface to an electronic version of the Yellow Pages [24]. In the IA, the YPA is used to perform personalized search by augmenting queries with the user's interests obtained from the Profile Assistant. Details of the original version of the YPA can be found in De Roeck *et al.* [24] in this volume.

The YPA pre-computes a set of indices to advertisements incorporating classifications, cross references and the free text of the advertisements. The interesting aspect of the Yellow Pages database is that it is *semi-structured*, by which is meant that the entries are a mixture of information indicating structure (such as classifications) and information with no structure (free text).

Within the IA, the YPA is used in conjunction with the user's profile to generate personalized responses. The profile is obtained from the Profile Assistant, and is represented as a hierarchical structure of keyword clusters [9]. Part of an example profile might contain the following:

Food: Italian
Work location: Colchester

Whenever the user requests a restaurant, for example, the YPA assumes that he/she is looking for an Italian restaurant unless another type is specified. A similar rule applies for the location of the restaurant. This aspect of the profile thus provides contextual information for the search with the aim of fleshing out the query to improve the relevance of results. These details can therefore be omitted for convenience when the user enters a query. Additionally, similar to the Web Assistant, the YPA can handle search requests initiated by the Coordinator.

The YPA in the IA has a front end similar to the Web Assistant, shown in Fig. 10 (the interface to the original YPA is much larger). The top text area is for entering any free form text as the search query, while results of the search are shown in the panel below the text area with a tabbed panel for each search result. The original query together with any automatic expansions is shown on the tab. In the example shown, the query '24 hour plumber' is augmented to '24 hour plumber in Colchester', using the location of the user from the profile.

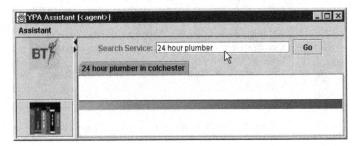

Fig. 10. YPA Interface

9   Diary Assistant

The Diary Assistant (DA) helps the user with time management by maintaining a schedule of tasks. The user is able to enter and edit tasks, move tasks from one day to another, and invoke the scheduling capabilities of the assistant. The main interface to the DA is designed to look like a standard paper diary, with each day divided into half hour slots starting from 9:00 through to 5:00, as shown in Fig. 11. In the display, the duration of each task is given in parentheses beside its description, in the form *hours:minutes*.

The DA uses ideas from fuzzy temporal reasoning, e.g. Dubois and Prade [25]. Users can specify preferences for the start time, duration and deadline of a task using terms that are interpreted as fuzzy functions. At present, the following fuzzy terms are supported: for time preferences *morning, afternoon, early morning, late morning, early afternoon, late afternoon, around t* and *about t* where *t* is a precise time, and when using the global scheduler, *early week, mid week*

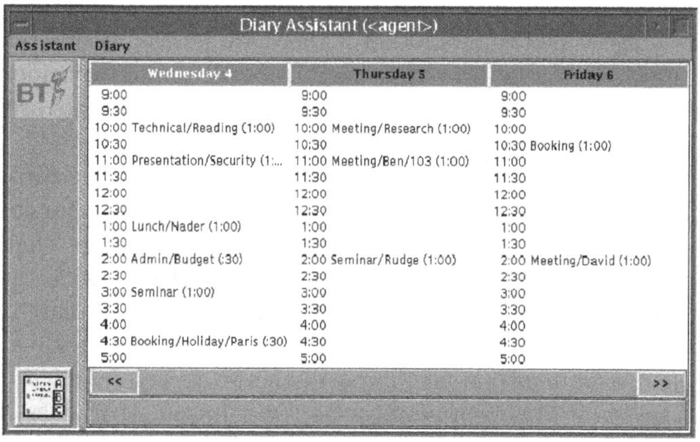

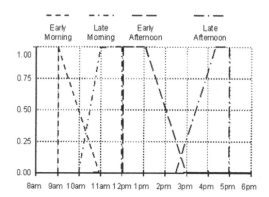

Fig. 11. Diary Assistant Interface

and *late this week*; and for durations *around d* and *about d* where *d* is a precise duration. The function denoted by each of these predicates is predefined. As an illustration, fuzzy functions for interpreting various predicates for day periods are shown in Fig. 12. The value of the function at a particular half-hour time indicates the degree to which that time meets the description of the fuzzy term.

Fig. 12. Sample Fuzzy Functions

The DA incorporates two schedulers: a *global* scheduler for allocating time slots to a set of tasks so as to maximize overall preference satisfaction, and a *local* scheduler that makes minimal adjustments to an existing schedule when adding a single new task. The global scheduler uses a standard AI depth first search algorithm with backtracking, and heuristic guidance to improve the efficiency of the search. The search uses heuristics in two ways: for defining the order in which tasks are considered and the order in which allocations to tasks are explored.

Firstly, tasks are ordered from most constrained to least constrained, where one task is more constrained than another if there are fewer possible time slots that satisfy the user's preference for that task. Secondly, when considering a single task in the context of a partial schedule, the possible time slots are explored in order of preference satisfaction.

The idea behind the use of local scheduling is to minimize disruption to an existing schedule when a *single* new task is added. The need for local search is that the diary entries often involve commitments by the user that should not be changed unless required for the satisfaction of preferences. A "hill-climbing" iterative improvement algorithm is used to implement local search. The procedure starts with a complete task allocation (here including a time slot for the new task), and examines one neighbour of this state (the one with the highest evaluation) to see if this represents a better solution. If it does, local search continues from this state; otherwise the best solution found is returned. The heuristic employed for generating neighbouring states is to consider each legitimate state computed by moving a sequence of tasks of up to length three either forwards or backwards by half an hour. Thus the aim is to minimize changes to *task sequences* in the user's schedules. In the construction of the initial solution which includes the new task added or moved, sequences of up to length three can also be moved forwards or backwards by half an hour, and tasks of imprecise preferred duration can be compressed (possibly in conjunction with moving a preceding or succeeding task half an hour forwards or backwards). This is because sometimes there is no gap in the schedule of sufficient length in which to place the new task; moving or shortening tasks sometimes creates such a gap.

At present, the "user model" of the DA consists of a collection of fixed fuzzy functions, one for each task type, each specifying a value between 0 and 1 for each hour in the week indicating the preference value for tasks of that type to be scheduled at that hour. In future work, we intend to investigate techniques for learning such preference functions. Further details of the Diary Assistant are given in Wobcke [ ] in this volume.

10   Integration

One of the main features of the IA is the co-ordinated behaviour produced by integrating the actions of more than one assistant. This occurs through the proactive aspect of the Co-ordinator in responding to some of the user's tasks by initiating plans of actions, some of which invoke the capabilities of the specialist assistants. In this section, we illustrate the complex behaviour underlying the selection, scheduling and execution of a simple plan.

The IA is organized as a collection of autonomous agents communicating using the open messaging architecture of Zeus [ ]. Fig. shows (some of) the interactions between the agents in the current version of the IA. An arrow in the figure indicates either the transfer of information or a request for information or to perform a task. Some interactions are a result of the system executing plans in the Co-ordinator plan library.

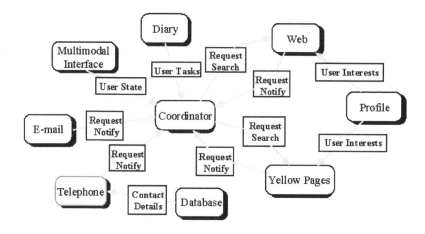

Fig. 13. Agent Interactions

In the IA, tasks in the user's diary, when confirmed by the user, trigger the plans of the Co-ordinator. We describe the simple example of a lunch booking entered in the diary for 1:00 on the current day. The plan related to the lunch booking contains three actions: (i) using the YPA to find a restaurant, (ii) finding the Web page of the person having lunch with the user, and (iii) reminding the user of the lunch appointment. Suppose that the user also enters a non-interruptible 1 hour meeting at 12:00 on the current day.

The whole process starts with the user's confirmation of the diary entries, when messages are sent from the Diary to the Co-ordinator giving the user's latest schedule. The first action of the Co-ordinator is to update its world model on the basis of this information. Then the Co-ordinator treats some of these user tasks, in particular the lunch booking, as goals to be acted upon. For each such goal, the Co-ordinator retrieves the appropriate plan of actions, and creates a new system task for each action in the plan parametrized according to additional information supplied by the user concerning the task (in this case, whom the lunch appointment is with). In this example, the YPA and Web searches are scheduled for the current time, while the reminder is scheduled for 11:55 (5 minutes before the user's non-interruptible meeting), which is 5 minutes before the latest time the user can be assumed to be reachable. The Co-ordinator then executes both the YPA search and Web search request actions, which simply involves sending request messages to the respective assistants.

The YPA augments the query given by the Co-ordinator (to find a restaurant in the user's locale) with the interests of the user (obtained from the user's profile) to search for a restaurant with a particular type of cuisine. The YPA accepts a natural language query such as, in this case, 'Italian restaurant in Ipswich'. The Web Assistant searches for the lunch partner's home page. When the YPA and Web assistants have finished searching, they must notify the user that the results are ready. However, the assistants each request permission from the Co-ordinator to interrupt the user, again by sending appropriate messages. Should the user be interruptible, permission will be granted by reply; assume otherwise. Then the Co-ordinator will schedule notifications to the user (that the output is ready) for the next available time that the user is interruptible, again based on information supplied from the diary, possibly overridden by the user via the interface. The Co-ordinator performs the notifications and reminders at the determined times.

11   Conclusions and Further Work

The Intelligent Assistant is a working prototype that gives a glimpse of what software agents can do to relieve a user from performing repetitive tasks, and more generally to help them organize work and improve productivity. The individual assistants, specialists in handling e-mail and telephone calls (communication management), Web and Yellow Pages search (information management), and agenda maintenance (time management), are each designed to have an intuitive but powerful user model under the control of the user, and to be adaptive to the user's changing preferences over time so as to minimize the need for direct manipulation. The IA is reactive to the users' commands, but is also capable of proactive behaviour through its planning and co-ordination mechanisms.

The following topics represent research challenges for the various aspects of the Intelligent Assistant.

- *Communication management*: Two issues are the use of more information (richer context) to better model the user's decision making and to learn structures of Bayesian networks representing enhanced priority models.
- *Information management*: One avenue for further work is to incorporate fuzzy query expansion in conjunction with the user profile to handle partial matches more reliably. The personal aspect is important because terms like 'cheap' do not have the same meaning for everyone, nor the same meaning in every context.
- *Time management*: One extension is to provide the Diary Assistant with a negotiation strategy that would enable a number of users to schedule a joint meeting by delegating this task to their agents. For the Co-ordinator, the user could be given more control over the IA's behaviour by allowing the plan library to be dynamically modifiable. Another aspect of the personalization of the IA involves learning plans of user actions. The Diary Assistant could use this information to improve task scheduling and, in commonly occurring situations, to suggest tasks that the user may wish to add to the agenda. The Co-ordinator may be able to suggest plans to be added to the plan library.
- *User Interface*: Further work is needed to develop a method to detect the high level "mood" of the user, a fairly easy task for humans but a challenging one for digital assistants. This would have a major effect on the accuracy of the user models, especially those for communication management, which would have a great impact on the usability of the system.

Acknowledgements

We gratefully acknowledge the contribution to research and development on the Intelligent Assistant made by Simon Case, Gilbert Owusu and Benoit Remael. The YPA is a BT project carried out at the University of Essex by Sam Steel, Udo Kruschwitz and Nick Webb. Thanks also to Nader Azarmi, to Divine Ndumu for help and support with the Zeus environment, and to Barry Crabtree and Stuart Soltysiak for the user profile software.

References

1. Maes P.: 'Agents that Reduce Work and Information Overload', Communications of the ACM, Vol. 37, No. 7, pp. 31-40 (1994).   ,   ,
2. Azvine B. and Wobcke W. R.: 'Human-Centred Intelligent Systems and Soft Computing', BT Technology Journal, Vol. 16, No. 3, pp. 125-133 (1998).   ,
3. Bonissone P. P.: 'Soft Computing: The Convergence of Emerging Reasoning Technologies', Soft Computing, Vol. 1, No. 1, pp. 6-18 (1997).
4. Nauck D., Klawonn F. and Kruse R.: 'Foundations of Neuro-Fuzzy Systems', Wiley, Chichester (1997).
5. Russell S. J. and Norvig P.: 'Artificial Intelligence: A Modern Approach', Prentice-Hall, Englewood Cliffs, NJ (1995).
6. Nwana H. S.: 'Software Agents: An Overview', The Knowledge Engineering Review, Vol. 11, No. 3, pp. 205-244 (1996).
7. Maes P.: 'Modeling Adaptive Autonomous Agents', Artificial Life Journal, Vol. 1, pp. 135-162 (1994).
8. Malone T. W., Lai K.-Y. and Grant K. R.: 'Agents for Information Sharing and Coordination: A History and Some Reflections', in 'Software Agents', ed., Bradshaw J. M., AAAI Press, Menlo Park, CA (1997).
9. Soltysiak S. J. and Crabtree I. B.: 'Automatic Learning of User Profiles—Towards the Personalisation of Agent Services', BT Technology Journal, Vol. 16, No. 3, pp. 110-117 (1998).   ,
10. Chin D. N.: 'Intelligent Interfaces as Agents', in 'Intelligent User Interfaces', eds, Sullivan J. W. and Tyler S. W., ACM Press, New York, NY (1991).
11. Dent L., Boticario J., McDermott J., Mitchell T. M. and Zabowski D. A.: 'A Personal Learning Apprentice', Proceedings of the Tenth National Conference on Artificial Intelligence (AAAI-92), pp. 96-103 (1992).
12. Kautz H. A., Selman B., Coen M., Ketchpel S. P. and Ramming C.: 'An Experiment in the Design of Software Agents', Proceedings of the Twelfth National Conference on Artificial Intelligence (AAAI-94), pp. 438-443 (1994).
13. Sycara K. P. and Zeng D.: 'Coordination of Multiple Intelligent Software Agents', International Journal of Cooperative Information Systems, Vol. 5, No. 2, pp. 181-211 (1996).   ,
14. Oates T., Nagendra Prasad M. V., Lesser V. R. and Decker K. S.: 'A Distributed Problem Solving Approach to Cooperative Information Gathering', Information Gathering from Heterogeneous, Distributed Environments: Papers from the 1995 AAAI Symposium, pp. 133-137 (1995).
15. Decker K. S., Lesser V. R., Nagendra Prasad M. V. and Wagner T.: 'MACRON: An Architecture for Multi-agent Cooperative Information Gathering', Proceedings of the CIKM-95 Workshop on Intelligent Information Agents (1995).

16. Wahlster W.: 'User and Discourse Models for Multimodal Communication', in 'Intelligent User Interfaces', eds, Sullivan J. W. and Tyler S. W., ACM Press, New York, NY (1991).
17. Moran D. B., Cheyer A. J., Julia L. E., Martin D. L. and Park S.: 'Multimodal User Interfaces in the Open Agent Architecture', Proceedings of the 1997 International Conference on Intelligent User Interfaces, pp. 61-68 (1997).
18. Georgeff M. P. and Lansky A. L.: 'Reactive Reasoning and Planning', Proceedings of the Sixth National Conference on Artificial Intelligence (AAAI-87), pp. 677-682 (1987).   ,
19. Jennings N. R.: 'Commitments and Conventions: The Foundation of Coordination in Multi-Agent Systems', The Knowledge Engineering Review, Vol. 8, No. 3, pp. 223-250 (1993).
20. Scahill F., Talintyre J. E., Johnson S. H., Bass A. E., Lear J. A., Franklin D. J. and Lee P. R.: 'Speech Recognition—Making It Work for Real', BT Technology Journal, Vol. 14, No. 1, pp. 151-164 (1996).
21. Tsui K. C. and Azvine B.: 'Intelligent Multimodal User Interface', in this volume.
22. Wobcke W. R.: 'Time Management in the Intelligent Assistant', in this volume.
    ,
23. Djian D. P.: 'Communication Management: E-mail and Telephone Assistants', in this volume.   ,
24. De Roeck A., Kruschwitz U., Scott P., Steel S., Turner R. and Webb N.: 'The YPA—An Assistant for Classified Directory Enquiries', in this volume.
25. Dubois D. and Prade H. M.: 'Processing Fuzzy Temporal Knowledge', IEEE Transactions on Systems, Man, and Cybernetics, Vol. 19, pp. 729-744 (1989).
26. Nwana H. S., Ndumu D. T. and Lee L. C.: 'ZEUS: An Advanced Tool-Kit for Engineering Distributed Multi-Agent Systems', Proceedings of the Third International Conference on the Practical Application of Intelligent Agents and Multi-Agent Technology, pp. 377-391 (1998).

The YPA - An Assistant
for Classified Directory Enquiries

Anne De Roeck[1], Udo Kruschwitz[1], Paul Scott[1], Sam Steel[1], Ray Turner[1], and
Nick Webb[2]

[1] Department of Computer Science, University of Essex
Wivenhoe Park, Colchester, CO4 3SQ, United Kingdom
{deroe,udo,scotp,sam,turnr}@essex.ac.uk
[2] Department of Computer Science, University of Sheffield,
Regent Court, 211 Portbello Street, Sheffield S1 4DP, United Kingdom
N.Webb@sheffield.ac.uk

Abstract. The YPA is a directory enquiry system which allows a user
to access advertiser information in classified directories [ ]. It converts
semi-structured data in the *Yellow Pages* machine readable classified
directories into a set of indices appropriate to the domain and task,
and converts natural language queries into filled slot and filler structures appropriate for queries in the domain. The generation of answers
requires a domain-dependent *query construction* step, connecting the indices and the slot and fillers. The YPA illustrates an unusual but useful
intermediate point between information retrieval and logical knowledge
representation.

1 Introduction

The YPA stands mid-way between full natural language analysis and information
retrieval. It does not attempt to build a deep representation of the facts in
the Yellow Pages. However, it goes considerably beyond keyword matching. It
does not treat all parts of a query alike, and it recognizes different functions
of different parts of the input text. It uses an on-line thesaurus *WordNet* [ ]
and cross-referencing to connect tokens in a query with tokens in the Yellow
Pages data. Different forms of a word are reduced to a base form where this is
straightforward.

The functionality it offers is intended to assist a Yellow Pages customer, or,
perhaps more realistically, a Talking Pages operator. Talking Pages is a service
in which a customer rings a call-centre operator and asks a question which the
operator then attempts to answer from a Yellow Pages like classified directory.
The goal is to narrow, rather than completely close, the gap between a user's
enquiry and the Yellow Pages data.

The system is a mixed initiative system. It allows free text input, and uses
robust, shallow, parsing to extract the important parts of a query. Free text

---

[1] Yellow Pages® and Talking Pages® are registered trade marks of British Telecommunications plc in the United Kingdom

B. Azvine et al. (Eds.): Intelligent Systems and Soft Computing, LNAI 1804, pp. 239– , 2000.
© Springer-Verlag Berlin Heidelberg 2000

query refinements are also possible later. However, when the system has a choice of possible replies, or sees a range of obvious possible query refinements, it may offer the user a range of options it has collected.

Though the system is described very much in the light of its applications to Yellow Pages, we believe that the techniques, both of constructing the *Backend* indices and of handling the *Frontend* interaction, will be applicable to many similar domains involving interactions with semi-structured data.

The paper first discusses what is needed from a Yellow Pages assistant (section) followed by a system overview (section), which also describes the function of each of the modules by reference to a running example. Section   deals with our most recent experiences including system evaluation. Finally section deals with conclusions and future work.

2   Motivation and Related Work

Finding information in a classified directory can be straightforward but requires prior knowledge of the indexing system employed by that directory. Take the example:

I want an Italian restaurant in Colchester that takes Visa.

Clearly the easiest route would be to take a local classified directory and look under the heading *Italian Restaurants* for the required addresses. However, several problems can occur, among them:

− There is no heading *Italian Restaurants* and under *Restaurants* the list of advertisements is very long but contains hardly any offering *Italian cuisine*.
− There are no *Italian restaurants* at all.
− None of the advertisements specifically say that they accept *Visa*.
− The best matches might be found under a heading *Pizzerias*.
− There could be an *Italian Restaurant* in *Wivenhoe*, just 3 miles outside *Colchester* which accepts *Visa* and says so.
− *Colchester* is not covered by the local directory.

The task of the YPA is to cut across the headings, allowing the user direct access to those advertisements which match their individual requirements. This task is made difficult by the problem of identifying within a query what it is that is of interest to a user is. For example:

I want a good Italian. - We are interested in *Italian.*

I want a pizza service. - We are interested in *pizza.*

In order to do this, we have to "narrow the gap" between the requirements of the user and the indices offered by the *Yellow Pages* domain.

From the user's end, we need to offer some natural language front end to soften the interface, coupled with some easily obtained common sense knowledge to reason about possible extensions to the user's input. From the *Yellow*

Pages domain, we build "knowledge-based" indices, capturing more accurately the nature of the information stored within individual advertisements.

Together these techniques will give us more power than simple information retrieval techniques, which although powerful in the right context would still be unable to find the entry *The Pasta Palace* under heading *Take Away Food* from an enquiry about *Italian restaurants*. In addition, our knowledge base will be easier to build and maintain than one built up through deep knowledge representation, using logic and theorem proving.

If we consider the YPA as a natural language dialogue system, we find it comparable to numerous previous systems. In the main these sophisticated systems (for example OVIS [ ], The Philips train timetable system [ ], Sundial [,], TRAINS [ ] and Verbmobil [ ]) are concerned with time and schedule information. These are heavily restricted domains, in terms of size and complexity of data. In addition, there are a number of systems which retrieve addresses from *Yellow Pages*. Most notable of these are *Voyager* (and its sibling, *Galaxy*) [,] and IDAS , an interactive directory assistance project funded by the European Union. IDAS has as a goal the effective disambiguation of user queries, and the narrowing of the search space of the query. This project is still in the development phase. *Voyager* and *Galaxy* have been around for some time, but the implementations are restricted to sample domains or small-scale address databases (e.g. 150 objects in the *Voyager* system [ ]). What seems to be the greatest commonality between these systems and the YPA is the fact that an interaction involves the system filling a set of slots — for instance, in a travel domain, start and finish time and place — and then reacting appropriately to the set of filled slots.

A separate issue is the *Backend* construction process which takes the raw data (the so-called *YP printing tape*) and creates a database that retains as much information and relations as possible for the online enquiry system. This was described in detail in De Roeck *et al.* [ ]. The input data is *semi-structured* in a sense that a record structure for the addresses and headings does exist but the internal structure of these entries is not formally defined. Usually this consists of partial English sentences, address information, telephone patterns, etc. Several types of advertisements exist: *free, line* and *semi-display* entries with *semi-display* advertisements carrying more information than just the name and the address of the advertiser. Standard *Information Retrieval* approaches do not help because the addresses are too short. Here is a typical *semi-display* entry as it appears in the printed directory (in this case listed under *Hotels & Inns*):

```
┌─ UDO, THE ──────────────────┐
│                             │
│   TOWN CENTRE BED & BREAKFAST   │
│   EN SUITE ROOMS-AMPLE PARKING  │
│     High St,Ipswich,01473 123456 │
└─────────────────────────────┘
```

―――――――

[2] http://www.linglink.lu/le/projects/idas

The actual source code in the *printing tape* does not give us much more structured information than what can be seen in the printed advertisement:

```
195SS15SBZS9810289N955030800 0 0150UDO,THE^
195SS15SBZS9810289B935020800C0    TOWN CENTRE BED & BREAKFAST^
195SS15SBZS9810289B935020800C0    EN SUITE ROOMS-AMPLE PARKING^
195SS15SBZS9810289B935020800C0    CHigh St,Ipswich,01473\$_123456^
```

The columns of coding on the left have considerable structure but are almost entirely about accounting and how the lines are to appear when printed. They contain very little about what is being advertised: that is almost entirely in the marked-up advertisement text on the right.

When comparing this data with a typical user request it is often hard to find advertisements which do actually satisfy the complete user query. The user might have asked for *hotels with en suite bathrooms*, something which cannot be found in the list of advertisements. But the above example is still a very good match.

We see the task of the dialogue system as narrowing the gap between a user request and what the index database of the system can supply.

Thus, the input data must be transformed into an appropriate representation which does allow matching of user queries to advertisements as effectively as possible combining various sorts of information like the name of the heading, the keywords in the free text of an entry (*TOWN CENTRE BED & BREAKFAST* ...), etc.

In order to obtain such a *Backend* database of indices we can distinguish two extreme positions for the construction process:

- *Knowledge Representation,* i.e. express the data in logic and do theorem proving in the online YPA system.
- *Information Retrieval,* i.e. use morphology and string matching.

There are at least two approaches for this sort of problem that should be mentioned here. *Publishers Depot* [ ] is a commercial product that allows the retrieval of pictures based on the corresponding caption. That means the documents are very short compared to standard *IR* tasks, just like in our case. On the other hand there has been work on *conceptual indexing* [ ]. A knowledge base is built that is based on the observation that there are few true synonyms in the language and usually there is a generality relationship like: *car −> automobile −> motor vehicle* which can be expressed as a *subsumption* relationship. Woods [ ] employs an example from the *Yellow Pages*:

- The *Yellow Pages* do not contain a heading "automobile steam cleaning".
- There are basic facts (axioms): (1) a *car* is an *automobile* and (2) *washing* is some kind of *cleaning*.

---

[3] http://www.picturequest.com

- The algorithm has to infer that *car washing* is some sort of *automobile cleaning*.

Such a knowledge base has been applied to precision content retrieval knowing that standard *Information Retrieval* approaches are not very effective for *short* queries [ ].

Our approach can be placed somewhere between the one used by Flank [ ] and Woods [ ].

A number of online directory enquiry systems are actually in use. Some of the existing systems that offer information one would expect from the *Yellow Pages* are: *Electronic Yellow Pages (U.K.)*, *Scoot (U.K.)* , *NYNEX Yellow Pages (U.S.A)* , *BigBook (U.S.A)* and *Switchboard (U.S.A)* . This type of commercial system functions quite differently from traditional *NLP* or *IR* systems. While they access large address databases of the same sort that we deal with, they all share a number of limitations:

- a very flat *Frontend* which offers at most pattern matching;
- a very simple lookup database which does not permit the access of free text hidden in the addresses;
- the inability to cope with words not found in the database (i.e. in the categories or names).

The intermediate position that we have chosen extracts relatively flat relations from the incoming data and uses text-retrieval-like methods for this *offline* process, while we can still apply theorem-proving-like methods in the *online* system.

3   Overall Structure of the YPA

The YPA is an interactive system. A conversation cycle with the YPA can be roughly described as follows. A user utterance (typed in via the *Graphical User Interface*) is sent to the *Dialogue Manager*. The *Dialogue Manager* keeps track of the current stage in the dialogue and controls the use of several submodules. Before handing back control (together with the relevant data) to the *Toplevel*, the input is first sent to the *Natural Language Frontend* which returns a so-called *slot-and-filler query*. The *Dialogue Manager* then consults the *Query Construction Component*, passing to it the result of the parsing process (possibly modified depending on the *dialogue history*, etc). The purpose of the *Query Construction Component* is to transform the input into a *database query* (making use of the *Backend* and possibly the *World Model*), to query the *Backend* and to return the retrieved addresses (and some database information) to the *Dialogue Manager*. Finally the *Dialogue Manager* hands back control to the *Toplevel* which for

---

[4] http://www.scoot.co.uk
[5] http://www.bigyellow.com
[6] http://www.bigbook.com
[7] http://www.switchboard.com

example displays the retrieved addresses. It could also put questions to the user which were passed to it by the *Dialogue Manager*, if the database access was not successful (i.e. did not result in a set of addresses). At this stage the cycle starts again.

Figure   shows the relationships of the modules in the YPA system.

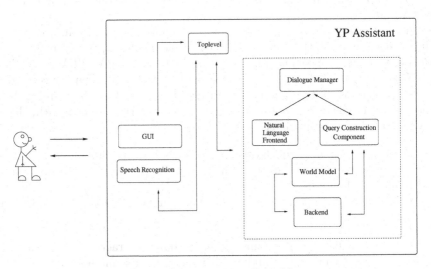

Fig. 1. Architecture of the YPA

We will now describe what each module does by taking the example *I want an Italian restaurant in Colchester that takes Visa* and following, more or less, the sequence of events in one interaction.

3.1   The Graphical User Interface

The *Graphical User Interface* is a form interface that allows a user to enter a query and then calls the *Toplevel*, which returns the content of an HTML page.

The input field is used to state a request for addresses from the *Yellow Pages*. The input query can be any English sentence or phrase or single word. Examples for possible queries are:

I want an Italian restaurant in Colchester.
Italian restaurants please!
RESTAURANTS in Colchester

The *Graphical User Interface* also provides different check boxes for the user to set parameters that influence the strategy of the YPA.

3.2   The Toplevel

The responsibility of the *Toplevel* lies in handling an incoming user request, forwarding the task to the *Dialogue Manager* and passing the returned output back to the *Graphical User Interface* in an appropriate format.

After connecting to the *Dialogue Manager* and waiting for its results, the *Toplevel* returns an HTML-page. This is a sample call:

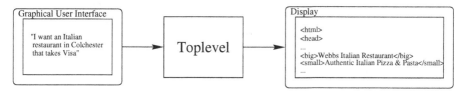

3.3   The Natural Language Frontend

The *Natural Language Frontend* [ ] is called directly by the *Dialogue Manager*. It consists of two components whose overall task is to transfer input strings from the user into slot and filler constructions. These two components, the *Parser* and the *Slot-Filler*, are described in more detail below.

The Parser Parsing methods for handling real NLP applications are being developed all the time. Notably, there are methods such as the LR parsing algorithm [ ], phrasal parsing as seen in the SPARKLE project [ ] and chunking [ ]. It is a primary aim of these systems that they return some linguistically correct parse tree for the input, and have the ability to choose correctly between syntactically (and semantically) ambiguous analyses. For example, the different attachments of prepositional phrases.

For our purposes, it made little difference in the construction of a query if input such as *Italian Restaurant* was seen as an adjective/noun construction or a compound of two nouns. Both terms would be used in the search regardless.

What was required by the *Yellow Pages* domain was not the linguistically correct syntactic tree structure, but the identification of those parts of the input which would allow us access to the meaning of the query, and that this process be a fast one. To that end, we began developing our own parsing process.

The requirement to handle ill-formed input meant that there was no need for a detailed grammar. Instead a simple DCG-like grammar was adopted, since it was easy both to understand and modify, and a basic bottom-up chart parser was implemented [ ].

We wanted to rapidly assign a "skeleton framework" to any input based on the closed class words. Any other words in the input would be given a limited freedom to try out different classes until one allowing a parse could be generated. As soon as one parse tree exists, it is accepted. We make no claim about the resolution of ambiguity on the basis of syntactic structure, but rather let the domain database react to such ambiguities as it sees fit.

All closed class words are listed as *hardwords*, other words were listed as *softwords*, in that we would prefer them to adopt particular word-class behaviour in the majority of situations. For example, the word 'phone' (listed in our lexicon as a *softword* verb) as in *I want to phone for a pizza*, compared to *I want to buy a phone*. In the first example we would want it to be a verb, and a noun in the second.

It was stipulated that any word that was not a hardword could also be a noun. This meant that any unknown words were identified as nouns, giving our system the powerful capability of dealing with previously unseen words. The loose nature of our grammar (in that it accepts structures such as prepositional phrases and noun compounds as complete sentences) helps to address a similar problem with unseen grammar constructions.

All this meant that the lexicon could consist of the prepositions and the determiners (as our *hardwords*), and those verbs which we extracted directly from the *Yellow Pages* as our suggested *softwords*, and nothing else.

As an example, here is the result of the parse process in brief for the query *I want an Italian restaurant in Colchester that takes Visa*:

```
[s,[np,[pron,i]],[vp,[v,want],[np,[det,an],
    [np,[n,italian],[np,[n,restaurant],
    [pp,[prep,in],[np,[n,colchester],
    [pp,[prep,that],[np,[n,takes],[np,[n,visa]]]]]]]]]]].
```

Once this brutal parse analysis has been attached to the input, it is passed to the next stage, the slot-filling process.

The Slot-Filling Process The notion of slots and fillers, or frames as they are sometimes called, has been around for some time [   ]. They are a way of specifying some semantic interpretation of user input as attributes of slots expressly identified by the domain.

A number of Natural Language Dialogue Systems have used a similar representation, notably Voyager [   ], ATIS [   ] and RailTel [   ]. An important difference between the use of the slot filler mechanism in these systems and in the YPA is the YPA's preservation of some syntactic structure.

The input parse tree is broken, where possible, into *subject, verb, object, modifiers*. Using this method, the parse tree in the example above would be split into the flatter structure:

subject	i
verb	want
object	an italian restaurant
modifiers	in colchester, that takes visa

Once the input is broken in this way, it is passed to the *domain dependent pragmatic analysis*. At this point, it becomes necessary to know about the behaviour and requirements of the domain.

Some mappings are straightforward. For example in this domain, as it is usually not necessary to know the subject information, this is discarded. The verb information maps directly into the transaction slot, and generally speaking the object maps into the goods slot.

With malformed input such as lone noun phrases (for example *parachuting centre*), it is assumed that the user has entered only the object and any modifiers.

Furthermore, domain-dependent knowledge is used to remove stop words from our slots - words such as *address* or *phone number* which we had identified through the construction of the back-end database as bearing little information content with relation to the domain. This gives us a final output structure for our example of:

```
[[transaction,[[]]],
 [goods,[[n(italian), restaurant]]],
 [payment,[[visa]]],
 [opening,[[]]],
 [street,[[]]],
 [location,[[colchester]]]]
```

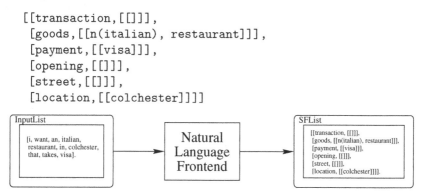

3.4   The Dialogue Manager

The interaction between user and machine can be roughly summarized as a filling of different slots in a *slot and filler* query with the information extracted from the user input, so that the database access finally retrieves an acceptable set of entries. In this process, the *Dialogue Manager* is the vital control module. Each stage in the dialogue with the user is characterized as a *dialogue state*. Every time the *Dialogue Manager* is called it performs the following tasks:

- calling the *Natural Language Frontend*
- evaluating the parsed input and determining the dialogue state (updating the *dialogue history*)
- performing all actions corresponding to the state transition.

The overall architecture of the *Dialogue Manager* is very similar to the *PURE* system [ ]. The user input is passed to the *Dialogue Manager*, which calls the *Natural Language Frontend* and, depending on the result, decides whether for instance the database should be accessed (calling the *Query Construction Component* and passing the current *slot and filler* query as an argument) or whether the dialogue should be restarted.

Our *Dialogue Manager* consists of a *Core Dialogue Manager* which is the domain-independent heart of the system and an extension (also domain-independent) which adds the basic functionality of a dialogue manager to a frame-based approach and which is called the *Default Dialogue Manager*. The administrator has to (1) set interfaces to the *Core Dialogue Manager* and the *Default Dialogue Manager* and (2) customize the system for the specific application.

The general idea about a domain independent basic dialogue manager is to have a core dialogue manager that covers all tasks to be handled by any similar dialogue system without having to access the *database system*. It should detect

- that a user wants to *quit* (or *restart*) the dialogue;
- *meta queries* (where the user asks for some help, etc);
- that a user uttered some *correction*.

The *Default Dialogue Manager* is this core engine expanded by adding coverage of the other states that can occur in a general spoken dialogue system:

- *mandatory slots* (which must be filled in order to submit a query to the database system) are not filled;
- *unknown concepts* occurred in the input;
- some *inconsistency* occurred;
- a database access was *successful*;
- a database access results in *too many matches*;
- a database access results in *too few matches*.

This outline compares to the two-layered dialogue architecture in Agarwal [ ], where the *Default Dialogue Manager* covers the upper layer of dialogue states, and where customization may refine those and add a second (domain-dependent) layer. Differences, however, are the set of dialogue states and the distinction made between the various possible states.

In order to keep the *Dialogue Manager* truly generic we do not assume anything about the structure of the query except that it is some sort of *slot and filler* list. In the YPA, we customized its current *Dialogue Manager* by defining the appropriate interfaces in the setup files.

Here is a sketch of the data flow in the *Dialogue Manager* in the case of our initial example:

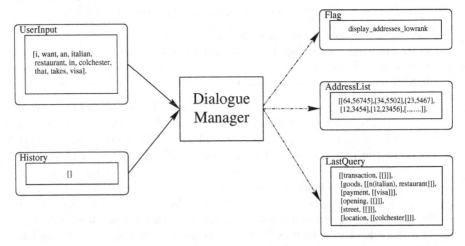

3.5   The Query Construction Component

The structure passed to the *Query Construction Component* is a *slot-and-filler* query. We believe that a large number of sample dialogues involve the construction of *slot-and-filler* structures, and there is nothing special about the slots (*goods, transaction, location*) used here apart from the fact that the *Query Construction Component* in this system knows how to convert them into queries suitable to be used with the indices in the *Backend*. The task is to match this query to a set of addresses by consulting different sources of knowledge, namely the transformed *Yellow Pages* data (part of the *Backend*) and knowledge sources which can be summarized as the *World Model*. While the *Backend* supplies indices as well as ranking values, the shallow *World Model* delivers information which can be employed on the *Backend* (e.g. for query expansion). It is therefore the task of the *Query Construction Component* to evaluate the various information sources (e.g. indices *versus* ranking values) and retrieve a set of addresses from the *Backend* if possible.

The constructed query is sent to the address database. If this results in a set of addresses (up to a maximum number defined by the administrator), then the *Query Construction* is finished. Otherwise there is a general strategy of successive relaxation of the query. A query that resulted in no matching addresses would for example be relaxed by ignoring slots which are not as important as others (e.g. *opening hours* as opposed to *goods & services*) or by exploiting syntactic information (prepositional phrases could be ignored). This all depends on how the component is set up. If too many addresses are retrieved, then the query will be further constrained if possible. If after query modification there is still no set of addresses, then an appropriate flag is passed back to the *Dialogue Manager*.

For the *Italian restaurant* example the input and output data could look like this:

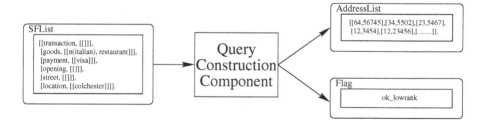

3.6   The Backend

Figure   reflects the data flow in the process of constructing the databases that form the *Backend* of the YPA.

The data extraction and transformation takes place in several steps.

The same extraction techniques result in significant differences in the results when applied to different parts of the input.

There are some general techniques we apply to all the data.

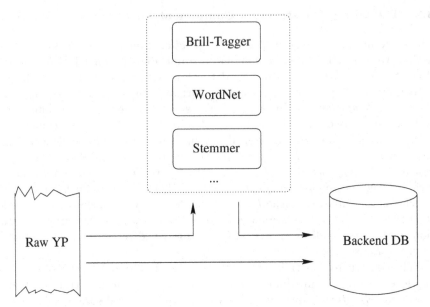

Fig. 2. Extraction of the YPA-Backend

Firstly, for part-of-speech tagging we use the Brill tagger [,] without training (using the supplied *lexical rule* and *contextual rule* files of the *Wall Street Journal Corpus* and the lexicon of both *Wall Street Journal* and *Brown Corpus*). This tagger is especially good for our purpose as we do need a contextual tagger, and one that is robust enough. Furthermore the tagging follows the *Penn Treebank* guidelines [ ] which makes the results comparable.

Secondly, we use *WordNet* [ ] for indexing the keywords. To do this, we use the *WordNet* interface that performs morphological reduction to base forms. We then apply a stemmer to further reduce the base forms delivered by *WordNet*. The result of the stemming does not have to be a proper lexicon entry [ ]. However, we can still make use of synonyms as provided by *WordNet*.

Thirdly, the *ID* for each entry in the data is the unique line number where this entry starts. Hence we automatically have a key for most of the relational tables to be created.

The *Backend* contains the information from the raw *Yellow Pages*. There are three subcomponents that form the *Backend*:

 - the *Relational Database*, which contains all the information extracted from the raw data file (the actual addresses, indexes, etc);
 - the *Information Retrieval Database*, which contains information about the extracted data (occurrences, term frequencies, etc);
 - the *Language Module*, which provides base forms for any word form.

The Relational Database The main purpose of the *Relational Database* is to represent the addresses that were extracted from the *Yellow Pages*. This is done fully automatically by applying a set of *UNIX* scripts to the *YP data file* exploiting the record structure of the entries as described in De Roeck et al [ ].

In the data file there are entries, whose type is determined by the values of certain fields in the record structure. These entries can be address entries as well as heading entries or reference entries of various types. What is used as the address database is the set of *free entries*, *line entries* and *semi display entries*.

Tables exist for address entries (complete addresses, company names, keyword indexes for the free text of addresses, keyword indexes for the company names, etc) and for headings used in the *Yellow Pages* (complete headings, keyword indexes, *see*-references and *see-also*-references).

While most of the relations are obvious something must be said about the *see*- and *see-also*-references. Each of the addresses fall under a unique heading. However, some headings are not followed by any address but instead contain a pointer to a set of other headings. This reference is called *see*-reference (for example the heading *Abortion Advice* makes a reference to *Clinics* and *Pregnancy Test Services*). The *see-also*-references are similar but there are still addresses listed under the heading (heading *Abattoirs* makes reference to *Horse Slaughterers* but also lists two addresses in the Colchester data file).

Additionally there are tables for relations which are not directly retrieved from the data file but derived by adding the information contained in the back cover of the *Yellow Pages* together with variations in the usage of town names detected in the actual addresses: *town indexes* and *dialling codes*.

The *town index* relation is used to map variations in the usage of town names onto a unique town index. This town index is used as the first argument in the *dialling code* relation, the second argument being the dialling code. For example the town index for the place Clacton-on-Sea is *clacton_on_sea* as it is mostly used in the addresses, but *'clacton on s'* and *clacton-o-s* denote the same location and therefore determining the dialling code for Clacton-on-Sea involves looking up the town index (*clacton_on_sea*) and then consulting the dialling code table with this key.

In the case of the *Italian restaurant* example, we get something like this:

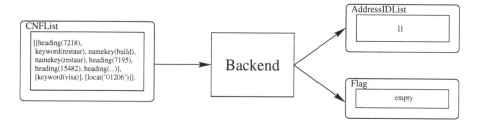

The returned flag *empty* indicates no matching addresses can be found (because there are no Italian restaurants that take Visa). However, it is the task of the *Query Construction Component* to evaluate this output and possibly query the *Backend* again with a modified query. In this case the requirement *keyword(visa)* is relaxed, leading to a revised query:

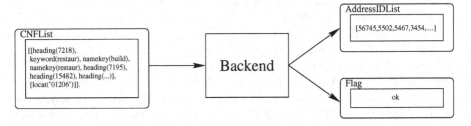

The Information Retrieval Component The tables in the *Information Retrieval Component* contain *meta information* about the data from the *Yellow Pages*, i.e. information about the distribution of keyword indexes in either the headings or addresses, etc. This data is for example used by the *Query Construction Component* to determine the weights for retrieved addresses. These relations express something like: "How many addresses would be retrieved if a certain index would be accessed?" for example:

"If using the keyword index *public_house*, then how many addresses would be retrieved?"

This relation is called *ranking*. The above example would access the table that contains the overall ranking, but the *Query Construction Component* might evaluate the usefulness of more detailed rankings, which are:

— ranking of keyword indexes in the free text of the addresses;
— ranking of keyword indexes in the company names;
— ranking of keyword indexes in the headings;
— overall ranking.

To take the example again, the keyword index *public_house* turns up only in two headings (ranking value 681, since that many addresses would be retrieved) and never in the free text or the name field of the data file (therefore no ranking entry in these two tables). The *overall* ranking appears to be the same as for the heading, but this is normally not the case.

Language Module The *Language Module* provides interfaces for the morphological reduction of *word forms* to *base forms* and for the reduction of *base forms* to *word stems*. These functions are useful when trying to access the *Relational Database* or the *Information Retrieval Component* since the indexes are constructed on the base of the *Language Module*.

The implemented *Language Module* accesses the *WordNet* library. This is of no interest for the interface predicates as these functions can be supplied by any other system, but in this case the *Backend Databases* would have to be rebuilt in order to match the stemmed base forms stored in the index files with the base forms used in the online dialogue.

3.7   The World Model

The function of the *World Model* is to allow query expansion and query modification. This is done either to retrieve addresses or to allow the user to choose various ways of modifying the original input if the query cannot be fired successfully. It contains both domain-independent data (a large lexicon containing various simple hierarchies (*WordNet* [ ])) and domain-dependent data (the heading structure from the *Yellow Pages* as well as knowledge acquired by the user, updated via the *YPA AdminTool*)). Other sources can be incorporated.

Parameters define the way *world knowledge* is applied. By default, synonyms and hypernyms of query terms are only used when there cannot be found any matching addresses otherwise. But the user can choose to always apply this *world knowledge* or never, or stick to the default.

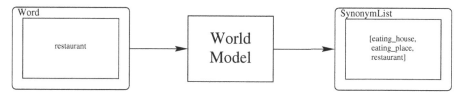

4   Recent Experiences

The YPA is not a single program but consists of two servers and several scripts which are responsible for the data and control flow between user and main server. It is accessible across the net, and the user interface is through a web browser. Figure   shows a screenshot of a reply to a query.

4.1   Evaluation

For the evaluation we used the YPA version 0.7 for the Colchester area with about 26,000 addresses.

To date, there have been two evaluations of the YPA system, the first focusing on technology issues, the second on the precision of the recalled addresses.

The first evaluation, that of the technology, reflects mostly on the behaviour of our robust *Natural Language Frontend* process.

The evaluation of such parsing strategies is an art in itself. There have been a large number of suggested methods for evaluating parsers for the purpose of guiding and monitoring the development of a parsing system (see Carroll et al [ ] for a good survey).

For the technology evaluation we used the method of *coverage*, where we calculate the percentage of sentences assigned an analysis from an unannotated corpus.

During a two-week period, members of BT's Intelligent Systems Research Group had access to the YPA via the World Wide Web. They were given an outline of the information the system contained, but not told how the system

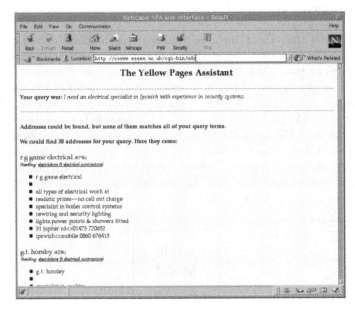

Fig. 3. Screenshot of an online dialogue

should be queried. Over this time, some 238 *unique* queries were collected by the administrators of the system. These queries were used to conduct the technology-focused evaluation of the YPA system. Each query was evaluated to see if it presented a list of addresses to the user, either first time or as the result of some dialogue with the system. If a list of addresses was not returned, we recorded the reason for this, and presented the figures as percentages of the total number of queries.

90% were successful from the parser point of view, although of those 22% failed at some later point in the system (incorrect query construction or spelling errors - note that these did not cause a parse failure, but failed to match information in the database). 10% were recorded as a *Frontend* failure - where either queries failed the parse completely, or information was misplaced, and put in incorrect slots.

This method of evaluation is very crude, given that the rules in the grammar allow a variety of parse trees, which might not necessarily be correct. Although linguistic correctness was not a requirement, it is equally important that we have some form of correct structural identification, as we aim to preserve some structural information throughout the slot-filling procedure.

It is often difficult to assess the performance of individual components of systems such as these (see Dybkjaer et al [29]), because the functionality of individual modules is often dependent on other modules within the system.

We also report on the second evaluation, that of the system as a whole, as this gives us an indication of the success of our goal to improve precision.

For the precision evaluation, we used a corpus of 75 queries, collected from the Talking Pages call centre in Bristol. Of these 75 queries, 62 (83%) asked for information about addresses contained within our sample set (that is, existed within the Colchester area). For those, we had a value of 74% of addresses returned being relevant to the input query.

The issue of how to deal with 'negative return queries', that is how to satisfactorily inform the user that no answers can be found, is one that we wish to address in the next stage of dialogue management development, and is probably a major factor in user satisfaction with any system.

These are the results of a very simplistic evaluation. One aspect for example is not reflected at all, that is the order and ranking values of the advertisements in a successful user query.

We continue with our evaluations of the YPA. At the moment we are most concerned about a more detailed evaluation, taking into account *recall* as well as *precision* values.

5   Conclusions and Future Work

We continue work on the YPA system. One of the interesting problems is to extract more structural information from richer data files. At the same time this will influence the other components in particular the *Query Construction Component* and the *Dialogue Manager*, because a more varied *Backend* database allows a refined query construction and a more user-friendly dialogue.

We also noticed that the function of the *Dialogue Manager* changed considerably in the process of the overall development of the YPA. More and more tasks which were initially located in the *Dialogue Manager* have been implemented as customizations of the *Query Construction Component*. It could well be that in future we will merge those two components to just one.

We are also making the developed data extraction tools more generic. We have recently created a similar system which can extract information from an advertisement such as the one below but still store it in the same *Backend* structure.

```
PRODUCTS AND SERVICES
* Authentic American themed restaurant and bar.
* International menu offering over 60 American, Tex Mex, Cajun
  and Italian dishes
* Specialities include BBQ ribs, Fajitas and our famous burgers
* Famous bar offering over 500 different cocktails and beers from
  around the world
  ...

PAYMENT METHODS
Cash, Cheque, Visa, Mastercard, American Express, Delta.

OPENING HOURS
```

```
12 Midday to 11.30pm   -  7 days a week
Open Bank Holidays and New Years Day
   ...
```

It proved to be very simple to convert the new data files once the set of scripts had been developed. Minimal customization of the scripts was needed.

A major task for the future is a deep evaluation of the system which involves another user trial once we have developed a framework for this.

6   Acknowledgements

This work has been funded by a contract from ISR group at BT's Adastral Park, Martlesham Heath, UK. Most of the data was provided by Yellow Pages. The authors want to thank K C Tsui and Wayne Wobcke for their helpful comments.

References

1. De Roeck A., Kruschwitz U., Neal P., Scott P., Steel S., Turner R. and Webb N.: 'YPA - an intelligent directory enquiry assistant'. BT Technology Journal, Vol. 16(3), pp. 145–155 (1998).   ,   ,
2. Miller G.: 'Wordnet: An on-line lexical database'. International Journal of Lexicography, Vol. 3(4) (1990). (Special Issue).   ,   ,
3. Nederhof M.-J., Bouma G., Koeling R. and van Noord G.: 'Grammatical analysis in the OVIS spoken-dialogue system'. In 'Proceedings of the ACL/EACL Workshop on "Interactive Spoken Dialog Systems: Bringing Speech and NLP Together in Real Applications"' (Madrid) (1997).
4. Aust H., Oerder M., Seide F. and Steinbiss V.: 'The Philips automatic train timetable information system'. Speech Communication, Vol. 17, pp. 249–262 (1995).
5. Peckham J.: 'A new generation of spoken dialogue systems: results and lessons from the SUNDIAL project'. In 'Proceedings of the 3rd European Conference on Speech Communication and Technology' (Berlin, Germany), pp. 33 – 40 (1993).
6. McGlashan S., Fraser N., Gilbert N., Bilange E., Heisterkamp P. and Youd N.: 'Dialogue Management for Telephone Information Systems'. In 'Proceedings of the International Conference on Applied Language Processing' (Trento, Italy) (1992).
7. Allen J., Schubert L., Ferguson G., Heeman P., Hwang C., Kato T., Light M., Martin N., Miller B., Posesio M. and Traum D.: 'The TRAINS project: a case study in building a conversational planning agent'. Journal of Experimental and Theoretical Artificial Intelligence, Vol. 7, pp. 7–48 (1995).
8. Wahlster W.: 'Verbmobil: Translation of Face-to-Face Dialogues'. In 'Proceedings of the 3rd European Conference on Speech Communication and Technology' (Berlin, Germany), pp. 29–38 (1993).

9. Zue V., Glass J., Goodine D., Leung H., Phillips M., Polifroni J. and Seneff S.: 'The VOYAGER Speech Understanding System: Preliminary Development and Evaluation'. In 'Proceedings of IEEE International Conference on Acoustics, Speech and Signal Processing' (Cambridge, MA, USA), pp. 73–76 (1990).

10. Zue V.: 'Toward Systems that Understand Spoken Language'. IEEE Expert Magazine, Vol. February, pp. 51–59 (1994).   ,

11. Glass J., Flammia G., Goodine D., Phillips M., Polifroni J., Sakai S., Seneff S. and Zue V.: 'Multilingual Spoken-Language Understanding in the MIT VOYAGER System'. Speech Communication, Vol. 17, pp. 1–18 (1995).

12. Flank S.: 'A layered approach to NLP-based Information Retrieval'. In 'Proceedings of the 36th ACL and the 17th COLING Conferences' (Montreal), pp. 397–403 (1998).   ,

13. Woods W. A.: 'Conceptual Indexing: A Better Way to Organize Knowledge'. Technical Report SMLI TR-97-61, Sun Microsystems Laboratories, Mountain View, CA (1997).   ,

14. Ambroziak J. and Woods W. A.: 'Natural Language Technology in Precision Content Retrieval'. In 'Proceedings of the 2nd Conference on Natural Language Processing and Industrial Applications (NLP-IA)' (Moncton, Canada), pp. 117–124 (1998).

15. Webb N., De Roeck A., Kruschwitz U., Scott P., Steel S. and Turner R.: 'Natural Language Engineering: Slot-Filling in the YPA'. In 'Proceedings of the Workshop on Natural Language Interfaces, Dialogue and Partner Modelling (at the Fachtagung für Künstliche Intelligenz KI'99)' (Bonn, Germany) (1999). http://www.ikp.uni-bonn.de/NDS99/Finals/3_1.ps.

16. Tomita M.: 'Efficient Parsing for Natural Language: A Fast Algorithm for Pratical Systems'. Kluwer Academic (1985).

17. Briscoe T., Carroll J., Carroll G., Federici S., Montemagni G. G. S., Pirrelli V., Prodanof I., Rooth M. and Vannocchi M. 'Phrasal Parser Software - Deliverable 3.1'. http://www.ilc.pi.cnr.it/sparkle.html, (1997).

18. Abney S.: 'Parsing by chunks'. In 'Principle-Based Parsing', S. A. R. Berwick and C. Tenny, Eds. Kluwer Academic Publishers (1991).

19. Gazdar G. and Mellish C.: 'Natural Language Processing in PROLOG: An Introduction to Computational Linguistics'. Addison Wesley (1989).

20. Minsky M.: 'A Framework for Representing Knowledge'. In 'The Psychology of Computer Vision', P. H. Winston, Ed. McGraw-Hill, New York, pp. 211–277 (1975).

21. Bannacef S. K., Bonneau-Maynard H., Gauvain J. L., Lamel L. and Minker W.: 'A Spoken Language System for Information Retrieval'. In 'Proceedings of the International Conference on Speech and Language Processing' (Yokohama, Japan) (1994).

22. Bannacef S. K., Devillers L., Rosset S. and Lamel L.: 'Dialog in the RAILTEL Telephone-Based System'. In 'Proceedings of the International Conference on Speech and Language Processing' (Philadelphia), pp. 550–553 (1996).

23. Agarwal R.: 'Towards a PURE Spoken Dialogue System for Information Access'. In 'Proceedings of the ACL/EACL Workshop on "Interactive Spoken Dialog Systems: Bringing Speech and NLP Together in Real Applications"' (Madrid), pp. 90–97 (1997).   ,

24. Brill E.: 'A simple rule-based part of speech tagger'. In 'Proceedings of the Third Conference on Applied Natural Language Processing, ACL' (Trento, Italy) (1992).

25. Brill E.: 'Some advances in rule-based part of speech tagging'. In 'Proceedings of the Twelfth National Conference on Artificial Intelligence (AAAI-94)' (Seattle, Wa.) (1994).

26. Santorini B.: 'Part-of-speech tagging guidelines for the Penn Treebank Project'. Technical report MS-CIS-90-47, Department of Computer and Information Science, University of Pennsylvania (1990).

27. Strzalkowski T.: 'Natural Language Information Retrieval: TREC-4 Report'. In 'Proceedings of the Fourth Text Retrieval Conference (TREC-4)' (NIST Special Publication 500-236) (1996).

28. Carroll J., Briscoe T. and Sanfilippo A.: 'Parser evaluation: a survey and a new proposal'. In 'Proceedings of the 1st International Conference on Language Resources and Evaluation' (Granada, Spain), pp. 447 – 454 (1998).

29. Dybkjær L., Bernsen N. O., Carlson R., Chase L., Dahlbäck N., Failenschmid K., Heid U., Heisterkamp P., Jönsson A., Kamp H., Karlsson I., v. Kuppevelt J., Lamel L., Paroubek P. and Williams D.: 'The DISC approach to spoken language systems development and evaluation'. In 'Proceedings of the 1st International Conference on Language Resources and Evaluation' (Granada, Spain), pp. 185 – 189 (1998).

Intelligent Multimodal User Interface

Kwok Ching Tsui and Behnam Azvine

Intelligent Systems Research Group
BT Labs, Adastral Park, Martlesham Heath
Ipswich IP5 3RE, United Kingdom
{kc.tsui,ben.azvine}@bt.com

Abstract. Research in human/computer interaction has primarily focused on natural language, text, speech and vision in isolation. A number of recent research projects have studied the integration of such modalities. The rationale is that many inherent ambiguities in single modes of communication can be resolved if extra information is available. This paper discusses issues related to designing and building a multi-modal system. The main characteristics of such a system are that it can process input and output from conventional as well as new channels. Examples of multi-modal systems are the *Smart Work Manager* [ ] and the *Intelligent Assistant* [ ]. Main components of the two systems described here are the reasoner, the speech system, the non-intrusive neural-network-based gaze-tracking system, the user presence detector and the integration platforms. The paper concludes with a discussion on the limitations and possible enhancements of the current system.

1   Introduction

The rapid growth in the use (and processing power) of computers both in the home and in the workplace has intensified the interaction between computers and human beings. The role of computers has evolved from merely a computational device to a centre for information processing. This is a direct result of the birth of the information age, which is not simply about adding traffic to the communications networks, but about added value [ ]. Computer users are required to have a lot more skills than in the past in order to handle the overload of information. It is surprising that the ways humans and computers interact have not changed too much since the first inception of computers. The introduction of mouse and graphical display systems is a step closer to natural human/computer communication. However, the interaction is still far more restricted than the way human beings communicate with each other.

It is important for computers to proactively assist humans, anticipate the effects of their action and learn from users' reactions. Recent advances in artificial intelligence (AI) research and computer hardware have made achievable the vision of a world in which computers work together in teams with humans acting as supervisors, who are called upon only in rare situations.

For a computer to effectively communicate with humans it must possess communication capabilities that are similar to those of a human, i.e. it must be able

B. Azvine et al. (Eds.): Intelligent Systems and Soft Computing, LNAI 1804, pp. 259–   , 2000.

see, hear and speak. It must also be able to understand and, if necessary, question. The key point is that it is the combination of these capabilities that allows humans to communicate effectively and naturally. Limiting the communication by blocking some of these channels clearly reduces the amount of information conveyed. This information, although redundant in some circumstances, can be vital in processing interactions such as: 'Put that there'.

The aim of the multi-modal user interface systems (MMUIs) described here is to provide computers with information about their external world using as many modalities as possible, equip them with human-like reasoning mechanisms, and facilitate adaptation to and learning from the user through observations and task-specific knowledge. The American Association for Artificial Intelligence has recommended intelligent interfaces to be one of several basic research initiatives with high potential for the next decade [ ]. An intelligent multi-modal system is defined here as a system that combines, reasons with and learns from, information originating from different modes of communication between humans and the computer. The fundamental research issues are:

- how to best capture the information from the outside world;
- how to extract knowledge from the information captured;
- how to use the knowledge to learn and reason;
- how to integrate robustly all the above components.

This paper describes the development of an intelligent multi-modal system called the Smart Work Manger (SWM) for a workforce scheduling application. The main components of the system are the reasoner, the speech system, the non-intrusive neural-network-based gaze-tracking system and the integration platform. The main characteristics of the SWM are that it can process input from speech and gaze information in addition to conventional means of keyboard and mouse, and its output is in the form of speech, text or graphics (Fig.). More recent enhancements to the MMUI include the addition of a user presence detector and simultaneous speech recognition. They are realised in the Intelligent Assistant [ ].

A brief summary of the application areas, namely, the workforce management system and the Intelligent Assistant, is provided in the next section. This is followed by a review of some multi-modal systems and discussion of the major engineering issues on the intelligent multi-modal interface. The core components such as the reasoner, the neural gaze-tracking system, the user presence detector and the the speech system are described in detail. The paper concludes with a discussion on some limitations of the current system.

2   The Application Areas

Complicated interaction with computers can be found in the work environment both at task and personal level. This section describes two application areas where a multi-modal user interface is able to help computer users.

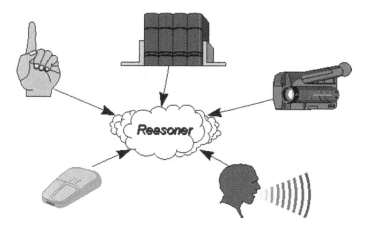

Fig. 1. A multi-modal system

2.1   The Workforce Management System

Work Manager is BT's workforce management system. The key component is the allocation algorithm called Dynamic Scheduler (DS) [5]. The purpose of the DS is to provide BT with the capability:

- to schedule work over a long period of time;
- to repair/optimise schedules;
- to modify the business objectives of the scheduling algorithms;
- to provide statistics from which the schedules can be viewed and their quality assessed.

Enormous amounts of information are produced by DS making the assessment of results via traditional management information systems extremely difficult. Data visualisation (DV) summarises and organises the information produced by DS, facilitating the real-time monitoring and visualisation of work schedules generated. Both the temporal and spatial dimensions of the information produced are visualised in the Gantt chart and the maps respectively, while statistical information is displayed on various forms and pie charts (see Fig. 2). When the system is used, the set of actions/queries during a complete session can be categorised into three classes:

- queries on scenario and schedule based on textual information display;
- queries on scenario and schedule based on the Gantt chart and the map;
- queries on the scheduling algorithms.

A grammar for these queries is defined as follows:

order/question + object_class + object_identifier + object_attribute

or

order/question + object_attribute + *of* + object_class + object_identifier

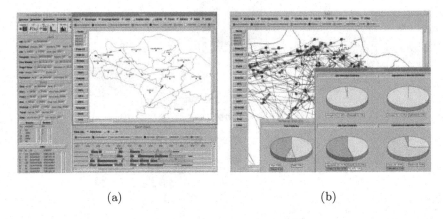

(a)   (b)

Fig. 2. Screen shots from the Data Visualisation tool

Examples:
```
{give me} + {technician} + {ab123} + {duration of lunch}
{what is} + {expected completion time} + of + {job} + {10}
{what is} + {duration} + of + {this job}
{show me} + {location in map} + of + {that technician}
```

2.2 The Intelligent Assistant

Computer users are becoming more reliant on their computers than ever before. This is mainly because today's computers are more powerful both in hardware and software terms. The intelligent assistant (IA) [2] is the electronic personal assistant of a computer user. It looks after the communication, information and time management needs of a user by employing multiple software agents to address each of them. The Email Assistant and Telephone Assistant filter and prioritise incoming emails and telephone calls for the user respectively. The Web Assistant and Yellow Pages Assistant search for information on the Internet for the user, taking the user's preferences and personal interests into consideration. The Diary Assistant schedules tasks and events for the user and provides a flexible way to user to specify the requirement of each diary entry. These software agents are in fact a family of adaptive agents built on top of the Open Messaging Architecture of Zeus.

Interacting with such a complex system using conventional means would normally requires the user to do a lot of typing and mouse clicking. The benefits of employing a multimodal user interface with speech and visual input is twofold. Firstly, the user is able to interact with the IA in a natural way. Secondly, the IA is able to perform infer information from the information collected from various input channels and act proactively and intelligently. For example, the telephone assistant will not put any telephone call through if the user is not at his/her desk.

3   Research Issues and Related Works

The biggest difference between human/human and human/computer communication lies at the degree of freedom and the availability of multiple channels. Humans communicate using verbal and non-verbal means and it is usually two ways. However, it is not the case with human/computer communication as computers are not equipped with the same capabilities as human beings. This limitation leads to the lack of 'naturalness' in human/computer interactions.

Modalities and media of communication are highly related in human/human and human/computer interaction. Media refer to the physical channels through which communication happens while modalities are the communication systems themselves. For example, natural language is a modality that uses speech as the medium. Multimodal communication often involves more than one medium. Following the previous example, printed text is another widely used medium that natural language employs. Similarly, more than one multimodal signal can be obtained simultaneously from the same medium.

There are several challenges in multi-modal user interface research. Firstly, understanding the messages coming from the sender via various media. Secondly, interpreting the messages in light of other information obtained from other modalities. Thirdly, carrying out actions appropriate to the messages. Fourthly, generating responses in accordance with the messages, the system's knowledge and the context of the interaction.

Research in human/computer interaction has mainly focused on natural language, text, speech, virtual reality and vision (mood recognition, head movement interpretation and gesture recognition) primarily in isolation. Recently there have been a number of research projects that have concentrated on the integration of such modalities using intelligent reasoners. The rationale is that many inherent ambiguities in single modes of communication can be resolved if extra information is available. A rich source of information for recent work in this area can be found elsewhere [,].

The CUBRICON system from Calspan-UB Research Centre is able to use a simultaneous pointing reference and natural language reference to disambiguate one another when appropriate. It also automatically composes and generates relevant output to the user in co-ordinated multimedia. The system combines natural language, text commands, speech and simulated gestures such as pointing with a mouse. The application area is military-based maps.

The XTRA system from DFKI (German Research Centre for AI) is an intelligent multi-modal interface to expert systems that combines natural language, graphics and pointing. It acts as an intelligent agent performing a translation between the user and the expert system. The most interesting aspect of this project is how free-form pointing gestures such as pointing with fingers at a distance from the screen has been integrated with graphics and natural language to allow a more natural way of communication between the user and the expert system.

The SRI system, from SRI International, combines natural language/speech with pen gestures such as circles and arrows to provide map-based tourist infor-

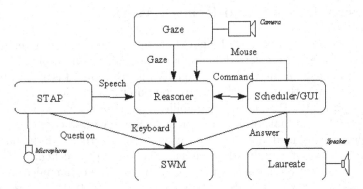

Fig. 3. An overview of the Smart Work Manager architecture

mation about San Francisco. At the heart of all the above systems is a reasoner that combines the general and task-specific knowledge in its knowledge base (a blackboard) with often vague or incomplete user requests in order to provide a complete query to the application [ ].

The MATIS project of IMAG Institute has a multi-modal input interface to an airline timetable information system [ ]. It has proposed a melting port approach to information fusion. Each melting point essentially has several attributes and contains a time-stamped events coming from a particular input source. The fusion engine that combines many melting points into one based on temporal relationship between events and an context. Time is important here as it provides a measurement of 'relatedness' of different events.

The Smart Work Manager utilises most of the functionality of the above systems. However, it is viewed as an initial attempt to understand the main issues involved in building a platform for such systems. Emphasis is put on the fusion of possibly redundant information for various channels, the application of fuzzy information processing in such complexity environment, and the introduction of gaze as a new channel of interaction.

The main module of the system is a front-end which spawns all the other modules. The user can type questions, correct poorly recognised spoken questions, get answers in text, and see the dialogue history. The overall architecture of SWM with the various modules and the communications between them is given in Fig. .

4   Engineering Issues

The general aim of this work is to study software architectures for building intelligent multi-modal systems. Before examining such an architecture used for the Smart Work Manager system, some of the general issues pertaining to the engineering of intelligent multi-modal systems are examined below.

Intelligent multi-modal systems use a number of input and output modalities to communicate with the user, exhibiting some form of intelligent behaviour in a particular domain. The functional requirements of such systems include the ability to receive and process user input in various forms such as:

- typed text from keyboard;
- hand-written text from a digitial tablet or light pen;
- mouse movement or clicking;
- speech from a microphone;
- focus of attention of the user's eye captured by a camera.

The system must also be able to generate output using speech, graphics, and text.

A system which exhibits the above features can be called a multi-modal system. For a multi-modal system to be called intelligent, it is essential that such a system is capable of reasoning in the chosen domain — automating human tasks, facilitating humans to perform tasks more complex than before and exhibiting a behaviour which can be characterised as intelligent by the users of the system.

A **modular** approach is necessary for breaking down the required functionality into a number of sub-systems which are easier to develop or for which software solutions already exist.

Another requirement for intelligent multi-modal systems is **concurrency**. The sub-systems must be running concurrently to process input which may come from more than one input device at the same time. For example, the user may be talking to the machine while at the same time typing text, moving the mouse or gazing at different parts of the screen. The same applies to the output produced by the system. An animation may be displayed while at the same time a speech synthesis program could be running in parallel explaining this animation.

Modular and concurrent systems require some type of **communication** mechanism, which enables information flow between the various sub-systems or modules. It is also desirable to have a **flexible** system that can be quickly adjusted to incorporate new and improved sub-systems.

Given the computational requirements of many of these sub-systems, of the various modules to be **distributed** over a network of computers instead of a single machine is also very important. This distribution of the computation implies that the overall system must be able to run on heterogeneous hardware, e.g. Unix workstations, PCs.

To address these requirements, a software platform has been developed which merges existing software from different sources into a single package suitable for building experimental intelligent multi-modal systems.

4.1   Development Platform: Parallel Virtual Machine

The core of the platform for building the Smart Work Manager is the Parallel Virtual Machine   (PVM) software package [ ]. PVM enables a collection of heterogeneous computers to be used as a coherent and flexible concurrent computational resource. The individual computers may be shared on local memory

---

[1] Home page: http://www.epm.ornl.gov/pvm/

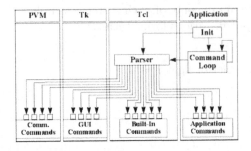

Fig. 4. The Tcl/Tk/PVM interpreter

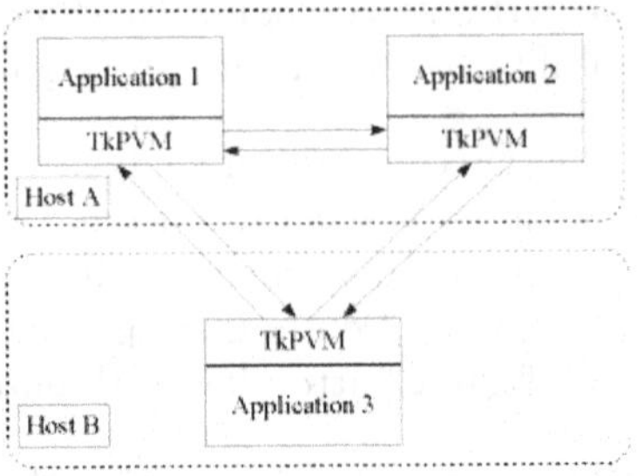

Fig. 5. A distributed system using Tcl/Tk and PVM

multiprocessors, vector supercomputers, specialised graphics engines, or scalar workstations, that may be interconnected by a variety of networks. It also supports user programs written in a large variety of user programming languages. Inter-process communication in PVM is via sockets, and is transparent to the user.

4.2   Programming Languages - Tcl/Tk and TkPVM

The Smart Work Manager is developed using Tcl/Tk. Tcl [ ] is a simple and easy-to-use scripting language suitable for integrating systems and also for rapid prototyping and development. The basic interpreter can be extended with extra application-specific commands by incorporating programs either written in C or other computer languages. Tk is a widely used extension to Tcl for building graphical user interfaces. The internal structure of the interpreter providing PVM, Tk, Tcl and application specific functionality is shown in Fig. .

   TkPVM provides all the necessary functionalities for using the PVM functions from within a Tcl script. Using TkPVM, Tcl scripts can be used as wrappers for applications to connect these applications to PVM. An example of a distributed system based on PVM is illustrated in Fig. . This is particularly important in the Smart Work Manager as all the systems that have to be integrated are written in different programming languages.

5   The Reasoner

The function of the reasoner can be stated as follows:

> Given inputs from all the channels, convert them to a valid command for the application. Consult the user only if necessary.

---

[2] Home page: http://www.sco.com/Technology/tcl/Tcl.html
[3] Home page: http://www.cogsci.kun.nl/tkpvm

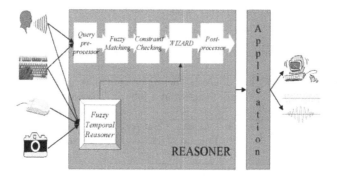

Fig. 6. The structure of the reasoner

In other words, it must:

- be able to handle ambiguities such as: 'give me this of that';
- have the capability to deal with conflicting information arriving from various modalities;
- be able to check the validity of a command based on a predefined grammar, that of which for the Smart Work Manager has been defined in section   .

The capabilities of the reasoner are to a large extent dependent upon the capabilities provided by the platform on which the reasoner is implemented. The platform used for the early version [ ] of the reasoner is CLIPS [   ], which is a well-known expert system shell with object-oriented, declarative and procedural programming capabilities and the fuzzy logic extension [   ]. The reasoner has since then been re-engineered using Fril [   ], an AI logic programming language which allows both probabilistic uncertainties and fuzzy sets to be included.

The reasoner handles ambiguities by using a knowledge base which is being continually updated by the information arriving from various modalities. The structure of the reasoner is shown in Fig.   . There are seven modules in the reasoner: fuzzy temporal reasoning, query pre-processing, fuzzy matching, constraint checking, resolving ambiguities (WIZARD), post-processing and learning. Table   contains some simple examples of interactions with the reasoner and how it works.

5.1 Fuzzy Temporal Reasoning

The fuzzy temporal reasoning module receives time stamped events from various modalities and determines the fuzzy temporal relationship between them. It determines to what degree two events have a temporal relationship using the certainty factors (CF).

The relationship with the highest CF will be chosen as the most likely relationship between the two events. This relationship can be used later by the

Table 1. Examples of interaction with the reasoner

Query	User action	Reasoning process
Show me technician ab123 location in map	None	Complete query, process command and send to application
Tell me the duration of this job	Mouse is clicked or eyes are focused on a job	'This job' is ambiguous, it is resolved using focus of attention. Context is updated.
Show me this of that technician	No focus. Context is 'technician ab123 end of day'	Two ambiguities, context is used to resolve them.
Show me this.	No focus. No context.	Everything is ambiguous, the user is asked to supply the missing parts. The context is updated.

reasoner to resolve conflicts between, and checking the dependency of, the modalities.

Specifically, an event or a process is specified temporally by two parameters, start time, t_s and end time, t_e. For two events A and B with their associated parameters $t_{sA}, t_{eA}, t_{sB}, t_{eB}$. The temporal relationship between events A and B can be specified by three parameters:

$$\delta_s = t_{sA} - t_{sB}, \tag{1}$$
$$\delta_e = t_{eA} - t_{eB}, \tag{2}$$
$$\delta_b = t_{eA} - t_{sB}. \tag{3}$$

With the assumption that A starts before or at the same time as B (i.e. $t_{sA} \leq t_{sB}$), there are a number of temporal relationships between A and B defined by the following rules:

1. If δ_b is negative then A has occurred **before** B,

   A • • • • • • • • • • • •

   B   ◇ ◇ ◇ ◇ ◇ ◇

2. If δ_b is zero then A has occurred **just before** B,

   A • • • • • • • • • • • •

   B   ◇ ◇ ◇ ◇ ◇ ◇

3. If δ_b is positive and δ_e is positive or zero then A has occurred **during** B,

   A ◇ ◇ ◇ ◇ ◇ ◇ ◇ ◇ ◇ ◇ ◇ ◇

   B   • • • • • •

4. If δ_s is zero and δ_e is zero then A has occurred **at the same time** as B,

   A • • • • • • • • • • • • •

   B ◇ ◇ ◇ ◇ ◇ ◇ ◇ ◇ ◇ ◇ ◇ ◇ '

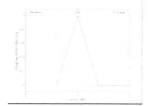

Fig. 7. PI membership function representation of 1

Fig. 8. Fuzzy definitions of Negative, Zero and Positive

Fig. 9. Mapping of the fuzzy time differences and fuzzy relationships

5. If δ_b is positive or zero and δ_e is negative then A **overlaps** with B.

A • • • • • • • • • • • • •

B   ◇ ◇ ◇ ◇ ◇ ◇

Systems using conventional technology implement these rules based on exact relationships between parameters of each event. When humans initiate the events, as is the case in the Smart Work Manager, events do not take place in strict order or in exact time-slots. The kind of reasoning required in such cases is fuzzy rather than exact, for example the relationship between speech and gestures is better represented by fuzzy relationships. What is important in such circumstances is the closeness of two events rather than the exact relationship between them. Below is a description of various stages of the processes that take place in the temporal reasoner.

First the temporal relationships (δs) are fuzzified using a PI membership function as shown in Fig. . Then the concepts of negative, zero and positive are fuzzified as shown in Fig. to allow the implementation of the rules. Finally, the fuzzified δs are mapped onto the three regions shown in Fig. . If the time differences fall on any single region then the temporal relationships will be simply determined by the corresponding rule in the rule base and an appropriate fact is inserted in the knowledge base. For example if δ_b is -20 then the following fact is inserted in the knowledge base by rule 1:

```
(occurred A before B).
```

However, for the majority of cases there will be an overlap between the PI membership functions and the positive, zero or negative regions. For example if δ_b is -2 then there could be two rules which fire and produce two facts with different degrees (Fig.):

```
((occurred A before B) 0.7)
((occurred A just_before B) 0.3).
```

In such cases a fuzzy match is calculated which determines the degree to which the time differences belong to each region and the corresponding facts are added to the knowledge base with their associated fuzzy matching (0.7 and 0.3 in the above example). When all the facts have been accumulated, defuzzification takes place. The principle here is that two events can only have one temporal relationship and therefore the relationship with the highest fuzzy match or certainty factor will be chosen as the most likely temporal relationship (e.g. (occurred A before B) in the previous example).

5.2   Query Pre-processing

In the query pre-processing module a sentence in natural language form is converted to a query which conforms to the system's predefined grammar. Redundant words are removed, keywords are placed in the right order and multiple word attributes are converted into single strings.

5.3   Fuzzy Matching

Fuzzy matching is implemented to handle minor typographic errors such as transposition. It considers each word as having three properties.

1. **The length of the Word**
   A word is similar to another word if it has a similar number of letters.
2. **Common letters**
   A word is similar to another word if they share the same letters. This returns a similarity metric of the percentage of letters in the longer word that are also in the shorter word. For example 'foo' and 'fool' have a common letter similarity metric of 75%.
3. **Letter Ordering**
   A word is similar to another word if the order of the letters is similar. For example 'chat' and 'chit' are similar because in both words 'c' is followed by 'h' and 't'; and 'h' is followed by 't'. Since there are 6 possible orderings and 3 of them are shared by both words, this metric makes them 50% similar.

The total similarity is defined in a somewhat *ad hoc* manner but it works well in practice. No word may be more than 1.5 times as long as a similar word. The final metric is then the sum of the common letters and letter ordering metrics divided by two. This is because the letter ordering metric gives lower similarity measures for smaller words.

5.4   Constraint Checking

The constraint checking module examines the content of the queries. If individual parts of the query do not satisfy predefined constraints then they are replaced by ambiguous terms (e.g. 'this', 'that') to be resolved later, otherwise the query is passed on to the next module.

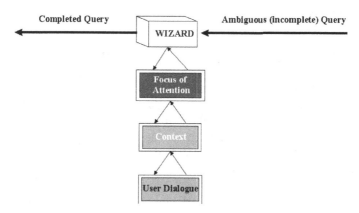

Fig. 10. Resolving ambiguities in the reasoner

It also checks the consistency of terms in the query. For example, duration of lunch is only valid when the query is about a technician. Entering this attribute when enquiring about a job will cause the reasoner to generate an error message and ask the user for correct input.

5.5   Ambiguity Resolution

The WIZARD is at the heart of the reasoner and resolves ambiguities. The ambiguities in the SWM take the form of reserved words such as 'this' or 'that', and they refer to objects that the user 'is' or 'has been' talking about, pointing to or looking at. The ambiguities are resolved in a hierarchical manner as shown in Fig. 10.

The context of the interactions between the user and the system, if it exists, is maintained by the reasoner in the knowledge base. When a new query is initiated by the user, it is checked against the context. If there are ambiguities in the query and the context contains relevant information, the context will be used to create a complete query which will be sent to the application interface for processing.

The reasoner contains a two-level context which stores two latest interactions regarding different objects, i.e. job and technician, or different identifiers, i.e. job numbers and technician identifications. The contexts are updated with every interaction in accordance to the structure of the grammar, i.e. object, identifier and attributes. This allows flexible interaction such as the following:

give me location in map of technician 123
duration of lunch *[of technician 123]*
what is the expected completion time of job 5
duration *[of job 5]*
[duration] job 6

    [duration of lunch] technician 30
    latest end time of *[job 6]*

When the system is engaging in a dialogue with the user and awaiting input through the speech recogniser or the keyboard, conflicting information can be obtained. The reasoner then uses the focus of attention, which is obtained from the user when pointing with the mouse or gazing at an object on the screen, as another mechanism to resolve ambiguities.

The focus of attention is always given the highest priority and the dialogue system the lowest. This means that the dialogue system will act as a safety net for the other modalities if all else fails, or if inconsistent information is received from the modalities.

In cases where text input is required, however, the dialogue system is the only modality used. In all other cases the dialogue system will be redundant unless all others fail, in which case a simple dialogue in the form of direct questions or answers will be initiated by the system. The WIZARD sends the completed queries to the post-processing module.

5.6 Post Processing

The post-processing module simply converts the completed queries in a form suitable for the application. This involves simple operations such as formatting the query or extracting key words from it.

5.7 Learning

The reasoner observes user's the interaction with the system and keeps a record of the pairwise likelihood of two queries (independent of object identifiers, i.e. job numbers and technician identification numbers) appearing one after the other by means of probabilities. It adapts the probabilities every time an interaction occurs. When a certain probability is higher than a user-defined threshold, the next query is issued automatically.

Several t ypes of information are in fact kept in the reasoner: the number of times a particular query is issued, the number of times and the probability of one query being followed by another, and other constraint information. Let $Q_1 \& N_1$ be the command and the associated count of the first command; $Q_2 \& N_2$ be the command and the associated count of the second command; $N_{1,2}$ is the number of times Q_2 has occurred after Q_1. The probability $P_{1,2}$ is calculated as:

$$P_{1,2} = \frac{N_2}{N_{1,2}}. \tag{4}$$

The use of probabilities allows the reasoner to accommodate changes in command sequence patterns over time and it is specific to the individual users. The current setup is that only the next query is suggested. This approach can be generalised to search for subsequent queries given the probability distribution described above. The only assumption here is that the completion of an query will not change the environment of the system, which is true in the case of the Smart Work Manager.

6   Non-intrusive Gaze-Tracking System

Gaze tracking has been a challenging and interesting task studied across several disciplines including machine vision, cognitive science and human/computer interaction [ ]. The main applications are in:

- videoconferencing [ ] for focusing on interesting objects and transmitting only these images through the communication networks;
- design of the new generation of non-command interface [,];
- the study of human vision, cognition, and attentional processes [ ].

Traditional methods are usually intrusive [ ] and involve a specialised high-speed/high-resolution camera, a controlled lighting source [ ], and electronic hardware equipment. Accurate extraction of eye movement information, along with speech, and gestures [ ] can potentially play an essential part in forming a fast and natural interface [,].

The objective of this subsystem is to develop a flexible, cheap, and adequately fast eye tracker using the standard videoconferencing setting on a workstation. The neural network based real-time non-intrusive gaze tracker determines the focus of attention of a user on a computer screen. This task can be viewed as simulating a forward-pass mapping process from the (segmented) eye image space to a predefined 2-D co-ordinate space. In general, the mapping function is nonlinear and highly sensitive to uncertain factors such as change of lighting, head movements and background object movement.

6.1   Methodology and System

The following two assumptions were made:

- the appearance of an eye is sufficient to determine the focus of attention;
- the user's head orientation generally conforms to the line of sight of the eyes.

The former is justified by human/human communications experience, while the latter is introduced to avoid the unnecessary many-to-one mapping situation when a person can look at an object on a screen from various head orientations.

Fig.   shows a schematic diagram of the system which works in an open plan office environment with a simple video camera mounted on the right hand side of the display screen. The analogue video signal from a low-cost video camera

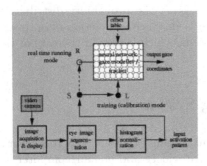

Fig. 11. The neural-network-based gaze-tracking system. S is switched between L and R during learning and real time operation

Fig. 12. User's face in the field of the camera. The rectangle area (100x60) in the image defines a search window for eye image segmentation

is captured and digitised using the SunVideo Card, a video capture and compression card for Sun SPARCstations, and the XIL imaging foundation library developed by SunSoft [4] [25].

For simplicity, only grey scale images are used in this system [5]. Fig. 12 shows a snapshot of the user's face in an open plan office environment under normal illumination. The objective of the eye image segmentation is to detect the darkest region in the pupil of the eye, and to segment the eye itself from the image (see Fig. 13). The current system uses only the image of the user's right eye. The histogram normalisation improves the contrast between important features (eye socket, pupil, reflection spot) which are used by the neural network during training.

Fig. 14 shows the three-layer feedforward neural network. Each of the 600 input units receives a normalised activation value from the segmented 40 5x15 eye image, and the 16 hidden units are divided into two groups of 8 units each. A split output layer of 50 and 40 units represents the (x, y) co-ordinates of a gaze point on the screen (low resolution grid of 50 by 40). The input units are fully connected to the hidden layer units which function as various feature detectors. All the hidden and output units assume a hyperbolic tangent transfer function:

$$f(x) = \frac{1 - e^{-x}}{1 + e^{-x}} \tag{5}$$

with $f(x)$ taking values between -1.0 and 1.0. A Gaussian-shaped coding method has been adopted for output activations, based on works published in the literature on autonomous vehicle guidance [27] and a similar gaze-tracking task [28].

---

[4] XIL is a cross-platform C functions library that supports a range of video and imaging requirements.

[5] Colour images could be used in the future to provide unique features which are not available from grey scale images [26]

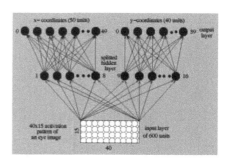

Fig. 13. Top: an example of the segmented eye image containing the pupil, cornea and the eye socket. Bottom: eye image after histogram normalisation

Fig. 14. The neural network architecture of the gaze tracker

It is interesting to note that by using the whole eye image directly as the input to the neural network modeller, a global holistic approach to the problem is taken, in contrast to the traditional explicit feature-based approach.

6.2   Experimental Studies

For data collection, the user visually tracks a blob cursor which travels along the computer screen in one of the two predefined paths, namely, either the horizontal or the vertical movements. Each data example consists of the (x, y) co-ordinates of the travelling cursor and the corresponding eye socket image after segmentation. The backpropagation algorithm is used to minimise is the summed squared error (SSE) of the average grid deviation (AGD), which measures the average difference between the current gaze predictions and the desired gaze positions for the training set after excluding a few wildcards due to the user's unexpected eye movements. A two-phase training method is used during training to make sure that the set of effective parameters was very well tuned, and neither underfitting nor overfitting of the network occurred.

This first phase initialises the network with small random weights and the network parameters are updated every few tens of training examples (avoid overfitting). This is followed by a fine-tuning phase where the network weights are updated once, after presenting the whole training set.

6.3   A Real-Time Gaze-Tracking System

After the training process, which has determined an optimal set of weights, captured eye images are fed into the network which outputs the (x, y) co-ordinates of the corresponding gaze point on the screen. The system works at about 20 Hz in its stand-alone mode on a SunUltra-1 Workstation. The average prediction accuracy on a separately collected test data set is about 1.5 degrees, which

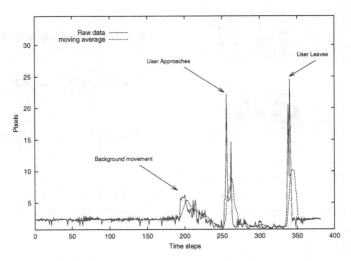

Fig. 15. Result of an experiment to detect user presence using a camera

corresponds to an error of around 0.5 inch on the computer screen. Due to the saccades of the eyes, data points output from the gaze-tracker is fairly unstable. Statistically analysis on data collected from a sliding window of 10 data points is used so that more reliable predictions are used by the reasoner.

7   User Presence Detection

The basic function of the presence detector is to determine whether or not the user is in front of the computer, using information from the camera and the keyboard/mouse. It is implemented in the Intelligent Assistant project. The results can be displayed on the window shown in Fig.   .

Assuming the user is at his/her desk working, the IA should interact with the user as usual. Conversely, no dialogue should be performed if the user is not at his/her desk, attending a meeting, for example. This kind of commonsense knowledge can be built in easily. The obvious source of the user's whereabouts is the diary, but the diary is unreliable as, for example, meetings can be cancelled or finish earlier/later than scheduled. The Diary Assistant cannot possibly keep up to date with such a dynamic environment unless the user enters every change to the original schedule once it is known. This requirement is unrealistic and adds unnecessary workload on the user.

The MMUI needs extra evidence to infer the user's presence. The most readily available information is keyboard and mouse activities. The MMUI can confidently deduce that the user is at the desk when keyboard or mouse activity is detected. It can then work out the appropriate screening action to take. Unfortunately, this approach is not foolproof, as the absence of keyboard/mouse activity does not conclusively imply the user is not there. He/she may be sitting right

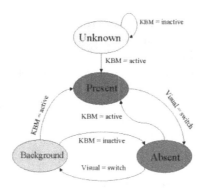

Fig. 16. State diagram for fusing keyboard/mouse activity and visual information

in front of the computer and reading background material for a presentation. In addition, the flow of keyboard/mouse information is intermittent as the user may pause for as long as he/she likes. This calls for another readily available information source: visual input from the camera that the gaze tracker uses. Grey scale images are used for the current purpose. By calculating the total difference between neighbouring frames in corresponding pixel positions, we are able to observe changes in the view of the camera. Fig.   shows the result of one of the experiments. The dotted line represents the inter-frame changes and the solid line is the moving average of ten time steps. The raw data is quite jittery but can be smoothed with the moving average. In both cases, spikes can be observed which signifies drastic changes between neighbouring frames.

The scenario in the experiment is that nobody sits in front of the camera until about time=200. There are few changes between frames apart from background activity such as people movement in the background and changes on a monitor that is within the view of the camera. The user then approaches the computer, sits down (time=260), does some work (between time=260 and time=360) and leaves (time=360). The two actions at time=260 and time=360 cause the biggest inter-frame difference. The moving average at those two points peaks at around 10.

The above simple experiment gives some useful hints as to what is available from this cheap image processing exercise. By setting a threshold to, for example, 6.5, we can confidently detect when the user comes to or leaves the computer. However, we cannot differentiate confidently between the two events. This is rectified by employing information from keyboard/mouse.

Fig.   is a state diagram showing the transition between 'Present' and 'Absent' states. When the system is first started, it is put into the initial state of 'Unknown' and only keyboard/mouse activity is considered. The system is put into the 'Present' state once the user starts using the keyboard or the mouse. Attention is then switched to the visual input to look for a 'switch' signal which corresponds to a change in scene of more than 6.5. Any keyboard/mouse activity while at the 'Present' state would only reinforce the system's belief of the user presence. It does not add extra information.

While in the 'Absent' state, both information sources are monitored. The presence of any keyboard/mouse activity would make the system go back to 'Present' state. However, detecting a 'switch' signal at the camera while there is no keyboard/mouse activity would put the system back to the 'Absent' state. Keyboard/mouse information takes precedence over camera input in this state.

8   Speech in Multi-modal Systems

The primary function of a speech recogniser in the multi-modal system is to recognise spoken commands in the form of complete sentences which can then be passed on to the reasoning module for further processing. In order to provide a speech interface as close to human interaction as possible, the commands have to be issued in a natural way as if the user is talking to another person. This requirement effectively precludes the possibility of employing keyword speech recognisers as the users are normally required to speak in a robot-like manner, speaking a word at a time. Another problem with keyword recognisers is the need for an interpreter that can understand the keywords and translate the string of keywords into a meaningful sentence. Error detection, context checking and discourse management would also be complicated.

A speech synthesiser is limited to provide feedback to the user regarding the result of the query in this current application. Due to the dynamic nature of the answers to the queries, pre-recorded messages are not useful. A speech synthesiser can further be developed for better communication between the computer and the user especially when the system needs to engage in a dialogue with the user.

The speech recogniser used in the multi-modal system is StapRec from BT's speech technology unit. StapRec is designed for use over telephone lines which have a limited audio bandwidth. It is speaker independent and works on connected word recognition. Laureate [ ] is used which is the text-to-speech synthesiser developed by BT. It is a platform-independent software with the aim of providing natural speech output. The provision of application programming interfaces in these packages allows development of applications without detailed knowledge of speech recognition and synthesis.

Laureate is being run in shell scripts under PVM in SWM and as an indepedent assistant in the IA. Initialisation is performed once. Whenever speech synthesis is required, the text is processed to produce an audio file which will then be played on the audio channel.

StapRec is run as two processes on the PVM platform — a speech recogniser and a voice activity detector, in the SWM. Speech data is passed to StapRec server once voice activity is detected. When a recognition result is available,

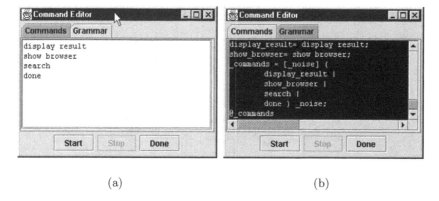

(a)   (b)

Fig. 17. Front end of the speech system that allows users to (a) define commands for an IA assistant, and (b) see the corresponding grammar for the speech recogniser. Once a speech recogniser is started, the 'process' button is changed to 'reconfigure', which should be used whenever new commands are added

it is passed to the reasoner for further processing before the actual query is performed.

This is enhanced in the IA project to allow parallel, multiple domain speech recognition. The speech recogniser operates in a multi-client/server mode. When a new client is connected, an independent speech server is started with the specific configuration instructions (including vocabularies). The IA, therefore, can provide a generic speech recognition capability to all other components that requires it. This also enables the user to define assistant-specific commands. The role of StapA is threefold.

1. Manage the job of starting, stopping and reconfiguring the set of speech recognisers.
2. Distribute the speech data streaming to all the speech recognisers that are accepting input.
3. Manage the voting system for selecting results from all the speech recognisers.

8.1   Speech Recogniser Management

StapA maintains a register of speech recognisers and their corresponding IA assistants. It also has information regarding the status of each recogniser. When the user has entered new commands for an IA assistant, new configuration files are generated and the corresponding speech recogniser is reconfigured (instead of starting a new recogniser). The register also helps StapA to locate the right recogniser to stop when the corresponding assistant exits. Fig. 17 shows the interface for (re)defining commands.

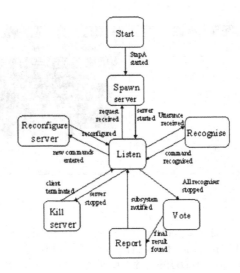

Fig. 18. State diagram of the speech (Stap) assistant

8.2   Speech Data Management

The register mentioned above contains the status of all the speech recognisers: recognising and recognition completed. StapA has an activity detector which activates the speech recognition process when there is speech data coming from the speech input channel (microphone). When this happens, StapA distributes (i.e. replicates and sends) the speech data to all recognisers that are operating. When all the recognisers have completed recognition, StapA determines the best output and all the recognisers are reset to prepare for the next utterance.

8.3   Selection of Speech Recogniser Results

The IA assistants have different command sets and corresponding speech recognisers, and therefore respond differently; some complete recognition earlier than others. During the speech recognition process, there is a score associated with the recognised sentence. Although this value is not an absolute score, it can be used as the basis of comparison between results from different recognisers dealing with the same utterance. A simple voting scheme is implemented which takes the best of all the valid (non-silence) results returned. The flow of control for the Stap Assistant is illustrated in Fig.   .

9   Conclusions

This paper has described an intelligent multi-modal user interface that delivers enhanced communications channels between human and computer in the context of BT's workforce management system. The contribution of this work is on the combination of multiple input modalities in order to support natural human/computer interactions. It has been demonstrated that soft computing techniques are useful tools for such applications. Specifically, the fuzzy temporal reasoner collects and reasons with redundant sources of information to infer the user's intention. Ambiguities are resolved by the reasoner with its context-sensitive fuzzy matching. This allows the user to be vague when issuing commands within the same context of current interaction, as happens in human interactions.

Another major contribution is the real-time non-intrusive gaze-tracking system based on powerful neural network modelling techniques. In contrast with other gaze-tracking systems, the current system works in an office environment under normal illumination, without resorting to any specialised hardware. The Smart Work Manager also has integrated speech input/output modules which has greatly enhanced the naturalness of the user interface.

System integration was a big engineering challenge of this project as almost all the modules in the system are written in different programming languages. By encapsulating individual modules within a generic wrapper written in a scripting language, the subsystems virtually become homogeneous entities. Robustness of the system is provided by a flexible PVM platform which allows seamless and efficient communication between subsystems running across a host of heterogeneous hardware. This forms a firm basis for future experiments when new or enhanced modules become available. Moreover, the modular design of the Smart Work Manager means individual components can easily be reused in other systems that require an intelligent multi-modal user interface.

One constraint of the current system is a restricted command set which is shared between the speech recognition system, the reasoner and the Work Manager system. An adaptive interface which supports automatic generation of grammar on new commands will certainly enhance the flexibility of the system. Part of this is also achieved by the speaker-independent speech recogniser. Constraints of the gaze tracking are relatively long training time, not coping well with the change of camera orientation, and apparent head movements. These are expected to be dealt with in future research work.

References

1. Tsui K., Azvine B., Djian D., Voudouris C. and Xu L.: 'Intelligent multi-modal systems'. BT Technol Journal, Vol. 16(3), pp. 134–144 (1998).   ,
2. Wobcke W., Azvine B., Djian D. and Tsui K.: 'The intelligent assistant: An overview'. In 'this volume'. Springer-Verlag (2000).   ,   ,
3. Negroponte N.: 'Being digital'. Coronet Books (1995).
4. Reddy R.: 'Grand challenges in AI'. ACM Computing Surveys, Vol. 27(3), pp. 301–303 (1995).
5. Lesaint D., Voudouris C., Azarmi N. and Laithwaite B.: 'Dynamic workforce management'. In 'UK IEE Colloquium on AI for Network Management Systems (Digest No 1997/094)' (London, UK) (1997).

6. Bunt H., Beun R.-J. and Borghuis T., Eds.: 'Multimodal Human-Computer Communication: Systems, Techniques, and Experiments (LNCS 1374)'. Springer-Verlag (1998).

7. Sullivan J. and Tyler S.: 'Intelligent user interfaces'. Frontier Series, New York, ACM Press (1991).

8. Cohen P., Cheyer A., Wang M. and Baeg S.: 'An open agent architecture'. In 'Proceedings of AAAI Spring Symposium' (Standford, CA.), pp. 1–8 (1994).

9. Nigay L. and Goutaz J.: 'A generic platform for addressing the multimodal challenge'. In 'Proceedings of CHI'95' (Denver), pp. 98–105 (1995).

10. Geist A., Beguelin A., Dongarra J., Jiang W., Manchek R. and Sunderam V.: 'PVM: Parallel Virtual Machine - A User's Guide and Tutorial for Networked Parallel Computing'. MIT Press (1994).

11. Welch B.: 'Practical programming in Tcl and Tk'. Prentice Hall (1994).

12. Giarratano J. and Riley G.: 'Expert Systems: Principles and Programming'. PWS-KENT Publishing Company (1989).

13. Orchard R.: 'FuzzyCLIPS Version 6.04 User's Guide'. Knowledge Systems Laboratory, Institute for Information Technology, National Research Council, Canada, (1995).

14. Baldwin J., Martin T. and Pilsworth B.: 'Fril - Fuzzy and Evidential Reasoning in Artificial Intelligence'. Research Studies Press Ltd (1995).

15. Velichkovsky B. and Hansen J.: 'New technological windows into mind: there is more in eyes and brains for human-computer interaction'. Technical report, Unit of Applied Cognitive Research, Dresden University of Technology, Germany (1996).

16. Yang J., Wu L. and Waibel A.: 'Focus of attention in video conferencing'. Technical Report CMU-CS-96-150, School of Computer Science, Carnegie Mellon University (1996).

17. Jacob R.: 'Eye tracking in advanced interface design'. In 'Advanced interface design and virtual environments'. Oxford University Press (1995).

18. Nielsen J.: 'Noncommand user interfaces'. Communications of the ACM, Vol. 36(4), pp. 83–99 (1993).

19. Zangemeister W., Stiehl H. and Freska C.: 'Visual attention and cognition'. North-Holland: Elsevier Science BV, Amsterdam (1996).

20. Stampe D.: 'Heuristic filtering and reliable calibration methods for video-based pupil-tracking systems'. Behaviour Research Methods, Instruments, Computers, Vol. 25(2), pp. 137–142 (1993).

21. Cleveland D. and Cleveland N.: 'Eyegaze eyetracking system'. In 'Proceedings of 11th Monte-Carlo International Forum on New Images' (Monte-Carlo) (1992).

22. Darrell T. and Pentland A.: 'Recognition of space-time gestures using a distributed representation'. In 'Artificial neural networks for speech and vision'. Chapman & Hall, London (1994).

23. Hansen J., Andersen A. and Roed P.: 'Eye-gaze control of multimedia systems'. In 'Symbiosis of human and artifact'. Elsevier Science (1995).

24. Starker I. and Bolt R.: 'A gaze-responsive self-disclosing display'. In 'ACM CHI'90 Conference Proceedings: Human Factors in Computing Systems' (Seattle, Washington), pp. 3–9 (1990).

25. Pratt W.: 'Developing visual applications: XIL - an imaging foundation library'. Sun Microsystems Press (1997).

26. Oliver N. and Pentland A.: 'Lafter: Lips and face real time tracker'. In 'Proceedings of Computer Vision and Pattern Recognition Conference, CVPR'97' (Puerto Rico) (1997).

27. Pomerleau D.: 'Neural network perception for mobile robot guidance'. Kluwer Academic Publishing (1993).
28. Baluja D. and Pomerleau D.: 'Non-intrusive gaze tracking using artificial neural networks'. Technical Report CMU-CS-94-102, School of Computer Science, Carnegie Mellon University (1994).
29. Page J. and Breen A.: 'The Laureate text-to-speech system - architecture and applications'. BT Technol Journal, Vol. 14(1), pp. 84–99 (1996).

Communication Management: E-Mail and Telephone Assistants

David Djian

Intelligent Systems Research Group
BT Labs, Adastral Park, Martlesham Heath
Ipswich IP5 3RE, United Kingdom
david.djian@bt.com

Abstract. Nowadays, office workers receive an increasing number of communications, mainly through e-mail and telephone. If not handled correctly, these can lead to a communication overload. This paper describes a system which helps a user to manage interruptions from incoming communications. It is based on a generic hierarchical priority model using causal probabilistic networks and taking into account the context of an interruption. The model was implemented in an e-mail and a telephone assistant. These assistants can learn the user's preference in a non-obtrusive manner and we show experimental results of successful adaptation to changing user's needs.

1 Introduction

In an office environment, human productivity is often reduced by frequent and/or untimely interruptions. There are two aspects to interruptions: how often they occur and when they occur. For instance, it can be a nuisance to receive too many phone calls or e-mail messages. The problem here is to decide which ones should have a higher priority to avoid information overload ("my phone keeps ringing" or "I can't keep up with all the e-mail messages I receive"). Another problem is the timing of an interruption. In extreme cases, just one phone call at the wrong time can be worse than several calls at a less busy time. Ideally, one would like to be notified of a high priority e-mail straight away, whereas most e-mails can be processed (read, replied to, archived) at given times of the day or the week. Such batch processing is sometimes the user's choice to reduce the nuisance of interruptions. Others prefer to check their e-mail very often, or as soon as a new message arrives. However, the fear of missing a high priority message is often undermined by the disappointment of interrupting a task to read what turns out to be a low priority message.

Current systems for e-mail and telephone which provide filing and filtering are usually knowledge based [ ] or rule-based. As noted by Payne *et al* [ ], the first shortcoming is that these systems require the user to define the rules. This leads to complex graphical user interfaces and in practice many people simply do not use them. Cohen [ ] reports a system which automatically learns rules

B. Azvine et al. (Eds.): Intelligent Systems and Soft Computing, LNAI 1804, pp. 284–   , 2000.
© Springer-Verlag Berlin Heidelberg 2000

to classify e-mail. However, these rules are crisp and do not take into account vagueness in representation. Suppose, for instance, that the system has a rule stating:

If (message size > 1 megabyte) Then priority is low

Two messages of size 999 kilobytes and 1.001 megabytes will be given respectively low and high priority. Intuitively, and all other things considered equal, their priorities should be *similar*. Also, rather than saying:

Refuse phone calls from Bob

people prefer to take into account the context of a call by saying:

Refuse **most** *phone calls from Bob, unless it's important*

Another source of uncertainty is intrinsic in the reasoning process. It is not so much a matter of providing a system which accepts and refuses phone calls or deletes e-mails, but rather a system which makes suggestions to the user about what it thinks the priority of an interruption should be. For this reason, we have used a probabilistic framework which handles explicitly the uncertainty associated with the observations leading to a suggestion, and with the suggestion itself. Horvitz *et al.* [ ] describe a similar framework. However, the main difference with our system is that it learns incrementally by watching the user's actions (and thus adapts itself to changing user's needs), rather than learning a classifier from batch data.

Finally, the timing associated with interruptions is an important factor. For instance in the current telephone call model, a call is made when the caller decides to get in touch with the callee, and the result will be either a conversation, no answer or voice mail. More telephony features can be used (e.g. divert on busy...) and the feature interaction problem has raised research issues which could lead to new call models, see for instance Rizzo and Utting [,], Montelius *et al.* [ ].

In this paper, however, we only consider the callee's telephone assistant who must deal with the call straight away. This is more general because it makes no asumption about whether the caller has a telephone assistant (TA) or not. The e-mail assistant on the other hand provides facilities for the user to deal with e-mails in batch. With the coordinator assistant (see the paper by Wobcke in this book), the system can even notify the user when batches are becoming large.

In the following sections, we present a generic priority model for interruptions, then we describe two assistants – for e-mail and telephone – which perform communication management on behalf of a user. We show experimental results on the behaviour of these assistants in real-world conditions. Finally, we discuss possible extensions to our system.

2   Generic Priority Model for Interruptions

2.1   Priority

The reason for introducing a priority model relates to the fact that two high-level features of interruptions are *importance* and *urgency*. For example, an interruption should be regarded as important depending on the content – who originated it, what it is about, etc. On the other hand, urgency is related to timing, e.g. how soon an action is required. Therefore the priority model aims at combining both aspects in order to compute a priority value for each incoming interruption.

2.2   Hierarchy

The information used to compute a priority has two components:

- information contained in the interruption itself;
- contextual information, which can be local to the assistant (e.g. telephone log) and global to other assistants (e.g. diary information).

2.3   Timing

Depending on the type of interruption, the timing constraints that the system should satisfy are different. For instance, e-mail messages can be processed in batch because the other party is not waiting for an interactive communication to be established. On the other hand, telephone calls require a decision to be made immediately and system response time must be kept short.

2.4   Bayes Nets

In order to represent the various modules in our priority model, we have chosen Bayes nets as a probabilistic model. There are two levels in a Bayes net (Fig.). Firstly, a directed acyclic graph (DAG) where nodes represent random variables and directed links represent a statistical dependency between variables. Secondly, the dependency is quantified by the conditional probability distribution of a node given its parents. In the example of Fig. , A and B are Boolean random

		A	not A
	B	P(B|A)	P(B| not A)
	not B	P(not B|A)	P(not B| not A)

Fig. 1. Bayes net and conditional probabilities table.

variables and the conditional probability distribution is represented by a table. Propagation algorithms, e.g. Pearl [ ] or Lauritzen and Spiegelhalter [ ], can compute posterior probabilities using Bayes rule.

The main advantages of Bayes nets are

- their sound probabilistic foundation;
- their capability to represent uncertainty explictly, for example where a production rule would state:

$$If\ A\ is\ true\ Then\ B\ is\ true$$

the Bayes net of Fig.   associates a degree of uncertainty quantified by $P(B|A)$;
- adaptation, where conditional probabilities can be updated with new observations.

In the following sections we describe the e-mail and telephone assistants in more detail.

3   Electronic Mail Assistant

3.1   E-Mail Priority Model

The purpose of the E-mail Assistant (EA) is to help the user to manage both incoming and outgoing e-mail messages. It proactively notifies the user of new incoming messages and provides advice about handling them depending on their priority, for example:

I suggest you read this message now, today, this week, this month or never

To do this, the EA automatically learns the user's preferences by watching how they handle similar incoming messages. This is an advantage over CAFE [   ] where the user has to specify rules in an unfriendly format. E-mail messages are kept in various lists corresponding to their level of priority: *now, today, this week, this month, never*. Once confident about the EA's performance, the user can delegate the automatic sorting of incoming messages and access them later from the various lists.

In order to compute a priority for incoming messages, the EA uses the Bayes net shown in Fig. .

The EA holds such a network for each known sender, rather than using concepts contained in the message [   ]. This gives more importance to the sender as a feature and introduces the concept of sender profile which can be used in other applications, e.g. telephone assistant.

The following variables are set according to features extracted from an e-mail message:

- message was sent to me (my e-mail address appears in message fields To, CC or Apparently-To);

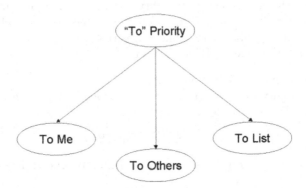

Fig. 2. Bayes net for e-mail priority associated with a sender.

– message was sent to mailing list (at least one of the mailing lists – specified in the configuration file – appears in message fields To, CC or Apparently-To);
– message was sent to others (at least one other e-mail address appears in message fields To, CC or Apparently-To, excluding mailing lists)

The priority is then refined by matching the subject keywords with the user's profile of interests. In case of a match, the message is moved from the current list to the next one with higher priority.

3.2   Implementation

E-mail facilities The Unix implementation of the EA (Fig.   ) picks up incoming e-mails at the mail server level by calling a PERL script for each message. This call is made in the .forward file. The script copies the message onto a local disk with an internal number and updates the current mail count in a file stored on the local disk as well. This processing is event-driven and provides the interface between the EA and the Unix platform. The EA creates a thread, which periodically checks the mail count. When it detects a change, it retrieves the corresponding message using the e-mail number and displays the e-mail pop window. The main reason for this implementation is to:

1. leave the user in control by having local copies of messages;
2. reduce the load on the mail server by delegating the reasoning process to the machine on which the client (EA) is running.

The EA is now integrated with the JavaMail package. This allows platform-independent handling of MIME messages. However, the current implementation is limited to Unix mail.

Assistant main window The main window of the EA (Fig.   ) contains a set of tabs which correspond to the various lists (now, today, this week, this month,

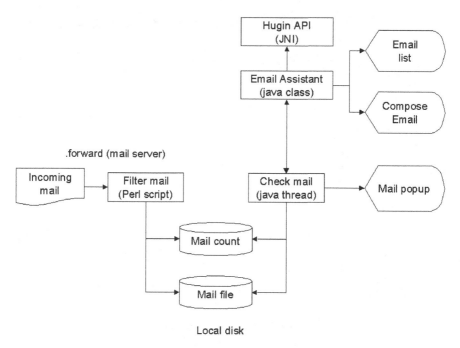

Fig. 3. Unix implementation.

never) and an extra tab for the current mail panel. The latter is used to display the current e-mail message. The top of the panel shows the message "From", "To" and "Subject" fields. The body of the message is displayed underneath.

At the bottom of the window is an area which displays the coloured envelopes associated with new incoming messages. The colours correspond to the level of priority (red: now, lighter shades of orange: today and this week, yellow: this month, black: never). By clicking on any of these, the user can see in a pop menu the header fields of the corresponding message, the suggested priority and the possible actions, i.e. read now, today, this week, this month or never (Fig.).

The *E-mail* menu offers some of the standard features of an e-mail client, e.g. the *Compose* option creates a window where the user can type the contents of the outgoing message. On top of that, the *Sort* option automatically takes the action suggested by the EA on the corresponding new incoming messages. Note that, in this case, the system updates its internal model (Bayes net) but each case is given less weight than a case where the user chooses an action explicitly. This is to prevent self reinforcement in the system and is described in section   . The *Reload* option reinitialises all the Bayes nets to prior probabilities, effectively forgetting what the EA has learnt from user feedback in the current session.

E-mail notification When the user receives an e-mail, the EA displays a pop-up window showing the "From", "To" and "Subject" fields and the suggestion

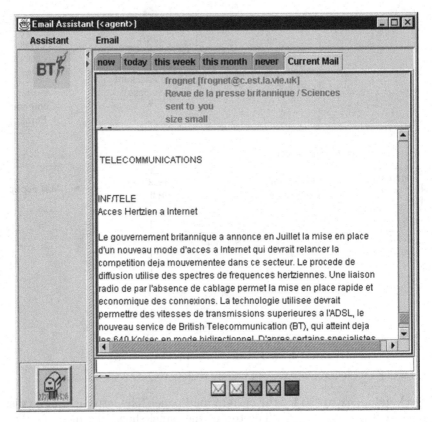

Fig. 4. E-mail assistant: main window.

of the EA (Fig.). It provides a button to execute the action suggested by the EA (quick shortcut). The user can access the same pop-up menu as the one described in the previous section (Fig.), and thus provide feedback to the system for learning current preferences.

3.3   Experimental Results

In this section, we show the system's trace for some e-mail messages.

Fast learning rate In this example, a message arrives and the prior probability distribution of the Bayes net associated with the sender is used to compute a priority. The state which has maximum probability in node *priority* in the Bayes net indicates the message's priority, in this case NOW:

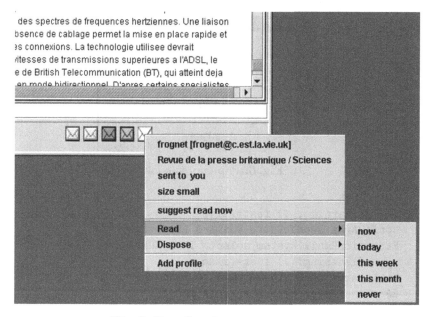

Fig. 5. E-mail assistant: pop menu.

```
EA: FROM: frognet [frognet@c.est.la.vie.uk]
EA: TO: you
EA:setToPriority suggest read NOW (0.42663652)
```

After being notified, the user chooses to read the message later today and the message is sent to the corresponding list:

```
NotifyArea:sendToLists email 9 read today
EA:actionEmail user selects TODAY
       (learning...) fast=true
```

The learning rate is fast because the user explicitly updates the priority and the example is given more weight. The next time a message from the same person arrives with similar features (who it was sent to), the EA computes a new priority according to the user's preference learnt during previous interactions:

```
EA: FROM: frognet [frognet@c.est.la.vie.uk]
EA: TO: you
EA:setToPriority suggest read TODAY (0.43717547)
```

Slow learning rate Once the user is confident about the way the EA handles their messages, they can delegate the sorting of all incoming messages:

```
NotifyArea:sendToLists email 1 read today
EA:actionEmail system selects THIS MONTH
```

Fig. 6. Pop mail window.

```
        (learning...) fast=false
NotifyArea:sendToLists email 3 read today
EA:actionEmail system selects THIS MONTH
        (learning...) fast=false
NotifyArea:sendToLists email 4 read now
EA:actionEmail system selects TODAY
        (learning...) fast=false
NotifyArea:sendToLists email 6 read this month
EA:actionEmail system selects NOW
        (learning...) fast=false
```

Here the learning is slow because the user did not explicitly select the actions to be taken and the model should be more stable. For this reason, each example is given less weight.

4   Telephone Assistant

4.1   Telephone Priority Model

The Telephone Assistant (TA) performs call screening on incoming phone calls and keeps a log of all the incoming calls whether they were blocked or not. It learns how the user handles incoming calls from various people and builds a context for each incoming call by looking at the user's diary and at the frequency of calls received from the caller. Finally, it provides easy access to the phone for outgoing calls, either by dialling the number on the keypad or by using name aliases.

When an incoming call is received, the TA uses the calling line identity (CLI) to search the database of contacts for the corresponding name of the caller. It uses this name and the context of the call to decide whether the call should be blocked or whether a notification showing the name of the caller should alert the user. According to the user's choice, calls coming from known people can be always blocked, always accepted or prioritised taking into account the context. The TA also learns from user's actions to refine the priority model associated with each known caller.

Bayes net for caller priority The caller priority Bayes net has a chain structure which contains a node for each person from which the user can receive a phone call and a special node for "Other" (Fig.). The initial conditional prob-

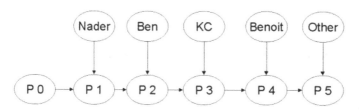

Fig. 7. Caller priority Bayes net.

abilities are set so that all the calls are accepted. The net can then adapt the probabilities by using user feedback when a call is accepted or not (TA main window).

Bayes net for context priority The context priority Bayes net incorporates information related to the call itself with contextual information to compute a priority (Fig.). The priority depends on whether the call is important as well

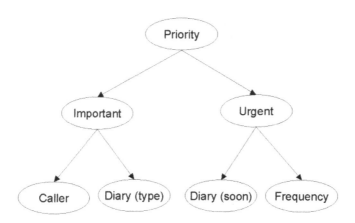

Fig. 8. Global priority Bayes net.

as whether it is urgent. The importance of a call depends on the caller's identity (the corresponding value is fed in from the caller priority net). Another factor affecting the importance of a call is whether or not the caller has a meeting with the user, and what type of meeting. For instance, a business meeting will affect the call's priority more than a leisure meeting such as a tennis game. A call is more urgent if the caller has frequently called the user in the past (information from the call log). Also, if there is a meeting with the caller scheduled in the diary, how soon this meeting is due to take place will increase the call's priority. In conclusion, this network builds a context by incorporating three levels of information:

- contained in the call itself: caller identity;
- local to the TA: call frequency in the call log;
- global to the whole system (see paper by Azvine *et al* in this book): diary information.

4.2   Implementation

The current implementation of the TA uses Callscape to interact with a PSTN (public service telephone network) analogue telephone line (Fig.   ).

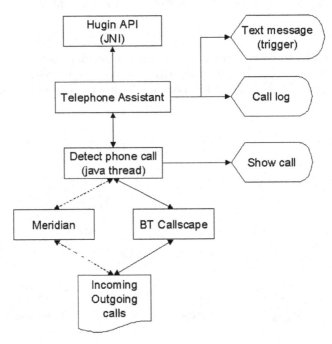

Fig. 9. TA architecture.

Callscape is a BT product providing computer telephony integration (CTI) and calling line identification. It comes as an external hardware device which connects to the serial port of a PC. Telephony events (lift receiver, incoming call, etc.) are passed to the PC application or can be generated by it (e.g. initiate phone call or hang up from PC).

Preliminary results were obtained with a Meridian digital phone line but the whole functionality has not been implemented yet. It uses a Meridian Communication Adapter as a hardware board added in the physical handset which also connects to the serial port of a PC.

The thread which detects phone calls provides a server front end to the Callscape client. The interface with the Callscape hardware is an ActiveX component with a Visual Basic layer to initiate the connection to the TA server. Incoming calls are signalled to the thread, which then notifies the TA with the calling line identity (CLI).

The main window of the TA interface (Fig.   ) contains a keypad to dial

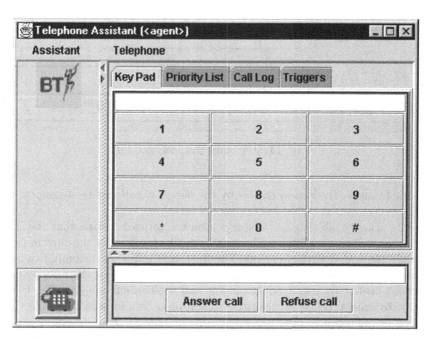

Fig. 10. TA main window: keypad.

phone numbers directly, and a text field where the user can type the name of the person to call.

The Call Log tab (Fig.   ) displays all incoming calls, whether they were blocked or displayed. Each call is shown as an item on a list. Each item displays the name of the person who called, the action taken by the system – displayed or blocked. The log tab becomes active automatically when the TA allows a call to go through to the user. The bottom panel flashes and displays the caller's identity (name, e.g. Wayne, or number). The user can then decide to accept the call or not by pressing the corresponding button. The TA adapts the priority model

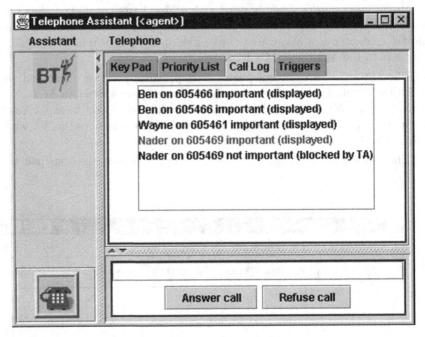

Fig. 11. TA main window: call log.

on-line by using the action chosen by the user, i.e. call was really important or not.

The priority tab (Fig.   ) displays a button for each person that the TA can phone, as well as a scrollbar and a text field, which represent the current priority of calls associated with a person. The button is red when incoming calls from this person are blocked, and green otherwise. The value of the priority can be updated on-line by user feedback in the call notification window. The user can decide to accept, refuse or prioritise calls from a certain person by selecting an option in the menu located below the corresponding button.

The user can also set triggers in the Trigger tab (Fig.   ) by associating a message with a caller's name or a number. When a new call arrives, the system checks for existing triggers and fetches the corresponding message. Although the current system does not play the message to the caller, this is the first step towards providing a fully customisable answering machine.

4.3   Experimental Results

When a call arrives, the system first translates the number with the name of the caller in the database, then checks for triggers. If no trigger is found, it computes a priority for the call using caller information, frequency of calls received from the same person and checks for a diary entry and diary type. The final priority is used to decide whether or not to accept the call and the call is logged:

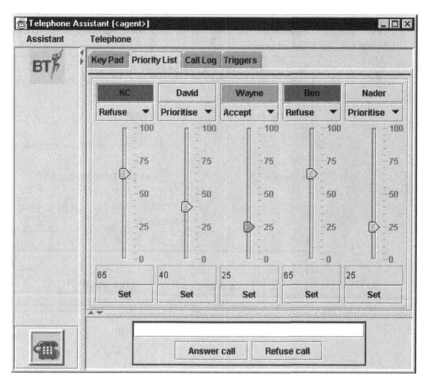

Fig. 12. TA main window: priority tab.

```
FileDB:performQuery
    getcondition:contacts:pname:pnum:605466
FileDB:performQuery result Ben
TA:checkTriggers NO trigger found
bnetHighPriorityCall:
    callerPriority 0.70000005 callFrequency 1.0
TA:diaryHasEntry KO : no entry found in diary for Ben
Log: inserting Ben on 605466
    priority 0.61252666 important (displayed)
```

The user can then override the system and decide to refuse the call. The next time the same person phones, their priority will have decreased. In this case, Ben is the only person who phoned so the call frequency in the log is unchanged:

```
FileDB:performQuery
    getcondition:contacts:pname:pnum:605466
FileDB:performQuery result Ben
TA:checkTriggers NO trigger found
bnetHighPriorityCall:
    callerPriority 0.6363636 callFrequency 1.0
```

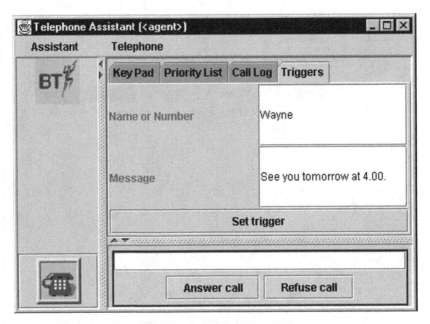

Fig. 13. TA main window: triggers.

```
TA:diaryHasEntry KO : no entry found in diary for Ben
Log: inserting Ben on 605466
       priority 0.6086705 important (displayed)
```

The following example shows the effects of a trigger in the reasoning process to compute a priority and in the personalisation of the system's behaviour according to the caller. Firstly, the user sets a trigger for a number or the name of a caller:

```
TA:setTriggerFromName: setting trigger Wayne 605461
```

When a call satisfying the trigger arrives, the TA retrieves the corresponding message which can be played to the user (personalised answering machine) and the call is accepted:

```
FileDB:performQuery
       getcondition:contacts:pname:pnum:605461
FileDB:performQuery result Wayne
TA:checkTriggers trigger found Wayne 605461
       See you tomorrow at 4:00
Log: inserting Wayne on 605461
       trigger important (displayed)
```

Finally, a caller can have a low priority and most calls will be blocked but the context of each will be taken into account:

```
TA:checkTriggers NO trigger found
FileDB:performQuery
     getcondition:contacts:pname:pnum:605469
FileDB:performQuery result Nader
bnetHighPriorityCall:
     callerPriority 0.26363632 callFrequency 0.25
diaryHasEntry: sending to DA Nader
TA:diaryHasEntry KO : no entry found in diary for Nader
Log: inserting Nader on 605469
     priority 0.47707465 not important (blocked by TA)
```

However, when the context changes, e.g. if the user has a meeting with the caller, then a different value is computed for the priority and the call is accepted:

```
FileDB:performQuery
     getcondition:contacts:pname:pnum:605469
FileDB:performQuery result Nader
bnetHighPriorityCall:
     callerPriority 0.26363632 callFrequency 0.4
diaryHasEntry: sending to DA Nader
TA:diaryHasEntry OK : 24/07/99 10:00 type: meeting
bnetHighPriorityCall:
     diarySoon 0.43189293 diaryType 0.74297200
Log: inserting Nader on 605469
     priority 0.7199749 important (displayed)
```

5   Conclusions and Future Work

We have described a generic priority model for incoming communications. Such a model is necessary to prevent a user from being interrupted too often and/or at the wrong time. Parts of this generic model have been implemented in two assistants which perform phone call and e-mail message prioritisation.

One of the reasons why these assistants are able to provide advanced services to the user is the integration within the whole platform (see paper by Azvine *et al* in this book).

Future enhancements of the EA will involve the integration with MAPI and the refinement of the reasoning process to compute message priority by considering more message features.

More general work will involve refining the Bayes nets by considering more information provided by the other assistants, as well as learning network structure and hidden variables (e.g. important and urgent in the global priority net used in the TA). Other soft computing techniques will be investigated to enrich the model. A general issue to be considered will be the explanation to the user, i.e. why the system took certain decisions, in human understandable terms. Finally, we will look at the ability for the user to update the priority model explicitly.

A patent has been filed regarding the work contained in this paper.

References

1. Motiwalla L.: 'An intelligent agent for prioritizing e-mail messages', Information Resources Management Journal, pp. 16-24 (Spring 1995).
2. Payne T., Edwards P. and Green C.: 'Experience with rule induction and k-nearest neighbor methods for interface agents that learn', IEEE Transactions on Knowledge and Data Engineering, Vol. 9, No. 2 (March-April 1997).
3. Cohen W.: 'Learning rules that classify Email', AAAI Spring Symposium on Machine Learning in Information Access, (1996).
4. Horvitz E., Jacobs A. and Hovel D.: 'Attention-Sensitive Alerting', Proceedings of UAI Conference on Uncertainty and Artificial Intelligence, Stockholm, Sweden, Morgan Kaufmann, San Francisco, pp. 305-313 (July 1999).
5. Rizzo M. and Utting I.: 'An Agent based model for the provision of advanced telecommunications services', TINA 95, Integrating Telecommunications and Distributed Computing - From Concept to Reality, pp. 205-218 (February 1995).
6. Rizzo M. and Utting I.: 'A Negotiating agents model for the provision of flexible telephony services', Proceedings ISADS 97 - Third Symposium on Autonomous Decentralized Systems, IEEE Computer Society Press, pp. 351-358 (April 1997).

7. Montelius J., Janson S., Gabrielsson J., Danne E., Bage G. and Eriksson M.: 'Intentions and intelligent screening in an agent based personal communication system', Presented at IATA'96 -Intelligent Agents in Telecommunication Applications, ECAI'96, Budapest (1996).
8. Pearl J.: 'Probabilistic reasoning in intelligent systems: networks of plausible inference', Morgan Kaufmann, San Mateo, California (1988).
9. Lauritzen S. and Spiegelhalter D.: 'Local computations with probabilities on graphical structures and their application to expert systems', Journal of the Royal Statistical Society, Vol. 50, pp. 157-224 (1988).
10. Takkinen J. and Shahmehri N.: 'CAFE: A conceptual model for managing information in electronic mail', Proceedings of the 31st Annual Hawaii International Conference on System Sciences, pp. 44-53 (January 1998).
11. Boone G.: 'Concept features in Re: Agent, an intelligent Email Agent', Second International Conference on Autonomous Agents (May 1998).

Time Management in the Intelligent Assistant

Wayne Wobcke

Intelligent Systems Research Group
BT Labs, Adastral Park, Martlesham Heath
Ipswich IP5 3RE, United Kingdom
wobckew@info.bt.co.uk

Abstract. The Intelligent Assistant (IA) is a system of software agents for helping the user with communication, information and time management. In this chapter, we discuss in detail issues related to time management. There are two distinct types of time management relevant to the IA: that concerning the user's management of his or her own time, and that concerning the coordination of actions performed by the various specialist assistants in the system (which affects the overall effectiveness of the system from the user's point of view). To aid the user in managing his or her own time, the IA includes a *Diary Assistant* which acts as a scheduler of tasks with the aim of satisfying the user's combined preferences for start times, durations and deadlines. The Diary Assistant offers ease of use by allowing preferences for a task to be specified using natural language terms such as *morning, afternoon, early morning* and *around 11:00*, which are interpreted by the system using fuzzy functions. To manage the system's time, the IA has a special *Coordinator* for regulating the communication from the system to the user and for planning system tasks. The Coordinator is the only component of the IA capable of scheduling the future actions of the assistants, and incorporates a novel agent architecture based on ideas from reactive scheduling called IRSA (*Intelligent Reactive Scheduling Architecture*). The Coordinator constructs and maintains the system's schedule of tasks using information about the user's schedule obtained from the Diary Assistant.

1 Introduction

The Intelligent Assistant (IA) is a collection of software agents for helping the user in aspects of communication, information and time management. The IA includes a number of specialist assistants: the Telephone Assistant for filtering telephone calls, the E-mail Assistant for prioritizing messages, the Web Assistant for web searches, the YPA for classified directory enquiries, and the Diary Assistant for calendar management. Each of these assistants has its own user interface and may need to repeatedly communicate with the user.

The work described in this chapter addresses issues of time management in the Intelligent Assistant. Time management in the IA takes two forms: first, the *Diary Assistant* helps the user manage his or her own time, and second, the IA has a *Coordinator* that helps to manage the system's time, both in controlling

B. Azvine et al. (Eds.): Intelligent Systems and Soft Computing, LNAI 1804, pp. 301–   , 2000.
© Springer-Verlag Berlin Heidelberg 2000

(to some degree) communication between the assistants and the user, and in scheduling the system's own future actions. Regulation of communication to the user is needed to prevent potential confusion and communication overload arising from a number of assistants attempting to grab the user's attention at the same time; the scheduling of the system's future actions concerns the efficient use of system resources (e.g. web search) and so relates to the timely presentation of information from the assistants. The two agents are thus very different, although they perform the same basic function, that of task scheduling.

The purpose of the Diary Assistant, being a tool under the user's control, is to construct schedules that satisfy the user's stated preferences for task start times, durations and deadlines. The system is personalized in taking into account user preferences when scheduling tasks. It makes use of fuzzy logic in allowing the user to specify preferences for the start time, duration and deadline of a task using simple natural language expressions such as *morning, afternoon, early morning, around 1:00*, etc. The assistant uses two scheduling algorithms: a *global* search is used when scheduling a set of tasks, while a *local* search is used when adding a single task to an existing day schedule.

The purpose of the Coordinator is to maintain information about the user's state and activities and to schedule future actions of the system: it is distinguished as the only agent in the IA with a scheduling capability. The Coordinator is an instantiation of a new agent architecture based on ideas from reactive scheduling. IRSA (*Intelligent Reactive Scheduling Architecture*) explicitly addresses questions relating to intentions in time, and focuses on the issues of intention maintenance and revision. IRSA extends the PRS system of Georgeff and Lansky [ ] to include a model of time, allowing the interpreter to schedule its own future actions and then to execute those actions at the scheduled times.

The organization of this chapter is as follows. The main body of the material is contained in two sections, section   describing the Diary Assistant and section   describing the Coordinator. In section   , after some motivating discussion, we present the interface to the Diary Assistant, the fuzzy evaluation function used by the schedulers, and the global and local scheduling algorithms. In section   , we give an overview of the abstract IRSA architecture, provide details of the implementation of the Coordinator, and present a scenario illustrating the integration of the assistants in the IA. We conclude in section   .

2   Diary Assistant

Present diary systems are of limited assistance: they act mainly as electronic versions of paper diaries that can be used as a record of appointments or for reminders of tasks to be done. In this section, we describe a *Diary Assistant* which helps its users schedule personal tasks. The system is personalized in taking into account user preferences when scheduling tasks. It makes use of fuzzy logic, along the line of Zadeh [ ], in allowing the user to specify preferences for

---

[1] An initial version of the Diary Assistant was implemented by Simon Case.

the start time, duration and deadline of a task using simple natural language expressions such as *morning, afternoon, early morning, around 1:00*, etc. Each preference is interpreted by the system using a predefined fuzzy function. The Diary Assistant uses two schedulers: a *global* scheduler that assigns timeslots to a set of tasks so as to maximize the overall satisfaction of preferences, and a *local* scheduler that allocates a timeslot to a single task so as to minimize disruption to an existing day schedule. Both algorithms make use of an evaluation function that computes the degree to which a partial schedule satisfies a set of user preferences. The local scheduler uses an iterative improvement strategy based on the heuristic of minimizing changes to task sequences, while the global scheduler uses a standard greedy search algorithm driven by the evaluation function.

The general motivation for our work on the Diary Assistant is the personal assistant metaphor promoted by Maes [ ] as characterizing a class of software agents that learn from the user as he or she performs a repetitive task over a period of time. The idea was that a system could adapt its behaviour to the user's habits by "looking over the shoulder" of the user, and hence could improve its performance with only minimal intervention. Some early systems were also known as *interface agents* because they typically provided a single point of contact between a user and a single software system such as a mail handler or calendar system. The calendar system described in Maes and Kozierok [ ] used a combination of memory-based reasoning and reinforcement learning to adapt to the user's habits in a very specific scenario, here deciding whether to accept, decline or request renegotiation of a proposed meeting time. Thus the system provided only minimal help to the user.

Another related system is the CAP system described by Dent *et al.* [ ]. This work derives from the "learning apprentice" metaphor, and uses a standard machine learning algorithm to learn the preferences of a single user for scheduling various types of meetings. In contrast to this system, our work focuses on task scheduling based on expressed user preferences, whilst learning those preferences is something which we have so far not investigated.

Our approach to specifying user preferences draws on what Zadeh [ ] calls 'computing with words'. In Zadeh's proposal, the vagueness of natural language terms is represented using fuzzy functions (functions whose range is the interval $[0,1]$), the idea being that the meaning of a word like *tall* is captured by associating a degree of satisfaction of the predicate for each actual height. So, for example, 1.9 metres may be tall to degree 1, while 1.8 metres may be tall to degree 0.9, etc. Our idea is that preferences expressed in natural language terms such as *early morning* also denote fuzzy functions; thus preferences can also be satisfied to greater or lesser degree. Fuzzy logic provides a simple way of combining preferences: in fuzzy logic, the degree of satisfaction of two preferences is the minimum of the degrees to which each preference is satisfied (although more complicated mechanisms are also possible).

The present work thus closely borrows from that on fuzzy scheduling, which has, however, been concerned mainly with job-shop scheduling and has not so far been combined with 'computing with words': perhaps the earliest work in this area is Prade [ ]. One theoretically motivated approach is described by Dubois, Fargier and Prade [ ], who present a constraint analysis algorithm adapted to fuzzy temporal intervals using the approach of Dubois and Prade [ ]; Kerr and Walker [ ] is an early application of fuzzy logic to job-shop scheduling, and Slany [ ] discusses alternative methods of combining multiple constraints. These systems are all designed for capturing and reasoning about the relative importance of constraints (rather than preferences) associated with release times and due dates of jobs: more precisely, that some "soft" constraints are free to be relaxed (to varying degrees), while other "hard" constraints are absolute. In addition, Türkşen [ ] gives an overview of three other ways that fuzzy methods can be applied in the design of scheduling systems.

The Diary Assistant makes use of a "local" scheduler for single user tasks. Our use of iterative improvement techniques for incremental scheduling is similar to its use in BT's Dynamic Scheduler, Lesaint *et al.* [ ], which applies the technique to a constrained version of the Vehicle Routing Problem. The method itself borrows more generally from work on reactive scheduling, e.g. Smith [,], which is primarily in the domain of job-shop scheduling. He proposes a general scheduling architecture, OPIS, based on a blackboard control structure; in addition to incremental scheduling, OPIS provides heuristics for schedule repair when a schedule becomes infeasible. However, both in Dynamic Scheduler and in OPIS, the heuristics for schedule modification are necessarily specific to the problem domain.

In the remainder of this section, we describe the interface to the Diary Assistant, the fuzzy evaluation function used by the system, and the global and local scheduling algorithms.

2.1   Interface

The interface to the Diary Assistant is designed to look like a standard paper diary, with each day divided into half hour slots from 9:00 a.m to 5:00 p.m. Each task has the following features: (i) preferred start time, (ii) preferred start day, (iii) duration (based on 30 minute slots), (iv) description, (v) deadline time, (vi) deadline day, and (vii) interruptible (a flag indicating whether the user is interruptible during the task). The description may be selected from a predefined hierarchy of task descriptions provided for convenience, such as *Meeting/Research*. The diary window displays three days, and the user can move the window one day into the past or the future by clicking on arrow buttons at the bottom of the screen. The main interface window is shown in Figure : the duration of each task is given in parentheses beside its description, in the form *hours:minutes*.

The system facilitates the easy addition, deletion and movement of tasks from one day to another. When a task is moved to a new day, the scheduler uses the original preferred start time, so the timeslot allocated to the task on the new day may differ from previously. For example, suppose an *early morning* task is scheduled at 9:30 a.m. on one day; if this task is moved to a completely free day, it will be scheduled at 9:00 a.m., the time at which the *early-morning* function

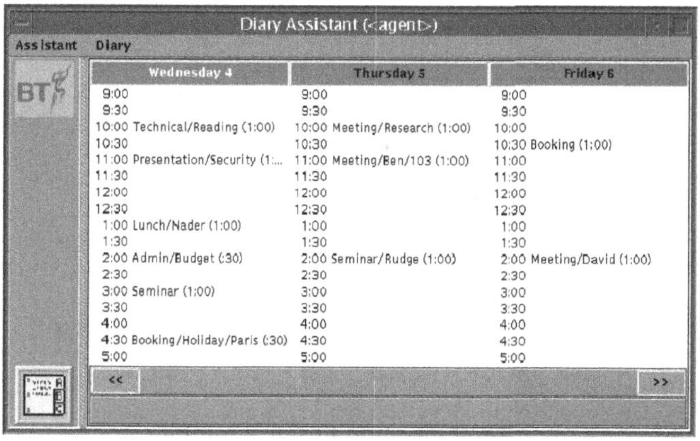

Fig. 1. Diary Assistant Interface

is maximized (see Figure 2 below). There is also a "To-Do" list containing tasks as yet unscheduled.

By clicking twice on a task, the user indicates that the task is to remain committed to its current timeslot, or, if the task is in the To-Do list, that it should remain unscheduled. The global scheduler, at the command of the user, reschedules all tasks on the To-Do list not indicated as remaining unscheduled. The local scheduler is used when a new task is added, when a task is moved from one day to another, and when the time, day, duration or deadline of a scheduled task is changed by editing.

2.2   Evaluation Function

Users can specify preferences for the start time, duration and deadline of a task using terms that are interpreted as fuzzy functions. At present, the following fuzzy terms are supported: for time preferences *morning, afternoon, early morning, late morning, early afternoon, late afternoon, around t* and *about t* where *t* is a precise time, and when using the global scheduler, *early week, mid week* and *late this week*; and for durations *around d* and *about d* where *d* is a precise duration, e.g. *around 1:00* (meaning a duration of around 1 hour). The function denoted by each of these predicates is predefined: it is our eventual aim to have these adaptively learnt by the system. As an illustration, fuzzy functions for interpreting various predicates for day periods are shown in Figure 2. As can be seen, the functions used are typically triangular and trapezoidal fuzzy functions.

The fuzzy function for the degree to which a time length *l* meets a duration of *around d* or *about d* is as follows.

$$
\mu_t(l) = \begin{cases} 1 & \text{if } l = d \\ 0.3 & \text{if } l = d \pm 30 \text{ minutes} \\ 0 & \text{otherwise} \end{cases}
$$

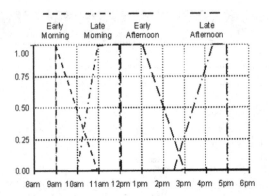

Fig. 2. Sample Fuzzy Functions

Because of the low value either side of the maximum (0.3), this function reflects a strong preference for changing a task's start time rather than shortening its duration (see below).

Finally, the degree to which a time s meets a deadline t is defined as follows, using the fuzzy function $\mu_{(-\infty,t]}$, assuming that μ_t is defined, see Dubois and Prade [ ].

$$\mu_{(-\infty,t]}(s) = \sup_{s \leq x} \mu_t(x) = \begin{cases} 1 & \text{if } s \leq t^* \\ \mu_t(s) & \text{otherwise} \end{cases}$$

where t^* is the latest timepoint x for which $\mu_t(x) = 1$, assuming that $\mu_t(x)$ is decreasing for $x \geq t^*$.

To combine these functions with a scheduling procedure, we need a way of computing the overall degree of satisfaction for several preferences that pertain to the same task, and a way of extending the evaluation function to cover several tasks in a partial task allocation. The general problem is one of aggregating preferences. Let P be a set of preference values which the user provides for a series of features. Here the features are the start time, duration and deadline of a diary task. Let T be a set of tasks and α be an allocation of timeslots (not necessarily of half hour length) to each task in T, so that $\alpha(t)$ is a timeslot for each $t \in T$. For each preference value $p \in P$, there is presumed to be a function μ_p giving the degree to which the timeslot s satisfies the preference p. It is natural to define the function μ_P representing the degree to which a timeslot s satisfies a set of preferences P as the minimum of the degrees to which s satisfies the individual preferences in P, since satisfying each of a set of preferences is analogous to satisfying the conjunction of those preferences. That is, we have assumed (along with both classical and fuzzy logic) that the preferences are independent. Thus we define:

$$\mu_P(s) = \min_{p \in P} \mu_p(s)$$

Note that if a timeslot violates any one of the preferences in P, the value of this function is 0.

Now the scheduling problem is to find an allocation α to a set of tasks that maximizes overall preference satisfaction. The scheduler typically operates with partial solutions (i.e. task allocations to a set of tasks that satisfy all preferences on those tasks). So that the search progresses towards a solution, we need a function μ for evaluating allocations to varying task sets T that is monotonic in T and α, i.e. if $T_1 \subseteq T_2$ and $\alpha_1 \subseteq \alpha_2$ then $\mu(T_1, \alpha_1) \leq \mu(T_2, \alpha_2)$. The function we choose is the summation function, although no doubt many other functions would work just as well. Thus we define (for a fixed set of preferences P):

$$\mu(T, \alpha) = \sum_{t \in T} \mu_P(\alpha(t))$$

In summary, equation ( ) is the function we use for evaluating partial task assignments, where T is a set of tasks and α is an allocation of timeslots to the tasks in T that satisfy all preferences on those tasks, and $\mu_p(s)$ is the degree to which a timeslot s satisfies a preference value p.

$$\mu(T, \alpha) = \sum_{t \in T} \min_{p \in P} \mu_p(\alpha(t)) \tag{1}$$

2.3   Global Scheduler

The Diary Assistant uses two schedulers: a *global* scheduler that allocates timeslots a set of tasks so as to maximize overall preference satisfaction, and a *local* scheduler that makes minimal adjustments to an existing schedule when adding (or editing) a single new task. The two scheduling algorithms are implemented in Fril, Baldwin, Martin and Pilsworth [ ], a logic programming language incorporating features of fuzzy inference, although the fuzzy aspects of Fril are not used to implement the evaluation function in this application.

We first describe the global scheduling algorithm. The system starts with a partial schedule for a set of tasks which the user has designated as fixed. The object is to find an assignment α to a set of tasks T such that $\mu(T, \alpha)$ is maximized. The problem, as with other scheduling problems, can be construed as a search problem. However, in contrast to other scheduling problems such as job-shop scheduling, the problem is relatively unconstrained, so there are typically many solutions that need evaluation. Hence the global scheduler uses a standard depth first search algorithm with backtracking, with heuristic guidance to improve the efficiency of the search.

The search uses heuristics in two ways: for defining the order in which tasks are considered and the order in which allocations to tasks are explored. Tasks are ordered from most constrained to least constrained, where one task is more constrained than another if there are fewer possible timeslots that satisfy the user's preference for that task. Note that the degree of satisfaction is not taken into account, just the number of possibilities: for example, an *early morning* task is more constrained than an *afternoon* task. Ties are broken arbitrarily. When considering a single task in the context of a partial schedule (an allocation of timeslots to the more constrained tasks), the possible timeslots are explored in order of preference satisfaction. This makes it highly likely, although there is no guarantee, that the first solution found by the scheduler (assuming one is found) maximizes the evaluation function μ defined in equation ( ): for efficiency, the first solution found is returned, even though this may not be optimal.

A sketch of the algorithm is given in Figure . It is assumed that a task allocation is represented as a set of pairs $\langle t : s \rangle$ where t is a task and s a timeslot. The first call to **Schedule** has T initialized to the set of all tasks ordered from most constrained to least constrained, and A to the empty set. The set S of free timeslots in an allocation that satisfy a preference p is ordered in decreasing degree of satisfaction of p.

Schedule(TaskSet T, Allocation A):
```
{
    if (T = {})
        return A;  % success
    else
        t = first(T); T = rest(T);
        p = user preference for t;
        S = free timeslots in A satisfying p;
        if (S = {})
            return null;  % backtrack
        else
            repeat
                s = first(S); S = rest(S);
                A' = Schedule(T, A ∪ {⟨t : s⟩})
            until (A' ≠ null) or (S = {});
            return A';
}
```

Fig. 3. Global Scheduling Algorithm

2.4   Local Scheduler

The idea behind the use of local scheduling in the Diary Assistant is to minimize disruption to an existing schedule when a *single* task is added or modified. The assumption here is that it is desirable to minimize as far as possible any confusion caused by moving diary entries, so tasks are not moved unless this is necessary for the satisfaction of preferences. Note that in the current system the day of a new task is supplied by the user, so the search is limited to a single day, and hence is much more constrained than global search.

We use a "hill-climbing" iterative improvement algorithm to implement local search. The algorithm presupposes a mechanism to compute the "neighbouring" solutions to a given solution state, which are typically found by modifying the solution by applying some simple heuristics (we use the term 'solution' here to indicate a task allocation that satisfies all the preferences). The heuristic we employ for generating neighbouring states is to consider each legitimate state computed by moving a sequence of tasks of up to length three either forwards or backwards by half an hour. The aim is to minimize changes to *task sequences* in the user's schedules. This is only one heuristic that we feel is intuitively reasonable. We prefer it to, for example, swapping tasks, either adjacent or nonadjacent. Of course the iterative improvement algorithm can operate with any heuristic.

A further issue is the construction of the initial solution. Here we also allow task sequences of up to length three to be moved forwards or backwards by half an hour, and tasks of imprecise preferred duration to be compressed (possibly in conjunction with moving a preceding or succeeding task half an hour forwards or backwards). This is because sometimes there is no gap in the schedule of sufficient length in which to place the new task; moving or shortening tasks sometimes creates such a gap.

A sketch of the modification algorithm is given in Figure . It is assumed that the initial solution A is found by the heuristic means of allowing movement and compression of tasks as described above. The score is just the value computed by the μ function, equation ( ), for complete solutions.

```
Schedule(Allocation A):
  {
      N = neighbouring solution states of A; ~
      if (N = {})
          return A;
      else
          A' = best state in N;
          if (score(A') ≤ score(A))
              return A;
          else
              return Schedule(A');
  }
```

Fig. 4. Local Scheduling Algorithm

The typical case where the use of local search improves the solution is when there are a number of relatively unconstrained tasks that require scheduling. For example, suppose there are two 1 hour afternoon tasks, which have been scheduled for 2:30 and 3:30. A new 1 hour afternoon task is to be added. The system initially assigns the new task to 1:30, then discovers that by moving all tasks backward by half an hour (i.e. the new task to 2:00, the 2:30 task to 3:00, and the 3:30 task to 4:00), the user's preferences are better satisfied.

3   Coordination in the Intelligent Assistant

The problem addressed in this section is the coordination of the various assistants in the Intelligent Assistant. Coordination is necessary first to avoid overloading the user with information from many assistants at the same time: this type of coordination essentially involves managing the communication from the assistants to the user. A more interesting aspect of coordination involves proactive behaviour: this refers to the system itself performing tasks on behalf of the user that require the action of more than one assistant (comprising simple plans of action). A subsidiary aspect of this type of coordination is the performance of actions at appropriate times. As a simple example, a reminder of a meeting should be given at a time close to the meeting and at a time when the user is likely to be available to receive the reminder. The reminder also has a deadline (the start time of the meeting) after which attempting the action is useless. Moreover, if the time of the meeting changes, the time of the reminder must also change. Thus temporal reasoning is a central part of coordination in this sense.

In this section, we describe the method of coordination we have developed to solve these problems. We have implemented a special *Coordinator* which is capable of scheduling and subsequently executing its own future actions: the Coordinator is distinguished within the IA as the only assistant with a scheduling capability. To support this facility, the Coordinator maintains a temporal database of the user's planned activities (obtained from the Diary Assistant), and uses this both to manage the system's interactions with the user and to schedule system actions related to the user's tasks. The Coordinator maintains this model as entries in the diary change, and reschedules its actions if necessary. An important point is that, due to the IA's messaging architecture, the Coordinator should not be regarded as a centralized controller: although the Coordinator can request other assistants to perform actions, the other assistants are autonomous to the extent that (i) they may not perform those actions, and (ii) they operate continuously, and hence for much of the time are operating under the direction of the user, rather than the Coordinator.

The Coordinator is based on a novel agent architecture that combines ideas from agent technology and reactive scheduling. As the name indicates, IRSA (*Intelligent Reactive Scheduling Architecture*), has much in common with previous architectures that follow Bratman's theory of intention, Bratman [ ], particularly IRMA, Bratman, Israel and Pollack [ ], and PRS, Georgeff and Lansky [ ], and exemplifies a cautious approach to the design of agent systems. In essence, IRSA extends the PRS system with a model of time, enabling the system to schedule and subsequently execute its own future actions. But where

---

[2]   An initial version of the Coordinator was implemented by Arash Sichanie.

the inspiration for PRS seems to be the multi-processing operating system with a view of a plan as an interruptible program, i.e. sequence of actions, the IRSA system views a plan as a set of actions each scheduled for execution at a particular point in the future. The architecture thus borrows from reactive scheduling, e.g. Smith [,], in its focus on intention maintenance and revision in response to changes in the world, in contrast to the PRS use of interrupt mechanisms to recover from plan execution failures. In support of these functions, the IRSA world model uses a temporal database to represent the future, while the PRS database typically contains information only about the current state of the world.

The Coordinator must maintain the timeliness of its scheduled actions. This sometimes means that tasks need to be rescheduled when the user task (goal) time is changed in the diary. For example, when the user changes the time of a meeting, the Coordinator must reschedule the reminder to the meeting. In the present implementation, this is done by simply deleting the goal and all its associated tasks (upon notification of the change from the diary), creating a new goal corresponding to the new time and then scheduling new tasks in response to the new goal. Another need for rescheduling occurs when the time comes for an action to be executed which involves notifying the user (such as issuing a reminder) but the user is not reachable for some reason (the Coordinator's model of the user's tasks is not necessarily complete). In this case, the notification is rescheduled for the next time the user is known to be reachable according to the presently available information (unless this time is past the task's deadline, in which case the goal is dropped).

The sense of "coordination" used for the IA is somewhat different from other senses used in the literature, which tend to involve negotiation or joint commitments between multiple agents using a protocol such as the contract net, c.f. Smith [ ], Jennings [ ]. It is closer to the sense of coordination in Sycara and Zeng [ ], who propose the TCA (Task Control Architecture), in which multiple task agents are connected to multiple interface agents and multiple information agents. This system has been applied to a number of problems where one task agent forms a plan that involves the action of other agents. However, in their applications, only one agent, an interface agent, communicates with any one user. Our work on the IRSA architecture is related to work on integrating planning and reacting in the AI planning literature, and in its use of scheduling to partial global planning, Durfee and Lesser [ ], and generalized partial global planning, Decker and Lesser [ ], which is also based on agents that employ scheduling algorithms. A major focus of that work is the coordination of a number of scheduling agents that negotiate to form a common schedule, although the agents do not execute their own schedules. Also many of the applications are scheduling-type examples in which resource optimization is the overall aim. At present, the IRSA agent implemented as the Coordinator of the IA does not coordinate its schedules with other similar agents, but only coordinates (in a more loose sense) the actions of itself and other autonomous nonscheduling agents. We sometimes refer to our notion of coordination as orchestration, as the Coordinator plays a role analogous to the conductor of an orchestra.

The remainder of this section is organized as follows. In section   , we give an overview of the abstract IRSA architecture. Details of the interpreter and the implementation are provided in section   . In section   , we illustrate the domain specific aspects of the architecture as instantiated as the Coordinator of the Intelligent Assistant through the use of a simple scenario.

3.1 IRSA Architecture

In this section, we describe our agent architecture which is called IRSA (*Intelligent Reactive Scheduling Architecture*). IRSA is both an abstract architecture, which is described in this section, and a concrete realization of this architecture, described in section   . So more precisely, it is the implementation of the architecture that meets the needs of schedule maintenance and revision, and the claim is that it does this in virtue of implementing the abstract architecture. Moreover, the abstract architecture leaves open the particular methods through which schedule maintenance and revision are implemented, as we believe that these are largely domain dependent.

In common with many agent architectures that aim to integrate planning with reactivity, e.g. Firby [ ], Ferguson [ ], Gat [ ], Lyons and Hendriks [ ], Müller and Pischel [ ], Bonasso *et al.* [ ], and especially Sloman [ ], IRSA is a layered architecture, consisting of three layers as shown in Figure : a reactive layer, a deliberative layer and a "meta-reasoning" layer.

The reactive layer is responsible for dealing with inputs from the environment that require an immediate response (by which we mean that there is insufficient time for any deliberation to influence the action taken). In the IA application, this "environment" consists only of the user and the other assistants, so the possible inputs are messages from other assistants, information about the user's state obtained from the multi-modal interface, and commands from the user. In general, this layer would also include filters and controllers.

The deliberative layer contains the IRSA architecture proper, which is described more fully in section   . It is responsible for accepting goals (which in the case of the IA correspond to user tasks), retrieving plans appropriate to those goals, scheduling actions in the plan(s), maintaining the plans as time progresses, and executing each scheduled action at the allocated time. Also included at this layer is a "world model" used when scheduling actions, and the system is responsible for maintaining the accuracy of this model: for example, in the IA when a user changes the time of a task using their diary, the Coordinator must both update the world model and reschedule the actions scheduled in response to that user task. The depiction of this layer in Figure is meant to emphasize the relationship between the IRSA architecture and the PRS system of Georgeff and Lansky [ ] and does not accurately reflect all the modules in the implementation (see section   below for these details).

The meta-reasoning layer is currently the least developed of the three layers in the present implementation. It includes a user model, which in the case of the Coordinator consists of the user's preferred times for performing various tasks. This enables the system to schedule actions in response to various

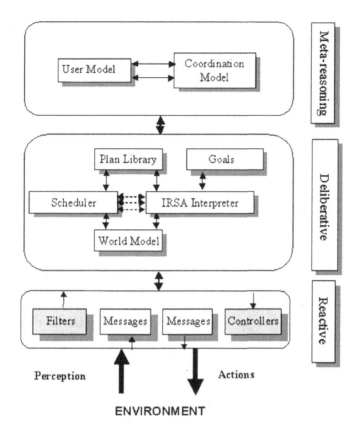

Fig. 5. IRSA Agent Architecture

system internal goals (such as issuing reminders to read low priority e-mails), which repeatedly arise and which we therefore call *recurrent* goals. The times are expressed using fuzzy terms, so an example fact in such a model is 'likes to read daily e-mail in late afternoon'. At a particular time each day (presently 11:00 p.m.), the Coordinator sets up internal goals corresponding to such tasks, e.g. *read daily e-mails*. However, the action corresponding to this goal is not to schedule a reminder to read daily e-mail, but rather to schedule a time at which the reminder will be scheduled. When determining the time for later scheduling, the user model is consulted so that (in this case), the scheduling action is performed some time before "late afternoon". Then at that time, the actual reminder is scheduled, and eventually, the reminder issued. The reason behind this "meta-scheduling" is that when the initial recurrent goal is generated (at 11:00 p.m.), the Coordinator is not assumed to have accurate information about the user's day, so scheduling the reminder then would be useless (or else the time of the reminder would require rescheduling in the event of a conflict). To avoid this, a scheduling event is scheduled for a time when the system can be expected to have more complete information.

The meta-reasoning layer also contains provision for a "coordination model", here referring to coordination of the activities of different IA users. The type of application we have in mind is multi-agent meeting scheduling, an obvious extension to the Diary Assistant requiring the coordination of multiple users.

3.2   Implementation

In this section, we focus on the deliberative layer of the IRSA architecture, which implements the planning/action interpreter of the system. As mentioned above, the IRSA interpreter is primarily an extension of the BDI interpreter of PRS, Rao and Georgeff [ ], that enables intentions to be scheduled at specific points in time. The implementation also represents an advance over PRS (at least of the UM-PRS implementation, Lee *et al.* [ ], in its use of Java threads for implementing concurrent processes. In fact, the goal reduction planner is only one of three threads forming the implementation of the deliberative layer. A second thread is used for executing the actions scheduled by the interpreter, and a third thread is responsible for updating the world model in response to changes in the environment (in this case, a change in the user's state).

The basic IRSA interpreter implements a goal reduction planner as shown in Figure . This thread takes each of the system's goals, retrieves a plan for the goal from a pre-specified plan library, and calls the scheduler to specify execution times for system tasks for each action in the plan. Goals mainly correspond to user tasks, so each goal comes with a deadline time (set to the start time of the user's task). Each plan in the plan library consists of a set of action templates for achieving a particular goal. Before a system task can be scheduled, the action template from which it derives must be instantiated to form an executable task using the parameters supplied with the specific goal. There are currently two types of scheduling for actions: either 'as soon as possible' or 'as late as possible before the deadline', the former typically being used for search tasks or notifications, and the latter for reminders (in this case, the scheduler determines a time which is 5 minutes before the user becomes unreachable from then until the action's deadline). System-generated "recurrent" internal goals are treated by the interpreter in exactly the same manner.

The IRSA execution module is illustrated in Figure . This thread repeatedly, at an interval appropriate to the application, checks whether there is a task that needs executing, then executes it. For the IA, the thread runs every 15 seconds, which is generally enough time to execute all tasks scheduled for a particular time. Note that the executor does not assume that there is only a single task scheduled for a particular time, but note also that the tasks are executed sequentially, not concurrently. The world monitor for the Intelligent Assistant is necessarily domain dependent, and is described in the next section.

The interpreter is also capable of simple "rescheduling" in response to changes in the world model. For example, when the user changes the time of a task in the diary, the Coordinator must reschedule the actions associated with the task.

```
Interpreter:
    {
        // basic goal reduction planner
        Goal = GoalList.getGoal();
        if (Goal ≠ null)
            {
                Plan = PlanLibrary.fetchPlan(Goal);
                if (Plan ≠ null)
                    Scheduler.schedule(Goal, Plan);
                Goal.setStatus(REDUCED);
            }
    }
```

Fig. 6. IRSA Interpreter

```
Executor:
    {
        // assumes now is the current time
        Task = TaskList.getTask(now);
        while (Task ≠ null)
            {
                executeTask(Task);
                Task.setStatus(COMPLETED);
                Task = TaskList.getTask(now);
            }
    }
```

Fig. 7. IRSA Execution Module

In the present implementation, this is done by simply deleting the goal and all its associated tasks, creating a new goal corresponding to the new time and then scheduling new system tasks in response to the new goal. This simple mechanism suffices for the relatively small plans currently used in this application.

3.3   Integration

In this section, we illustrate the integration and coordination of the assistants in the Intelligent Assistant. The IA is designed as a multi-agent system consisting of various specialist "assistants" in the areas of time, information and communication management. For communication management, the IA includes specialist Telephone and E-mail assistants, used respectively for filtering telephone calls and prioritizing e-mail messages. For information management, the IA includes a Web Assistant (for web search) and the YPA (for Yellow Pages® lookup).

Communication between agents in the IA is implemented using the open messaging architecture of Zeus, Nwana, Ndumu and Lee [ ]. The interaction between the various agents is shown in Figure , which shows the types of messages or kind of information sent between components of the system.

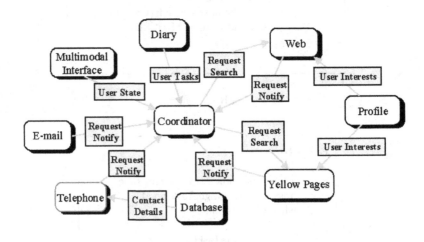

Fig. 8. Agent Interactions

The world monitor of the Coordinator is responsible for maintaining information about the user's state and future activities. One aspect of the world state is the user's willingness to accept interruptions from the system. The Coordinator includes a simple interface allowing the user to accept or refuse all interruptions, telephone calls, and e-mail notifications; the user may change state at any time (selecting to accept/refuse all interruptions entails accepting/refusing telephone calls and e-mails). To maintain consistency, the world monitor checks this parameter every second. The system also maintains an up to date model of the user's tasks based on information from the diary. Since the diary is organized into half hour chunks, information concerning the user's interruptibility based on the diary need only be updated on the half hour.

In the IA, tasks in the user's diary, when confirmed by the user, trigger the plans of the Coordinator. We describe the simple example of a lunch booking entered in the diary for 1:00 on the current day. The plan related to the lunch booking contains three actions: (i) using the YPA to find a restaurant, (ii) finding the web page of the person having lunch with the user, and (iii) reminding

---

³ Yellow Pages® is a registered trade mark of British Telecommunications plc in the United Kingdom.

the user of the lunch appointment. Suppose that the user also enters a non-interruptible 1 hour meeting at 12:00 on the current day.

The whole process starts with the user's confirmation of the diary entries, when messages are sent from the Diary Assistant to the Coordinator giving the user's latest schedule. The first action of the Coordinator is to update its world model on the basis of this information. Then the IRSA Interpreter treats some of these user tasks, in particular the lunch booking, as goals to be acted upon. For each such goal, the interpreter retrieves the appropriate plan of actions, and calls the scheduler which creates a new system task for each action in the plan parametrized according to additional information supplied by the user concerning the user task (in this case, who the lunch appointment is with). In this example, the YPA and Web searches are scheduled for the current time, while the reminder is scheduled for 11:55 (5 minutes before the user's non-interruptible meeting), which is 5 minutes before the latest time the user can be assumed to be reachable. The IRSA Execution Module then executes both the YPA and Web Search Request actions, which simply involves sending request messages to the respective assistants.

The YPA augments the query given by the Coordinator (to find a restaurant in the user's locale) with the interests of the user (obtained from the user's profile) to search for a restaurant with a particular type of cuisine. The YPA accepts a natural language query such as, in this case, 'Italian restaurant in Ipswich'. The Web Assistant searches for the lunch partner's home page. When the YPA and Web assistants have finished searching, they must notify the user that the results are ready. However, the assistants each request permission from the Coordinator to interrupt the user, again by sending appropriate messages. Should the user be interruptible, permission will be granted by reply; assume otherwise. Then the Coordinator will schedule notifications to the user (that the output is ready) for the next available time that the user is interruptible, again based on information supplied from the diary, possibly overridden by the user via the interface. This occurs through the creation of new internal goals, then a plan being retrieved by the interpreter (as discussed above), and times for the notification tasks being set by the scheduler. Finally, the Coordinator performs the notifications and reminders at the determined times.

An added complication is that the Coordinator user interface enables the user to override the system's current information concerning interruptibility (when there is no entry in the diary covering a particular time, the user is assumed to be interruptible). Supposing this has been done when a notification is to be executed, the scheduler is invoked to reschedule the task for the next time the user is interruptible (i.e. based on the then available information, which may be different from when the task was originally scheduled), provided also that the deadline for the task has not passed. It may be that because of this, some notifications never get issued; this is unavoidable. The way this is implemented at present is that the program for executing the notification first tests whether the user is interruptible, then if not, makes an explicit call to the scheduler to reschedule the task.

4   Conclusion and Further Work

Time management is an important and intricate aspect of the Intelligent Assistant, involving both the construction of user schedules in an intuitive and predictable way and the planning and execution of system tasks so as to minimize demands on the user's attention and maximize the usage of system resources. The coordination of assistants is complicated by the fact that the assistants are all autonomous, i.e. techniques based on centralized, or even distributed, planning are not appropriate. We have used a novel agent architecture based on ideas from reactive scheduling as the basis of the Coordinator. IRSA extends the PRS architecture with temporally specific beliefs, goals and intentions; the IRSA interpreter is capable of scheduling its own future actions and then executing those actions at appropriate times. In addition to strengthening the temporal reasoning capability of the system, current work on the Coordinator concerns the investigation of both general and domain specific heuristics for rescheduling in dynamic settings, and in particular, in the domain of the Intelligent Assistant.

The Diary Assistant in the IA helps the user schedule tasks based on their stated preferences. Preferences for start times, durations and deadlines can be specified using simple natural language terms such as *morning*, *afternoon*, etc., which are interpreted using predefined fuzzy functions, enhancing usability. The system includes two scheduling algorithms: a *global* scheduler allocates timeslots to a set of tasks so as to maximize overall satisfaction of the user's preferences, and a *local* scheduler allocates a timeslot to a single task so as to minimize disruption to an existing day schedule. Thus the Diary Assistant is particularly geared towards the incremental task scheduling necessitated by repeated interactions with the user.

Three topics are the subject of current research related to the Diary Assistant. First, we intend to enable the user to specify plans of action, or more generally, constraints between tasks. Although this can be handled by augmenting the global and local scheduling algorithms described in this paper, the possibility of using constraint solving techniques is one that must also be considered. Second, we aim to investigate approximate scheduling, by which we mean scheduling at more than one level of granularity, and incrementally refining an approximate schedule as time progresses and more information becomes available. The intuition here is that sometimes the Diary Assistant is overly specific in allocating specific timeslots to tasks before the user is ready to commit to a final time. The idea is to develop an algorithm that can determine efficiently whether an approximate schedule is feasible or infeasible: by an *approximate schedule*, we mean an allocation of tasks to intervals at larger granularity than half-hour slots, such as days or weeks. Third, we intend to investigate learning user profiles, both the fuzzy functions representing the user's preferences for different types of task, and constraints on combining the preferences for different tasks based on the context provided by related entries in the diary.

Acknowledgements

We gratefully acknowledge the contribution to research and development on the Intelligent Assistant made by Ben Azvine, David Djian, Kwok Ching Tsui, Simon Case, Gilbert Owusu, Benoit Remael and Arash Sichanie.

References

1. Georgeff M. P. and Lansky A. L.: 'Reactive Reasoning and Planning', Proceedings of the Sixth National Conference on Artificial Intelligence (AAAI-87), pp. 677-682 (1987).   ,   ,

2. Zadeh L. A.: 'Fuzzy Logic = Computing with Words', IEEE Transactions on Fuzzy Systems, Vol. 4, pp. 103-111 (1996).   ,

3. Maes P.: 'Agents that Reduce Work and Information Overload', Communications of the ACM, Vol. 37, No. 7, pp. 31-40 (1994).

4. Maes P. and Kozierok R. A. E.: 'Learning Interface Agents', Proceedings of the Eleventh National Conference on Artificial Intelligence (AAAI-93), pp. 459-465 (1993).

5. Dent L., Boticario J., McDermott J., Mitchell T. M. and Zabowski D. A.: 'A Personal Learning Apprentice', Proceedings of the Tenth National Conference on Artificial Intelligence (AAAI-92), pp. 96-103 (1992).

6. Prade H. M.: 'Using Fuzzy Set Theory in a Scheduling Problem: A Case Study', Fuzzy Sets and Systems, Vol. 2, pp. 153-165 (1979).

7. Dubois D., Fargier H. and Prade H. M.: 'Fuzzy Constraints in Job-Shop Scheduling', Journal of Intelligent Manufacturing, Vol. 6, pp. 215-234 (1995).

8. Dubois D. and Prade H. M.: 'Processing Fuzzy Temporal Knowledge', IEEE Transactions on Systems, Man, and Cybernetics, Vol. 19, pp. 729-744 (1989).   ,

9. Kerr R. M. and Walker R. N.: 'A Job Shop Scheduling System Based on Fuzzy Arithmetic', Proceedings of the Third International Conference on Expert Systems and the Leading Edge in Production and Operations Management, pp. 433-450 (1989).

10. Slany W.: 'Scheduling as a Fuzzy Multiple Criteria Optimization Problem', Fuzzy Sets and Systems, Vol. 78, pp. 197-222 (1996).

11. Türkşen I. B.: 'Scheduling System Design: Three Fuzzy Theory Approaches', in 'Fuzzy Information Engineering', eds, Dubois D., Prade H. M. and Yager R. R., John Wiley & Sons, New York (1997).

12. Lesaint D., Azarmi N., Laithwaite R. and Walker P.: 'Engineering Dynamic Scheduler for Work Manager', BT Technology Journal, Vol. 16, No. 3, pp. 16-29 (1998).

13. Smith S. F.: 'OPIS: A Methodology and Architecture for Reactive Scheduling', in 'Intelligent Scheduling', eds, Zweben M. and Fox M. S., Morgan Kaufmann, San Francisco, CA (1994).   ,

14. Smith S. F.: 'Reactive Scheduling Systems', in 'Intelligent Scheduling Systems', eds, Brown D. and Scherer W., Kluwer Academic Publishers, Dordrecht (1994).
    ,

15. Baldwin J. F., Martin T. P. and Pilsworth B. W.: 'Fril – Fuzzy and Evidential Reasoning in Artificial Intelligence', Research Studies Press, Taunton (1995).

16. Bratman M. E.: 'Intention, Plans and Practical Reason', Harvard University Press, Cambridge, MA (1987).

17. Bratman M. E., Israel D. J. and Pollack M. E.: 'Plans and Resource-Bounded Practical Reasoning', Computational Intelligence, Vol. 4, pp. 349-355 (1988).
18. Smith R. G.: 'The Contract Net Protocol: High-Level Communication and Control in a Distributed Problem Solver', IEEE Transactions on Computers, Vol. C-29, pp. 1104-1113 (1980).
19. Jennings N. R.: 'Controlling Cooperative Problem Solving in Industrial Multi-agent Systems Using Joint Intentions', Artificial Intelligence, Vol. 75, pp. 195-240 (1995).

20. Sycara K. P. and Zeng D.: 'Coordination of Multiple Intelligent Software Agents', International Journal of Cooperative Information Systems, Vol. 5, No. 2, pp. 181-211 (1996).
21. Durfee E. H. and Lesser V. R.: 'Using Partial Global Plans to Coordinate Distributed Problem Solvers', Proceedings of the Tenth International Joint Conference on Artificial Intelligence, pp. 875-883 (1987).
22. Decker K. S. and Lesser V. R.: 'Designing a Family of Coordination Algorithms', Proceedings of the First International Conference on Multi-Agent Systems, pp. 73-80 (1995).
23. Firby R. J.: 'Adaptive Execution in Complex Dynamic Worlds', Yale University Technical Report YALEU/CSD/RR #672 (1989).
24. Ferguson I. A.: 'Toward an Architecture for Adaptive, Rational, Mobile Agents', in 'Decentralized AI 3', eds, Werner E. and Demazeau Y., Elsevier, Amsterdam (1992).
25. Gat E.: 'Integrating Planning and Reacting in a Heterogeneous Asynchronous Architecture for Controlling Real-World Mobile Robots', Proceedings of the Tenth National Conference on Artificial Intelligence (AAAI-92), pp. 809-815 (1992).
26. Lyons D. M. and Hendriks A. J.: 'A Practical Approach to Integrating Reaction and Deliberation', Proceedings of the First International Conference on AI Planning Systems (AIPS), pp. 153-162 (1992).
27. Müller J. P. and Pischel M.: 'An Architecture for Dynamically Interacting Agents', International Journal of Intelligent and Cooperative Information Systems, Vol. 3, No. 1, pp. 25-45 (1994).
28. Bonasso R. P., Kortenkamp D., Miller D. P. and Slack M.: 'Experiences with an Architecture for Intelligent, Reactive Agents', in 'Intelligent Agents II', eds, Wooldridge M. J., Müller J. P. and Tambe M., Springer-Verlag, Berlin, pp. 187-202 (1996).
29. Sloman A.: 'Exploring Design Space and Niche Space', in 'SCAI-95', eds, Aamodt A. and Komorowski J., IOS Press, Amsterdam (1995).
30. Rao A. S. and Georgeff M. P.: 'An Abstract Architecture for Rational Agents', Proceedings of the Third International Conference on Principles of Knowledge Representation and Reasoning (KR'92), pp. 439-449 (1992).
31. Lee J., Huber M. J., Kenny P. G. and Durfee E. H.: 'UM-PRS: An Implementation of the Procedural Reasoning System for Multirobot Applications', Proceedings of the AIAA/NASA Conference on Intelligent Robotics in Field, Factory, Service, and Space, pp. 842-849 (1994).
32. Nwana H. S., Ndumu D. T. and Lee L. C.: 'ZEUS: An Advanced Tool-Kit for Engineering Distributed Multi-Agent Systems', Proceedings of the Third International Conference on the Practical Application of Intelligent Agents and Multi-Agent Technology, pp. 377-391 (1998).

Machine Interpretation of Facial Expressions

Simon J. Case[1], Jim F. Baldwin[2] and Trevor P. Martin[2]

[1] Intelligent Systems Research Group, BT Labs
Adastral Park, Martlesham Heath, Ipswich IP5 3RE, United Kingdom
simon.case@bt.com
[2] Artificial Intelligence Group, Department of Engineering Mathematics
University of Bristol, Bristol BS8 1TR, UK
{trevor.martin,jim.baldwin}@bristol.ac.uk

Abstract. Facial expressions are an important source of information for human interaction. Therefore, it would be desirable if computers were able to use this information to interact more naturally with the user. However, facial expressions are not always unambiguously interpreted even by competent humans. Consequently, soft computing techniques in which interpretations are given some degree of support would seem appropriate. This paper describes how the mass assignment approach to constructing fuzzy sets from probability distributions has been applied to i) the low-level classification of pixels into facial feature classes based on their colour to segment a facial image into possible facial feature regions, ii) to make a final decision on which combination of these regions correctly extracts the facial features, and iii) to generate rules which classify the emotional content of the image according to values taken from these extracted regions.

1 Introduction

Facial expressions are an important part of human/human interaction. Currently, however, the information which may be derived from these expressions is not used by computers for the following two reasons. Firstly, there is the formidable task of extracting a useful characterization of a face from its image. Secondly, facial expressions and the emotional states or events that they signify are ambiguous and vague. This paper will discuss both of these aspects. We will discuss how 'natural' facial features can be used in classifying and utilizing expressions. We will also describe a set of methods for extracting facial features from an image which uses fuzzy sets derived from a small set of sample images.

1.1 The Importance of Facial Expressions

When communicating with other humans we use many forms of communication. The most obvious is speech; however, this is often accompanied or supplanted by other

B. Azvine et al. (Eds.): Intelligent Systems and Soft Computing, LNAI 1804, pp. 321-342, 2000.
© Springer-Verlag Berlin Heidelberg 2000

methods. In particular there is the tone with which someone says something, as well as the facial and bodily expressions that accompany it. Indeed, when it comes to guessing how someone has reacted to something or how they are feeling, expression analysis is not only less intrusive, but also more accurate. If we consider the usual response to the question *"Are you OK?"* (i.e. *"I'm fine"*), we can see how little we use words to communicate our emotional state.

The information which we use all the time when communicating with others is currently not available to a computer. At present we interact with computers either via the keyboard or with the aid of a mouse. The interaction is one way, in the form of a command from the user to the computer. However, it would be more desirable if the computer could:

- initiate courses of action which are dependent on the mood of the user — in this case the facial expression would be used as a condition for undertaking the action;
- pro-actively suggest and implement commands which the user would approve of but has not yet specified — facial expression could be used here to monitor the user's response to the action.

This would extend the input modalities of the computer allowing a more 'natural' interaction with the user.

Further applications of an expression recogniser might also include a pain-detector in which the expression of a patient would be monitored in order to warn the carer, and a lip-reader to aid speech analysis.

1.2 The Ambiguity of Facial Expressions

The human face can generate around 50,000 distinct facial expressions, which correspond to about 30 semantic distinctions [1]. Clearly the human face is extremely expressive. Given this, a number of outcomes are possible: we might expect a mapping of many expressions to a few emotions. We can also expect that a given expression may be mapped to more than one emotional state, because the different states share the same expression. Finally, at any given time the subject may be in more than one emotional state, in which case we would expect a mapping from one expression to different emotional states.

Furthermore, different gradations of emotional states are experienced. For example we may be *extremely angry* or just a *bit upset*. So we can expect a degree of vagueness as to whether someone is in a particular emotional state or not.

2   Outline of a Method for Facial Expression Interpretation

Because of the ambiguity of facial expressions and the underlying emotions, interpretation of a given facial expression is not simply a matter of classification into one type. Rather we should expect it to belong to several classes with varying memberships. We propose that a given expression should belong to one or more classes with a corresponding degree of support for each class. Thus an expression might be considered to be bored with a support of 0.8 and sad with a support of 0.4. A given expression can then be conveniently classified using rules.

```
e.g.        subject is happy
                    if      the lip shape is happy
                    and     the eye shape is happy
            with support S
```

The question then is how to assign supports for a given expression. This will depend on the measurable features we select from the face and the method of generating the support from these features.

2.1   Calculating the Support

The information required for this application will come from various sources:

- visual information from the lips;
- visual information from the eyes;
- behavioural information about the user;
- other potential sources of information e.g. keyboard typing speeds.

Using information from different sources can greatly increase the complexity of the classification since each extra source increases the dimensionality of the data. Furthermore, for some of the sources data will be scarce. For example, behavioural information will come as and when the user performs certain series of actions. If, on the other hand, we use intermediate classifications for each source and then combine these, we will require less data since we will be classifying on a sub-space of the entire classification feature space and we will reduce the complexity of each classification. We can write a program to do this in FRIL, a support logic programming language.

Intermediate classifications can be made using basic FRIL rules in which the fuzzy sets have been generated from data according to mass assignment theory [2-5] and using the data-browser [6, 7]. In this case the rules will have the form:

```
((shape of lip is lipshape1
           if     width    is        shape1_lip_width
                  height1 is         shape1_lip_height1
                  height2 is shape1_lip_height2
                  height3 is shape1_lip_height3
                  height4 is shape1_lip_height4))
```

where *width, height1*, etc, are the measured values from the image and *shape1_lip_width*, etc, are fuzzy sets generated by the data-browser. The resulting evidences can then be combined using either the evidential logic rule or the extended FRIL rule.

In its current state the system uses only lip and eye information to make an intermediate classification on the emotional response of the user. These rules have the form:

((expression is E if LX LY RX RY OLH ILH LEW REW REH)
     (is_a_member LX of class [-4:0 –1:1 3:0])
     (is_a_member LY of class [-5:0 –2:1 –1:0])
     ...
     (is_a_member REH of class [-5:0 –3:1 –1:0])
)

where E is the emotional response and LX-REH are measurements made from the image.

These rules can be combined with those from different sources in the form of a probabilistic decision tree. In this case we would use the extended FRIL rule, which can be generated from data using the mass assignment ID3 algorithm [8]. If some sources are more discriminatory for one class than for others *evidential logic rules* [6, 9, 10] may be used. They can be generated from data using the data-browser and semantic discrimination as described in Baldwin [11].

3   Region Segmentation Based on Colour Information

3.1   The Use of Colour for Facial Feature Extraction

The extraction of facial features from an image is not a trivial task. As well as the problems encountered for any computer vision task, extracting facial features has the following problems:

- facial features are not geometrically simple;
- facial features vary in shape among individuals;
- facial features are highly deformable even for one individual;
- facial features should be extracted under varying lighting conditions.

As has been noted above, the features we wish to extract are the eyes and mouth. Of these the mouth is particularly difficult to extract because the greyscale values of the mouth in an image are typically very similar to those of the skin. Therefore, it is not possible to reliably find the boundaries of the lips from a grey-scale image. Consequently edge-detection on the grey-scale image is not a viable method.

However, these boundaries could be located if an appropriate transform could be found. In this case we are looking for a transform from the RGB values which would:

- vary according to the closeness of the colour to the facial feature;
- be insensitive to changes in lighting conditions.

Similar approaches to feature extraction using chromaticity information can be found in Coianiz et al [12] and Yang et al [13].

3.2   Selecting an Appropriate Colour Transformation

To reduce sensitivity to lighting conditions we require an initial transform from RGB values to values in which the chromaticity is separated from the intensity. Many such transforms exist, such as HSV and YIQ values. However, we have found that using normalized red and green values as described in Terzopoulos [1] have given the best results . In this case the initial transform is:

R_normalized=R/(R+G+B)
G_normalized=G/(R+G+B)

where R, G and B are the RGB values.

To meet the first condition, examples of skin, lips and eyes were isolated by hand from a set of training images as examples of facial features. The individual pixel values were converted into normalized red and normalized green. For each colour transform fuzzy sets were formed for each facial feature using the data-browser method. Resulting images of the skin class can be seen in Figs. 1—3. Here the intensity of the image corresponds to membership of the skin class such that a white pixel has a high membership and a black pixel has a low membership. Clearly the normalized colour sets are more succesful at separating skin from not-skin pixels, and this is in general the case for all classes. The normalized colour sets generated for the eye, lip and skin classes can be seen in Figs. 4 and 5 where the y-axis corresponds to the membership of the set and the x-axis to the normalized colour.

  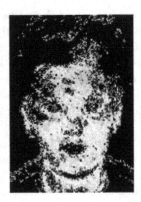

Fig. 1. Fuzzy image generated from hue values   **Fig. 2.** Fuzzy Image generated from IQ values   **Fig. 3.** Fuzzy Image generated from normalized colour values

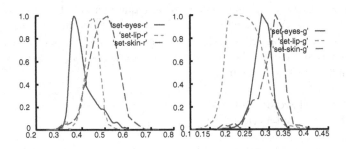

Fig. 4. Fuzzy sets for normalized red   **Fig. 5.** Fuzzy sets for normalized green

Once these sets have been formed we can give a support for membership of a particular facial feature set for any novel pixel.

3.3 Resulting Colour Spaces

For illustrative purposes colour spaces for each class can be generated as is shown in Figs. 6, 7 and 8. The axes are the normalized red and green values and the intensity is the rescaled product of the degree of membership in the normalized red and green fuzzy sets such that white indicates the highest membership in the class and black indicates the lowest.

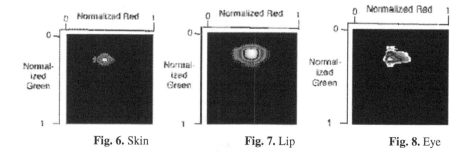

Fig. 6. Skin   **Fig. 7.** Lip   **Fig. 8.** Eye

The most striking feature of these results is the surprising uniqueness of skin colour. It might be expected that the variation in skin colour would be greater than that of lip colour, but as can be seen in Fig. 6, it occupies a very small area of the colour space in comparison to the lip class (Fig. 7).

It can also be seen that the eye space is small and centred around the values of 0.333 for both normalized colours. This will correspond to a whitish colour which is what should be expected.

The smallness of the skin and eye spaces implies that both are good candidates for discrimination of classes on the basis of colour.

3.4   Resulting Fuzzy Images

Figs. 9 to 12 show the results of classifying pixels using the fuzzy sets. The degree of membership in each class is shown by the intensity of each pixel. As before, white pixels have a high membership and dark pixels have a low one.

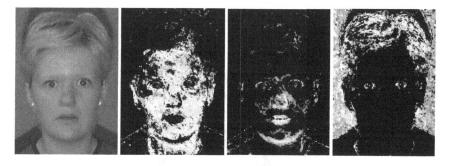

Fig. 9. Original image   **Fig. 10.** Skin image   **Fig. 11.** Lip image   **Fig 12.** Eye image

3.5   Improving the Lip Image

As can be seen from the resulting colour-maps and images there is a degree of inter-section between the lip and skin pixel sets. An improvement to the lip image can be made by asserting that a pixel is a lip pixel if it belongs to the lip class and not to the skin class, i.e. lip pixel membership becomes:

$$(\chi_{\text{red-norm-lip}} * \chi_{\text{green-norm-lip}}) * (1 - (\chi_{\text{red-norm-skin}} * \chi_{\text{green-norm-skin}}))$$

where $\chi_{\text{red-norm-lip}}$ represents membership in the fuzzy set for normalized red for the lip class.

The resulting image for the example can be seen in Fig. 13.

Fig. 13. Fuzzy lip image

3.6 Using Intensity Information

The use of intensity (defined as 0.3*R + 0.59*G+0.11*B) has been avoided so far because of its sensitivity to lighting conditions. This can be seen in Fig. 14, where the light source is on one side. This has caused pixels on the left-hand side to have a lower membership in the skin class, but this lower membership is in fact due to differing lighting conditions across the face.

Fig. 14. Fuzzy skin image generated from normalized colour and fuzzy intensity sets

This illustrates the general point that using the data-browser method to generate fuzzy sets for intensity values is inappropriate because of the difficulty in obtaining enough data. Indeed, we would need the training data to be evenly spread around the possible intensity space.

On the other hand, we would not expect extreme intensity values to belong to any of the classes since facial features are neither very reflective nor very absorbent. From small amounts of data we can estimate higher and lower bounds for the intensity values. These can be implemented as crisp sets and used in addition to the normalized colour sets in classifying novel pixels.

Figs. 15 and 16 show the improvement which can be made when using intensity information. Fig. 12 shows the skin image generated only from the normalized colour values, and Fig. 13 shows the same image generated from colour values with upper and lower bounds for intensity. In particular removing extreme intensity values prevented misclassification of pixels which come from the hair in the original image.

Fig. 15. Fuzzy image generated from normalized colour sets

Fig. 16. Fuzzy image generated from normalized colour sets and crisp intensity set

3.7   Using Rough Positional Information

As well as colour information we also know that the facial features all occupy regular positions relative to each other. Since skin pixels are so well classified we can use the expected positions of the other features relative to the centre of the skin to improve their classifications.

We need to know the direction and the distance of objects either from a certain point or from each other. For this, we use the centre of the skin image as defined by the average skin pixel co-ordinate as the centre point of the face. Since we expect the distributions of the skin pixels in the x and y axes to be symmetrical about the mean, we find the standard deviation from these axes, which is then used as a scaling factor. Fuzzy sets are generated for the scaled distance of the lip pixels from the centre of the face in x and y axes. These sets can be seen in Figs. 17 and 18. The dark lines represent the positional fuzzy sets for the eyes and the lighter lines represent those for the lips. The y-axis corresponds to the membership of the class and the x-axis the rescaled distance. Again because of the lack of data the sets have been estimated.

These sets are then used in conjunction with the normalized colour fuzzy sets and the crisp intensity sets in novel images. Figs. 19 and 20 show the results of applying these sets to the sample image (Fig. 9).

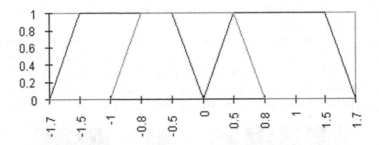

Fig. 17. X-axis positional fuzzy sets for eye and lip pixels

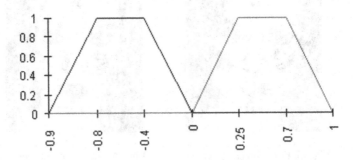

Fig. 18. Y-axis positional fuzzy sets for eye and lip pixels

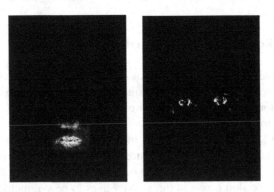

Fig. 19. Lip image using   **Fig. 20.** Eye image using
positional sets   positional sets

3.9   Isolating the Lip Region

As can be seen from Figs. 19 and 20 the final fuzzy images may retain small mis-classified regions. However, it is known that the lips should form a solid object in the image plane. Therefore, the horizontal and vertical projections of an ideally classified image should cross the x or y value axis at only two points, i.e. non-zero x or y projection values should be consecutive. This can be seen in Figs. 21 and 22, in which the abscissa corresponds to the vertical or horizontal projection value and the ordinate represents the x or y value in the image. For the purposes of this paper we shall refer to consecutive non-zero projection values as projection sections. In Figs. 21 and 22 there is one section per image starting at C_1 and ending at C_2.

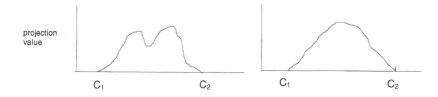

Fig. 21. Y-value in image   **Fig. 22** X-value in image

Consequently if there is more than one section in either projection then one of these sections can be considered to be misclassified. We assume that the smaller section is misclassified and remove any of the pixels that fall within this range. This is repeated iteratively on the x and y axes until no more pixels are removed. This will remove any misclassified region which is separated from the correctly classified region in either the x or y directions.

The lip region is then considered to be the union of all those regions which remain.

The corners of this region are found by locating the zero crossings of the horizontal projection of the final fuzzy lip image (C_1 and C_2 in Fig. 22), and then finding the average y value of the lip pixels with these x values.

4   Extracting Facial Feature Values

4.1   Selecting the Best Eye Regions

In the majority of cases there will be several regions misclassified as eye regions. It is necessary therefore to select only the most likely regions. Correctly classified eye regions come in two different types as shown in Figs. 23 and 24. *Eye type 1* corresponds to the situation in which the *eye centre* region (pupil and iris) splits the white of the eye into two distinct regions. This is the situation which occurs in the majority of cases. *Eye type 2* corresponds to the situation in which the eye centre region merely occludes a part of the eye white region but does not divide it into two distinct regions.

In our method eye regions are selected using common-sense fuzzy rules on eye and eye centre regions along with information gained from the lip region extracted as described above. The reasoning steps taken are:

i.   divide the image into two parts corresponding to the left and right halves of the face;

ii. in each part of the image find all potential eyes, each of which will have a support representing the likelihood that it is an eye;

iii. find all pairs of eyes and find their supports from the support for each eye and their relative distance and orientations.

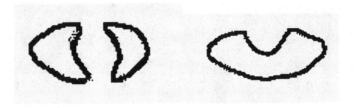

Fig. 23. Eye type 1   **Fig. 24.** Eye type 2

4.2   Dividing the Image into Two Parts

We expect to find an eye for each half of the face, consequently we need to divide the image into two parts corresponding to the left and right halves of the face. This is achieved by using information which can be extracted from the lip region. We find the line connecting the two corners of the lip region $l1$. We then find the line $l2$ which is normal to $l1$ and intersects it at the midpoint of $l1$. This will divide the image in two parts such that one will contain the left eye and the other will contain the right.

4.3   Finding all Potential Eyes

Potential eyes are found using eye-regions, eye centre regions and information from the lip region. As has been noted above, the underlying eye in the image can be split into two or three regions. In the type 1 case the white of the eye is split into two regions, with a third region corresponding to the eye centre. In the type 2 case the white of the eye is found as a single region with the second region corresponding to the eye centre. For the two types different reasoning strategies are required.

4.4   Type 1 Eyes

For type 1 eyes we look at three regions: the left eye white region (*lew*), the eye centre region (*ec*) and the right eye white region (*rew*). Given three such regions we make the following common-sense observations:

- the regions should be close to each other;
- *lew* is to the left of *ec* which is to the left of *rew*;
- the centres of each region should be in a line roughly parallel to *l1*, the line connecting the corners of the mouth;
- in the case of the left eye *lew* should be slightly further away from the line *l2* than *ec* which should be slightly further away from *l2* than *rew*, the reverse being the case for the right eye.

These observations can be easily converted into two Fril rules corresponding to the left and right eyes.

In these rules *close to*, *roughly parallel to* and *slightly further away from* are fuzzy relations between two regions R1 and R2. The support for R1 being *close to* R2 is found by finding the largest width of the two regions. This is treated as the scalar. The Euclidean distance between the centre points of these regions is found and divided by the scalar. The resulting value is then matched against a fuzzy set generated from previous examples using the data-browser method [6, 7].

The support for R1 being *roughly parallel to* R2 is found by finding the polar-angle between the centre points of R1 and R2. This is then matched to a fuzzy set generated by the data-browser method.

The support for *slightly further away from l2* is found by finding the distance between the centre point of R1 and *l2* (d1) and that from R2 and *l2* (d2) and dividing d1 by d2. There is no need to re-scale here. This value is then matched to a fuzzy set generated by the data-browser method.

4.5   Type 2 Eyes

For type 2 eyes we look at only two regions: the eye white region (*ew*) and the eye centre region (*ec*). Given these regions we make the following common-sense observations:

- the region *ec* should be *approximately contained within ew*;
- the centre points of *ec* and *ew* should be approximately the same distance from the line *l2*.

The fuzzy relation the *same distance from l2* is found in a similar manner to slightly further away from *l2*. The fuzzy relation *approximately contained within* is found by finding what percentage of the area of *ec* is within *ew*. The resulting value is then matched against a fuzzy set in which 100% has a support of 1 and 0% has a support of 0.

4.6   Finding Eye Pairs

By this stage potential eyes have been found with supports calculated from the fuzzy relations used in finding the eyes combined with the likelihood of each region being eye or eye centre using colour information.

However, type 2 eyes are found using different rules than type 1 eyes. This corresponds to being a separate source of information. This implies that the typical support for a type 2 eye will be of a different order to that of a type 1 eye. Support for type 2 eyes must therefore be adjusted so that one type does not swamp the other. This is achieved by finding the mean values of type 1 and type 2 eyes from a set of training images. Type 2 values are then found to be:

Type 2 value = original Type 2 value * ((mean Type 1 value)/(mean Type2 value))

It is next necessary to find the final eye-pairs, i.e. a pair of left eye and right eye. This is achieved by using the following common-sense observations:

- the line connecting the left and right eyes is parallel to that connecting the corner of the lips and approximately in a plane — consequently the centre-points of the eyes should *be approximately parallel to l1*;
- similarly the centre-points of each eye should *be at approximately the same distance from* the line *l2*.

The fuzzy relations *parallel to* and *approximately the same distance from* are found as described above. The final eye-pair is that which has the highest support.

4.7   Re-orientation

We require the system to detect emotional expressions under a limited range of subject poses. In keeping with the commonsensical approach of our method we assume the eyes and lips to be on an approximate plane. Once the eyes have been selected we have a number of points which may be used as an estimate for the current orientation of the subject. The current method selects three of these points: the centre of each eye and the centre of *l1*. These are then used with previously recorded positions of these points in a face on, eyes level (mug-shot) pose to find the parameters of an affine transform. These parameters are then used to transform the detected eye and lip regions so that they approximate the mug-shot approach.

In this way all orientations in which both eyes and lips are seen can be transformed to one standard orientation. This negates the need for expression detection rules for all orientations.

4.8   Finding the Final Lip Parameters

It is now necessary to select an appropriate representation for the isolated lip pixels. This representation should be expressive enough to capture the important mouth movements and simple enough to allow easy classification of these movements. We have chosen a parameterized model of the mouth similar to those defined elsewhere [12, 14].

The final lip shape is defined as four half ellipses which meet at the corners of the mouth, as illustrated in Fig. 25. Solid lines show the actual lip shape. Dotted lines show the model. The shape has five parameters: the height of each ellipse and the width which is the same for all the ellipses. This should express the height of each lip, the separation of the lips and the width of the whole mouth.

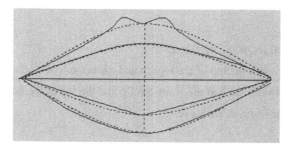

Fig. 25. Lip model superimposed on actual lip shape

To find where the centre of each lip starts and finishes a 5-pixel wide vertical strip is made through the middle of the lips. Zero-crossings of this strip are then considered to be potential height parameter values. To decide which combination of parameters is correct we assign a score to each one. Since the parameterized model should tell us where lip and not lip pixels should be, the score is simply the sum of those pixels within the lip area in the parameterized model which are also classified as lip in the fuzzy image and those pixels which are outside or between the lips in the parameterized model which are also classified as not lip in the fuzzy image. The best scoring combination of parameters is considered to be the final lip shape.

4.9   Finding the Final Eye Measurements

Facial expressions result from muscle movements around the eye and mouth areas. Our method assumes that these movements will result in changes in the height and width of the eyes. If P is the set of all points in the regions corresponding to an eye (*lew, ec, rew* in the type 1 case, and *ew, ec* in the type 2 case) and then:

Height = max(y of P)-min(y of P)
Width = max(x of P)-min(x of P)

5   Finding the Expression Type

5.1   Selecting Facial Features

The main muscles used in facial expressions are centred around the eye and the mouth. Consequently extracting measurements, such as width and height for these features will give a quantitative expression of their shape. Further information can be obtained from the eyebrows which reflect the muscle movement in the forehead more strongly than the eyes, but at this stage we propose only to investigate how much information can be derived from the eyes and lips alone.

In our method a face is classified as belonging to one or more of the following emotions: {afraid, angry, disgusted, happy, sad, surprised}. This classification is made according to the ten following features as derived from the extracted facial features outlined above:

- the x and y values of the lip corners;
- the height between the top of the top lip and the bottom of the bottom lip;
- the height between the bottom of the top lip and the top of the bottom lip;
- the height and width of each eye.

6   Expression Interpretation from Features

Given the re-oriented features outlined above, interpretation proceeds as follows:

- rescale the extracted features;
- compare the feature values to reference values taken from the null face of the subject;
- generate rules from training examples;
- classify novel images according to the rules.

The feature values are rescaled in both the vertical and horizontal directions. Since the image has been re-oriented so that the eyes are level, we use the length of the line connecting the centre of the eyes as the horizontal scalar. Similarly, after re-orientation the line connecting the centre of the lip with the centre of the horizontal scalar is vertical. We use this as the vertical scalar. Both of these can be seen in Fig. 26.

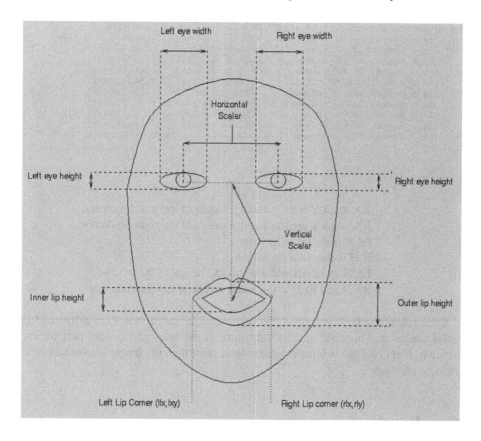

Fig. 26. Expression measures

Our method assumes that expression information is contained in the changes of the face. Taking the feature values in themselves might not lead to correct emotional expression since i) expression information is more likely to be contained in changes of the facial features than the features themselves, ii) the null face of some subjects may be classified as belonging to a given emotion, e.g. we can think of subjects whose normal expression is considered sad when this does not reflect their emotional reaction. In order to take these facial changes into account, we take an image of the subject showing the null face. The resulting feature values are the rescaled values of the null face subtracted from their corresponding rescaled values in an image with emotion content.

Fril rules are generated for each emotional state from sets of example values in a similar manner to those generated for the colour sets above. A sample rule is:

```
((expression is angry if LX LY RX RY OLH ILH LEW LEH REW REH)
    (is_a_member LX of class [-4.5595:0 -1.20236:1 2.78604:0])
    (is_a_member LY of class [-4.31624:0 -2.44107:1 -1.00622:0])
    (is_a_member RX of class [-6.22426:0 -0.172611:1 5.30892:0])
    (is_a_member RY of class [-6.66667:0 -2.62561:1 0.606061:0])
    (is_a_member OLH of class [-1.72575:0 1.95821:1 8.54849:0])
    (is_a_member ILH of class [-13.8739:0 -3.40568:1 1.26126:0])
    (is_a_member LEW of class [-13.2384:0 -3.3743:1 2.14393:0])
    (is_a_member LEH of class [-5.55556:0 -2.59048:1 0.505051:0])
    (is_a_member REW of class [-5.97826:0 -2.06147:1 0.543478:0])
    (is_a_member REH of class [-5.38164:0 -3.23934:1 -1.40799:0])):((1 1)(0
0))
```

In this example:

LX and LY are the x and y values of the left lip corner.
RX and RY are the x and y values of the right lip corner.
OLH is the outer lip height.
ILH is the inner lip height
LEW and LEH is the width and height of the left eye
REW and REH is the width and height of the right eye

Once rules have been generated, the re-oriented, rescaled values are extracted from novel images and matched against the values in the rules giving a support for each emotion. If no rule has a support greater than zero, then the image is assumed to express no emotion.

6   Results

6.1   Feature Extraction Results

The method was tested on a set of images of subjects taken under uncontrolled indoor lighting conditions with a flash camera. The subjects were oriented so they were more or less facing the camera. The resulting images were passed on to the lip extraction system as whole images.

The eye region detection rules were trained on 19 images and tested on 23 images. The results can be seen in Table 1. As can be seen, the system finds the lips in nearly all the test and training images. Eyes are correctly detected in most of the training sets, but problems were found with the test set.

An analysis of the images with mis-detected eye regions showed that in the large majority of cases mis-detection was due to the absence of the eye-white regions. This happened for two reasons: narrowing of the eyes in some expressions occluded the eye-white area, and the eye white colour in some of the test regions was different from that generated from the training images.

In order to test the eye detection rules the images with missing eye-white areas were removed. In this case the detection algorithm found the eye areas in over 90% of the cases demonstrating that the eye detection rules are reliable.

Table 1. Feature Extraction Results

	Number of Images	Correct Detection		
		Lip	Eye	Both
Training	19	19 (100%)	18 (94%)	18 (94%)
Test	23	22 (96%)	12 (52%)	12 (52%)
Test with eye regions present	14	14 (100%)	13 (92%)	13 (92%)

A set of sample images applied to the feature extraction system can be seen in Figs. 27-30. The sample images show both closed (Figs. 27, 28 and 29) and open lips (Fig. 30). The white lines in the images show where the lip extraction system considers the lips and eye to be. Close-up views of the eye areas from these images can be seen in Figs. 31-34 and Figs. 35-38 show close-up views of the lip areas. In general there is a good fit to the image.

   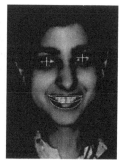

| Fig. 27 | Fig. 28 | Fig. 29 | Fig. 30 |

Figs 27-30: Feature location in whole image

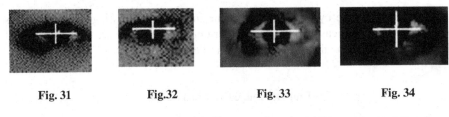

Fig. 31   **Fig.32**   **Fig. 33**   **Fig. 34**

Figs 31-34: Close-ups of eye location

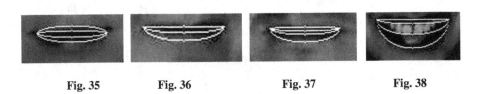

Fig. 35   **Fig. 36**   **Fig. 37**   **Fig. 38**

Figs 35-38: Close-ups of lip location

6.2   Expression Recognition Results

Expression recognition rules were generated on 13 images in which features had been correctly extracted. A total of 6 rules were generated with a maximum of three examples per rule. These rules were then tested against 13 sample images from which the features had been correctly detected.

The results can be seen in Table 2. The second column shows the number of images in which the emotional content shown in the image was found to have a support of greater than zero. However, these figures also include images in which other emotions were also detected, some of which have a higher support than the correct emotion.

The second column shows the number of images in which the emotion shown in the image derived the highest support. This is the true classification result.

It can be seen that in their current state the rules can detect the presence of the displayed emotion with a reasonably high accuracy. However, it cannot disambiguate it well from other emotions. In fact the true classification result (third column) is disappointingly low. The low result on the training set indicates that a more complex set of rules is needed.

Table 2. Emotion Classification Results

	Number of Images	Emotion Correctly Detected	Number in which correct emotion had most support (true classification)
Training	20	19 (95%)	14 (70%)
Test	13	10 (77%)	5 (38%)

7   Conclusions

This paper has outlined the ambiguous nature of facial expressions and drawn attention to the possible causes of these ambiguities. We have proposed a set of methods with which expressions can be characterized and which reflects this indeterminacy.

We have also derived a method for extracting the relevant facial features from an image. The method relies on colour information to extract possible lip and eye areas and then reasons on combinations of these areas to find the best interpretation of the image. In general lip areas are extracted very reliably and with a close fit to the image. On the other hand eye regions are not reliably detected from their colour information. If, however, the regions are present then the eye detection rules work well. This indicates that the region segmentation must be improved if the method is to be robust.

The emotion classification rules can detect emotional content but do not disambiguate well between other emotions. However, the rules were generated from very small data sets which necessitated a simplistic approach to classification and in this respect the results were encouraging.

References

1. Terzopoulos D. and Waters M.: 'Analysis and Synthesis of Facial Image Sequences Using Physical and Anatomical Models', IEEE PAMI, Vol.15, No.6 (June 1993).
2. Baldwin J.F.: 'Combining Evidences for Evidential Reasoning', International Journal of Intelligent Systems, Vol. 6, pp. 569-616 (1991).
3. Baldwin J.F.: 'A Theory of Mass Assignments for Artificial Intelligence', Proc. IJCAI Workshop on Fuzzy Logic, Australia (1991).
4. Baldwin J.F.: 'A New Approach to Inference Under Uncertainty for Knowledge Based Systems', in 'Symbolic and Quantative Approaches to Uncertainty', eds., Krues R. and Siegel P., Springer Verlag Lecture Notes in Computer Science 548, pp. 107-115 (1991).
5. Baldwin J.F.: 'The Management of Fuzzy and Probabilistic Uncertainties for knowledge based systems', in 'Encyclopedia of A.I.', ed., Shapiro S. A., John Wiley (2nd ed.) pp. 528-337 (1992).

6. Baldwin J.F., Martin T.P. and Pilsworth B.W.: 'FRIL-Fuzzy and Evidential Reasoning in Artificial Intelligence', Research Studies Press (1995).
7. Baldwin J.F. and Martin T.P.: 'A Fuzzy Data-browser in FRIL', in 'Fuzzy Logic', ed., Baldwin J. F., John Wiley and Sons (1996).
8. Baldwin J.F., Lawry J. and Martin T.P.: 'A mass assignment based ID3 algorithm for decision tree induction', International Journal of Intelligent Systems, Vol. 12, No. 7, pp. 523-552 (1997).
9. Baldwin J.F.: 'Evidential Support Logic Programming', Fuzzy Sets and Systems, Vol. 24, pp. 1-26 (1987).
10. Baldwin J.F.: 'Evidential Reasoning under Probabilistic and Fuzzy Uncertainties', in 'An Introduction to Fuzzy Logic and Applications in Intelligent Systems', eds., Yager R. R. and Zadeh L. A., Kluwer Academic Publishers (1991).
11. Baldwin J.F.: 'Knowledge from Data using Fril and Fuzzy Methods', in 'Fuzzy Logic', ed., Baldwin J. F., John Wiley and Sons (1996).
12. Coianiz T., Torresani L. and Caprile B.: '2D deformable models for visual speech analysis', Technical Report, Istituto per la Ricerca Scientifica e Tecnologica (1995).
13. Yang J., Wu L. and Waibel A.: 'Focus of attention in video conferencing', Technical Report, CMU-CS-96-150, School of Computer Science, Carnegie Mellon University (June 1996).
14. Rao R. and Mersereau R.: 'Lip Modelling for Visual Speech Recognition', Technical Report, School of Electrical Engineering, Georgia Institute of Technology (1996).

Modelling Preferred Work Plans

Neill R. Taylor

Department of Mathematics
King's College, London, WC2R 2LS, UK
ntaylor@mth.kcl.ac.uk

Abstract. We developed simulations of temporal sequence storage and generation by multi-modular neural networks based on the frontal lobes system. Possible architectures for the storage and retrieval of temporal sequences are investigated using a cartoon version of the frontal lobes i.e. the ACTION net. This architecture is used to learn preferred work plans in relation to the sequences that
a user performs to solve work tasks.

1   Introduction

Temporal sequence storage and generation is important during our everyday lives. The
sequences of actions that we perform to accomplish tasks are learnt as schemata, and
are then used in planning solutions. Hence schemata are required to be set up for planning.

The problem tackled here is to plan a user's work schedule in a manner that takes
account of the user's own preferences. Such a system will not only plan the order in
which work is tackled at a high level, but also at a low level within a work task. Where
all planning is based upon data of the user's own preferred working patterns. This
requires the tasks the user performs to be learnt, as well as the temporal sequence of
sub-tasks that are required to complete a particular task; these are the schemata of a
user's work actions. Where write report, e-mail maintenance, etc, are examples of
tasks, and appropriate sub-tasks for the latter can include: read e-mail, follow web
link, reply, archive, then the user's preferences for performing tasks in certain orders
are learnt, in order to use the schemata in forming a planned work schedule.

There are a number of neural networks that achieve temporal sequence storage and
generation. Time-delay neural nets [1, 2] implement Hakens embedding theorem
which states: "Measurements of a time series produced by an underlying dynamical
system can always allow the underlying dynamics to be reconstructed by using an
embedding vector of a time-lagged set of the elements of the measured series." Recurrent models include: the spin-glass approach of Hopfield [3], nets with context neu-

B. Azvine et al. (Eds.): Intelligent Systems and Soft Computing, LNAI 1804, pp. 343-357, 2000.
© Springer-Verlag Berlin Heidelberg 2000

rones [4, 5] and extensions to the Elman net [6, 7], the crumbling history approach [8, 9]. We do not use the above models in our system. The Hopfield model has problems with the length of sequence that can be generated, with length 3 sequences the longest that can be generated with accuracy. The Elman net approach uses associative chaining to generate sequences, this leads to multiple representations for the same outputs, which is computationally expensive. The crumbling history approach will encounter problems during planning due to its method of sequence generation. It uses the last output of the model as the next input. During a competitive process between different modules, disrupting the output (i.e. generating the incorrect output) produces a competition between sequences different from those originally intended. We require a system to learn long sequences, in a manner that is computationally less expensive than Elman nets, and where sequence generation is accomplished in an 'internal' manner once the sequence generation has been started. So we turn to the frontal lobes of primates.

The frontal lobes are composed of complex cortical and sub-cortical structures. Humans can learn, with practice, temporal sequences of long length (most humans normally learn sequences of length 7 ± 2); additionally evidence from single-cell recordings during motor sequence generation of monkeys [10, 11] suggest that chunking occurs during sequence learning. Chunking is the process by which short subsequences of actions are linked together to provide a memory of all the actions performed by that 'chunk'. This allows the use of the chunking neurones to perform a sub-sequence wherever it occurs in a total sequence. So multiple representations of sub-sequences do not occur. To solve the sequence learning part of the problem, stated above, we use a model based on the structure of the frontal lobes.

We begin, in section 2, with a description of a neural network which performs basic temporal sequence storage and generation by learning short sequences of up to length four. In section 3 we describe how, by using the short sequence learner, longer sequences can be learnt and regenerated. How these learnt sequences can be used to learn the user's work preferences is described in section 4.

2   The ACTION Network

2.1   Architecture

As mentioned above the first stage of building the system is to develop a network capable of temporal sequence storage and generation of work actions. The structure used for this is the ACTION network [12, 13], a recurrent neural network. This is a cartoon version of the frontal lobes cortical and sub-cortical structures, where it is termed the basal ganglia-thalamocortical circuit. The frontal lobes are important for working memory maintenance and a number of separate circuits exist [14]. The motor circuit is important for generating, from memory, temporal sequences of motor actions [10, 11].

Different versions of the ACTION net have been used to solve a variety of tasks, from psychological delayed response tasks [15-17] to sequences of motor actions with delays [18, 19]. Fig. 1 shows the frontal regions modelled for the ACTION net version used here. The ACTION net comprises two cortical regions — the supplementary motor cortex (SMA) and the pre-motor cortex (PMC) — the basal ganglia, thalamus (THL) and sub-thalamic nucleus (STN). The basal ganglia is composed of two layers, the striatum (STR) and the globus pallidus, which is modelled as its internal and external segments, GPi and GPe, respectively. Neurophysiological and psychological studies have suggested that the SMA is responsible for movements from memory while the PMC generates movements from visual instruction [10, 11, 20, 21], and both are necessary to learn a new sequence [20, 21]. The neurones modelled are mean firing rate with all but IN and OUT neurones being leaky integrators. This model can hold activity over long periods of time due to the many closed loops that exist within its structure. Most of the sub-cortical structure provides for a competition of excitatory input and inhibitory input on to the GPi via the STN and STR respectively. When the GPi is inhibited this releases the inhibition exerted by it on the THL, which then allows the THL to become spontaneously active. Active thalamic neurones then cause reverberation of activity between SMA and THL. This leads to sustained activity over long time periods, which can be turned off by removing the inhibition on GPi from the STR; thus the GPi becomes positively excited inhibiting THL once again. This removes the chance of reverberating activity between SMA and THL. The net effect of the complete basal ganglia is as a dis-inhibitor.

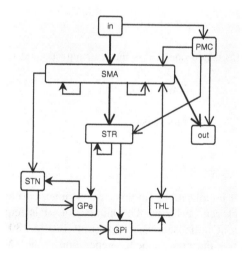

Fig. 1. The ACTION network, where SMA is supplementary motor area, PMC pre-motor cortex, STN sub-thalamic nucleus, GPe external region of globus pallidus, GPi internal region of globus pallidus, THL thalamus, STR striatum, IN input layer and OUT output layer. Open arrowheads indicate excitatory weights, closed arrowheads inhibitory connections. Thicker arrows indicate adaptive weights

2.2   Training

The system consists of a number of ACTION net modules with each module learning a sequence of up to four work actions. The adaptable weights are: IN to SMA, SMA to OUT, and SMA to STR, which is a reduction from previous models [18, 19].

Each work action is represented by a specific number, and it is these numbers which are used as inputs to each module. The output of the module must regenerate the input. Training begins with the presentation of the first two inputs of the sequence, the correct outputs must be generated in response to the external stimuli. Once this can be performed correctly the module is presented with the first input, in response to which it is required to produce the first output followed by the second output, where the second is generated internally by the network. Hence the first input is used to initiate the sequence regeneration and is known as the 'seeding' input. When the length two sequence can be generated by seeding, the first three inputs are presented to the net and again the correct three outputs must be played out in the correct order. After this the net is seeded again and the three outputs must be correctly generated with the second and third generated internally. This is repeated for the length four sequence. If the wrong output is generated, training returns to the previous stage.

Weights are updated using Hebbian and reinforcement learning rules, so the information the network receives is whether the output was correct or incorrect, not what the output should have been. A reinforcement learning rule, for a weight w_{ij} is of the form:

$$\Delta w_{ij} = r \, \varepsilon \, u_i u_j \tag{1}$$

where u_k is the output of neurone k, ε is the learning rate and r is the reward defined by:

$$r = \begin{cases} 1, & \text{if output is correct} \\ -1, & \text{otherwise} \end{cases} \tag{2}$$

2.3   Results

Using suitable weight initialisations (in this case symmetrical) and parameter choices, length four sequences can be learnt. The number of trials required for the training process, using different initialisations, range from 180 to 1800. Fig 2 shows some neurones that are active during a sequence generation in the SMA region of the AC-TION net. Simulations have shown that certain regions are important in being able to learn and generate sequences. For instance removing the indirect loop (STN and GPe) through the basal ganglia of Fig. 1, leads to a reduction of sequences that can be learnt. No other regions can be removed from the structure of Fig. 1. The direct route through the basal ganglia, the route using STR and Gpi, could be modelled as one layer. Then this combined region has to excite the THL, and excitation is not the same as disinhibition, which is the action of the direct route. It appears that the competition of the

direct and indirect routes through the basal ganglia is important for sequence generation.

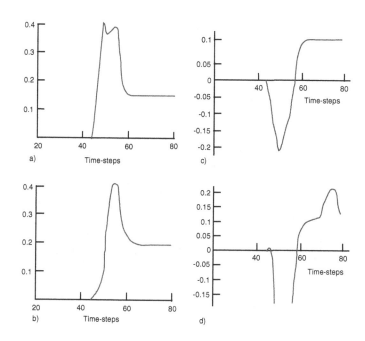

Fig. 2. Activities of four neurones recorded from the SMA neurone during generation of a
length four sequence over 80 time-steps. Graph (a) shows a neurone that is responsible for the
generation of the first output of the sequence, which occurs between time-steps 40 and 50; (b) is
a neurone that generates the second output of the sequence, between time-steps 50 and 60; (c) is
responsible for the generation of the third output between time-steps 60 and 70, (d) is
responsible for the generation of the fourth output between time-steps 70 and 80

3   Longer Sequences

At this stage the system can only learn work sequences of up to length four. By using
ACTION net modules in a hierarchical system, sequence length can be built up in
powers of four. Hence, using two levels of ACTION modules means sequences of up
to length 16 can be learnt and regenerated. The highest level ACTION nets are termed
the first level or first order chunking modules which excite the low order modules
(Fig. 3).

   The only difference in architecture between chunking modules and lower order
modules is the inclusion of connections from the chunking module OUT layer to the
low order IN layers.

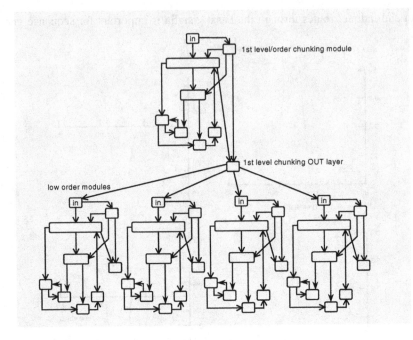

Fig. 3. The arrangement of ACTION nets to generate sequence of length 1 to 16, showing the 1st level chunking module and the four low order modules

The chunking modules' outputs therefore act as a seeding pattern to the low order modules. So while the low order modules are trained on a continuous sequence of up to length four, the chunking modules are trained to generate the first then every fourth subsequent input in response to seeding with the first input. Hence, for the sequence {1,2,3,...,14,15,16} four low order modules are trained to generate one of the sequences {1,2,3,4}, {5,6,7,8}, {9,10,11,12}, {13,14,15,16} while the first order chunking module is trained to generate {1,5,9,13} which are the four seeding inputs of the low order nets.

The whole sequence is generated in the correct order by seeding the chunking module, the outputs of the chunking module are hidden and the sequence generation is controlled by the low order modules.

The benefit of this hierarchical structure of ACTION nets is the reusability of low order modules by many chunking modules. A complete sequence will only be learnt once — there is no need to have a number of chunking modules that produce exactly the same sequence. However, a user might solve a particular task in a number of different ways, depending on what the work entails. So within a group of sequences, which can solve the same task, there may be sub-sequences which are common. Rather than represent the sub-sequence by many low order modules it is advantageous for space and speed to reuse the low order module that can already generate the sub-sequence. Fig. 4 indicates four chunking modules, all of which are possible user solutions to a particular task, which have common sub-sequences.

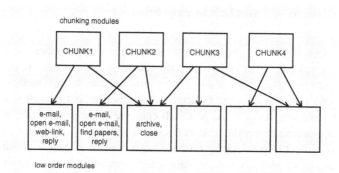

Fig. 4. The arrangement of chunking reusing low order modules; each box represents an AC-TION net of the form of Fig. 1, with each chunking module representing a different solution to an e-mail task

4   Learning User Preferences

Sections 2 and 3 have described the basis of the system for learning the sequences that a user performs to solve work tasks. Now we turn to learning the orders in which the user prefers to perform work. The user preferences are used by the system to order a pool of outstanding work tasks in a manner the user would have chosen. Two possible solutions are discussed: (a) sequences of task level and (b) task level, both of which use a competitive process between chunking modules. The preferences learnt form the salience, which is the level of preference for an object compared to other objects. In the case of method (a) the salience will be the preference of one specific order of sequence tasks over another order of the same tasks, for example the preference of performing the task order e-mail maintenance, write report, simulations over the sequence: simulations, e-mail maintenance, write report. For method (b) the salience is the preference of a particular task over all other tasks within a particular pool of tasks. So, using the same tasks: e-mail maintenance, write report, simulations, the chunking modules that code these tasks compete to find the most active and hence which task should be performed first.

4.1   Architecture

The architecture is the same for both methods of competition, involving the addition of inhibitory connections between the striata of the chunking modules (Fig. 5). All existing modules are connected to all other modules via these weights, with no self-recurrence.

4.2   Sequences of Tasks Level Competition

The sequences of tasks level of competition requires that the sequences that are learnt and regenerated consist of tasks. Then the stored sequences are the user's preferred working patterns. There are a number of problems with this method. Due to the method of sequence generation, by seeding with the first pattern, all sequences which start with one of the tasks in the pool will compete in the competition whether or not the sequence contains only the tasks resident in the pool.

This could lead to plans being produced that contain all tasks, those contained in the pool and others that are not, or plans which contain only some of the tasks in the pool. For example, using the previous set of tasks — e-mail maintenance, write report, simulations — another sequence of tasks — e-mail maintenance, web search, meeting, paper review — will also be activated even though it contains only one task belonging to the pool.

This method of learning user preferences cannot generalise if the pool contains a particular group of tasks that the system has not been trained on. In this case, if the pool is 'e-mail maintenance, write report, simulations, meeting', this may be a group of tasks that the system has not seen during the period of observing the user; hence there will not be an ACTION net that has stored the preferred order of these tasks, but there will be ACTION nets that have information of preferred orders of sub-sets of this pool, such as the tasks: e-mail maintenance, write report, simulations.

So we move to competition at the individual task level.

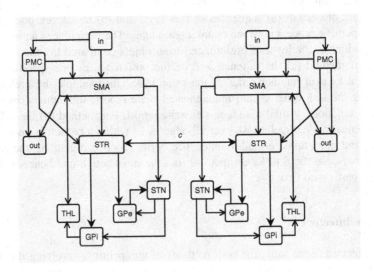

Fig. 5. The competitive inhibitory weights connecting the striata of ACTION nets, with the competitive weight denoted c

4.3   Task Level Competition

In this case the sequences involved in the competition are those that represent the different stages used to solve one task. Hence the sequence regenerated consists of the task, followed by the order of sub-tasks used to solve that task. Now if all the tasks present in the pool are presented to the system the only sequences that will be regenerated are those that begin with one of the tasks in the pool; additionally, generalisation can occur.

For the pool: e-mail maintenance, write report, simulations, meeting, even though these tasks have not all been seen together, there may be some existing relationships. For instance if 'e-mail maintenance, write report, simulations' have been performed together by the user and so have 'e-mail maintenance and meeting', this gives the system some information of how the tasks are related in preference.

Even if the task meeting has not been seen with any of the other tasks in the pool, it will be ordered as an ACTION net provided that its required solution has been activated.

Training To train the user preferences the sequence in which the user likes to perform certain tasks is used as a template. The task name is used to 'seed' all sequences that begin with that input. Hence during salience training all task names contained within the data stream are presented to the system at the same time. One module, for one of the tasks in the preferred ordering, will be the winner (i.e. most active) at the end of the sequence regeneration. This winner is then compared with the template and weights are updated according to a modified reinforcement training law. The competitive weights which are negative are denoted c_{ij}, which identifies the weight from module j to module i. The update rule is defined as:

$$c_{i*j} = c_{ij} + 0.5 \text{ reward act}_j \text{ act}_{i*} \tag{3}$$
$$c_{ji*} = c_{ji*} - 0.5 \text{ reward act}_j \text{ act}_{i*} \tag{4}$$

where

$$\text{reward} = \begin{cases} 1, & \text{if winning module matches template} \\ -1, & \text{otherwise} \end{cases} \tag{5}$$

and $i*$ represents the winning module, and act_k is the average output of a striatal neurone during the competitive process from module k.

Equation (3) therefore has the effect of changing the weights to the winning module. These become less negative if the winner is correct, remembering that these connections are inhibitory, hence reducing the combined inhibitory action. If the winner is wrong the weights are made more negative to it such that it will not win the competition in the next trial. Equation (4) controls the weights from the winning module to all other modules that were excited. If the winner is correct the inhibitory weights are strengthened to all other active modules, if wrong then the weights are weakened.

Equations (3) and (4) only act to change the competitive weights of active modules, hence previously learnt saliencies for tasks not involved in the current competition are not altered.

Once the competitive weights have been learnt such that the first task of the data stream is the winner when that particular pool of tasks is presented, then that task is removed from the pool and training continues using the same method with the remaining tasks.

For example, given a pool of tasks {e-mail, simulations, meeting, write report, web search, paper review} with a preferred user order of 'simulations, paper review, e-mail, web search, meeting, write report', training commences with input to the trained chunking modules of all of the tasks in the pool. We require from this first stage that an ACTION net generating simulations be the winning module. Training continues using the above equations until this is the case. The next training phase removes simulations from the pool of tasks to leave the following pool tasks {e-mail, meeting, write report, web search, paper review} for which the preferred order is 'paper review, e-mail, web search, meeting, write report'. The training must then modify the weights such that paper review is the next winner. The task paper review is then removed from the pool of tasks and training continues as previously for the remaining four tasks, using their preferred order.

Producing a Plan from a Pool of Tasks We wish now to order a pool of tasks, in a manner that the user will find acceptable, given that the system has learnt a number of the user's preferred work patterns. To order this pool of tasks, all of the tasks are input to the chunking modules. The chunking modules, with any of the tasks as their seeding input, become active and a winning module is found, which has as its first output a certain task. This task is then put first in the current work plan and removed from the pool of tasks. The resulting pool of tasks is then input and a new winner found, which is the second entry to the work plan; this new winner is then removed from the pool. This method of competition and winner removal continues until only one task is remaining in the pool, at which point it is placed last in the proposed work plan.

Results We have presented to trained systems preferred work orderings of 2-tasks, 4-tasks, 6-tasks and 8-tasks (5 simulations for each). In every case the preferred ordering was learnt and could be regenerated. Table I shows the average trials required to learn the preferred sequence order for the different numbers of tasks.

Table 1. Sequence learning

Number of Tasks	Average Trials
2	1.4
4	4.4
6	8.4
8	20.6

Fig. 6 shows two graphs of the average results obtained from the 8-task case. Fig. 6(a) indicates the average number of trials required to get the nth task in the correct position given that the previous $n - 1$ tasks are already correctly ordered. The second graph indicates the average number of tasks that are in their correct positions (this does not require, for position n, the previous $n - 1$ positions to be ordered correctly) at each stage when a new position is filled correctly. Fig. 6(a) shows that, for larger numbers of tasks, as a task is correctly ordered, the general trend for the number of trials to correctly order the next task becomes smaller. It also shows that to train the third to the eighth preferred tasks takes on average 10.5 trials which is an increase of two trials from ordering 6 tasks only. This indicates that due to incorrect tasks winning early on in the ordering process, tasks can be inhibited too much and weights have to be re-learnt.

While Fig. 6(b) indicates that once 4 tasks are correctly ordered, 7 tasks on average are correctly ordered (the number of correct orderings actually range from 5 to 8, with no modules having 7 tasks correctly ordered as this is impossible). We find that for long enough sequences of tasks 6 and 10 (in addition to 8), the results of Fig. 6(a) are generally repeated.

For length four the average number of trials required to train each position is nearly the same.

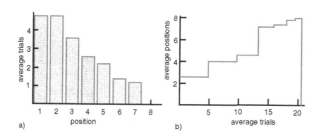

Fig. 6. Average results obtained from the 8-task case

Fig. 7 displays as a graph the average number of trials, for length 2, 4, 6, and 8 sequences over 20 simulations each, taken to learn the preferred order of the tasks. The rough doubling in the average number of trials, from length 4 (5.15 trials) to length 6 (9.5 trials) to length 8 (20.45 trials), suggests that on average 40 trials will be necessary to train the saliencies of 10 tasks.

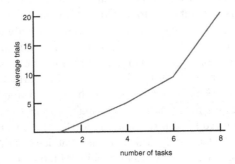

Fig.7. Number of trials to learn the preferred order of tasks

5   Training the Entire System

At this stage we have described the architectures used to learn sequences of a task and its composite sub-tasks, and how basic user preferences can be learnt between the trained modules in order to plan work in isolation. We have not described the mechanism of how, given a data stream consisting of tasks and sub-tasks, which describes a user's daily use, a complete system can be built up.

An example of the data stream is: ***e-mail maintenance***, *open e-mail, reply, archive, close*, ***write report***, *open word processor, save, close, etc*, where tasks are in bold italic and sub-tasks italic. So the sequences the system would be trained on would be: ***e-mail maintenance***, *open e-mail, reply, archive* and then ***write report***, *open word processor, save, close*.

The e-mail sequence would be trained first. So the sequence is: ***e-mail maintenance***, *open e-mail, reply, archive, close*. We wish to see if this complete sequence exists, so the task name ***e-mail maintenance*** is presented to the system. All modules that are seeded by that input will become active and generate their respective sequence. The generated sequences can then be compared with the presented sequence. If the complete sequence does not already exist then the length 3 and 4 sub-sequences contained within the sequence '***e-mail maintenance***, *open e-mail, reply, archive, close*' are checked against the previously played off sequences, to investigate whether any low order module generates exactly that sequence. If a sub-sequence has previously been learnt, then no new low order module is trained for that sub-sequence. For example if the sequence ***e-mail maintenance***, *open e-mail, reply* was generated by a low order module, a new low order module would only be trained on the remainder of the sequence, *archive, close*. Length 1 and 2 sub-sequences are not checked to save time as well as forming too many modules with only 1 or 2 outputs. The low order modules have now been trained for this sequence; these have to be linked together by a chunking module. In this case, the sequence on which the chunking module is trained is *e-mail maintenance*, *archive* which are the seeding inputs of the 2 low order modules. If no sub-sequences had existed the training sequence would have been *e-mail maintenance*, *close*, but this has been changed by the existence of the **sequence** *e-mail maintenance*, *open e-mail*, *reply*. Once the chunking module has been trained, the sequence *e-mail maintenance*, *archive* is presented to the system again to excite the correct chunking module outputs and the two lower order modules that generate the total sequence, so training the weights from the OUT layer of the chunking module to the IN layers of the lower order modules. Now when the chunking module is seeded with the input *e-mail maintenance* the total output is the original sequence *e-mail maintenance*, *open e-mail*, *reply*, *archive*, *close*. This method is then repeated for all the remaining task sequences in the data stream.

The data stream also provides the user's preferences for task order which can be extracted by removing all sub-task entries. In our example this would give the sequence: *e-mail maintenance*, *write report*, etc. All newly created chunking modules have the competitive c weights initialised to all other chunking modules, which also create the reciprocal weights. Before salience training begins the system is tested to see if the preferences can be generated already; if the correct order can be generated, then training is dispensed with.

As mentioned before the user may solve a task in more than one way, if this occurs it is most likely that there is one method that the user prefers, hence this needs to be taken account of during saliency learning. This can be achieved by a separate set of competitive weights that are trained in the same manner as above. These competitive weights though would connect chunking modules that generate different solutions to the same task. Hence, the main competitive process determines in which order the tasks should be tackled, while the second competitive process determines which particular method should be used to solve a task.

6   Generating and Using a Plan

With a system trained in the manner of the previous section, a basic plan can be generated for a pool of tasks using the method described in section 4.3. Due to the method of learning saliencies at the task level, if the pool of tasks is such that the system has never been trained on such a pool, it can generalise, using the user information it has learnt to produce its best 'guess'. When the work plan has been produced, each task is played off as required for the sub-tasks to be generated — this may cause competition again between schemata for the same task.

7   Conclusions

We have detailed a system to solve a particular problem, namely to schedule work in a user friendly way having learnt the user's habits. The system can learn a user's schemata of any length simply by adding more layers of chunking modules. The chunking used attempts to balance between reusing existing learnt sub-sequences and learning many short sequences, by reusing modules that generate short sequences. User preferences of work ordering can be learnt, so far up to 10 tasks long. The forming of plans from schemata can be generalised.

Further work is required to include context of user mental state due to time of day or day of the week. Context will also aid in the selection of the correct schema to solve a task from multiple solutions.

References

1. Waibel A.: 'Modular construction of time-delay neural networks for speech recognition', Neural Computation, Vol. 1, pp. 39-46 (1989).
2. Waibel A., Hanazawa T., Hinton G., Shikano K. and Lang K.: 'Phoneme recognition using time-delay neural networks', IEEE Transactions on Acoustics, Speech and Signal Processing, Vol. 37, pp. 328-339 (1989).
3. Hopfield J. J.: 'Neural networks and physical systems with emergent collective computational abilities', Proceedings of the National Academy of Sciences, USA, Vol. 79, pp. 2554-2558 (1982).
4. Jordan M. I.: 'Attractor dynamics and parallelism in a connectionist sequential machine', Proceedings of the Cognitive Science Society (Amhurst, MA), pp. 531-546 (1986).
5. Elman J. L.: 'Finding structure in time', Cognitive Science, Vol. 14, pp. 179-212 (1990).
6. Wang D. L. and Arbib M. A.: 'Complex temporal sequence learning based on short-term memory', Proceedings of the IEEE, Vol. 78, No. 9, pp. 1536-1543 (1990).
7. Wang D. L. and Arbib M. A.: 'Timing and chunking in processing temporal order', IEEE Transactions on Systems, Man, and Cybernetics, Vol. 23, pp. 993-1009 (1990).
8. Reiss M. and Taylor J. G.: 'Storing temporal sequences', Neural Networks, Vol. 4, pp. 773-787 (1991).
9. Taylor J. G. and Reiss M.: 'Does the Hippocampus Store Temporal Patterns?', Neural Network World, Vol. 2, pp. 365-384 (1992).
10. Tanji J. and Shima K.: 'Role for the supplementary motor area cells in planning several movements ahead', Nature, Vol. 371, pp. 413-416 (1994).
11. Halsband U., Matsuzaka Y. and Tanji J.: 'Neuronal activity in the primate supplementary, pre-supplementary and premotor cortex during externally and internally instructed sequential movements', Neuroscience Research, Vol. 20, pp. 149-155 (1994).
12. Taylor J. G.: 'Modelling the Mind by PSYCHE', Proc ICANN'95, eds, Soulie F. and Gallinari P., Paris, EC2 & Co (1995).
13. Taylor J. G. and Alavi F.: 'A basis for long-range inhibition across cortex', in 'Lateral Interactions in Cortex: Structure and Function', eds., Sirosh J., Miikulainen R. and Choe Y, The UCTS Neural Networks Research Group, Austin TX (1996), electronic book, http:www.cs.utexas.edu/users/nn/web-pubs/htmlbook96.
14. Alexander G. E., DeLong M. R. and Strick P. L.: 'Parallel organisation of functionally segregated circuits linking basal ganglia and cortex', Annual review of Neuroscience, Vol. 9, pp. 357-381 (1986).
15. Monchi O. and Taylor J. G.: 'Computational Neuroscience Models to Complement Brain Imaging Data for the Understanding of Working Memory Processes', in 'Connectionist

Representations', eds., Bullinaria J. A., Glasspool D. W. and Houghton G., Springer, London, pp. 142-154 (1997).

16. Monchi O. and Taylor J. G.: 'A Model of the Prefrontal Loop that Includes the Basal Ganglia in Solving the Recency Task', Proc of WCNN'95, Vol. 3, pp. 48-55, Hillsdale N.J., L Erlbaum & INNS Press (1995).

17. Monchi O. and Taylor J. G.: 'A hard-wired model of coupled frontal working memories for various tasks', Information Sciences Journal, Vol. 113, No. 3/4, pp. 221-243, Elsevier Science (1998).

18. Taylor N. R.: 'Modelling Temporal Sequence Learning', University of London, Thesis (1998).

19. Taylor N. R. and Taylor J.G.: 'Experimenting with models of the frontal lobes', in 'NCPW5 Connectionist Models in Cognitive Neuroscience', eds., Humphreys G. W., Olson A. and Heinke D., Perspectives in Neural Computation series, Springer-Verlag, pp. 92-101 (1998).

20. Passingham R. E.: 'Two cortical systems for directing movement', in 'Motor Areas of the Cerebral Cortex', CIBA Foundation Symposium No. 132, John Wiley, Chichester, pp. 151-164 (1987).

21. Passingham R. E.: 'The Frontal Lobes and Voluntary Action', Oxford University Press, Oxford (1993).

Author Index